FLSA · IRS
ADA · OSHA
NLRA · COBR
· WARN · FIC
· FUTA · OWPA
MHPA · NMHP
· EAP · CDA
ERISA · CCP
· EPA · ADR
CRA · ADEA
TITLE VII · SS
· RA · IRCA
PDA · DFW
· WCA · INS
HIPAA · DOL
USERRA · OT
MSDS · SHAR
SECTION 530
FMLA · EEO
· FLSA · IRS
ADA · OSHA
NLRA · COBR
· WARN · FIC
· FUTA · OWPA
MHPA · NMHP
· EAP · CDA

What Every Business Manager
and HR Professional Should Know
About ...

Federal
Labor and Employment
Laws

A complete guide written in plain English
that explains how the laws affect your business

7th Edition

PDA · DFW
· WCA · INS
HIPAA · DOL
USERRA · OT
MSDS · SHAR
· SECTION 53
· FMLA · EEO
· FLSA · IRS
ADA · OSHA
NI RA · COBR

Louis P. DiLorenzo
Sheldon I. London

WME BOOKS
a division of
Windsor Media Enterprises, LLC
Rochester, New York
USA

What Every Business Manager
and HR Professional Should Know About ...
Federal Labor and Employment Laws
A complete guide written in plain English
that explains how the laws affect your business

ISBN 0-9777297-3-7

Cover Design/Page Layout/InteriorDesign: Tom Collins

Published by:
WME Books
Windsor Media Enterprises, LLC
Rochester, New York
USA

Available online at: www.WMEBooks.com, as well as other booksellers and distributors worldwide.

Special Sales:

This and other WME Books titles are available at special discounts for bulk purchases, for use in sales promotions, or as premiums. Special editions, including personalized covers, excerpts of existing books, and corporate imprints, can be created in large quantities for special needs or projects.

For more information, please contact:

Special Book Orders
Windsor Media Enterprises, LLC
282 Ballad Avenue
Rochester, NY 14626

1-877-947-BOOK (2665)

info@wmebooks.com

Summary of Contents

Getting the Most Out of This Book

We've provided several ways for you to access the material in this book. A detailed Table of Contents that starts on the next page. There is an Index at the back. Along the way, you'll find many tables, checklists, FAQs, and practical tips. To help you find these items quickly, we've set them off in boxes and tagged them with the following icons:

 – Checklists to help you keep track of important items.

 – Noteworthy Items with important rules, tips, or guidelines.

 – "Dos and Don'ts" listing actions to take and those to avoid.

 – Frequently Asked Questions ... *and Answers!*

Online Resources

For the latest news, updates, links, and lively discussion, visit us on our Blog:

www.LaborAndEmploymentLawBlog.com

We're planning to provide a variety of free online resources that will be accessible through the blog. The publisher will host the blog so that the authors, teachers, students, managers, and professionals can connect with each other and share ideas and information.

We invite you to ask questions, challenge us, share your insights, examples, and "war stories" – all of which will make this book more valuable to you.

We'll do our best to keep up with you, offer answers to your questions, find new material to post, and connect you with others in the field.

The blog will grow and evolve (as blogs tend to do), so we suggest you come back regularly. Or, better yet, subscribe to the free email or RSS feeds.

Table of Contents

7 - Americans with Disabilities Act   115

8 - Age Discrimination   133

9 - Occupational Safety and Health — 141

10 - National Labor Relations Act: Unfair Labor Practices, Union Organizing, and the Collective Bargaining Process — 155

11 - Employee Health and Insurance Laws — 177

12 - Miscellaneous Laws Affecting the Workplace   199

13 - Drug and Alcohol Abuse in the Workplace   215

14 - Workplace Investigations   229

Introduction

In 1978 Mr. Sheldon London, an attorney in Washington, D.C., wrote a book entitled ***How To Comply With Federal Employee Laws***. He created it primarily for his clients to help them better understand the complex issues that surround federal employment laws. The guidebook was to become a national best seller in the business marketplace.

I met Shelly some 19 years later. When the human resource manager in our publishing company acquired a later edition of the book, she found it to be invaluable in helping her establish company policies and best practices programs for our employees. Prompted by her enthusiasm, we thought it might be something that we could publish and market nationally. We met with Shelly who enthusiastically embraced our idea. In 1998, a new edition of ***How To Comply With Federal Employee Laws*** was released.

The book was highly acclaimed. Over the next two and one-half years, over 85 national and regional professional business associations would endorse and promote the guidebook to its memberships. The Society for Human Resource Management listed it as one of its "best sellers" for three consecutive years. Fifty professors at 45 prominent business schools throughout the country incorporated the guidebook into their human resource management curricula, using it as a course reference for employment laws. Business managers and human resource professionals from both large and small companies throughout the country discovered the reference book they needed. In 1999, the prestigious *Washington Kiplinger Letter* proclaimed it to be an outstanding employment law reference for business.

I was given the task of directing the national marketing for the 1998 edition. Perhaps two stories best describe my experience.

One afternoon I received a call from the HR Director of a heating and cooling company in Ohio. His company had just acquired 11 small companies, and it was his job to consolidate the employment programs and culture of each subsidiary into one homogeneous organization. "I have just visited your Website," he said. "I wish I had found it earlier. It would have saved me over four hours of searching the Internet to find an employment law reference book I could use. How quickly can you send me a copy of ***How To Comply With Federal Employee Laws***?" One week later he called again and ordered 11 more copies.

At a national tradeshow, a number of people stopped by our booth to look at our new publication. As they were reviewing the book, a bystander proclaimed, "I have a copy of that book, and it is the best book ever written about federal employment laws." I said nothing, because there was nothing more to say.

While working as the Marketing Advisor for Windsor Media Enterprises (WMEBooks), I had the opportunity to meet Mr. Louis DiLorenzo during the summer of 2005. An extremely talented lawyer, counselor and public speaker, Lou directs a 53-person employment law division of the New York law firm, Bond Schoeneck & King.

In early 2006, I posed the idea to both Shelly and Lou about co-authoring a new edition of Shelly's book. Within a month, the three of us met to discuss the possibilities. The result is what you now hold in your hands, *What Every Business Manager And HR Professional Needs To Know About ... Federal Labor And Employment Laws*. Keeping that earlier experience in mind, we are confident that readers will consider this edition "the best guidebook ever written on federal employment laws."

You will find this guide easy to read and easy to understand. The authors have included checklists to help you organize your programs and have provided numerous questions and answers that offer sound guidance. It's not meant to replace a lawyer, but rather to provide you with information to help you better interact with your outside counsel and build a positive work environment.

Two friends of mine, Mr. Shelly London and Mr. Lou DiLorenzo are businessmen that just happen to be attorneys. They have co-authored an extraordinary business reference that will help thousands of businesses and organizations in the months to come.

George Kittredge, Marketing Advisor
Windsor Media Enterprises, LLC (WMEBooks)
Rochester, NY
July 2006

Employees/ Independent Contractors 1

Critical Classification

In every chapter of this book covering compliance with federal employee laws, the first question an employer must answer is whether an individual's proper classification is as an employee or an independent contractor. The consequences flowing from that determination are immense. Whether it is the relatively new Family and Medical Leave Act, any of the unemployment insurance laws, the Fair Labor Standards Act, the federal tax consequences under the Federal Insurance Contribution Act (FICA) and the Federal Unemployment Tax Act (FUTA), or the income tax withholding requirements under the Internal Revenue Code, the classification decision is critical.

For the purpose of this Chapter, the discussion is limited to the definitions of and the procedures for determining whether an individual is an independent contractor or an employee under the Fair Labor Standards Act (FLSA) and the Internal Revenue Code (IRC). It is the latter area that has been the focus of enormous public interest, including vigorous legislative efforts to amend the IRC with a far simpler statutory formula to help determine the proper classification of individuals.

FLSA Determinations

It is no easy matter to determine whether an individual is an employee or an independent contractor. There have been many legal challenges over the years by employers, and the Supreme Court has been asked on a number of occasions to resolve controversies arising out of the dilemma employers face in defining whether a worker is an "independent contractor" or an "employee."

The Supreme Court has been careful to point out that there is no single rule, factor or test which determines whether an individual is an independent contractor or an employee for purposes of the FLSA. It is the totality of the circumstances surrounding the relationship that controls. Among the circumstances considered by the Supreme Court to be significant are the following:

1. The nature of the relationship of the services to the principal's business. In this connection, the more the work is routine, requiring industry and efficiency, the less indicative of independence and non-employee status.

2. The permanency of the relationship. The less permanent, the more persuasive that it is not an employer-employee relationship.

3. The amount of individual investment in facilities and equipment. Obviously, the greater the investment by the individual, the more likely there will be a determination of independent contractor status.

4. The opportunity for profit and loss. Risk of gain or loss, not just compensation for time spent at work, is a strong indication of an independent business relationship in an open market competition.

5. The degree of independent business organization and operation. This is a crucial

test and goes to the heart of the question whether there is the requisite degree of independence. This factor has been described as the difference between merely contracting for a result or controlling the methods or means by which the result is achieved. The employer does not have to actually control the details and ways of accomplishing tasks in order for individuals to be considered "employees." There need only be the right to exercise that control.

6. The degree of independent initiative or judgment. If the task performed is identical to one performed by an employee, and no amount of personal initiative would change the condition of work or the job to other than that of an employee's, then there is no basis to find an independent contractor relationship.

Questions to Determine Independent Contractor Status

Yes No

☐ ☐ Does the enterprise set the hours of work?

☐ ☐ Does the enterprise dictate the methods by which the task is to be implemented?

☐ ☐ Does the enterprise pay an hourly wage?

☐ ☐ Does the enterprise supply material and tools?

☐ ☐ Does the enterprise furnish space, telephone, or secretarial services?

☐ ☐ Does the enterprise set fixed, geographical limits on work?

The courts have held that "yes" answers to these questions indicate an employer-employee relationship. While each case will be determined by its own facts, each "yes" answer to the above questions lessens the likelihood of a finding of independent contractor status. The employer-employee relationship is tested by economic reality rather than technical concepts.

IRS Common Law Test

Under the Internal Revenue Service ("IRS") common law test, an individual generally is an employee if the person for whom the individual performs services has the right to control and direct that individual, both as to the result to be accomplished by the work and as to the details and means by which that result is accomplished. The most important factor under the common law test is the degree of control, or rights of control, which the employer has over the manner in which the work is to be performed.

In determining whether the necessary degree of control exists in order to find that an individual is an employee, the courts and the IRS ordinarily evaluate and weigh all of the facts of a particular situation. The decision as to the weight to be accorded any single factor depends upon both the activity under consideration and the purpose underlying the use of the factor as an element of the classification decision. Because of the particular attributes of a specific occupation, any number of facts may be considered inapplicable.

In all, the IRS has identified 20 factors it may consider in any given situation. As the test is very fact specific, it is virtually impossible to predict with any degree of certainty the outcome of a particular situation, or whether any specific combination of factors will result in a favorable outcome. It should be noted that this is an area in which "form" will not prevail over "substance."

As a Congressional committee observed, the 20 common law factors used by the IRS to make reclassification decisions are "extremely subjective and are often inconsistently applied by the IRS." Obviously, the IRS certainly has a bias towards finding the existence of an employer-employee relationship because that finding forms the basis for the most efficient and effective method for collecting taxes in its system. The 20 factors are set forth in the next several pages.

The 20 Factors of the Common Law Test

1. Instructions

    Employees. An employee is required to comply with instruction about when, where, and how to work. Even if no instructions are given, the control factor is present if the employer has the right to give instructions.

    Independent Contractor ("IC's"). IC's determine on their own on how they will proceed in accomplishing an assigned task. An IC is under no obligation to comply with instructions as to how to perform an assigned task, only that they accomplish it.

2. Training

    Employees. An employee is trained to perform services in a particular manner.

    Independent Contractors. IC's ordinarily use their own methods to accomplish the required task and receive very little or no training from the party which retains their services.

3. Integration

    Employees. An employee provides services that are an integral part of the employer's operations.

    Independent Contractors. IC's services are generally not part of the core operations of the engaging party.

4. Services rendered personally

    Employees. Employees are personally required to perform their services and may not assign another individual to perform their tasks.

    Independent Contractors. IC's may or may not personally render the required services, as they are permitted to engage others to do the work.

5. Hiring assistants

    Employees. An employee works for an employer that directly hires, supervises, and compensates the individuals performing the work. Employees do not hire assistants to help perform the required task.

    Independent Contractors. An IC may hire, supervise, and pay assistants under a contract that requires the former to provide materials and/or labor, and is responsible for the contracted results.

6. Continuing relationship

    Employees. An employee has a continuing relationship with an employer on what is hoped to be a long-term basis.

    Independent Contractors. IC's typically enter temporary relationships and move from assignment to assignment.

7. Set hours of work

    Employees. An employee has set hours of work established by an employer.

    Independent Contractors. IC's are masters of their own time; they set their own hours of work.

8. Full-time work

    Employees. An employee normally works full-time for an employer.

    Independent Contractors. IC's work when and for whom they choose; and may be engaged by more than one entity at one time.

9. Work done on premises

Employees. An employee works on the employer's premises, or works at a location chosen by the employer.

Independent Contractors. IC's typically work off the engaging firm's premises, unless the particular tasks need to be done at the engaging firm's place of business.

10. Order or sequence set

Employees. An employee performs services in the sequence set by an employer, a manifestation of the employer's direction and control over the method used to perform the work.

Independent Contractors. IC's decide the method to be used in performing the required task, including the sequence of activities.

11. Reports

Employees. An employee submits interim reports to an employer to keep the employer informed as to the method being used to perform the work. This reporting obligation tends to demonstrate that the individual is subject to direction and control.

Independent Contractors. IC's generally do not submit interim reports; they are only responsible for reporting completion of the work.

12. Payments

Employees. An employee is paid by the hour, week, or month.

Independent Contractors. IC's are normally compensated by a flat rate for a project or a manner different than the engaging firm pays its employees. However, if the general practice in certain trades and professions is to pay on the basis of a unit of time, the method of payment will not be given great weight.

13. Expenses

Employees. An employee's business and travel expenses are paid for by an employer.

Independent Contractors. Typically, IC's pay their own business and traveling expenses. However, it is customary in certain trades and professions for IC's to bill their clients for disbursements such as travel, photocopying and other incidental expenses. Payment of disbursements, in addition to the fee for services, does not create an employment relationship.

14. Tools and materials

Employees. An employer furnishes employees the necessary tools, material, and other equipment needed to complete the task.

Independent Contractors. IC's generally furnish their own tools and materials.

15. Investment

Employees. Employees generally have no investment in equipment or facilities. This demonstrates a lack of independence from the hiring firm and is an additional indicia of a employer-employee relationship.

Independent Contractors. IC's have an investment in the equipment and facilities used in their line of work.

16. Profit or loss

Employees. Employees are typically paid for their time and labor and are not responsible for ensuring that their revenue exceeds their expenses.

Independent Contractors. For an IC, a given assignment presents an opportunity for a profit (revenue exceeding expenses) or a loss (expenses exceeding revenues). In other words, there is risk and reward associated with being an IC.

17. Works for more than one person or firm

Employees. While an employee can have more than one job at a time, employers can demand exclusive employment and prohibit an employee from working for another employer.

Independent Contractors. IC's usually offer their services to multiple, unrelated entities at the same time. Having more than one client or customer at a particular time is persuasive evidence of IC status.

18. Offers services to general public

Employees. Employees offer their services only to their employers.

Independent Contractors. IC's offer their services to the general public.

19. Right to fire

Employees. An employee can be terminated by an employer at will.

Independent Contractors. An IC can be only terminated in accordance with terms of the agreement of engagement. For example, an IC who fails to perform in accordance with the contract terms is in breach, which may be a basis for termination.

20. Right to quit

Employees. An employee can quit his or her job at any time without incurring liability for uncompleted tasks or assignments.

Independent Contractors. An IC usually agrees to perform a specific task and is responsible for its satisfactory completion, or is legally obligated to take responsibility for the damages caused by their failure to complete the job.

The IRS Employment Audit

An IRS audit of a business which involves the possible reclassification of independent contractors as employees, presents three different tax liabilities. First, is the employer's responsibility to withhold and submit income taxes from the wages paid to an employee. Second, is to pay the employer's share and withhold the employee's share of Federal Insurance Contributions Act (FICA) taxes. Finally, the employer is responsible for making payments under the Federal Unemployment Tax Act (FUTA).

Once an audit is completed, the agent will "write up" the audit findings. The taxpayer generally learns the audit results when a notice of deficiency arrives in the mail, advising that taxes and penalties are owed.

Typically, the audit will cover a three-year period. In addition to the deficiency, the IRS will assess a penalty for failure to deposit payroll taxes in a timely manner.

The taxpayer has several courses of action, including internal IRS appeals and, ultimately, litigation. In any case, the taxpayer will have some opportunity to respond to the agent's findings.

Highlights from the IRS Training Manual

The IRS Training Manual provides detailed instructions to field staff on how to conduct a classification audit. The Training Manual expressly recognizes that either worker classification — independent contractor or employee — can be a valid and appropriate business choice.

Highlights taken from the IRS Training Manual provide insight as to the method used by the IRS in determining independent contractor or employee status during a classification audit.

1. **Behavioral Control**. Virtually every business will impose on individuals, whether independent contractors or employees, some form of instruction (for example, requiring that the job be performed within specified time frames). According to the IRS, this fact alone is not sufficient evidence to determine the individual's status.

   As with every relevant fact, the goal is to determine whether the business has retained the right to control the details of an individual's performance or instead has given up its right to control those details. Accordingly, the weight of "instructions" in any case depends on the degree to which instructions apply to how the job gets done rather than to the end result.

   a. *Types of Instructions* – Instruction about how to do the work may cover a wide range of topics, for example:

      - when to do the work
      - where to do the work
      - what tools or equipment to use
      - what workers to hire to assist with the work
      - where to purchase supplies or services
      - what work must be performed by a specified individual (including ability to hire assistants)
      - what routines or patterns must be used
      - what order or sequence to follow

   b. *Prior Approval* – The requirement that an individual obtain approval before taking certain actions is an example of an instruction concerning how the job gets done.

   c. *Degree of Instruction* – The more detailed the instructions the individual is required to follow, the more control the business exercises over the individual, and the more likely it is the business has retained the right to control the methods by which the individual performs the work. An absence of detail in instructions reflects less control.

   d. *Presence of Instructions or Rules Mandated by Governmental Agencies or Industry-Governing Bodies* – If a business requires its individuals to comply with rules established by a third party (for example, municipal building codes related to construction), the fact that such rules are imposed by the business should be given little weight in determining the individual's status. However, if the business develops more stringent guidelines for an individual in addition to those imposed by a third party, more weight will be given to these instructions in determining whether the business has retained the right to control.

   e. *Instructions by Customer* – If the customer tells the business that engages the individual how the work is to be done, the IRS advises its staff that this type of evidence must be evaluated with great care.

If the business passes on the customer's instructions about how to do work as its own, the business may have adopted the customer's standards as its own. The IRS advises its staff not to disregard these instructions and standards merely because they originated with the customer.

f. *Suggestions vs. Instructions* – A true suggestion does not demonstrate the existence of the right to direct and control. For example, a dispatcher may suggest avoiding highway X because of traffic congestion. If the driver is free to accept or reject the suggestion, it is a true suggestion and not an instruction. However, if compliance with the suggestion is mandatory, then the suggestions is, in fact, an instruction.

g. *Nature of Occupation* – The nature of an individual's occupation also affects the degree of direction and control necessary to determine worker status. Highly trained professionals such as doctors, accountants, lawyers, engineers, or computer specialists may require very little, if any, training and/or instruction on how to perform their services. Generally, such professional workers who are engaged in the pursuit of an independent trade, business, or profession in which they offer their services to the public are independent contractors, and not employees, even if some instruction is provided.

h. *Nature of Work for Instructions* – An employment relationship may also exist when the work can be done with a minimal amount of direction and control, such as work done by a stockperson, store clerk, or gas station attendant. The absence of a need to control should not be confused with the absence of a right to control. According to the IRS, the key fact to consider is whether the business retains the right to direct and control the individual, regardless of whether the business actually exercises that right.

i. *Business Identification as Instructions* – In the past, requiring an individual to wear a uniform or to put a business logo on a vehicle was typically viewed as the type of instruction consistent with employee status. However, in view of increasing concerns about safety and security, many businesses now provide customers with some reassurance about the identification of those people gaining access to their homes or work places.

The IRS has told its examiners that wearing a uniform or placing the business' name on a vehicle is a neutral fact in analyzing whether an employment relationship exists.

j. *Evaluation Systems* – Like instructions, evaluation systems are used by virtually all businesses to monitor the quality of work performed by individuals, whether they are independent contractors or employees. Thus, in analyzing whether a business' evaluation system provides evidence of the right to control work performance or the absence of such a right, the IRS tells its field staff to look for evidence of how the evaluation system may influence the individual's behavior in performing the details of the job. If, for example, an evaluation system measures compliance with performance standards concerning the details of how the work is to be performed, the system and its enforcement are evidence of control over the individual's behavior.

k. *Training* – Training is a classic means of explaining detailed methods and procedures to be used in performing a task. Periodic or ongoing training provided by a business about procedures to be followed and methods to be used indicates the business wants the services performed in a particular manner. This type of training is strong evidence of an employer-employee relationship.

2. **Financial Control**. Economic aspects of the relationship between the parties are frequently analyzed in determining the individual's status and illustrate who has financial control over the activities undertaken. The items frequently explored include:

- significant investment
- unreimbursed expenses
- services available to the relevant market
- method of payment
- opportunity for profit or loss

These items bear on the issue of whether the recipient has the right to direct and control the means and details of the economic aspects of how the individual performs services. While the first four items are important in their own right, they also affect whether there is an opportunity for the realization of profit or loss.

a. *Economic Dependence* – Although economic aspects of the relationship between an individual and a business are significant in determining an individual's status, it is equally important to understand that some features of the economic relationship are not relevant. According to the IRS, the question to be asked is whether the recipient has the right to direct and control business-related means and details of the individual's performance.

b. *Significant Investment* – A significant investment is evidence that an independent contractor relationship may exist. The IRS notes, however, that a significant investment is not necessary

for independent contractor status. Some types of work simply do not require large expenditures. Further, even if large expenditures (such as costly equipment) are required, an independent contractor may rent the equipment needed at fair rental value.

c. *No Dollar Limitation on Investment* – There are no precise dollar limits that must be met in order to have a significant investment. However, the investment must have substance. As long as the individual pays fair market or fair rental value, the individual's relationship to the seller or lessor of the equipment is irrelevant. The size of the individual's investment and the risk borne by the individual are not diminished merely because the seller or lessor receives the benefit of the individual's services.

d. *Business Expenses* – The extent to which an individual chooses to incur expenses and bear their costs has an impact on the individual's opportunity for profit or loss. This constitutes evidence that the individual has the right to direct and control the financial aspects of the business' operations. Although not every independent contractor needs to make a significant investment, almost every independent contractor will incur an array of business expenses, either in the form of direct expenditures or in the form of fees for pro rata portions of one or more expenses. These may include:

- rent and utilities
- tools and equipment
- training
- advertising
- payments to business managers and agents
- wages or salaries of assistants

- licensing/certification/professional dues
- insurance
- postage and delivery
- repairs and maintenance
- supplies
- travel
- leasing of equipment
- depreciation
- inventory/cost of goods sold

e. *Reimbursed Expenses* – Businesses often pay business or travel expenses for their employees. However, independent contractors' expenses may also be reimbursed. Independent contractors may contract for direct reimbursement of certain expenses or seek to establish contract prices that will reimburse them for these expenses. The IRS advises its field staff to focus on unreimbursed expenses, which better distinguish independent contractors and employees, inasmuch as independent contractors are more likely to have unreimbursed expenses.

f. *Unreimbursed Expenses* – If expenses are unreimbursed, then the opportunity for profit or loss exists. Fixed, ongoing costs that are incurred regardless of whether work is currently being performed are especially important. However, employees may also incur unreimbursed expenses in connection with the services they perform for their businesses. Thus, relatively minor expenses incurred by an individual, or more significant expenses that are customarily borne by an employee in a particular line of business, such as an auto mechanic's tools, would generally not indicate an independent contractor relationship.

g. *Services Available* – An independent contractor is generally free to seek out

business opportunities. Indeed, the independent contractor's economic prosperity depends on doing so successfully. As a result, independent contractors often advertise, maintain a visible business location, and are available for hire.

Of course, these activities are not essential for independent contractor status. An independent contractor with special skills may be contacted by word of mouth, without the need for advertising. An independent contractor who has negotiated a long-term contract may find advertising equally unnecessary and may be unavailable to work for others for the duration of the contract. Further, other independent contractors may find that a visible business location does not generate sufficient business to justify the expense. Therefore, the absence of these activities is a neutral fact.

h. *Method of Payment* – The IRS notes that the method of payment may be helpful in determining whether an individual has the opportunity for profit or loss. An individual who is compensated on an hourly, daily, weekly, or similar basis is guaranteed a return for labor. This is generally evidence of an employer-employee relationship, even when the wage or salary is accompanied by a commission. However, in some lines of business, such as law, it is typical to pay independent contractors on an hourly basis. Performance of a task for a flat fee is generally evidence of an independent contractor relationship, especially if the individual incurs the expenses of performing the services. The timing as to when payments are made (daily, weekly, or monthly) is not relevant. A commission-based individual may be either an independent contractor or employee. The individual's status may depend on his or her ability to realize a profit or incur a loss as a result of services rendered.

i. *Realization of Profit and Loss* – The ability to realize a profit or incur a loss is probably the strongest evidence that an individual controls the business aspects of services rendered. The other factors already considered -- significant investment, unreimbursed expenses, making services available, and method of payment are also relevant in this regard. If the individual is making decisions which affect his bottom line, it follows that the individual likely has the ability to realize profit or loss.

It is sometimes asserted that because an individual can receive more money by working longer hours or receive less money by working fewer, the individual has the ability to incur a profit or loss. This type of income variation, however, is also consistent with employee status and does not distinguish employees from independent contractors.

j. *Not All Facts Required* – Note that not all of the financial control factors need to be present in order for the individual to have the ability to realize profit or loss. The IRS cites, for example, an individual who is paid on a straight commission basis, makes business decisions, and has unreimbursed business expenses likely would have the ability to realize profit or loss even if the individual does not have a significant investment and does not market services.

3. **Relationship of the Parties**. Courts often consider the intent of the parties in determining the nature of their relationship. This is most often embodied in their contractual relationship. Thus, a written agreement describing the individual as an independent contractor is viewed as

evidence that the parties intended to create an independent contractor relationship.

a. *Contractual Designation* – The contract, however, is not, in and of itself, determinative of an individual's status. The facts and circumstances under which an individual performs services will determine the individual's status. This means the substance of the relationship, not the label given by the parties, governs the individual's status. The contract may, however, provide relevant evidence in ascertaining methods of compensation, expenses that may be incurred, and the rights and obligations of each party with respect to how work is to be performed.

In addition, if it is difficult to determine whether an individual is an independent contractor or an employee, the intent of the parties, as reflected in their contract, may be an effective way to resolve the issue. The contractual designation of the relationship has been described as being "very significant in close cases."

b. *Form W-2* – Issuing a W-2 Form indicates one or both parties believe that the individual is an employee.

c. *Incorporation* – Questions sometimes arise as to whether an individual who creates a corporation through which services are rendered can be an employee of a business that engages the corporation. Provided that the corporate formalities are properly followed and at least one non-tax business purpose exists, the corporate form is generally recognized for both state law and federal law, including federal tax purposes.

However, the fact that an individual receives payment for services from a business through the individual's corporation does not automatically require a finding of independent contractor status with respect to those services.

For example, a professional athlete who attempted to assign a salary received from the team to a wholly-owned professional corporation was nevertheless held by the Tax Court to be a common law employee of the team, rather than an independent, professional corporation.

d. *Employee Benefits* – Providing an individual with employee benefits traditionally associated with employee status has been an important fact in several recent court decisions. Receipt of employee benefits, such as paid vacation days, paid sick days, health insurance, life or disability insurance, or a pension, constitutes evidence of employee status. The evidence is strongest if the individual is provided with employee benefits under a tax-qualified retirement plan, IRC Section 403(b) annuity or cafeteria plan. By statute, these employee benefits can only be provided to employees.

e. *State Law Characterization* – State laws, or determinations of state or federal agencies, may characterize an individual as an employee for purposes of various benefits. IRS staff are instructed to disregard characterizations based on these laws or determinations because the laws or regulations involved may use different definitions of employee or be designed to achieve particular policy objectives.

f. *Discharge/Termination* – The circumstances under which a business or an individual can terminate their relationship has been considered relevant evidence concerning the type of relationship the parties intended to create.

Under a traditional analysis, a business' ability to terminate the work relationship at will and without penalty provided a highly effective method to control the details of how work was performed and, therefore, tended to indicate employee status. Conversely, in the traditional independent contractor relationship, the business could terminate the relationship only if the individual failed to provide the agreed upon service, thus indicating the parties' intent that the business not have the right to control how the work was performed, only that it be performed.

Because determining the nature of the right to discharge/terminate is often unclear in practice, and depends primarily on interpreting contract and labor law, the IRS advises its field staff that this type of evidence should be evaluated with great caution.

g. *Permanency* – Courts have considered the existence of a permanent relationship between the individual and the business as relevant evidence in determining whether there is an employer-employee relationship.

h. *Indefinite Relationship* – If a business engages an individual with the expectation that the relationship will continue indefinitely, rather than for a specific project or period, it is generally considered evidence of their intent to create an employment relationship.

i. *Long-Term Relationship* – A relationship created with the expectation that it will be indefinite should not be confused with a long-term relationship. A long-term relationship may exist between a business and either an independent contractor or an employee.

The relationship between the business and an independent contractor may be long-term for several reasons:

• the contract may be a long-term contract

• contracts may be renewed regularly due to superior service, competitive costs, or lack of alternative service providers.

A business may also have a relationship with an employee that is long-term, but not indefinite. This could occur if temporary employment contracts are renewed or if a long-term, but not indefinite, employment contract is entered into. As a result, according to the IRS, a relationship that is long-term, but not indefinite, is a neutral fact that should be disregarded.

j. *Temporary Relationship* – According to the IRS, a temporary relationship is also a neutral fact that should be disregarded. An independent contractor will typically have a temporary relationship with a business, but so will employees engaged on a seasonal, project or "as needed" basis.

k. *Regular Business Activity* – The courts have looked at whether the services performed by the individual, and the extent to which those services are performed, are a key aspect of the regular business of the company.

According to the IRS, in considering this evidentiary fact, the mere fact that a service is desirable, necessary, or even essential to a business does not mean the service provider is an employee. An appliance store needs individuals to install electricity and plumbing in the store building. However, this work can be done equally well by independent contractors or employees.

In contrast, the work of an attorney or paralegal is part of the regular business of a law firm. If a law firm hires an attorney or paralegal, it is likely the firm will present the work as its own. As a result, there is an increased probability that the law firm will direct or control their activities.

Common Sense Suggestions to Avoid Adverse IRS Determinations

If one engages independent contractors, the best way to prevent a problem is to ensure that the relationship with them is a professional and well documented one.

Remember, an independent contractor is just that, independent. The standards one applies to dealing with other non-employees should apply. For that reason, relationships with independent contractors should be carefully reviewed.

Here are a number of suggestions:

1. Avoid the appearance of "employment" by calling a meeting of independent contractors. Meet with them one-on-one. Also, keep proper separation from regular company staff meetings. Do not hold employee-type instructional or training meetings for independent contractors.

2. Keep corporate logos, insignia, or signs off independent contractors' trucks and at the job site.

3. You may provide company shirts or other items of clothing imprinted with company name so as to promote consumer safety and security concerns. This reflects today's realities.

4. Provide materials to independent contractors at a bona fide price that reflects, at a minimum, the cost of the material and overhead. Furnish an invoice for these materials.

5. Do not have a policy preventing the independent contractor from working for other customers, including competitors (stated or unstated) unless there are trade secret or other compelling reasons.

6. If a job performance is deficient, then the independent contractor who did it should be given the opportunity to correct or cure the defect, or stand the risk of financial penalty.

7. It is recommended that a separate file be kept for each independent contractor containing a copy of the contractual agreement (ideally, it should be for each work order), copies of 1099 Forms, certificates of insurance, etc. If there ever is an audit, these documents will be critical.

8. Require each contractor to submit an invoice prior to payment.

9. Do not automatically deduct expenses or make chargebacks without independent contractor approval.

10. Issue payments to independent contractors on the same schedule as other vendors.

11. An independent contractor should be able to negotiate rates for extra work for the customer and decide whether to accept such work.

12. If a company vehicle is used, there must be a fair payment for its use. It is far more preferable to insist the contractor provide all the necessary equipment. If this is not possible, then be certain adequate rent is paid for equipment use.

13. Do not advertise that contractors work exclusively for one firm.

14. Remember, independent contractors hire their own assistants.

15. Contractor preference or construction practices should determine scheduling.

16. Require proof of liability insurance from contractors.

17. If one has both independent contractors and regular employees who do similar work, distinguish the treatment of each in as many ways as practicable. For example, employees can earn overtime premium pay.

18. An independent contractor should never be threatened as a result of an inability or an unwillingness to be available for work. Obviously, you can choose those who have performed well and reliably in the past. You do not have to conduct a lottery for the jobs if there are more independent contractors available than there are jobs needed to be performed.

19. Be careful with terminology. Employees are paid on the basis of payroll agreements; the payment for the independent contractor is based upon the terms of a contract. Remember, you can terminate employees but, in the case of independent contractors, you may choose to end the "contractual agreement." You should not "fire" independent contractors.

20. Do not specify that certain individuals be part of work crews of independent contractors.

21. If state licenses are required for independent contractors to perform services, make sure independent contractors furnish proof they have secured the necessary license.

22. When communicating with independent contractors, do not use the same types of communications you send to employees. For example, do not terminate the contractual relationship with an independent contractor with the same termination letter you would send an employee.

23. Do not hand out employee work rules or employee handbooks or manuals to contractors. If there are certain workplace rules or policies you wish to apply to independent contractors (*e.g.*, sexual harassment or drug free workplace), incorporate them by reference in the contract or republish them as contractor policies.

Section 530 – Statutory Safe Harbor

A statutory safe harbor known as IRC § 530 provides that a business may engage individuals and treat them as independent contractors, even though the relationship might not meet the IRS test. First, the company engaging the individual must meet certain procedural requirements:

1. The individual must not have been treated as an employee at any time.

2. All Federal tax returns required (e.g., Forms 1099) for the individual must have been filed.

3. The safe harbor is not available if the company has treated any individual holding a substantially similar position as an employee.

If these procedural requirements are met, one of the following conditions must also apply before the IRS will recognize the availability of the Safe Harbor:

1. There is a past IRS audit of the company, and there was no assessment of employment taxes of individuals holding positions substantially similar to the positions now in question. The provision does not affect the ability of taxpayers to rely on prior audits that commenced before January 1, 1997, even though the audit was not related to employment tax matters;

2. There is a judicial precedent, a published ruling, or a letter ruling on technical advice with respect to the taxpayer, that indicates the individual may be treated as an independent contractor; or

3. It has been a long-standing recognized practice of a significant segment of the industry to treat the individuals as independent contractors.

It is not necessary for the business to expressly claim Section 530 relief for it to be applicable. In order to correctly determine tax liability, as required by the IRS' mission, the IRS must explore the applicability of Section 530 even if the business does not raise the issue.

The IRS must, at (or before) the commencement of an audit involving worker classification issues, provide the taxpayer with written notice of the provisions of Section 530. In many cases, the portion of an audit involving worker classification issues will not arise until after the examination of the taxpayer has begun. In that case, the notice need only be given at the time the worker classification issue is first raised with the taxpayer.

Section 530 Process

The IRS takes the position that it must first determine whether the individuals are employees or independent contractors before applying Section 530. The IRS reasons that Section 530 is limited in scope to the business' liability for FICA, FUTA, and federal income tax withholding, as well as any interest or penalties attributable to that employment tax liability. It does not change the worker's status for purposes of other tax provisions, including those that apply to pensions and other employee benefit plans.

Additionally, the IRS claims Section 530 relief does not extend to the worker. Only the business is eligible for relief.

Thus, the worker who is determined by the IRS to be an employee remains liable for the employee's share of FICA tax. Often, the worker will have filed and paid his or her own employment tax. If the worker paid self-employment tax (SECA), he or she may file a claim for refund for the difference between SECA tax and the employee share of FICA.

Substantive Consistency

Section 530 does not apply if the business or a predecessor treated the individual, or any individual holding a substantially similar position, as an employee at any time after December 31, 1977. In other words, treatment of the class of individuals must be consistent with the business' belief that they were independent contractors.

According to the IRS, a substantially similar position exists if the job functions, duties, and responsibilities are substantially similar, and the control and supervision of those duties and responsibilities is substantially similar.

Examples of treatment consistent or inconsistent with the business entity's belief as to independent contractor status, include:

1. The withholding of federal income tax or FICA tax from an individual's wages is treatment of the worker as an employee, whether or not the tax is paid to the Government.

2. Filing a Form 940, 941, 942, 943, or W-2 with respect to an individual, whether or not tax was withheld from the individual, is treatment of the individual as an employee for that period.

3. The filing of a delinquent or amended employment tax return for a particular tax period is not treatment of the individual as an employee if the filing was a result of IRS compliance procedures. However, filing the returns for periods after the period under audit is "treatment" of the individual as an employee for those later periods, regardless of the time at which the return was filed.

4. It is the IRS' view that only federal tax treatment as an employee is relevant. Thus, if a business treats individuals as employees for state unemployment or state withholding tax purposes, that is not "treatment" for purposes of determining whether the provisions of Section 530 have been satisfied.

5. Section 530 specifically states that the treatment by predecessor entities will be taken into account when evaluating substantive consistency. This ensures that the substantive consistency rule is not avoided by the formation of new entities.

6. If the business begins to treat misclassified individuals as employees, relief may be granted under Section 530 for the years it treated them as independent contractors, provided it meets all the requirements (reporting and substantive consistency and reasonable basis) for the years prior to the change in treatment.

7. The IRS recognizes that some individuals perform services in dual capacities. For example, a business' bookkeeper might be separately engaged to design and print an advertising brochure. The fact that the bookkeeper is treated as an employee with respect to the bookkeeping services does not preclude application of Section 530 if it is determined that the bookkeeper is an employee, and not an independent contractor, with respect to the design and printing services.

The IRS tells its field staff: "Remember that if the business establishes the existence of a safe haven, the business must show reliance on the safe haven. Section 530 requires that the reliance must be reasonable. At the time you conduct a worker classification examination, you should explore with the business why it treated the workers as independent contractors. The business's stated reasons should be set forth in your workpapers. This is important if the case is unagreed, as it provides invaluable information to the appeals officer or attorney. However, the business's stated reasons should also be recorded in agreed cases, as the business may later file a claim for refund."

Prior Audit

A business is treated as having a reasonable basis under § 530 if it relied on a prior audit.

A taxpayer may not rely on an audit commenced after December 31, 1996, unless such audit included an examination for employment tax purposes of whether the individual involved (or any individual holding a position substantially similar to the position held by the individual involved) should be treated as an employee of the taxpayer.

The prior audit safe haven does not apply if the relationship between the business and the workers is substantially different from that which existed at the time of the audit.

The prior audit safe haven is limited to past audits conducted on the business itself. Therefore, a business is not entitled to relief based upon a prior audit of any of its workers. Nor would a subsidiary corporation usually be entitled to relief based upon a prior audit of its separately filing parent corporation. Even if a consolidated return was filed in the year the parent was audited, the subsidiary would only be entitled to relief if the subsidiary was examined in connection with the parent.

If a corporation which was previously audited begins conducting a new line of business, that corporation is not entitled to relief based upon the audit of the corporation's original line of business. However, if there has only been a change of form and the successor entity is in the same line of business, the corporation may nevertheless be entitled to Section 530 relief if the corporation can demonstrate, in some other manner, any reasonable basis for not treating the worker as an employee.

A business will be able to claim that it was subject to a prior audit if the IRS previously inspected the business' books and records. Mere inquiries or correspondence from a Service Center will not constitute an audit.

If, for example, a correspondence contact was made to verify a discrepancy disclosed by an information matching program, such as Information Returns Processing, self-employment tax, and similar Service Center programs, such contacts do not constitute a prior audit. They are referred to as adjustments. However, if correspondence contacts entailed the examination or inspection of the business' records to determine the accuracy of deductions claimed on a return, such contacts do constitute an audit for purposes of Section 530.

Judicial Precedent

Another safe haven provided by Section 530 is judicial precedent. To obtain relief under this section, the business must demonstrate reasonable reliance on a judicial precedent, a published ruling, technical advice relating to that business, or a letter ruling to that business.

Because the business must show reasonable reliance, the facts in the judicial precedent or published ruling relied upon must be similar to the business' situation. The facts need not be identical and the precedent relied upon need not deal with exactly the same industry as the business'. In addition, the judicial precedent or published ruling relied upon must have been in existence at the time the business began treating workers as independent contractors.

As long as these requirements are met, one case is sufficient to establish a precedent that creates a safe haven. This is true even if case law can be found to support either side of the independent contractor/employee issue.

A technical advice memorandum (TAM) or a private letter ruling (PLR) addressing the employer-employee relationship can be used by the business to which it was issued for purposes of the judicial precedent safe haven. If a private letter ruling is issued to a member of a group of related corporations, the business may rely upon the ruling only if it is specifically addressed to that business entity. Note that each corporation included in a related group is considered a separate business entity.

A private letter ruling issued to a business may not be relied upon by its successor. However if there has merely been a change in form, the business may have some "other reasonable basis" on which it could rely. Even a private letter ruling or determination letter issued to the business itself cannot be relied upon if the facts were materially misstated or omitted. Further, if there has been a substantial change in the facts since the ruling or determination was obtained, the precedent does not apply.

Since Section 530 offers relief from having to establish the federal common law standards for employer-employee relationships, only federal court decisions and revenue rulings interpreting the IRC are relevant. Businesses are not entitled to the judicial precedent safe haven based upon state court decisions. The term "published rulings" refers to revenue rulings which are intended for general use by all businesses. Neither rulings by state administrative agencies, including agencies which regulate employment, nor rulings from federal agencies other than the IRS, can be used to support a judicial precedent safe haven.

Industry Practice

Proof of a long-standing, recognized practice of a significant segment of the industry to treat certain individuals as independent contractors may lead to the establishment of the § 530 safe harbor. The elements of "significant segment" and "long-standing" have their own safe harbor tests.

The safe harbor test for a "significant segment" of the taxpayer's industry is defined as 25 percent or more of an industry (determined without including the taxpayer in the calculation). As this percentage is intended to be a "safe harbor," a lower percentage may constitute a "significant segment" of the taxpayer's industry based on the particular facts and circumstances.

An industry practice will be considered "long-standing" if it has continued for more than 10 years. An industry practice in existence for a shorter period of time may be considered "long-standing" based on the particular facts and circumstances.

The IRS takes the position that an industry generally consists of businesses located in the same geographic or metropolitan area which compete for the same customers. For example, the landscaping industry will generally consist of businesses within a single metropolitan area. However, if the area includes only one or a few businesses in the same industry, the geographic area may be extended to include contiguous areas in which there are other businesses competing for the same customers. If businesses compete in regional or national markets, the geographic area may include the competitors in that region or throughout the United States. For example, the commercial film production industry competes in a national market.

In addition to showing that the business followed an industry practice at the time it began treating individuals as independent contractors, the business must also show that its reliance on the industry practice was reasonable.

Reasonable reliance consists of two concepts, reasonableness and reliance, which are simple to state but not always simple to establish. The IRS first asks whether the business claiming the industry practice safe haven actually relied upon industry practice.

1. **Reliance** — According to the IRS, a claim of reliance on industry practice necessarily

requires that the business establish that it knew of the industry practice at the time the independent contractor treatment began. Thus, the date the business' independent contractor treatment began must be determined. It must then be established that the long-standing industry practice existed at that time in order to be relied upon. Evidence of the year the business began its treatment of the individuals as independent contractor is proven by the business' first filing of Form 1099's for those individuals. Evidence of when an industry's long-standing practice began and of the business' knowledge of that practice is more difficult to identify and substantiate.

2. **Establishing Industry Practice** — Reliance on industry practice with respect to independent contractor treatment can result from the business' general knowledge of competition in the industry or from communications with competitors or business advisers knowledgeable about the industry. According to the IRS, the fact that a formal survey was not conducted when independent contractor treatment began is relevant to, but not conclusive of, whether the business relied on industry practice.

The fact that a current survey confirms long-standing industry practice can buttress other evidence that the business relied on industry practice during the relevant period. IRS agents are instructed to discuss with the business, before it begins its survey, the desired sample size, method of selecting the sample, and questions to be asked. The survey should be verifiable or, if anonymity for the businesses contacted is sought, it should be conducted by an independent third party.

3. **Establishing Reliance** — Whether the business relied on industry practice can be established by several types of evidence such as business records, corporate minutes,

unanimous consents in lieu of directors' meetings, or statements from individuals themselves establishing the reasons given to them by the business when establishing their status as independent contractors.

Section 530 Coverage

Under Section 530(d) relief is not available in the case of a worker who, pursuant to an arrangement between the business and a client, provides services for that client as any of the following:

- engineer;
- designer;
- drafter;
- computer programmer;
- systems analyst; or
- other similarly skilled worker engaged in a similar line of work.

1. **Corporate Officers** - Officers of corporations generally are included within the definition of an employee. However, an officer is not considered to be an employee of the corporation if two requirements are met: (1) the officer does not perform any services or performs only minor services; and (2) the officer is not entitled to receive, directly or indirectly, any remuneration.

The officer must meet both requirements to be excepted from employee status. In determining whether services performed by a corporate officer are considered minor or nominal, examine the character of the service, the frequency and duration of performance, and the actual or potential importance or necessity of the services in relation to the conduct of the corporation's business.

2. **Statutory Employees** - If a worker is not an employee under the usual common law rules or a corporate officer, the worker and the business may nevertheless still be subject to employment taxes if an individual works in one of four occupational groups who, under certain circumstances, are considered employees for FICA tax. These groups are:

   - agent-drivers or commission-drivers;
   - full-time life insurance salespersons;
   - home workers; or
   - traveling or city salespersons.

   These workers are referred to as "statutory employees." While workers in these four occupational groups are considered employees for FICA tax purposes, they are not employees for federal income tax withholding purposes.

   The regulations defining a statutory employee have three general requirements. They are:

   a. The contract of service contemplates that the worker will personally perform substantially all the work.

   b. The worker has no substantial investment in facilities other than transportation facilities used in performing the work.

   c. There is a continuing work relationship with the business for which the services are performed.

   Workers in the following three occupations will not be treated as employees for FICA, FUTA, or federal income tax withholding purposes provided they meet certain qualifications. These workers are referred to as "statutory non-employees":

   - qualified real estate agents;
   - direct sellers; and
   - companion sitters.

Fair Labor Standards Act – Minimum Wage/Overtime 2

Legislative Purpose

In 1938, Congress enacted the Fair Labor Standards Act (FLSA). For the first time, it was the law of the land to permit Congress to regulate the minimum standards for hours and wages of covered employees. The legislative history reveals a congressional intent to lessen the historic high unemployment of the depression years by shortening workweek hours and spreading available work among a greater number of workers. The principle was simple: a fair day's pay for a fair day's work. Congress wanted to discourage, if not eliminate, substandard wages by establishing a minimum wage and a premium for overtime.

In its nearly seven-decade existence, the FLSA has been amended numerous times by Congress, reflecting ever-expanding coverage of the work force to the extent it is estimated that well over 90 percent of the full-time and part-time nonsupervisory workers in the private sector are now covered by the law. The Wage and Hour Division, an integral part of the Employment Standards Administration of the U.S. Department of Labor, is responsible for the administration of the FLSA.

Coverage

The FLSA defines employee coverage by reference to three basic tests. Meeting any one of the following tests is sufficient for coverage.

1. Any employee engaged in interstate or foreign commerce is covered.

2. Any employee producing goods for interstate commerce is covered. By later amendment, the law specifically includes those nonproduction workers whose activities are closely related or directly essential to production (e.g., maintenance, custodial, and clerical workers). Thus, FLSA coverage would ensue in virtually all interstate manufacturing businesses, regardless of size or sales volume.

3. Any employee of an "enterprise," which is defined as an entity with a common business purpose, engaged in commerce or in the production of goods, or which has employees handling, selling, or otherwise working on goods or materials, is covered so long as the enterprise has annual gross sales of $500,000. [Note that tests (1) and (2) predicate coverage on the activities of the individual employee, but in test (3) employer coverage of the employees is determined by what the enterprise does; once an enterprise is covered, all employees, regardless of position, are subject to the FLSA.]

It is this "enterprise" standard that is used to cover retail and wholesale businesses. Additionally, employees of hospitals, schools, and institutional care facilities are considered to be employees of an enterprise, for which there is no sales dollar volume threshold for coverage.

Some FLSA "Coverage" Issues and Answers

1. A domestic service worker (any employee in a private home) is covered if that employee receives wages from one employer of $50 or more in a calendar quarter, or if that employee is employed for more than eight aggregate hours in a workweek in one or more households.

2. Both casual babysitting (less than 20 hours per week) and companionship services (not including the services of trained personnel like registered nurses) in the case of the aged or infirm are not covered.

3. To determine the applicability of the $500,000 sales volume test for a retail business, the gross receipts from all sales (excluding excise and sales tax) during a 12-month period immediately preceding the calendar quarter in question will be counted. At the beginning of each calendar quarter, volume for the preceding 12 months is determined. This is known as the "rolling quarter" method. When the statutory dollar volume levels are met, enterprise coverage applies from that time on or until such time as the dollar volume tests are not met. A new business would project annual sales based on its first quarter sales to determine whether it is covered.

4. The "enterprise" test includes all of the related activities of the employer achieved by unified operations or common control for a common business purpose. If this relationship exists, then all facets of an employer's business would be taken in aggregate to determine if the threshold dollar sales volume has been reached.

5. While courts have liberally interpreted the coverage provisions of the FLSA, the burden of proving that coverage is placed on the employee in wage law suits and on the Secretary of Labor in wage recovery litigation.

6. Where there is a bona fide desire by individuals to volunteer and donate their time for public, charitable, religious, or humanitarian service without the expectation of compensation, there would not be an employment relationship.

7. A true, unincorporated family business which employs only family members (parent, spouse, child, or other member of the immediate family) is not a covered enterprise.

Federal Minimum Wage Rate Changes
(1938-2006)

Year	Rate
1938	$0.25/Hour
1939	$0.30/Hour
1945	$0.45/Hour
1950	$0.75/Hour
1956	$1.00/Hour
1961	$1.15/Hour
1962	$1.25/Hour
1967	$1.40/Hour
1968	$1.60/Hour
1974	$2.00/Hour
1975	$2.10/Hour
1976	$2.30/Hour
1978	$2.65/Hour
1979	$2.90/Hour
1980	$3.10/Hour
1981	$3.35/Hour
1990	$3.80/Hour
1991	$4.25/Hour
1996	$4.75/Hour
1997	$5.15/Hour*

*Note: the scope of this book is limited to federal law. Federal requirements are considered a floor. If state laws impose greater requirements, the more stringent state law requirements must be met. Therefore, a review of applicable state minimum wage, overtime, child labor and other wage and hour requirements is essential.

The *U.S. Dept. of Labor in the 21st Century* website provides links to current state law rates at: www.dol.gov/dol/topic/wages/minimumwage.htm

Opportunity Wage

The 1996 amendments to the Fair Labor Standards Act provided for an "Opportunity Wage." Employees under 20 years of age may be paid $4.25 per hour during their first 90 consecutive calendar days of employment as long as their work does not displace other workers. An employer is subject to sanctions if an opportunity wage is used to displace employees or otherwise reduce hours, wages or employment benefits. After 90 consecutive days of employment or the employee reaches 20 years of age, whichever comes first, the employee must receive a minimum wage of $5.15 per hour.

What the FLSA Does Not Regulate

While the Fair Labor Standards Act does set basic minimum wage and overtime pay standards and regulates the employment of minors, there are a number of employment practices which the Act does not regulate. For example, the Act does not require:

- vacation, holiday, severance, or sick pay;
- meal or rest periods, holidays off, or vacations;
- premium pay for weekend or holiday work;
- pay raises or fringe benefits;
- a discharge notice, reason for discharge, or immediate payment of final wages to terminated employees; and
- any limit on the number of hours of work for persons 16 years of age and over.

Hours Worked

The original FLSA contained no definition of "working time" for the purpose of computing the minimum wage. The U.S. Supreme Court has set down a rule to the effect that working hours include all time during which an employee is engaged in physical or mental effort controlled or required by his or her employer and pursued primarily for the benefit of the employer and the business. If the employer "suffers or permits" the employee to perform services on its behalf, the time is considered "working time". The Supreme Court also ruled that any time an employee spent at a plant, after punching in, to get to the job and to get ready, was a part of the hours worked, but time which the employee merely spent waiting because he or she arrived early was not compensable.

After these two decisions, many workers pressed to recover overtime pay to cover the time spent from the moment one arrived on the plant premises to the time one left. Known as the "portal-to-portal" pay litigation, the intense controversy led to congressional enactment of the Portal-to-Portal Act (1947). This law, in part, was designed to prevent legal actions by employees to recover pay for non-productive time. The law established the guideposts to determine what constitutes the "workday." This Act confined the employer's obligation to pay wages for the employee's principal activity, unless there is a contract, custom, or practice requiring pay for these peripheral activities. For example, the time employees spent "donning and doffing" safety equipment and clothing was considered working time. In addition, the Supreme Court recently ruled that where workers have to don and doff protective gear in order to do their work, the time that they have to spend walking from the changing room to their work stations is compensable work.

A 1996 amendment to the Portal-to-Portal Act allows employers and employees to agree on the use of employer-provided vehicles to commute to and from work at the end of the workday, without the commuting time being treated as hours of work.

In general, all the time an employee is actually at work, or required to be on duty and not use the time for his or her own purposes, is compensable. A Circuit Court of Appeals has ruled that the

Department of Labor's regulation requiring compensation for meal breaks "during which a worker performs activities predominantly for the benefit of the employer" is valid even when the workers provide a passive service (e.g., security). In the court's view, being present and watchful is an "indispensable" service to the employer. Travel away from home is clearly work time when it cuts across the employee's work day. The employee is simply substituting travel for other duties. The table below illustrates how Department of Labor interpretations, court rulings, and legislative history have determined the status of some common workplace activities and whether they count as "hours worked." However, as with any generalization, there are exceptions. The determinations represent the prevailing rule.

Defining the "Workweek"

The workweek – seven consecutive, regular, recurring, 24-hour periods totaling 168 hours – is the unit of time used for determining compliance with the minimum wage. The computation and recording of hours worked is to be done on a workweek basis, and the employee must be paid, free and clear, compensation equal to at least the minimum wage for each hour worked in the workweek. It may begin on any day of the week and any hour of the day established by the employer. As long as the average hourly earnings for non-overtime hours in each workweek equal the minimum wage, the requirement is considered satisfied for that week. Average hourly earnings above the minimum in one workweek may not be used to offset earnings below the minimum wage in another workweek.

An employer can change the payday of its employees so long as the change is intended to be permanent, is done for legitimate business purposes, does not evade minimum wage and overtime requirements, and does not cause an unreasonable delay in payment of wages.

Official Rulings on "Hours Worked" for Compensation

Activity	Compensable Hours Worked	Noncompensable Hours Worked
Washing up after work		✓
Changing clothes		✓
Coffee break (less than 20 minutes)	✓	
Putting on Safety Equipment	✓	
Meal period*		✓
Staff training/ meeting	✓	
Voting time		✓

*Any time the employee is required or permitted to perform any duties while eating, the time will be compensable.

Minimum Wage Compliance

Let's examine some typical wage computations in which the minimum wage payment is the issue:

1. In the case of an employee hired on an hourly rate basis, it is required that the rate equal the statutory minimum.

2. In the case of a commission employee (e.g., commissions are the sole basis of compensation), the individual's earnings must be at least equal to the minimum wage rate for each of the hours worked, exclusive of overtime.

3. In the case of an employee who is paid an hourly rate for a portion of the workweek and a commission for the balance, earnings at the hourly rate which exceed the minimum may not be applied to make up differences

in the commission earnings during the other part of the week.

4. In the case of a piece-rate worker, earnings must equal at least the legal hourly minimum over the course of the workweek.

Deductions From Wages

While it is true the FLSA provides for the "free and clear" payment of the minimum wage for each workweek in cash or its equivalent each payday, the law does recognize one specific exception. Deductions are permitted for "reasonable cost" or "fair value" of "board, lodging, or other facilities." The FLSA has been interpreted to mean that "reasonable costs" of furnishing board, lodging, or other facilities may not include any profit to the employer.

Compensation for overtime hours is disregarded in determining whether the deductions made by the employer are legal. Thus, deductions for "board, lodging, or other facilities" are legal, and so long as the cash wage and the "reasonable cost" equal the minimum wage, there is no violation. Certain taxes assessed against the employee and collected by means of a wage deduction are not "wages" under FLSA. Included in this category are an employee's contribution to Social Security (FICA), federal and state unemployment insurance, and other state and local taxes. An employee may authorize the employer to make deductions to turn over to some third party; when voluntarily assigned, these deductions are not violations of the law (e.g., union dues, purchase of savings bonds, and insurance premiums).

Deductions from an employee's wages for cash shortages are considered illegal to the extent that they reduce the wages of the employees below the required minimum or reduce the overtime compensation due under FLSA. There has been a court ruling involving deliberately misappropriated monies in the case

of repayment of these funds by an employee. There is no violation of FLSA rules as long as the criminal action has been determined in court.[1]

In circumstances where an employee must wear a uniform, the financial burden of furnishing and maintaining (including laundry and repairing) the uniform may not be imposed upon the employee if the result would be to lower wages to below the minimum wage or overtime compensation required by FLSA. In cases where the employer merely prescribes a general type of ordinary basic clothing and permits some diversity in details of dress, the clothing is not considered a uniform. The Wage and Hour Division has ruled that when an employee is required to purchase a uniform, that individual must be reimbursed for the cost of the uniform to the extent that the expense cuts into the required minimum wage or overtime compensation. This reimbursement must be made promptly on the next immediate payday, and may not be spread over the life of the uniform.

Tip Credit

The cash wages paid a "tipped" employee by an employer must be at least $2.13 per hour, if the employer claims a tip credit against one's minimum wage obligation. The employer, however, would be required to make up any difference between the minimum wage and the combination of $2.13 plus tips to ensure that each employee makes at least the minimum wage.

A "tipped employee" is any employee engaged in an occupation in which he or she customarily and regularly receives more than $30 a month

---

1. There are a number of state labor statutes prohibiting any deduction from an employee's paycheck unless authorized in writing and for the benefit of the employee.

in tips. The law requires that (1) the employer must inform tipped employees about this tip credit allowance before the credit is utilized; (2) the employees must be allowed to retain all tips (individually or through a pooling arrangement), and this is so regardless of whether the employer elects to take a credit for tips received; and (3) the employer must be able to show that the employee receives at least the minimum wage in the combination of direct wages and the tip credit. An employer may not take a greater tip credit in overtime hours than in straight time hours.

A compulsory charge for service – for example, 15 percent of the bill – is not a tip. Such charges are part of the employer's gross receipts, and where service charges are imposed and the employees receive no tips, the employer must pay the entire minimum wage and overtime as required by the Act.

Learners, Apprentices, and Handicapped Workers

The FLSA provides discretion to the Wage and Hour Administration to permit the employment of learners, apprentices, and handicapped workers at hourly wages lower than the prevailing minimum wage. There is no exemption from the overtime pay provision for these workers.

The Administration must issue a certificate to the employer before that employer can make use of the exemption. An "apprentice" is a person at least sixteen years of age who is employed to learn a skilled trade through a registered apprenticeship program. Training is provided through structured on-the-job training combined with supplemental related theoretical and technical instruction.

A "handicapped worker" is one whose earning capacity is impaired by age, physical or mental deficiency, or injury. The learning period will normally not exceed 240 hours for any qualifying occupation. The subminimum wage rate is 95 percent of the prevailing minimum wage. These workers may be engaged by commercial establishments or by "sheltered workshops." The FLSA allows for a subminimum no less than 50 percent of the minimum wage, but the Act requires an employer to pay wages commensurate with those paid nonhandicapped workers in the area, taking into consideration the type, quality, and quantity of work produced.

The "learner" is a beginner at a skilled occupation. In order for a certificate to be issued, there must be a showing that the lower wage is necessary to prevent the loss of employment opportunities. It was not the purpose of the FLSA to make the employment of learners more advantageous to the employer than the employment of experienced workers.

Trainees

To answer the question, "When are trainees considered 'employees' under FLSA?" it is necessary to examine all of their activities. If all of the following elements are present, then the trainees would not be considered "employees." The tests are derived from two U.S. Supreme Court cases involving the status of trainees:

1. Both the employer and trainees understand that the trainees are not entitled to compensation during the time spent for training.

2. The trainees are not necessarily entitled to a job at the conclusion of the training period.

3. The training is not unique and is merely like a vocational school's work experience period.

4. The training is primarily for the benefit of the trainee.

5. The employer derives no obvious advantage from the activities of the trainees; indeed, operations may be impeded by them.

6. The trainees neither replace regular employees nor work under their supervision.

Full-Time Students and Subminimum Wage

The FLSA provides for a minimum wage of 85 percent of the prevailing minimum for full-time students engaged in work at retail-service establishments, on farms, and at higher educational institutions. Certificates will be issued to employers applying for this preferential treatment so long as there is no lessening of opportunities for employment among full-time workers.

To minimize paperwork and to encourage small retail and service business, the FLSA allows these employers to engage up to six full-time students by merely notifying the Department of Labor. In this instance, only the following steps would be necessary:

1. Complete a simple application and send it to a Regional Office of the Wage Hour Division of the Department of Labor. It must contain the employer's name, address, type of business, and date the business began;

2. Affirm that no more than six full-time students will be employed on any workday, and that student employment will not reduce the full-time employment opportunities of other individuals; and

3. Post a copy of the application where employees can see it.

A full-time student must be enrolled at a bona fide educational institution. The student permitted to work at subminimum wage may not work more than five hours a day, nor for more than 40 hours a week when school is not in session. When school is in session, there is a 20-hour-a-week limit. An exception is when there is a school holiday and the business is open, in which case the student may work an additional eight hours.

If more than six full-time students will be employed, then it is necessary to obtain prior approval by the Wage Hour Administration. The certification process requires an inordinate amount of paperwork. A separate application is required for each business location. Certificates are issued for periods up to one year and must be renewed annually. For these large business users of full-time students, the law will allow up to 10 percent of the total hours of all employees. Some allowance in the summer is given for seasonal business and for firms which compete with those that employ full-time students at subminimum wage rates.

There are some special recordkeeping requirements for employers using this subminimum rate. The employee's records should contain school information, and, upon graduation, a certificate from the next school to be attended stating that the student has been accepted as a full-time student. The monthly hours of full-time students at subminimum wage and the total hours of all employees during the month should be kept for three years.

Child Labor

Congress wanted to keep the channels of commerce free from child labor, and it accomplished this with a child labor provision in the Fair Labor Standards Act. The coverage of the child labor rules embraces business involved in producing, manufacturing, mining, handling, transporting, or in any other manner working on goods shipped in commerce. The penalty for child labor violations allows up to an $11,000 civil penalty for each employee who was the subject of such a violation.

The provisions include lists of hazardous occupation orders for both farm and nonfarm jobs declared by the Secretary of Labor as being too dangerous for minors to perform. Regulations governing youth employment in nonfarm jobs are set out in the chart below.

An employer wanting to protect against unintentional violations of the child labor requirements should obtain a certificate of age for each minor employed. Age or employment certificates (work permits) are accepted as proof of age in most states and are available from state labor offices.

Overtime Pay

Compared to the relatively straightforward rules governing minimum wage, the rules governing overtime pay are complicated and confusing. The overtime pay premium (one and one-half times the regular rate) applies to all hours worked above 40 in a workweek. Each workweek is a separate unit for overtime purposes; with very few exceptions, hours may not be averaged over two or more weeks. There is no absolute limit on the number of hours an employee may work in any workweek. The FLSA does not require that an employee be paid

Permissible Nonfarm Work

AGE	JOB	HOURS OF WORK
18 years or older	Any job, hazardous or not	Unlimited
16-17 years old	Any nonhazardous job	Unlimited
14-15 years old*	Outside of school hours in various nonmanufacturing, nonmining, honhazardous jobs	No more than 3 hours on a school day, 18 hours in a week, 8 hours on a non-school day, or 40 hours on a non-school week. Work may not begin before 7 a.m. nor end after 7 p.m., except from June 1st through Labor Day, when evening hours extend until 9 p.m.

* Under a special provision, 14- and 15-year-olds enrolled in an approved Work Experience and Career Exploration Program may be employed for up to 23 hours in school weeks and 3 hours on school days (including work during school hours).

Fourteen is the minimum age for most nonfarm work. However, at any age, youths may deliver newspapers; perform in radio, television, movie, or theatrical productions; or work for parents in their solely owned nonfarm business (except in manufacturing or hazardous jobs).

NOTE:

The Drive for Teen Employment Act, allows 17-year-olds to operate an auto or truck (under 6,000 pounds) on public roadways so long as such driving is occasional and incidental to the employee's employment. This exception to what the Department had considered a prohibited activity has numerous conditions (i.e., daylight driving, no more than 20 percent of workweek, and limits on length of trips); accordingly, checking with the U.S. Department of Labor regulations, and any applicable state law requirements, would be appropriate.

overtime compensation for working more than eight hours in a day, or for work on Saturday or Sunday, holidays, or regular days of rest.

Overtime compensation need not be paid weekly; instead, it must be paid on the regular pay date for the periods in which such work weeks end. If there is a problem in completing the overtime computations by the end of the pay period, the FLSA will be satisfied if the employer pays the excess overtime compensation as soon as possible. In no event may payment be delayed beyond the next payday.

In recent years, there has been a growing number of court rulings involving employers who keep workers "on call," and whether that practice requires overtime for the "on call" time. While there has been a variance in the courts' rulings, an employer is generally going to be responsible for overtime where the "on call" rules prevent employees from effectively using the time for personal pursuits.

The Regular Rate

The "regular rate" of pay has been declared by the U.S. Supreme Court as the hourly rate actually paid the employee for the normal, non-overtime workweek. The "regular rate" is a rate per hour. Yet, the FLSA does not require employers to compensate on an hourly basis; accordingly, piece-rate, salaried, and commission workers must have their compensation converted to an hourly rate. The regular hourly rate of pay is normally determined by dividing an employee's total remuneration (less the statutory exclusions discussed later) in any workweek by the total number of hours worked. The following examples illustrate the determination of the regular rate.

1. **Hourly Rate Employees** – If an employee is employed solely on the basis of a single hourly rate, the hourly rate is the "regular rate." For overtime hours the employee must be paid, in addition to the straight-time for hourly earnings, a sum determined by multiplying one-half the hourly rate by the number of hours worked over 40 in the week. If, for example, the hourly rate is $7.00 and one works 46 hours in a week, the employee would be entitled to receive $343.00 (46 hours at $7.00 and 6 at $3.50). Stated another way, 40 hours times $7.00 plus 6 hours times $10.50 (time and one-half).

2. **Hourly Rate and Bonus** – If the employee in the above example received in addition to the earnings at the hourly rate a bonus of $20.00, the regular rate of pay would be $7.43 an hour (46 hours at $7.00 equals $322.00 plus the $20.00 bonus, making a total of $342.00); this total divided by 46 hours yields a rate of $7.43. The employee would then be entitled to receive a total wage of $364.10 (46 hours at $7.43 plus 6 hours at $3.72).

3. **Piece Rate** – The regular rate of pay for an employee paid on a piecework basis is obtained by dividing the total weekly earnings for the week in which he or she worked more than 40 hours by the total number of hours worked in the same week. The employee is entitled to an additional 1½ times this regular rate for each hour over 40, in addition to the full piecework earnings.

Example: An employee paid on a piecework basis works 45 hours in a week and earns $330.00. The regular pay rate for that week is $330.00 divided by 45, or $7.33 an hour. In addition to the straight time pay, the employee is entitled to $3.67 (half the regular rate) for each hour over 40. Another way to compensate pieceworkers for overtime, if agreed to before the work is performed, is to pay 1½ times the piece rate for each piece produced during overtime hours. The piece rate must be the one actually paid during non-overtime hours and must be enough to yield at least the minimum wage per hour.

4. **Day Rates and Job Rates** – An employee may be paid a flat sum for a day's work or for doing a particular job, without regard to the number of hours worked in the day or at the job, and receive no other form of compensation. In such a case, the employee's regular rate is found by totaling all the sums received at such day rates or job rates in the workweek and dividing by the total hours actually worked. The employee is then entitled to extra half-time pay at this rate for all hours worked over 40 in the workweek.

5. **Employee Paid on a Salary Basis** – If an employee is employed solely on a weekly salary basis, the regular hourly rate of pay is computed by dividing the salary by the number of hours which the salary is intended to compensate. For example, if an employee is hired at a salary of $300.00 and if it is understood that this salary is compensation for a regular workweek of 35 hours, or $8.57 an hour, when overtime is worked, the employee is entitled to receive $8.57 for each of the first 40 hours and $12.86 (time-and-one-half) for each hour thereafter. If an employee is hired at a salary of $300.00 for a 40-hour week, the regular rate is $7.50 an hour.

6. **Salary for Periods Other Than a Workweek** – Where the salary covers a period longer than a workweek, such as a month, it must be reduced to its workweek equivalent. A monthly salary can be converted into its equivalent weekly wage by multiplying by 12 (the number of months) and dividing by 52 (the number of weeks). A semi-monthly salary is converted into its equivalent weekly wage by multiplying by 24 and dividing by 52.

7. **Fixed Salary for Fluctuating Hours** – The regular rate of an employee whose hours of work fluctuate from week to week, who is paid a stipulated salary with the clear understanding that it constitutes straight-time pay for all hours worked (whatever their number and whether few or many), will vary from week to week. The regular rate is obtained for each week by dividing the salary by the number of hours worked in the week. It cannot, of course, be less than the applicable minimum wage in any week. Since straight-time compensation has already been paid, the employee must receive additional overtime pay for each overtime hour worked in the week at not less than one-half this regular rate. Take the example of an employee who works no more than 50 hours and is compensated on a fluctuating workweek basis at a weekly salary of $400.00. If during the course of four weeks the employee works 40, 44, 50, and 48 hours, the regular hourly rate of pay in each of these weeks is $10.00, $9.09, $8.00 and $8.33, respectively. Since straight-time pay for all hours worked has already been paid, only additional half-time pay is due. For the first week, the employee is due $400.00; for the second week, $418.20 ($400.00 plus four hours at $4.55); for the third week, $440.00 ($400.00 plus 10 hours at $4.00); for the fourth week, $433.36 ($400.00 plus eight hours at $4.17). A 1998 Circuit Court decision concerning this method of calculating overtime, ruled that the employee does not have to understand the manner in which overtime pay is calculated, so long as the employer provided a reasonably clear and accurate explanation of this compensation system.

8. **Employees Working at Two or More Rates** – When an employee in a single workweek works at two or more different types of work for which different straight-time rates have been established, the regular rate for that week is the weighted average of such rates. That is, the earnings from all such rates are added together and the sum

is then divided by the total number of hours worked at all jobs.

9. **Payments Other Than Cash** – When payments are made to employees in the form of goods or facilities which are regarded as part of wages, the reasonable cost to the employer or the fair value of such goods or facilities must be included in the regular rate. When, for example, an employer furnishes lodging to employees in addition to cash wages, the reasonable cost or the fair value of the lodging (per week) must be added to the cash wages before the regular rate is determined.

10. **Commission Payments** – Commissions (whether based on a percentage of total sales or sales in excess of a specified amount or on some other formula) are payments for hours worked and must be included in the regular rate. This is so regardless of whether the commission is the sole source of the employee's compensation or is paid in addition to a salary or hourly rate. It does not matter whether the commission earnings are computed daily, weekly, monthly, or at some other interval.

11. **Commission Paid on a Workweek Basis** – When a commission is paid on a workweek basis, it is added to the employee's other earnings for that workweek, and the total is divided by the total number of hours worked in the workweek to obtain the employee's regular rate for the particular workweek. The employee must then be paid extra compensation at one-half of that rate for each overtime hour worked.

12. **Deferred Commission Payments** – If the calculation and payment of the commission cannot be completed until some time after the regular payday for the workweek, the employer may disregard it until the amount of commission can be determined. When the commission is computed, the additional overtime compensation must be paid. To compute this additional overtime compensation, the commission is apportioned back over the work weeks of the period during which it was earned. The employee must then receive additional overtime pay for each week during the period in which overtime was worked. If it is not possible or practical to allocate the commission on the basis of the amount of commission actually earned each week, some other reasonable and equitable method must be adopted. One such method is to allocate an equal amount of commission earnings to each workweek in the period in which the commission was earned; another is to allocate equal amounts to each hour worked in that period. For the weekly basis:

a. If the commission computation period is one month, multiply the commission payment by 12 and divide by 52 to get the amount of commission allocable to a single week.

b. To figure the increase in the hourly rate, divide the commission for each week by the total number of hours worked in that week. Additional overtime due is computed by multiplying one-half of this figure by the number of overtime hours worked in the week.

For example, if there is a monthly commission payment of $320.00, the amount of commission allocable to a single week is $73.85 ($320.00 times 12 equals $3,840.00, divided by 52 equals $73.85). In a week in which an employee works 48 hours, dividing $73.85 by 48 yields an increase to the regular rate of $1.54. Multiplying one-half of this figure by eight overtime hours gives the additional overtime pay due of $6.16 on the commission payment. Thus, if the individual had an hourly rate of $8.00, the eight hours for overtime premium would be $114.48.

Exclusions From the "Regular Rate"

The FLSA specifically excludes a number of categories of payments from the computation of the "regular rate." It is important to qualify each exclusion payment since any amount paid to an employee not specifically covered by these exclusions must be added to the total compensation received by the employee before the regular rate of pay is computed.

- **Overtime pay for hours in excess of a daily or weekly standard** – Many employment contracts provide overtime pay for hours worked over eight per day or 40 per week. Such extra compensation paid for the excess hours, whether or not at time and one-half, is excludable from the regular rate and may be credited toward statutory overtime payments.

- **Premium pay for work on Saturdays, Sundays, and other special days** – Extra compensation provided by a premium rate of at least time and one-half which is paid for work on Saturdays, Sundays, holidays, or regular days of rest, or on the sixth or seventh day of the workweek as such, may be treated as overtime pay. If the premium rate is less than time and one-half, the extra compensation paid must be included in determining the regular rate of pay and cannot be credited toward statutory overtime due.

- **"Clock Pattern" premium pay** – A collective bargaining agreement or other employment contract may, in good faith, establish certain hours of the day as the basic, normal or regular workday (not exceeding eight hours) or workweek (not exceeding 40 hours) and provide for the payment of a premium for work outside such hours. The extra pay will be treated as an overtime premium as long as the premium rate is not less than one and one-

half times the rate established in good faith by the contract or agreement for like work performed during the basic, normal or regular work day or workweek.[2]

- **Non-overtime premium** – Lump sum payments which are paid without regard to the number of hours worked are not overtime premiums and must be included in the regular rate. For example, where an employer gives eight hours pay for a particular job whether it is performed in eight hours or in less time, the extra premium of two hours' pay received by an employee who completes the job in six hours must be included in the regular rate.

- **Discretionary bonuses** – A bonus need not be included in the regular rate if the employer retains discretion both (1) that a bonus will be paid, and (2) that the amount is not determined until the end, or near the end, of the bonus period.[3]

- **Gifts and Christmas and special occasion bonuses** – If a bonus paid at Christmas or on other special occasions is a gift, it may be excluded from the regular rate even though it is paid with regularity so that the employees are led to expect it. It may be excluded even though the amounts paid to different employees or groups of employees vary with the amount of the salary or regular hourly rate.

- **Reimbursement for expenses** – When an employee incurs expenses on the employer's behalf or where the employee is required to spend sums solely for the

---

2. A shift differential, often providing added compensation for those working the second or third shift, would be included in the regular rate.

3. Non-discretionary bonuses such as for production or attendance must be included in the regular rate.

convenience of the employer, payments to cover such expenses are not included in the employee's regular rate of pay.

- **Pay for certain idle hours** – Payments that are made for occasional periods when the employee is not at work due to vacation, holiday, illness, failure of the employer to provide sufficient work (for example, because of machinery breakdown or materials shortage), or other similar causes, where the payments are in amounts approximately equivalent to the employee's normal earnings for a similar period of time, and are not made as compensation for the hours of employment, may be excluded from the regular rate of pay.

- **Pay for foregoing holidays and vacations** – In some instances, employees are entitled to holiday or vacation pay but forego the holiday or vacation and work on that day or period. If they receive their customary rate (or higher) for their work on the holiday or vacation day, the additional sum given as holiday or vacation pay is excluded from the regular rates of pay.

- **Profit-sharing and thrift or savings plans** – Payments made by an employer on behalf of an employee to a bona fide profit-sharing plan or trust, or bona fide thrift or saving plan, may be excluded from the regular rate of pay.

- **Benefit plans** – Contributions irrevocably made by an employer to a trustee or third person pursuant to a bona fide plan for providing retirement, life, accident, or health insurance or similar benefits, such as Supplemental Unemployment Benefits, may be excluded from the regular rate of pay for purposes of computing overtime pay.

Overtime Calculations in Special Situations

How Deductions Affect the Regular Rate – Deductions made for such items as "board, lodging, or other facilities" furnished employees, union dues, savings bonds, and charitable contributions do not affect the regular rate. The employee's regular rate is computed before the deductions are made.

Fixed Sum for Varying Amounts of Overtime – A lump sum paid for work performed during overtime hours, without regard to the number of overtime hours worked, does not qualify as an overtime premium even though the amount of money paid is equal to or greater than the sum owed on a per-hour basis. For example, no part of a flat sum of $90.00, to employees who work overtime on Sunday, will qualify as an overtime premium, even though the employees' straight-time rate is $8.00 an hour and the employees always work less than eight hours on Sunday. Similarly, where an agreement provides for six hours pay at $8.00 an hour, regardless of the time actually spent for work on a job performed during overtime hours, the entire $48.00 must be included in the employees' regular rate. If the rule were otherwise, an employer desiring to pay a fixed salary regardless of the number of overtime hours worked could merely label as overtime pay a fixed portion of such salary, sufficient to take care of compensation for the maximum number of hours that would be worked. The same reasoning applies to payment of a flat sum for a special job performed during overtime hours. Extra compensation paid in the form of a lump sum for varying numbers of overtime hours must be included in the regular rate and may not be credited against statutory overtime compensation due.

Salary for Workweek Exceeding 40 Hours – A fixed salary for a regular workweek longer than 40 hours does not discharge the statutory obligation. For example, an employee may be hired to work a 44-hour workweek for a weekly salary of $300.00. In this instance the regular rate is obtained by dividing the $300.00 straight-time salary by 44 hours, which results in a regular rate of pay of $6.82 per hour. The employee is then due additional overtime computed by multiplying the four overtime hours by one-half the regular rate of pay ($3.41) or $13.64.

Overtime Pay May Not Be Waived — The requirement that overtime must be paid after 40 hours a week may not be waived by agreement between the employer and employees. Similarly, an agreement that only eight hours a day or only 40 hours a week will be counted as working time will clearly fail.

Computing Overtime Pay on the Rate Applicable to the Type of Work Performed in Overtime Hours — A simpler method of computing overtime pay for employees paid piece rates or at a variety of hourly rates is provided in Section 7(g)(1) and (2) of the FLSA. The regular rate may be computed at a piece rate not less than one and one-half times the bona fide piece rate applicable to the same work when performed during non-overtime hours. In the case of an employee performing two or more kinds of work, for which different hourly rates have been established, the regular rate may be computed at rates not less than one and one-half times the bona fide rate for the same work when performed during non-overtime hours. Under these methods, there must be an agreement or understanding with the employees before performance of the work.

Special Overtime Provision for Hospital Employees — Under Section 7(j) of the FLSA, hospitals and residential care establishments may, pursuant to a prior agreement or understanding with their employees, utilize a fixed work period of 14 consecutive days in lieu of the workweek for the purpose of computing overtime, if they pay time and one-half the regular rate for hours worked over eight in any

workday or 80 in the 14-day period, whichever is the greater number of hours. This arrangement is commonly referred to as the 8/80 rule.

Guaranty Wage Contracts

The FLSA does permit a wage plan that provides for a constant wage, even though overtime is worked. It is known as the "Belo Plan," named after the company that successfully argued its merits to the U.S. Supreme Court. Later, Congress amended the FLSA to provide specifically for this type of plan.

The Belo Plan is designed for salaried employees who work irregular hours, but there are a number of restrictions. Under a Belo Plan, the employer and the employee agree on an hourly rate of pay which is substantially less than the employee's average hourly earnings in an ordinary week. The employee is promised this hourly rate for the first 40 hours each week, not less than time and one-half this rate for overtime hours, with a guarantee of a certain weekly salary regardless of the number of hours the employee works.

A Belo Plan is appropriate when the employee's job demands irregular hours of work. It requires:

1. A written agreement between the employer and the employee.
2. The specification of the employee's regular hourly rate.
3. A guarantee of time and one-half the regular rate for hours worked over 40.
4. A guaranteed weekly salary, regardless of the hours worked.
5. The guaranteed weekly salary may not cover more than 60 hours per week.
6. When the employee's earnings at the regular rate for 40 hours and time and one-half for additional hours exceed the amount of the guarantee, the employee must be paid the excess over the guarantee.

Retail/Service Commission-Paid Employees

There is a special provision of the FLSA that allows an employee of a "retail or service establishment" paid on a commission basis or whose compensation includes commissions to be exempt from the payment of overtime providing two conditions are met:

1. The regular rate of pay of this employee must be more than one and one-half times the prevailing minimum wage, and

2. More than half of the compensation for a "representative period" (not less than one month) must represent commissions on goods or services.

The term "retail or service establishment" means that a business must engage in the selling of goods or services and 75 percent of its sales of goods or services must be recognized as traditionally in a "retail" concept. Further, not over 25 percent of its sales of goods or services may be for resale. The purpose of this exemption was to relieve a retail employer from the obligation of paying overtime compensation to employees who typically sell "big ticket" items, such as home furnishings, floor covering, and major appliances. It is a good policy to have a written agreement with commission salespersons acknowledging that the compensation plan is based upon Section 7(i) of the FLSA; and, therefore, no overtime will be paid. The "representative period" to test an employee's compensation may not be shorter than a month and should be of sufficient length to reflect, fairly, as many factors as possible. The period chosen should be long enough to stabilize the measure of the balance between the portions of the employee's compensation which respectively represents commissions and other earnings (bonuses and contest prizes) against purely seasonal or plainly temporary changes. The exemption is given to individuals and not to commission salespersons as a category

of employees. A written agreement between a commission salesperson and an employer should at least contain these elements:

1. Definition of the pay period (e.g., a calendar month);

2. The pay date for each pay period;

3. The hourly rate for every hour worked (e.g., may not be less than one and one half times the prevailing minimum wage);

4. Definition of the representative period, and statement of the basis of the Section 7(i) exemption from the overtime provisions; and

5. Both parties should sign and date the agreement.

Overtime Exception for State and Local Government Employees

Congress addressed the significant concerns of state and local governments and their employees by amending the overtime pay provisions of the FLSA as they apply to public employees. The amendments permit state and local governments to compensate their employees for overtime hours worked with compensatory time off in lieu of overtime pay, at a rate of one and one-half hours for each hour of overtime worked.

The amendments provide that the use of compensatory time in lieu of overtime pay must be pursuant to some form of collective bargaining agreement or other agreement or understanding between the employer and the employee prior to the performance of work, and that compensatory time may be accrued up to a maximum of 240 hours for most public employees. This does not include those employees engaged in public safety, emergency response, and seasonal activities, who may accrue compensatory time up to 480 hours. For hours worked in excess of the accrued maximum amounts, an employee is to receive overtime pay. The amendments also exclude, from the definition of "employee," individuals who volunteer their services to state and local governments without compensation but who receive a nominal fee, reasonable benefits, or reimbursement for expenses.

An employee is permitted to use accrued compensatory time within a reasonable period after it is requested, if to do so would not unduly disrupt the operations of the employing public agency.

Payment for accrued compensatory time upon termination of employment is to be calculated at the average regular rate of pay for the final three years of employment, or the final regular rate received by the employee, whichever is the higher.

Exemptions from FLSA Overtime Provisions

Industry/Occupation
of Employees

Administrative, executive, and professional	Exempt
Commission salespersons of retail or service establishments	Exempt
Domestic service workers residing in the employer's residence	Exempt
Farm workers	Exempt
Hospitals/nursing homes	Limited exemptions
Railroad and airline workers	Exempt
Seamen	Exempt
Auto, truck, trailer, farm implement, boat or aircraft salespersons, partsmen, and mechanics employed by non-manufacturing dealers	Exempt
Outside salespersons	Exempt
Retail-service establishments	Limited exemptions

"Compensatory time" and "compensatory time off" are defined as hours when an employee is not working and which are paid for at the employee's regular rate of pay. These hours are not counted as hours worked in the week in which they are paid.

Under regulations effective in 2004, public sector employers may now establish pay systems that include salary deductions for absences of less than a day for certain exempt employees. Such a pay system must be "established by statute, ordinance, or regulation, or by a policy or practice extablished pursuant to principles of public accountability, under which the employee accrues personal and sick leave." The pay system may require that deductions from pay shall be taken for absences for personal reasons or illness or injury when leave is not used by the employee because (1) permission for leave has not been sought or has been sought and denied; (2) accrued leave has been exhausted; or (3) the employee chooses to use leave without pay.

"White Collar" Employees

The FLSA provides for an exemption from both the minimum wage and overtime pay provisions for employees engaged in an executive, administrative, or professional capacity, or for the position of an outside salesperson. The Department of Labor established the criteria which designates these individuals. Regulations governing the "white collar" exemption were revised in August 2004.

The determination of an individual's exemption is dependent upon one's duties and is largely a question of fact. The regulations provide that an employee's title is irrelevant; the exemption is based upon job duties and not titles.

Salary Basis

Under the August 2004 revised regulations, to qualify for exemption, employees generally must be paid not less than $455 per week on a salary basis. These salary requirements do not apply to outside sales employees, teachers, and employees practicing law or medicine. Exempt computer employees may be paid at least $455 on a salary basis *or* on an hourly basis at a rate not less than $27.63 an hour.

Being paid on a "salary basis" means an employee regularly receives a predetermined amount of compensation each pay period on a weekly, or less frequent, basis. The predetermined amount cannot be reduced because of variations in the quality or quantity of the employee's work. Subject to specified exceptions, an exempt employee must receive the full salary for any week in which the employee performs any work, regardless of the number of days worked. Exempt employees do not need to be paid for any workweek in which they perform no work. If the employer makes deductions from an employee's predetermined salary, e.g., because of the operating requirements of the business, that employee is not paid on a "salary basis." If the employee is ready, willing, and able to work, deductions may not be made for time when work is not available.

The exceptions to the "docking" pay rules include the following circumstances:

1. Absences of a day or more for personal reasons other than sickness or accident.

2. Absences of a day or more because of sickness or disability, if the employer has a plan, policy or practice providing compensation for loss of salary due to sickness or disability.

3. Absences due to industrial accidents, if the employee is compensated for loss of salary in accordance with an applicable compensation law.

4. Penalties imposed in good faith for violation of major safety rules.

5. Partial days taken under the authority of the Family and Medical Leave Act.

6. Deductions from vacation or sick leave credits, provided that the deductions do not reduce the compensation for any week in which some work is performed.

7. Deductions may not be made for absences of an employee caused by jury duty, attendance as a witness, or temporary military leave. Note, however, that an employer may take an offset against other weekly pay received as jury or witness fees or military pay.

8. Unpaid disciplinary suspensions of one or more full days imposed in good faith for workplace conduct rule infractions.

Also, an employer is not required to pay the full salary in the initial or terminal week of employment.

Effect of Improper Deductions from Salary

The employer will lose the exemption if it has an "actual practice" of making improper deductions from salary. Factors to consider when determining whether an employer has an actual practice of making improper deductions include, but are not limited to: the number of improper deductions, particularly as compared to the number of employee infractions warranting deductions; the time period during which the employer made improper deductions; the number and geographic location of both the employees whose salary was improperly reduced and the managers responsible; and whether the employer has a clearly communicated policy permitting or prohibiting improper deductions. If an "actual practice" is found, the exemption is lost during the time period of the deductions for employees in the same job classification working for the same managers responsible for the improper deductions.

Isolated or inadvertent improper deductions will not result in loss of the exemption if the employer reimburses the employee for the improper deductions.

Safe Harbor

Under the revised regulations, if an employer (1) has a clearly communicated policy prohibiting improper deductions and including a complaint mechanism, (2) reimburses employees for any improper deductions, and (3) makes a good faith commitment to comply in the future, the employer will not lose the exemption for any employees unless the employer willfully violates the policy by continuing the improper deductions after receiving employee complaints.

Employers are strongly urged to implement an appropriate, safe harbor policy.

Fee Basis

Administrative, professional and computer employees may be paid on a "fee basis" rather than on a salary basis. If the employee is paid an agreed sum for a single job, regardless of the time required for its completion, the employee will be considered to be paid on a "fee basis." A fee payment is generally paid for a unique job, rather than for a series of jobs repeated a number of times and for which identical payments repeatedly are made. To determine whether the fee payment meets the minimum salary level requirement, the test is to consider the time worked on the job and determine whether the payment is at a rate that would amount to at least $455 per week if the employee worked 40 hours. For example, an artist paid $250 for a picture that took 20 hours to complete meets the minimum salary requirement since the rate would yield $500 if 40 hours were worked.

The new regulations eliminated the old "long" and "short" test for the white-collar exemptions and replaced them with a single test for each exemption.

Exemption Rules for Executive Employees

To qualify for the executive employee exemption, all of the following requirements must be met:

1. The employee must be compensated on a salary basis (as defined in the regulations) at a rate not less than $455 per week;

2. The employee's primary duty must be managing the enterprise, or managing a customarily recognized department or subdivision of the enterprise;

3. The employee must customarily and regularly direct the work of at least two or more other full-time employees or their equivalent; and

4. The employee must have the authority to hire or fire other employees, or the employee's suggestions or recommendations as to the hiring, firing, advancement, promotion, or any other change of status of other employees must be given particular weight.

Exemption Rules for Administrative Employees

To qualify for the administrative employee exemption, all of the following requirements must be met:

1. The employee must be compensated on a salary or fee basis (as defined in the regulations) at a rate not less than $455 per week;

2. The employee's primary duty must be the performance of office or non-manual work directly related to the management or general business operations of the employer or the employer's customers:

3. The employee's primary duty includes the exercise of discretion and independent judgment as to matters of significance.

Exemption Rules for Professional Employees

The specific requirements for exemption as a bona fide professional employee are summarized below. There are two general types of exempt professional employees: learned professionals and creative professionals.

Learned Professional Exemption – To qualify for the learned professional exemption, all of the following requirements must be met:

1. The employee must be compensated on a salary or fee basis (as defined in the regulations) at a rate not less than $455 per week;

2. The employee's primary duty must be the performance of work requiring advanced knowledge, defined as work which is predominantly intellectual in character and which includes work requiring the consistent exercise of discretion and judgment;

3. The advanced knowledge must be in a field of science or learning; and

4. The advanced knowledge must be customarily acquired by a prolonged course of specialized intellectual instruction.

Creative Professional Exemption – To qualify for the creative professional exemption, both of the following requirements must be met:

1. The employee must be compensated on a salary or fee basis (as defined in the regulations) at a rate not less than $455 per week; and

2 The employee's primary duty must be the performance of work requiring invention, imagination, originality or talent in a recognized field of artistic or creative endeavor.

Exemption Rules for Outside Salespersons

To qualify for the outside sales employee exemption, both of the following requirements must be met:

1. The employee's primary duty must be making sales (as defined in the FLSA), or obtaining orders or contracts for services or for the use of facilities for which a consideration will be paid by the client or customer; and

2 The employee must be customarily and regularly engaged away from the employer's place or places of business.

The salary requirements of the regulation do not apply to the outside sales exemption. An employee who does not satisfy the requirements of the outside sales exemption may still qualify as an exempt employee under one of the other exemptions if all the criteria for that exemption are met.

Remedial Education Exemption

The 1989 FLSA Amendments provided a limited, special exemption for up to 10 hours in any workweek from the overtime provisions of the FLSA for remedial education. The latter term is limited to individuals who lack a high school diploma or educational attainment at the eighth grade level. The program must be designed to provide reading and other basic skills at an eighth grade level or below and does not include job-specific training.

Computer Industry Exemption

To qualify for the computer employee exemption, the following requirements must be met:

1. The employee must be compensated either on a salary or fee basis at a rate not less than $455 per week or, if compensated on an

hourly basis, at a rate not less than $27.63 an hour;

2. The employee must be employed as a computer systems analyst, computer programmer, software engineer or other similarly skilled worker in the computer field performing the duties described below;

3. The employee's primary duty must consist of any of the following:

   • The application of systems analysis techniques and procedures, including consulting with users, to determine hardware, software or system functional specifications;

   • The design, development, analysis, documentation, creation, testing or modification of computer systems or programs, including prototypes, based on and related to user or system design specifications;

   • The design, documentation, testing, creation or modification of computer programs related to machine operating systems; or

   • A combination of the aforementioned duties, the performance of which requires the same level of skills.

The computer employee exemption does not include employees engaged in the manufacture or repair of computer hardware and related equipment. Employees whose work is highly dependent upon, or facilitated by, the use of computers and computer software programs (e.g., engineers, drafters and others skilled in computer-aided design software), but who are not primarily engaged in computer systems analysis and programming or other similarly skilled computer-related occupations identified in the primary duties test described above, are also not exempt under the computer employee exemption.

FLSA Recordkeeping

Employers are required to keep records on wages, hours, and other items for at least six years. Most of the information is of the kind generally maintained by employers in ordinary business practice and in compliance with other laws and regulations. The records may be kept in any particular form including microfilm and other source documents such as an automatic word or data processing memory. With respect to an employee subject to both minimum wage and overtime pay provisions, the following records must be kept:

1. Personal information, including employee's name, home address, zip code, occupation, sex, and birth date (if under 19 years of age).

2. Hour and day when workweek begins.

3. Total hours worked each workday and each workweek.

4. Total daily or weekly straight-time earning.

5. Regular hourly pay rate for any week when overtime is worked.

6. Total overtime pay for the workweek.

7. Deductions from or additions to wages.

8. Total wages paid each pay period.

9. Date of payment and pay period covered.

Records required for exempt employees differ from those for non-exempt employees, and special information is required about employees working under uncommon pay arrangement or for whom lodging or other facilities are furnished.

In addition to these general recordkeeping requirements, the FLSA imposes recordkeeping requirements for employees subject to miscellaneous exemptions under the law. The specific terms of each such exemption covering these workers must be documented. Those with special recordkeeping requirements include:

1. Employees exempt from both overtime pay requirements and minimum wage.

2. Employees exempt from overtime pay requirements.

3. Employees of hospitals and residential care facilities compensated for overtime work on the basis of a 14-day work period.

4. Employees working under a "Belo" contract.

5. Board, lodging, or other facilities.

6. Tipped employees.

7. Learners, apprentices, messengers, students, or handicapped workers.

8. Individual homeworkers.

9. Agricultural employees. Timeclocks are a good means of recording work hours, but they are not required. If there is a timeclock, note that in addition to the timecard punches, the number of hours worked and the workweek should be written down. These figures may be noted on the timecard itself or on another record.

Timecard punches often do not show the true hours of an employee's work. Often, workers arrive early at the plant for personal reasons and punch in right away, but they do not start work until their shifts begin. This kind of early punching may be disregarded in counting hours worked. On the other hand, workers who punch in and out with their shifts may be engaged in set-up work before or after punching. In that case, the time doing the make-ready work should also be counted. This also would be true of work done during lunch hours. If an employee works but does not punch a card, the time spent on the job still must be counted as hours worked. As far as the law is concerned, the important thing is whether the employer "suffered or permitted" the employee to work, not whether a time record device has been correctly used.

When workers are credited with more or fewer hours of work than the timecard punches show, and when there is a discrepancy of more than a few minutes, a brief note should be made on the timecard to explain the difference. This will avoid disputes about the time actually worked. Basic employment and earning records (i.e., timecards) must be preserved for two years. It is well settled that when an employer fails to keep adequate records of its employees' compensable work periods, employees seeking recovery for overdue wages will not be penalized due to their employer's recordkeeping default.

The Wage and Hour Division of the Department of Labor requires that its poster be displayed in a conspicuous place at each business location so employees may readily observe it.

Enforcement

The Wage and Hour Division administers and enforces the law with respect to private employment. The Wage and Hour Division's enforcement of the FLSA is carried out by compliance officers stationed across the United States. As the Division's authorized representatives, they have the authority to conduct investigations and gather data on wages, hours, and other employment conditions or practices in order to determine compliance with the Act. Where violations are found, they also may recommend changes in employment practices in order to bring an employer into compliance with the law.

It is a violation of the FLSA to fire or in any other manner discriminate or retaliate against an employee for filing a complaint or participating in a legal proceeding under the law.

Wage and Hour inspectors carry an official identity card with their photograph and the signature of the Wage and Hour administrator.

Inspections may be made on the initiative of the Department of Labor as part of a random pattern of inspection or upon complaints from any source. If made upon the complaint of an individual or individuals, the names of the complainants (e.g., employees, competitors) will not be revealed. The courts have ruled that any benefit to the employer does not equal the need and right of government informers to remain anonymous. Inspectors may not only examine payroll records but, in addition, may ask to interview employees.

An employer under investigation for a violation is entitled to see those passages in the Wage and Hour Division's Field Operations Handbook which may inform the employer of the government's interpretation of the law. Certain portions of that handbook which deal with the department's enforcement strategies and methodology are not available even under the provisions of the Freedom of Information Act. In any case, where there are alleged violations, it is strongly advised that the inspection be made with the employer's accountant and/or attorney present.

Where no violations are found, the field investigator will advise the employer, and that is the end of the matter. On the other hand, where violations are found, the employer is entitled to a complete written report detailing the violations, the back-wage liability, if any, and other remedial actions believed necessary to bring the employer into compliance.

Confronted with alleged violations of the FLSA, it is appropriate to have a conference, with counsel present to discuss the matter with the investigator. The employer will be given a "Summary of Unpaid Wages" owed employees. At this point, the investigative conclusions should be carefully checked for accuracy. If the matter is settled at this point by the payment of back wages, then the case will be closed.

Let us assume that a substantial difference of opinion between the investigator and the employer remains. The employer can then request a conference with the investigator's immediate supervisors or even an official at the regional office level.

When the dispute remains unresolved, there is recourse available at the national office of the Wage and Hour Division of the Department of Labor in Washington. While it is a time-consuming process, one finds the greatest amount of latitude at this administrative level. In the absence of any resolution, the Department of Labor will instruct the Solicitor of Labor to bring an appropriate type of action which will often include injunctive relief to prevent future violations.

Department of Labor's Internet Services

Businesses can now get advice on their rights and responsibilities under a number of federal employment laws from the Department of Labor's "elaws" (Employment Laws Assistance for Workers and Small Business), an interactive expert system on workplace laws enforced by the Department.

With the advent of "elaws" the Department of Labor now ranks among the best federal agencies for providing information and technical assistance.

The "elaws" have been designed to be particularly helpful to smaller businesses that do not have professional staff dedicated to following and understanding the latest regulatory developments of the Department of Labor.

Each "elaws" system is a computer program that mimics the interaction an individual might have with a human expert. The "elaws" advisors, most of which will run interactively directly from the Internet, give advice and provide information on a specific law or regulation based on a worker's or employer's particular situation.

"Elaws" uses the technology of the new workplace to help workers and their employers, particularly small business, to solve their employment law problems before they ever reach the Labor Department.

The Department of Labor presently has the following elaws online, all of which can be accessed from www.dol.gov/elaws:

- Drug-Free Workplace Advisor
- Family & Medical Leave Act (FMLA) Advisor
- Federal Contractor Compliance Advisor
- FirstStep Employment Law Advisor
- FLSA Child Labor Rules Advisor
- FLSA Coverage & Employment Status Advisor
- FLSA Hours Worked Advisor
- FLSA Overtime Security Advisor
- FLSA Section 14 (c) Advisor (Special Minimum Wage)
- Health Benefits Advisor
- MSHA Online Forms Advisor
- MSHA Training Plan Advisor
- MSHA Fire Suppression & Fire Protection Advisor
- OSHA Confined Spaces Advisor
- OSHA Fire Safety Advisor
- OSHA Hazard Awareness Advisor
- OSHA Lead in Construction Advisor
- OSHA Software Expert Advisors
- Poster Advisor
- Small Business Retirement Savings Advisor

- Uniformed Services Employment & Reemployment Rights Act (USERRA) Advisor
- Veterans' Preference Advisor
- e-VETS Resource Advisor

Penalties and Other Relief Measures

The FLSA provides for the following methods of recovering unpaid minimum and/or overtime wages:

1. The Secretary of Labor may bring suit for back wages and an equal amount as liquidated damages.

2. An employee may file a private suit for back pay and an equal amount as liquidated damages, plus attorney's fees and court costs.

3. The Secretary may obtain an injunction to restrain any person from violating the law, including the unlawful withholding of proper minimum wage and overtime compensation.

An employee may not bring suit if he or she has been paid back wages under the supervision of the division, or if the Secretary has already filed suit to recover the wages.

A two-year statute of limitations applies to the recovery of back pay, except in the case of willful violation, in which case a three-year statute applies.

Willful violations may be prosecuted criminally and the violator fined up to $10,000. A second conviction may result in imprisonment. Violators of the minimum wage and overtime provisions are subject to a civil monetary penalty of up to $1,000 for each violation.

Equal Pay Act 3

Legislative Purpose

A significant amendment to the FLSA occurred in 1963. Congress passed the Equal Pay Act, prohibiting unequal wages for women and men who work in the same establishment, for equal work on jobs which require equal skill, effort, and responsibility, and which are performed under similar working conditions.

Coverage

With a few inconsequential exceptions, the Equal Pay Act now covers most employees, including executive, administrative, and professional employees as well as U.S. government employees who had initially been exempted from coverage. The Equal Pay Act is designed to eliminate any wage rate differential based on sex; nothing in the law is intended to prohibit differences in wage rates based not on sex, but wholly on other factors. The equal pay standards do not rely upon job classifications or titles, but rather depend on actual job requirements and performance. The focus of any equal pay inquiry is the job itself and the worker's hour-by-hour duties and responsibilities. While the Equal Pay Act was motivated by concern for the historically weaker bargaining position of women, the law by its expressed terms applies to both sexes. The law is enforced by the Equal Employment Opportunity Commission (EEOC).

Establishment

The law uses "establishment" to mean a distinct place where employees work. Therefore, the obligation to comply with the equal pay provisions must be determined separately with reference to those employees at that particular location. Thus, disparities in wage rates between men and women working at different branch operations of a business are not relevant under the statute as the prohibition is against unequal pay at the "same establishment".

Wages

Wages paid an employee include all payments made to the employee as remuneration for employment. Vacation and holiday pay, premium payments of any kind, and fringe benefits are also included. [Note, however, that payments which do not constitute remuneration for employment are not "wages" (e.g., expense reimbursements).]

Fringe Benefits

Fringe benefits are considered to be remuneration for employment; therefore, it is unlawful for an employer to offer different fringe benefits to men and women performing equal work at the same establishment. Fringes include medical, hospital, accident, and life insurance, retirement benefits, profit sharing, bonus plans, leave, etc.

Among the key points in the EEOC regulations are the following:

1. When an employer conditions benefits to employees and their spouses and families on whether the employee is the "head of the household" or "principal wage earner" in the family unit, the overall implementation of the plan will be closely scrutinized.

2. It is unlawful for an employer to make available benefits for the spouses or the families of employees of one gender when the same benefits are not made available for the spouses or families of the opposite gender employees.

3. It shall not be a defense to a charge of sex discrimination in benefits, under the Equal Pay Act, that the cost of such benefits is greater with respect to one sex than the other.

4. It is unlawful to have a pension or retirement plan which establishes different optional or compulsory retirement ages based on sex, or which otherwise differentiates benefits on the basis of sex.

The Supreme Court has ruled that retirement benefits constitute "wages" and EEOC regulations make it clear that wages include "all payments made to an employee as remuneration for employment."

Determining "Equal Work"

Congress intended that jobs requiring "equal pay" should be substantially equal with respect to skill, effort, and responsibility and performed under similar working conditions.

In determining whether employees are performing equal work within the meaning of the Equal Pay Act, the amounts of time which employees spend in the performance of different duties are not the sole criteria. The Courts have indicated that in addition to differences in time spent, it is also necessary to consider the degree of difference in terms of skill, effort and responsibility required in the jobs. These factors are so uniquely interrelated that a general, mathematical formula or standard based solely on the percentage of time spent performing various duties, cannot be set to determine the equality of jobs.

Consequently, a mere finding that one job requires employees to expend greater effort for a certain percentage of their working time than employees performing another job would not in itself establish that the two jobs do not constitute equal work.

Similarly, the performance of jobs on different machines or equipment would not necessarily result in a determination that the work so performed is unequal within the meaning of the statute if the equal pay provisions otherwise apply. If the difference in skill or effort required for the operation of such equipment is inconsequential, payment of a higher wage rate to employees of one sex because of a difference in machines or equipment would constitute a prohibited wage rate differential.

Where greater skill or effort is required from the lower paid sex, the fact that the machinery or equipment used to perform substantially equal work is different does not defeat a finding that the Equal Pay Act has been violated. Likewise, the fact that jobs are performed in different departments or locations within the establishment would not necessarily be sufficient to demonstrate that unequal work is involved where the equal pay standard otherwise applies. This is particularly true in the case of retail establishments. Unless a showing can be made by the employer that the sale of one article requires such a higher degree of skill or effort than the sale of another article, so as to render the equal pay standard inapplicable, it will be assumed that the salesmen and saleswomen concerned are performing equal work. Although the equal pay provisions apply on an establishment basis (the jobs to be compared are those in the particular establishment), all relevant evidence that may demonstrate whether the skill, effort, and responsibility required for the jobs in the particular establishment are equal should be considered, whether this relates to the performance of like jobs in other establishments or not.

The law uses three tests – equal skill, effort, and responsibility. These terms are considered to constitute three separate tests. Each of them, however, must be satisfied in order for the equal pay law requirements to apply.

1. **Equal Skill**. Here, the analysis includes experience, training, education, and ability. Skill should be measured in terms of the performance of the job. Possession of a skill not needed to meet the requirement of the job is not a relevant factor in determining the quality of skill. It is, after all, the skill required to do the job that is being scrutinized and not the skill possessed by the worker. Similarly, the efficiency of the employee's performance on the job is not, in itself, an appropriate factor to consider in evaluating an individual's skill.

2. **Equal Effort**. The measure of the physical or mental exertion needed for the performance of a job is the key here. Jobs may require equal effort in performing them even though the effort may be displayed in different ways in two otherwise similar jobs. Differences only in the kind of effort required of the job in such a situation will not justify wage differentials among employees.

   The occasional or sporadic performance of an activity which may require extra physical or mental exertion is not alone sufficient to justify a finding of unequal effort. Suppose, however, that men and women are working side by side in a factory line assembling parts. Suppose, further, that one of the men who performs the operations at the

end of the line must also lift the assembly as he completes his part of it, and place it on a waiting pallet. In such a situation, a wage rate differential might be justified for the person (but only for that person) who is required to expend the extra effort in the performance of the job, provided that the extra effort is substantial and is performed over a considerable portion of the work cycle.

3. **Equal Responsibility**. For this test, the degree of accountability in the performance of the job with emphasis on the importance of the job obligation is paramount. To illustrate this test, assume that there are sales clerks engaged primarily in selling identical or similar merchandise, but are given different responsibilities with respect to that duty. For example, suppose that one employee of such a group is authorized and required to determine whether to accept payment for purchases by personal checks from customers. The person having the authority to accept personal checks may have an additional degree of responsibility which may materially affect the business operations of the employer. In this situation, payment of a higher wage rate to this employee would be permissible.

Similar Working Conditions

Employees performing jobs requiring equal skill, effort, and responsibility are likely to be performing them under similar working conditions. However, in situations where some employees whose work meets these standards have working conditions substantially different from those required for the performance of other jobs, the equal pay principal would not apply. For example, if some salespersons are engaged in selling a product exclusively inside a store and others employed by the same establishment spend a large part of their time selling the same product away from the establishment, the working conditions would be dissimilar even though they sell the same product.

Also, where some employees do repair work exclusively inside the shop and others spend most of their time doing similar repair work in customers' homes, there would not be a similarity in working conditions. On the other hand, slight or inconsequential differences in working conditions that are essentially similar would not justify a differential in pay. Such differences are not usually taken into consideration by employers or the collective bargaining process in setting wage rates.

Exceptions to Equal Pay Standard

The Equal Pay Act provides three specific exceptions and one broad exception to its general standard requiring that employees doing equal work be paid equal wages, regardless of sex. Under these exceptions, if it can be established that a differential in pay is the result of a wage payment made under a seniority system, a merit system, a system measuring earnings by quantity or quality of production, or that the differential is based on any factor other than sex, the differential is expressly excluded from the statutory prohibition of wage discrimination based on sex. These exceptions recognize that there may be legitimate factors that can justify a wage differential among employees performing equal work on jobs which meet the statutory tests of equal skill, effort, and responsibility and similar working conditions. An employer who asserts one of these exceptions to a claimed violation of the Equal Pay Act has the burden of providing the facts establishing the defense.

Additional duties may not be a defense to the payment of higher wages to one sex where the higher pay is not related to the extra duties. The Commission will scrutinize such a defense to

determine whether it is bona fide. For example, an employer cannot successfully assert an extra duties defense where:

1. Some employees of the higher paid sex receive the higher pay without doing extra work;

2. Members of the lower paid sex also perform extra duties requiring equal skill, effort, and responsibility;

3. The extra duties do not in fact exist;

4. The extra duties consume a minimal amount of time and are of peripheral importance; or

5. Third persons (i.e., individuals who are not in the two groups of employees being compared) who perform the extra duties as their primary job are paid less than the members of the higher paid sex for whom there is an attempt to justify the pay differential.

The term "red circle" rate is used to describe certain unusually higher wage rates which are maintained for reasons unrelated to sex. An example of bona fide use of a "red circle" rate might arise in a situation where a company wishes to transfer a long-service employee, who can no longer perform his or her regular job because of a disability, to different work which is now being performed by opposite gender employees at a lower rate of pay.

Under the "red circle" principle the employer may continue to pay the employee his or her present salary, which is greater than that paid to the opposite gender employees, for the work both will be doing.

Under such circumstances, maintaining an employee's established wage rate, despite a reassignment to a less demanding job, is a valid reason for the differential even though other employees performing the less demanding work would be paid at a lower rate. Here the differential is based on a factor other than sex. However, where wage rate differentials have been or are being paid on the basis of sex to employees performing equal work, rates of the higher paid employees may not be "red circled" in order to comply with the Equal Pay Act. To allow this would only continue the inequities which the law was intended to address.

Equal Pay Enforcement

For a full explanation of EEOC enforcement procedures, please refer to Chapter 4, (EEOC Enforcement Procedures).

Anti-Discrimination Laws and the Equal Employment Opportunity Commission

4

Legislative Purpose

With the historic passage of the Civil Rights Act of 1964, which contains Title VII – Equal Employment Opportunity – the law of the land became equal opportunity for all in the crucial area of employment rights. Congress had found a historical pattern of restriction, exclusion, discrimination, segregation, and inferior treatment of minorities and women in many employment areas. There was clear evidence that denial of equal rights in employment had led to higher unemployment, lesser occupational status, and the consequent of lower income levels for minorities and women. Title VII of the Civil Rights Act provides, therefore, the legal basis for individuals to pursue the work of their own choice and to advance in that work, subject only to consideration of their individual qualifications, talents and energies.

Congress developed a new national policy which made it an unlawful employment practice for an employer, labor organization or placement agency:

1. To fail or refuse to hire or to discharge any individual, or to discriminate against any individual with respect to compensation, terms, conditions, or privileges of employment because of such individual's race, color, religion, sex, or national origin; or

2. To limit, segregate, or classify employees or applicants for employment in any way which would deprive or tend to deprive any individual of employment opportunities or otherwise adversely affect his or her status as an employee, because of such individual's race, color, religion, sex, or national origin.

To enforce this anti-discrimination law, the Equal Employment Opportunity Commission was created. There are five bipartisan Commissioners, appointed by the President and confirmed by the Senate for a fixed term of five years, responsible for overseeing the Commission.

Coverage

Title VII of the Civil Rights Act applies to any employer engaged "in an industry affecting commerce" who has 15 or more employees for each working day in each of 20 or more calendar weeks in the current or preceding year. In 1972, Title VII was amended to include federal, state, and local public employers and educational institutions.

In 1997, a unanimous U.S. Supreme Court decision allowed an individual who was given a negative job reference the right to sue his former employer under Title VII. The Court, in interpreting what it termed the ambiguous classification of "employee," decided that it included former employees. To do otherwise would "undermine the effectiveness of Title VII by allowing the threat of post-employment retaliation to deter victims of discrimination from complaining to EEOC, and would provide a perverse incentive for employers to fire employees who might bring Title VII claims."

The Supreme Court also decided in 1997 the method for determining whether there are a sufficient number of employees to trigger Title VII coverage. The Court decided that all employees should be counted using the payroll method. A company's list of workers includes anyone the company has an "employment relationship" with, whether or not that person is at work on a given day. "What is ultimately critical is the existence of an employment relationship." The employee need not actually receive compensation. While this ruling affects only the smaller employers who are close to the threshold for coverage, it does have ramifications for other laws (e.g., Age Discrimination, Americans with Disabilities Act, etc.) having similar threshold provisions.

Types of Discrimination — An Overview

The original impetus for the ban on racial discrimination was to protect the minority race. However, the U.S. Supreme Court has held that the protection extends to all individuals, including Caucasians, when race is used as a criterion in an employment decision. Thus, reverse discrimination suits brought by non-minorities are recognized by Title VII.

The prohibition against discrimination based on color would include an employment decision made among minority candidates based on possession of the lightest complexion and the most Caucasian-like features. Distinctions in employment practices based on sex, male or female, are illegal unless the job requires specific physical characteristics necessarily possessed by only one sex. The law recognizes a very narrow exception for a "bona fide occupational requirement" such as employment

of a wet nurse. In 1978, Congress enacted the Pregnancy Disability Amendment to Title VII, which further defined sex discrimination to include disparate treatment of pregnant women for all employment-related purposes. (The Pregnancy Disability Amendment is discussed in greater detail later in this chapter.)

The fastest growing area of sex discrimination cases involve sexual harassment. Though not mentioned specifically or defined in Title VII, the Supreme Court in 1986 identified and defined this activity as a form of sex discrimination prohibited by Title VII. The Court identified two types of sexual harassment; quid pro quo, and hostile environment. For a more detailed discussion of this form of sex discrimination, please refer to Chapter 6.

The prohibition against basing an employment decision on one's religious beliefs or practices is broad in scope. In this instance, neutrality or non-discrimination is not enough; there must be an accommodation of the religious needs of employees and job applicants. The prohibition against employment discrimination based upon national origin prohibits discrimination based on ethnicity or ancestry for all persons residing in the United States – citizens and non-citizens. An employer may deny employment for lack of citizenship, but only to the extent that the refusal does not have the effect of discrimination on the basis of national origin.

The U.S. Supreme Court has held that workplace harassment is merely a form of discrimination. Therefore, a "hostile environment" based on a person's gender, race, religion, national origin, age, or disability is as illegal under Title VII as sexual harassment.

No single factor is essential to establishing hostile environment harassment. The record as a whole and the totality of the circumstances will be examined. Among the elements considered will be the frequency of the discriminatory conduct, its severity, whether it is physically threatening or humiliating, and whether it unreasonably interferes with an employee's work.

Burden of Proof and Theories of Discrimination

There are basically two theories available to prove discrimination, disparate treatment and disparate (or adverse) impact. Disparate treatment involves an allegation of discriminatory treatment due to a protected characteristic. A claim that termination occurred because the employee was Italian or Jewish would be a claim of disparate treatment – the employee was treated disparately, or differently, because of ethnicity or religion. It is proven by direct or circumstantial evidence.

In order to establish a prima facie case of disparate treatment, a plaintiff has the burden to prove:

1. Membership in a protected class;

2. Application and qualification for a job for which the employer was seeking applicants;

3. Rejection, despite the applicant's qualifications; and

4. The employer's continued solicitation of applicants with qualifications equal to the plaintiff's.

Of course, the courts consider these elements to be flexible and modify them, on a case-by-case basis, to differing factual situations. For example, in a layoff situation, the issue is whether plaintiff was selected despite having qualifications equal to those retained.

If this low threshold is met, the burden shifts to the employer to articulate a legitimate reason for the adverse employment action. If the employer articulates a non-discriminatory reason for the action taken, the plaintiff is given the opportunity to prove the stated reason is not the true reason for the action. This

final opportunity has been described as the opportunity to prove that the stated reason is, in fact, a pretext for discrimination. Although there is a shifting burden analysis, the ultimate burden of proving discrimination remains on the plaintiff.

Disparate (or adverse) impact involves a policy or practice which, although neutral on its face, adversely affects members of a protected group. Such a case is established through the use of statistics. EEOC uses a four-fifths rule of thumb, the courts recognize more sophisticated inferential statistical models. Examples of policies neutral on their face but having adverse impact include layoff policies based upon selection of the highest paid, high school degrees, test scores, etc. If the disparate impact is established, the burden shifts to the employee to prove the business necessity of the policy.

Race Discrimination

Race discrimination, like all employment discrimination, requires a showing that an employee was discriminated against because of his or her race. While there is nothing wrong with firing an employee who is a sub-standard performer or engages in misconduct, there is everything wrong with firing an employee because he or she is of a certain race. Racial discrimination protection is given to persons of all races. That is, a black manager can be charged with racial discrimination against a white employee in the same manner that a white manager can be charged with discriminating against a black employee.

Sex Discrimination

The sex discrimination prohibition in Title VII is much broader than the Equal Pay Act protections. Under Title VII, there are no strict requirements that the equal work be in the same establishment and require the same skill, effort and responsibility under the same working conditions. Further, the non-discrimination prohibition covers all employment related practices, not just pay.

The principle of nondiscrimination requires that individuals be considered on the basis of individual capacities and not on the basis of any characteristics generally attributed to the members of a group. For example, the refusal to hire a woman based on the assumption that the turnover rate among them is higher than men is illegal. It is illegal to make employment decisions in reliance upon stereotype concerning someone's sex (or other statutorily protected characteristic).

State laws preferential to one sex over the other are superseded by Title VII and are, therefore, unlawful. Further, it is illegal to have separate lines of progression or a seniority system based on sex just as it is illegal to discriminate between men and women with regard to fringe benefits.

Favoritism, unfair treatment and unwise business decisions do not violate Title VII unless based on prohibited discrimination. Thus, where a male supervisor selects a female employee for a promotion because of his romantic involvement with her, these circumstances do not create liability to other, more qualified females, who are not subjected to a sexually hostile work environment. A consensual romantic relationship between a supervisor and an employee, while not a good idea for a number of reasons, is not prohibited under Title VII.

Hostile Environment Discrimination

The 1993 Supreme Court decision alluded to above expanded hostile environment harassment beyond sexual to embrace gender, race, religion, national origin, age, and disability. Note, however, that welcomeness of conduct is usually not an issue in situations of harassment that is not sexual in nature, such as harassment due to ethnicity or religion; in such situations, it is usually clear that the comments are perceived as abusive. While no single factor is essential to establish hostile environment harassment, violations are established by examining the record as a whole and the totality of the circumstances. Among the elements reviewed are the frequency of the discriminatory conduct, its severity, whether it is physically threatening or humiliating, and whether it unreasonably interferes with an employee's work performance. Harassment is merely considered a method or means by which discrimination is carried out. Therefore, hostile environment harassment based on any protected characteristics such as race, color, sex (whether or not of a sexual nature), religion, national origin, protected activity, age, or disability is illegal. If the harassment is committed by non-supervisory personnel (such as co-workers, third parties, contractors, etc.) the employer, once the employer learns of the harassment, must promptly investigate the allegations and, if harassment exists, take appropriate action to eliminate it. In non-supervisory harassment, the obligations are triggered when the employee knows or should know the harassment exists. In harassment committed by supervisors, employers are generally vicariously liable for the conduct.

Religious Discrimination Guidelines

Denying or limiting equal opportunities to individuals without reasonable effort to accommodate their religious beliefs or practices is a violation of Title VII. Section 701(j) of Title VII established an obligation by employers to reasonably accommodate the religious practices of an employee or prospective employee unless doing so would create an undue hardship upon the employer. In the U.S. Supreme Court's decision in *Trans World Airlines, Inc. v. Hardison* (1977), the Court ruled against a religious observer who could not work on the sabbath because the required accommodation would have involved violating the seniority rights of other workers and the regular payment of overtime pay to the replacement workers. Although the *Hardison* decision reaffirmed the employer's responsibility to accommodate, the extent of the duty was unclear. To help explain the extent of the duty, the EEOC has published revised Guidelines on Discrimination Because of Religion; the major elements of which are summarized below:

Accommodations – The employer is obligated to accommodate an employee's or prospective employee's religious practices once the employer has been notified of the need. The employer must offer the alternative which would least disadvantage the employment opportunities of the religious observant and not cause undue hardship to the employer.

In a religious discrimination case involving an interpretation of "reasonable accommodation," the Supreme Court ruled that an employer must make a "reasonable" effort to accommodate a worker's religion, but need not adopt the employee's suggested accommodation. In that case, the employer provided for three religious holidays and three days of personal leave, all with pay. The employee, who celebrated six religious holidays a year, argued that he wanted to take three personal days instead of unpaid leave for the remaining three religious holidays. The employer's policy was that personal days could not be used for religious holidays. The Court ruled that an employer's duty to accommodate the employee's religious belief under Title VII of the 1964 Civil Rights Act does not require the employer to accept the accommodation preferred by the employee. In another case, the Court struck down a Connecticut law that required employers to give employees their sabbath day off. The Court found that the law unconstitutionally promoted religious worship.

Alternatives – Examples of scheduling alternatives specified by the guidelines include the use of voluntary substitutions and swaps, flexible schedules, lateral transfers, and change of job assignments.

Union Dues – When an employee's religious practices prohibit payment of union dues to a labor organization, the employee must not be made to pay union dues but may be permitted to pay a sum equivalent to the dues to a charitable organization.

Undue Hardship – Under the guidelines, an employer may assert undue hardship to justify a refusal to accommodate an employee's need to be absent from his or her scheduled duty hours if the employer can demonstrate that the accommodation would require more than a minimal cost. This would be determined by an examination of all the facts and must be in accordance with the *Hardison* decision. Also, undue hardship may be shown where the accommodation would require a variance from a bona fide seniority system in order to accommodate an employee's religious practices.

Selection Practices – The guidelines address selection practices which tend to exclude individuals because of their religious beliefs. Under the guidelines, unlawful practices by employers include scheduling of examinations and other selection activities during a period which conflicts with an individual's religious practices (or beliefs), and pre-employment inquiries which ascertain an applicant's availability to work during certain time periods.

National Origin Discrimination Guidelines

The Commission broadly defines national origin discrimination as including, but not limited to, the denial of equal employment opportunity because of an individual's place of origin; or because an individual has the physical, cultural, or linguistic characteristics of a national origin group. The Commission will examine, with particular concern, charges alleging that individuals have been denied equal employment opportunity for reasons which are grounded in national origin considerations, such as: (a) marriage to, or association with, persons of a national origin group; (b) membership in or association with an organization identified with, or seeking to promote the interests of, national origin groups; (c) attendance or participation in schools, churches, temples, or mosques generally used by persons of a national origin group; or (d) because an individual's name or spouse's name is associated with a national origin group.

The "Speak English Only" Rule – The Commission will presume that a rule requiring employees to speak only English at all times in the workplace may violate Title VII as a burdensome term and condition of employment. Requiring employees to speak only in English at certain times would not be discriminatory if the employer shows that the rule is justified by business necessity. When the employer believes that the rule is justified by business necessity, the employer should clearly inform employees of the circumstance in which they are required to speak only in English and the consequences of violating the rule. Notice of such a rule is necessary because it is common for individuals whose primary language is not English to inadvertently slip from speaking English to speaking their native tongue. Any adverse employment decision against an individual based on a violation of the rule will be considered as evidence of discrimination if an employer has not given effective notice of the rule.

Accent – The Commission has determined that an employer must show a legitimate non-discriminatory reason for the denial of employment opportunity because of an individual's accent or manner of speaking. Investigations will focus on a claimant's qualifications to do the job and whether the claimant's accent or manner of speaking would have a detrimental effect on job performance. Requirements that employers or applicants be fluent in English may also violate Title VII if they are adopted for discriminatory reasons or applied in a discriminatory manner, or if they have the effect of excluding individuals of a particular national origin and are not related to successful job performance.

Harassment – The Commission has consistently held that harassment on the basis of national origin is a violation of Title VII. It holds that an employer has an affirmative duty to maintain a working environment free of harassment on the basis of national origin. This rule, which has been adopted by the courts in race and sex cases, clearly applies equally to national origin.

Ethnic slurs and other verbal or physical conduct relating to an individual's national origin constitutes harassment when this conduct (1) has the purpose or effect of creating an intimidating, hostile, or offensive work environment; (2) has the purpose or effect of unreasonably interfering with an individual's work performance; or (3) otherwise adversely affects an individual's employment opportunities.

An employer is responsible for its acts and those of its agents and supervisory employees under Title VII, regardless of whether the acts were specifically authorized or forbidden by the employer and regardless of whether the employer knew or should have known of the acts.

The guidelines for determining whether harassment exists distinguish between the employer's responsibility for the acts of its agents or supervisors and the responsibility it has for conduct among fellow employees. Liability for acts of national origin harassment between fellow employees in the workplace exists only when the employer, or its agents or supervisory employees, knows or should have known of the conduct, and the employer cannot demonstrate that it took immediate and appropriate corrective action. In certain circumstances, where an employer may be shown to have the necessary control, it may also be responsible for the acts of non-employees with respect to harassment of employees in the workplace on the basis of national origin.

Hiring Non-Nationals – With the enactment of the Immigration Reform and Control Act of 1986, Congress for the first time made it unlawful for an employer to hire individuals who are not legally authorized for employment in the United States. (For an expanded description of this law, please refer to Chapter 12, Immigration Control - Verification of Employment.) After the adoption of these new requirements, Congress became concerned that some employers might overreact and refuse to hire individuals who appeared or sounded "foreign." Although Congress recognized that the existing prohibitions on national origin discrimination in Title VII of the Civil Rights Act would cover much of the potential discrimination, Congress also included in the Act a new non-discrimination provision, to be enforced by the Department of Justice, which prohibits national origin discrimination by small employers not covered by Title VII and discrimination because of citizenship status by all employers with four or more employees.

While the Immigration Act prohibits discrimination on the basis of citizenship in some circumstances, it specifically states that it is not a violation of the Immigration Act to prefer a citizen over an alien where both are equally qualified. Employers should be aware, however, that such citizenship preferences may

still violate Title VII if they have the purpose or effect of discriminating on the basis of national origin.

Affirmative Action Guidelines

The legislative purpose of Title VII was to encourage voluntary action without recourse to legal proceedings and, for that reason, the EEOC has encouraged voluntary affirmative action to improve opportunities for minorities and women. Therefore, in providing guidelines for affirmative action programs, the EEOC offers what could be an affirmative good faith defense to any subsequent equal employment discrimination charge. The Commission recommends that such a plan be in writing and be dated so that it could serve as credible evidence of an employer's compliance efforts in case of a subsequent challenge.

The Supreme Court has strongly endorsed the use of affirmative action, including specific hiring goals, to remedy past employment discrimination. The Court has authorized federal judges to set goals and timetables requiring employers who have engaged in past discrimination to hire or promote specific numbers of minorities. It has also permitted private and public sector employers the ability, under defined circumstances, to voluntarily adopt specific goals for their work forces without court orders.

In a 1987 decision, the Supreme Court held that in hiring and promotion decisions, employers may sometimes favor women and members of minorities over better qualified men and whites in order to achieve better balance in their work force. The decision upheld a California city's affirmative action plan for women and minority group members.

The ruling was the Court's first involving affirmative action plans which give job preferences to women over men. The Court rejected a discrimination claim by a man who said he had been the victim of illegal sex discrimination when a less qualified woman was promoted instead of him. The decision also marked the first time the Court had clearly held that in a case where there was no proof of past discrimination against women or minorities by a particular employer, the employer may use racial and sexual preferences in hiring and promoting to bring its work force into line with the make up of the local population or relevant labor market. "In determining whether an imbalance exists that would justify taking sex or race into account, a comparison of the percentage of minorities or women in the employer's work force with a percentage in the area labor market or general population is appropriate in analyzing jobs that require no special expertise."

Pregnancy Discrimination Guidelines

The Pregnancy Discrimination Act of 1978 makes it clear that discrimination on the basis of pregnancy, childbirth, or related medical conditions constitutes unlawful sex discrimination under Title VII.

The basic principle of the Act is that women affected by pregnancy and related conditions must be treated the same as other applicants and employees on the basis of their ability or inability to work. The Equal Employment Opportunity Commission has issued guidelines, including questions and answers, interpreting the Act. They provide guidance as to what employment practices would be considered by the Commission as violating the Act. Adoption of the Family Medical Leave Act has provided additional leave protection for giving birth or adopting a child.

Frequently Asked Questions
Relating to Pregnant Employee Rights

Provide Another Job

Q. If, for pregnancy-related reasons, an employee is unable to perform the functions of her job, does the employer have to provide an alternative job?

A. An employer is required to treat an employee temporarily unable to perform the functions of the job (because of her pregnancy-related condition) in the same manner as it treats other temporarily disabled employees, whether by providing modified tasks, alternative assignments, disability leave, leave without pay, etc. For example, a woman's primary job function may be the operation of a machine, and, incidental to that function, she may carry materials to and from the machine. If other employees temporarily unable to lift are relieved of these functions, pregnant employees also unable to lift must be temporarily relieved of the function.

How to Determine if She Can Work

Q. May an employer place on leave a pregnant employee who claims she is able to work, or deny leave to a pregnant employee who claims she is disabled from work?

A. An employer may not single out pregnancy-related conditions for determining an employee's ability to work. However, an employer may use any procedure used to determine the ability of all employees to work. For example, if an employer requires its employees to submit a doctor's statement concerning their inability to work before granting leave or paying sick benefits, the

FAQs – Pregnant Employee Rights [(continued)]

employer may require employees affected by pregnancy-related conditions to submit such statements. Similarly, if an employer allows its employees to obtain doctors' statements from their personal physicians for absences due to other disabilities or return-dates from other disabilities, it must accept doctors' statements from personal physicians for absences and return-dates connected with pregnancy-related disabilities.

Length of Leave

Q. Can an employer have a rule which prohibits an employee from returning to work for a predetermined length of time after childbirth?

A. No.

Stay off Until Delivery?

Q. If an employee has been absent from work as a result of a pregnancy-related condition and recovers, may her employer require her to remain on leave until after her baby is born?

A. No. An employee must be permitted to work at all times during pregnancy when she is able to perform her job.

Keep Job Open?

Q. Must an employer hold open the job of an employee who is absent on leave because she is temporarily disabled by pregnancy-related conditions?

A. Unless the employee on leave has informed the employer that she does not intend to return to work, her job must be held open for her return on the same basis as jobs are held open for employees on sick or disability leave for other reasons.

Status During Leave

Q. May an employer's policy concerning the accrual and crediting of seniority during absences for medical conditions be different for employees affected by pregnancy-related conditions?

A. No. An employer's seniority policy must be the same for employees absent for pregnancy-related reasons as for those absent for other medical reasons.

Fringe Benefits

Q. For purposes of calculating such matters as vacations and pay increases, may an employer credit time spent on leave for pregnancy-related reasons differently than time spent on leave for other reasons?

A. No. An employer's policy with respect to crediting time for the purpose of calculating such matters as vacation and pay increases cannot treat employees on leave for pregnancy-related reasons less favorably than employees on leave for other reasons. For example, if an employee on leave for medical reasons is credited with the time spent on leave when computing entitlement to vacation or pay raises, an employee on leave for pregnancy-related disability is entitled to the same kind of time credit.

FAQs – Pregnant Employee Rights (continued)

Hiring

Q. Must an employer hire a woman who is medically unable, because of a pregnancy-related condition, to perform a necessary function of a job?

A. No. An employer can refuse to hire a woman because of her pregnancy-related condition so long as she is unable to perform the major functions necessary to do the job.

Only Marrieds Protected?

Q. May an employer limit disability benefits for pregnancy-related conditions to married employees?

A. No.

All Female Workforce

Q. If an employer has an all-female workforce or job classification, must benefits be provided for pregnancy-related conditions?

A. Yes. If benefits are provided for other conditions, they must be also be provided for pregnancy-related conditions.

Income Maintenance

Q. For what length of time must an employer who provides income maintenance benefits for temporary disabilities provide such benefits for pregnancy-related disabilities?

A. Benefits should be provided for as long as the employee is unable to work for medical reasons unless some other limitation is set for all other temporary disabilities, in which case pregnancy-related disabilities should be treated the same as other temporary disabilities.

Long-Term Disability

Q. Must an employer who provides benefits for long-term or permanent disabilities provide such benefits for pregnancy-related conditions?

A. Yes. Benefits for long-term or permanent disabilities resulting from pregnancy-related conditions must be provided to the same extent that such benefits are provided for other conditions which result in long-term or permanent disability.

Fringe Benefits

Q. If an employer provides benefits to employees on leave, such as installment purchase disability insurance; payment of premium for health, life, or other insurance; or continued payments into pension, savings or profit-sharing plans, must the same benefits be provided for those on leave for pregnancy-related conditions?

A. Yes, the employer must provide the same benefits for those on leave for pregnancy-related conditions as for those on leave for other reasons.

Vacation

Q. Can an employee who is absent due to a pregnancy-related disability be required to exhaust vacation benefits before receiving sick leave pay or disability benefits?

A. No. If employees who are absent because of other disabling causes receive sick leave pay or disability benefits without any requirement that they first exhaust vacation benefits, the employer cannot impose this requirement on an employee for a pregnancy-related cause.

Pre-Employment Inquiries

Employment application forms and pre-employment interviews have traditionally been instruments for screening out, at an early stage, "unsuited" or "unqualified" persons from consideration for employment and often have been used in such a way as to restrict or deny employment opportunities for women and members of minority groups.

The law, interpreted through court rulings and EEOC decisions, prohibits the use of all pre-employment inquiries and qualifying factors which disproportionately screen out members of minority groups or members of one sex, are not valid predictors of successful job performance, and cannot be justified by "business necessity."

In devising or reviewing application forms or in seeking information from job applicants, employers should ask themselves: (1) Will the answers to these questions directly or indirectly reveal information concerning an applicant's membership in a protected class? (2) Will the answers to this question, if used in making a selection, result in disparate treatment or disparate effect on minorities and/or members of one sex (e.g., disqualify a significantly larger percentage of members of a particular group than others)? and (3) Is this information really needed to judge an applicant's competence or qualification for the job in question?

The concept of business necessity has been narrowly defined by the courts. When a practice is found to have discriminatory effects, it can be justified only by showing that it is necessary to the safe and efficient operation of the business, that it effectively carries out the purpose it is supposed to serve, and that there are no alternative policies or practices which would better or equally well serve the same purpose with less discriminatory impact.

Title VII specifically excludes from its discrimination ban any employment practices based upon giving and acting upon the "results of any professionally developed ability test, provided that such test, its administration, or action upon the results is not designed, intended, or used to discriminate because of race, color, religion, sex, or national origin." In a technically complex guideline, the EEOC states that the use of any selection procedure which has an adverse impact on the hiring, promotion, or other employment or membership opportunities of members of any race, sex, or ethnic group will be considered to be discriminatory and inconsistent with Title VII, unless the selection procedure has been validated. The guidelines also explain validity studies and establish certain minimum technical standards for them.

An employer needs to be able to demonstrate through statistical evidence that any selection procedure which has a "disparate effect" on groups protected by the law is job related (i.e., validation tests indicate that the selection procedure validly predicts successful performance for the type of job in question). For example, if a valid written civil service examination is given for law enforcement applicants, one would expect the best officers to score the highest on the test. A correlation study, comparing performance evaluations (later success on the job) with the prediction of success (the written test) will prove, or disprove, the test's validity. If this cannot be shown or if the employer cannot or does not wish to perform a technical validation study, the use of the selection procedure should be discontinued or altered in such a way that there is no longer a discriminatory effect. Even when a procedure having an adverse impact can be validated, it may not be used if there are other procedures which would accomplish the same goal and have less of a discriminatory effect.

Data Required for Legitimate Business Purposes

An employer may justifiably seek and obtain information regarding a job applicant's race, sex, or ethnicity if needed for implementation of affirmative action programs, court-ordered or other government reporting or recordkeeping requirements, and for studies to identify and resolve possible problems in the recruitment and testing of members of minority groups and/or women to insure equal employment for all persons.

Data on such matters as marital status, number and age of children, and similar matters, which could be used in a discriminatory manner in making employment decisions but which are necessary for insurance, reporting requirements, or other business purposes, can and should preferably be obtained after a person has been employed, not by means of an application form or pre-employment interview or process.

The employer, however, must be able to demonstrate that such data was collected for legitimate business purposes. Such information should be kept separate from the regular permanent employee records to insure that it is not used to discriminate in making personnel decisions. To protect against the improper use of such information by their selected officials, employers should consider collecting the facts by the use of a "tear-off sheet." After completing the application and the tear-off sheet, the latter is separated from the application, not provided to the decision-makers, and used only for purposes unrelated to the selection decision. The tearoff sheet should contain a statement about the purpose for which the information is being collected and that the information will not be made available or used for making employee selections. This should help allay applicant concern that the information will be used to discriminate on a prohibited basis.

It is reasonable to assume that all questions on an application form or in a pre-employment interview are used for some purpose and that selection or hiring decisions are made on the basis of the answers given. Seeking information other than that which is relevant to evaluate effectively a person's qualification for employment increases the potential exposure to charges of discrimination in legal proceedings. Therefore, applications should be reviewed to insure that only relevant, lawful questions are asked and persons conducting interviews are properly trained.

Race, Color, Religion, Sex, or National Origin – Pre-employment inquiries concerning race, color, religion, sex, or national origin are not considered independent violations of the law. However, inquiries which either directly or indirectly disclose such information, unless otherwise explained, may constitute evidence that discrimination prohibited by Title VII has occurred. Some states' fair employment practice laws expressly prohibit direct or indirect inquiries on employment applications concerning the applicant's race, color, religion, sex, or national origin or indirectly reveal such information. In some states, it may also be considered illegal to seek related data (former name, past residence, names of relatives, place of birth, citizenship, education, organizational memberships and activities, a photograph, and color of eyes and hair) which could indirectly reveal similar information. Denial of equal employment opportunity to individuals because of marriage to or association with persons of a specific national, ethnic, or racial origin, or because of attendance at schools or churches, or membership in organizations identified with particular racial or ethnic groups, may be considered a violation of Title VII. Charges presented to the EEOC alleging such discrimination will be examined with particular concern to determine if, indeed, the alleged discrimination was based on race or national origin.

Height and Weight – The Equal Employment Opportunity Commission and the courts have ruled that minimum height and weight requirements are illegal if they screen out a disproportionate number of minority-group individuals (e.g., height requirements have been found to disproportionately screen out Spanish-surnamed or Asian Americans) or women, and the employer cannot show that these standards are essential to the safe and proper performance of the job in question.

Marital Status, Number of Children, and Provisions for Child Care – Questions about marital status, pregnancy, future child-bearing plans, and number and age of children are frequently used to discriminate against women and may be a violation of Title VII if used to deny or limit employment opportunities for female applicants. Employers are cautioned against use of such non-job-related questions. Information needed for tax, insurance, or Social Security purposes may be obtained after employment. It is a violation of Title VII for employers to require pre-employment information about child care arrangements from female applicants only. The U.S. Supreme Court has ruled that an employer may not have different hiring policies for men and women with pre-school children.

English Language Skill – When the use of an English language proficiency test has an adverse effect upon a particular minority group and English language skill is not a requirement of the work to be performed, there is a violation of Title VII.

Educational Requirements – The U.S. Supreme Court has found an employer's requirement of a high school degree discriminatory where statistics showed such a requirement operated to disqualify blacks at a substantially higher rate than whites, and there was no evidence that the requirement was significantly related to successful job performance. This same standard applies to any adverse impact on a group protected under Title VII with respect to educational attainment, unless job-relatedness or business necessity can be established.

Friends or Relatives Working for the Employer – Information about friends or relatives working for an employer is not relevant to an applicant's competence. Requesting such information may be unlawful if it indicates a preference for friends and relatives of present employees and the composition of the present work force is such that this preference would reduce or eliminate opportunities for women or minority group members. Such "word-of-mouth" recruiting efforts may have adverse impact and not survive business necessity scrutiny. Also, a "nepotism" policy which prohibits or limits employment opportunities of a spouse or other relative also may be illegal if it has an adverse impact on job opportunities for either women or men as a group and is not narrowly drawn to reflect business necessity. For example, a prohibition against persons working in a supervisory – subordinate relationship and the option for either employee to terminate employment would probably survive challenge.

Arrest Records – Because members of some minority groups are arrested substantially more often than whites in proportion to their numbers in the population, making personnel decisions on the basis of arrest records has a disproportionate effect on the employment opportunities of members of these groups. Further, since an arrest, unlike a conviction, is not proof of criminal activity or misconduct, it cannot be job related. The courts and the commission, accordingly, have held that without proof of business necessity, an employer's use of arrest records to disqualify job applicants is unlawful discrimination. Even if an employer does not consider arrest information, the mere request for such information tends to discourage minority applicants and will, therefore, be considered suspiciously by the Commission.

The EEOC recently issued a policy statement on arrest records staing the bottom line: refusing to hire any and all applicants based on arrest record will be found to be discrimination under Title VII of the Civil Rights Act. Since it is generally presumed employers ask only questions which are deemed relevant to employment decisions, routinely asking job applicants about arrest records on an employment application or in a job interview may violate Title VII, unless further inquiry is made about the circumstances surrounding an arrest.

An arrest alone is not reliable evidence that a person actually committed a crime. Even where the conduct alleged in an arrest record is related to the job at issue, the EEOC states the employer must investigate whether the arrest is proof of a particular conduct. The employer should conduct its own investigation into the surrounding circumstances, offer the applicant or employee an opportunity to explain, and, if the person denies engaging in the conduct, make follow-up inquiries to evaluate the person's credibility. The purpose of the investigation is to determine whether the conduct that led to the arrest, which would make the employee ineligible for the job, did in fact occur.

This does not mean information about arrests can never be used to make an employment decision. As with conviction records, arrest records may be considered as evidence that conduct occurred which renders an applicant unsuitable for a particular position, the EEOC explains. But, to use an arrest record to support a refusal to hire, the employer must consider the relationship of the arrest charges to the position applied for, and determine the likelihood the conduct actually occurred.

Even asking for conviction records, which do provide reliable proof a person engaged in illegal acts, carries some risks. National law enforcement statistics indicate blacks and Hispanics are convicted in numbers disproportionate to whites. Basing employment decisions on conviction records could thus have an adverse impact on minority groups and, therefore, must be job related. While convicted child molesters can be denied jobs as nursery school teachers and embezzlers need not be offered jobs as bank tellers, job relatedness is not always that easy to determine.

Conviction Records – A conviction for a felony or misdemeanor may not, by itself, lawfully constitute an absolute bar to employment. However, an employer may give fair consideration to the relationship between a conviction and the applicant's fitness for a particular job. Conviction records should be cause for rejection only if their number and nature would cause the applicant to be unsuitable for the position. If such inquiries are made, they should be accompanied by a statement that a conviction record will not necessarily be a bar to employment and that factors such as age and time of the offense, seriousness and nature of the violation, and rehabilitation will be taken into account.

Discharge from Military – Employers should not, as a matter of policy, reject applicants with less than honorable discharges from military service. Minority service members have had a higher proportion of general and undesirable discharges than nonminority members of similar aptitude and education.

Thus, an employer's requirement that to be eligible for employment ex-members of the armed services must have been honorably discharged has a disparate effect upon minorities and may be a violation of Title VIII.

One federal district court has held that an employer may inquire about an applicant's military service record if information regarding discharge status is used not in making a hiring decision, but in deciding whether further investigations should be made into the applicant's background and qualifications. If further inquiry reveals nondiscriminatory grounds for denying employment, the employer may then refuse to hire the applicant.

Since a request for this information may discourage minority workers from applying and, therefore, be grounds for a discriminatory charge, employers should avoid such questions unless "business necessity" can be shown. As in the case of conviction records discussed above, questions regarding military service should be accompanied by a statement that a dishonorable or general discharge is not an absolute bar to employment and that other factors will affect a final decision to hire or not to hire.

National Security — It is not unlawful to deny employment to an individual who does not fulfill the national security requirements.

Economic Status — Rejection of applicants because of poor credit ratings might have a disparate impact on minority groups and has been found unlawful by the Commission, unless business necessity can be shown.

Inquiries as to an applicant's financial status, such as bankruptcy, car ownership, rental or ownership of a house, length of residence at an address, or past garnishments of wages, if utilized to make employment decisions, may likewise violate Title VII.

Availability for Work on Weekends or Holidays — Employers and unions have an obligation to accommodate the religious beliefs of employees and/or applicants, unless to do so would cause undue hardship. The EEOC has determined that the use of pre-employment inquiries that establish an applicant's availability has an exclusionary effect on the employment opportunities of persons following certain religious practices. Questions relating to availability for work on Friday evenings, Saturdays, or holidays should not be asked unless the employer can show

that the questions have not had an exclusionary effect on its employees or applicants who would need an accommodation for their religious practices, that the questions are otherwise justified by business necessity, and that there are no alternative procedures which would have a lesser exclusionary effect.

EEOC Enforcement Procedures

An Overview – The Equal Employment Opportunity Commission's representatives have full investigatory powers to:

1. Enter and inspect the place of employment, review records, and interview employees;

2. Advise employers regarding any changes necessary or desirable to comply with the law (if a violation of the law is found, the EEOC will attempt to negotiate a settlement to make the employees whole and eliminate the discriminatory practice);

3. Subpoena witnesses and order production of documents;

4. Supervise back wage payments; and

5. Initiate and conduct litigation.

Typically, information is submitted in person, by telephone, or by mail to an EEOC field office. When the information involves a violation, a charge is drawn up with EEOC assistance, if desired, which generally contains the following information:

1. The full name, address, and telephone number of the person making the charge;

2. The full name and address of the employer; and

3. A clear and concise statement of the facts, including pertinent dates constituting the alleged unlawful employment practices.

The EEOC, in a "Memorandum of Understanding," has given the Department of Labor power to seek relief from federal contractors that discriminate against workers based on gender, race or religion. Accordingly, employees of federal contractors will now be permitted to file discrimination claims with the Department of Labor, which has the power to review the employment practices of some 200,000 federal contractors. The Department's new authority allows for it to negotiate a voluntary settlement once a complaint is filed, although it would still be prohibited from suing employers to recover damages.

The Typical "Charge" Process – Most often, complaints are filed by the aggrieved individual(s), but the EEOC regulations allow complaints to be filed on behalf of the EEOC. Normally, the aggrieved party will be interviewed by an Equal Opportunity Specialist (EOS) during the initial intake interview. At that time, the complaining party will be asked to complete a questionnaire which calls for information such as the name, address, and telephone number of the employer, the place where he or she applied for the job, the name of the employee's supervisor (if the individual was an employee), the date that the alleged discrimination occurred, and the nature of the discrimination.

A complaint must be filed within 180 days of the alleged discriminatory act. If there is a state or local fair employment practice agency in the area, the employee has up to 240 days, and in some cases 300, but if the complaint is not filed on time, the EEOC cannot investigate it.

The EOS will investigate the allegation so that a proper charge may be written. An employee is counseled about the EEOC investigation procedures as well as any rights they may have under the Age Discrimination Act and the Equal Pay Act.

The identity of a complainant, a confidential witness, or the aggrieved party on whose behalf a charge is filed will ordinarily not be disclosed without prior written consent.

Once the charge is filed, the employer will be notified within 10 days and will be advised as to the date, place, circumstances, and identity of the person filing the charge. The employer will normally be asked to come to the EEOC office for a fact-finding conference to discuss the allegation in the charge. That conference is conducted by an Equal Opportunity Specialist. Evidence may be presented by both the employee and the employer. The employer may bring along any witnesses who have actual knowledge of the incident. The aggrieved party's witness will have been interviewed prior to the conference. Only those people who have firsthand knowledge of the incident are permitted to speak at the conference. The effort will be to amicably resolve the charge at this fact-finding conference. If it turns out that this is impossible, the charge will be investigated further. The EEOC has a Continued Investigation and Conciliation Unit which will further investigate the charge, if necessary. If this group has reasonable cause to believe that discrimination has occurred, the EEOC will notify the aggrieved party and the employer. At this point, the EEOC will begin the conciliation efforts required under the statute. Most charges filed with the EEOC, even when the Commission decides to sue, are conciliated or settled before the case actually goes to trial. At all stages of the investigation, the Commission is required by law to attempt to bring the matter to a resolution agreeable to all parties without costly litigation.

If the Commission's investigation shows no reasonable cause to believe that discrimination has occurred, both the aggrieved party and the employer will be notified. The aggrieved party will be issued a "right to sue" letter which permits a private court suit.

If there is reasonable cause to believe discrimination took place and conciliation efforts fail, the Commission or an aggrieved party can file a lawsuit in federal district court.

Title VII and the ADA requires that the federal government refer charges of discrimination to state or local agencies, if the charge meets certain criteria. Depending on the state or local agency's work-sharing agreement with the Commission, a charge may be processed either by the EEOC or the state or local agency.

The dramatic increase in the number of EEOC complaints charging employers with illegal discrimination has driven home to employers that they are exposed to increasing amounts of liability, which includes punitive damages, for the conduct of employees and managers. The conduct includes all aspects of the employment relationship, including remarks or comments. The costly consequences of inattention reinforce the importance of effectively handling and responding to a charge of discrimination filed with the EEOC. There is clear evidence to show that properly handling the charge at its early stages can markedly reduce, and possibly even eliminate, potential liability.

EEOC Views on Arbitration

The EEOC supports voluntary arbitration and other alternative approaches to resolve employment discrimination disputes. To this end, the EEOC has been running an alternative dispute resolution pilot program, which uses volunteer mediators. On the other hand, mandatory arbitration of workplace discrimination claims is opposed by the EEOC and the agency will challenge the legality of these practices.

In the EEOC's view, mandatory arbitration, by its nature, does not allow for the development of civil rights law. Since judicial review of arbitration decisions may not be written or made public, the system affords no opportunity to build precedent or provide for meaningful review. Mandatory arbitration also has other "inherent limitations" such as the private nature of the process which "allows for little public accountability" of either the arbitrators themselves or the decision-making process.

The EEOC contends that the lack of public disclosure not only weakens deterrence, but also prevents assessment of whether individual employers' practices are in need of reform.

The EEOC's policy guidelines assert that mandatory arbitration systems also contain "structural biases" against employees because "the employer has an advantage over the employee, who is less able to make an informed selection of an arbitrator or be savvy regarding the system." Also, the arbitrator, paid by the parties, is likely to be influenced by the fact that the employer is the potential source of future business.

EEOC Mediation

In 1999, EEOC launched a new initiative to significantly expand its voluntary mediation program. Mediation is a form of Alternative Dispute Resolution (ADR) that is offered by the EEOC as an alternative to the traditional investigative or litigation processes. Mediation is an informal process in which a neutral third party assists the opposing parties to reach a voluntary, negotiated resolution of a "charge" of discrimination. The decision to mediate is completely voluntary for the charging party and the employer. Mediation gives the parties the opportunity to discuss the issues raised in the charge, clear up misunderstandings, determine the underlying interests or concerns, find areas of agreement and, ultimately, to incorporate those areas of agreement into resolutions. A mediator does not resolve the charge or impose a decision on the parties. Instead, the mediator helps the parties to reach a mutually acceptable resolution.

If either party declines to participate in mediation, the charge of discrimination will be processed just like any other charge. Only mediators who are experienced and trained in mediation and equal employment opportunity law are assigned to mediate EEOC charges.

EEOC has a staff of trained mediators. The EEOC also contracts with professional external mediators to mediate charges filed with EEOC. All EEOC mediators, whether internal staff or external mediators, are trained to be neutral unbiased professionals with no stake in the outcome of the mediation process. Mediation will usually take place early in the process prior to an investigation of the charge.

The EEOC maintains strict confidentiality in its mediation program. The mediator and the parties must sign agreements that they will keep everything that is revealed during the mediation confidential. The mediation sessions are not tape-recorded or transcribed. Notes taken during the mediation are destroyed. Any records or other documents offered by either party during the mediation are also destroyed. Furthermore, in order to ensure confidentiality, the mediation program is insulated from the EEOC's investigative and litigation functions. EEOC mediators only mediate charges and are precluded from performing any other functions related to the investigation or litigation of charges of discrimination. Mediations conducted by EEOC staff will usually take place at the EEOC's offices in space reserved for mediation. External mediators will arrange a mutually convenient time and place for the mediation after consultation with both parties.

While it is not necessary to have an attorney or other representative in order to participate in EEOC's mediation program, either party may choose to do so. The mediator will decide what role the attorney or representative will play during the mediation. The mediator may ask that they provide advice and counsel, but not speak for a party or directly question the other side. If a party plans to bring an attorney or other representative to the mediation session, he or she can discuss this with the mediator prior to the mediation session. The majority of mediations are completed in one session, which usually lasts from one to five hours. There is no

fee for the mediation. An agreement reached during mediation is enforceable in court just like any other settlement agreement resolving a charge filed with the EEOC.

The EEOC evaluates each charge to determine whether it is appropriate for mediation, considering such factors as the nature of the case, the relationship of the parties, the size and complexity of the case, and the relief sought by the charging party. Charges determined by the EEOC to be without merit are not eligible for mediation.

If a charge is not resolved during the mediation process, the charge is returned to an investigative unit, and is processed just like any other charge. Since the entire mediation process is strictly confidential, information revealed during the mediation session cannot be disclosed to anyone, including other EEOC personnel. Therefore, it cannot be used during any subsequent investigation.

Penalties

A court that finds an employer deliberately has engaged in or is engaging presently in an unlawful employment practice (e.g., Title VII Civil Rights Act of 1964, as amended, the Equal Pay Act, the Age Discrimination in Employment Act) may issue an injunction forbidding the employer to continue that practice. It may require, in addition, appropriate affirmative action. This may include, but is not limited to, reinstatement or hiring of employees, with or without back pay for a period up to two years prior to the filing date of the charge. The court may also employ other equitable relief.

The Civil Rights Act of 1991 significantly expanded the remedies available in employment discrimination cases. It significantly increased remedies for women, the disabled, and federal employees for violations of their civil rights. Perhaps the most important change in terms of impact on employers are the rights to trial by jury, compensatory and punitive damages

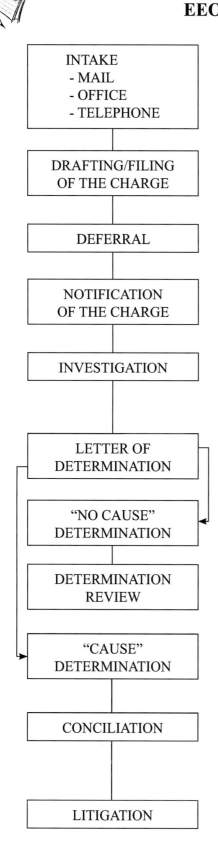

EEOC Charge Process Flow Chart

INTAKE - MAIL - OFFICE - TELEPHONE	Rendering Assistance to persons who may wish to file charges or complaints under Title VII, Age Discrimination in Employment Act (ADEA), or Equal Pay Act (EPA).
DRAFTING/FILING OF THE CHARGE	Interview to set forth the alleged discriminatory practices, collect information related to the allegations, and discuss EEOC procedures.
DEFERRAL	Title VII requires deferral to a state or local human rights agency meeting Federal standards. Either the EEOC or the deferral agency will process the charge.
NOTIFICATION OF THE CHARGE	Respondent must be notified within 10 days of receipt of charge.
INVESTIGATION	Investigator attempts to secure as much relevant information as possible regarding the charge from both the charging party and the respondent. Investigator may conduct an on-site investigation. Title VII and the ADEA permit settlement during processing of charges.
LETTER OF DETERMINATION	A Letter of Determination is issued on whether discrimination occurred. Conclusion is based on findings and analysis of evidence gathered during its investigation.
"NO CAUSE" DETERMINATION	Based on evidence uncovered in the investigation, the Commission determined there was no violation of the statutes the EEOC enforces.
DETERMINATION REVIEW	The charging party can request staff in a headquarters office to review the determination of "No Cause."
"CAUSE" DETERMINATION	Based on evidence uncovered in the investigation, the Commission determined there was a violation of one or more of the statutes the EEOC enforces.
CONCILIATION	The objective of conciliation is to achieve an informal resolution of all violations found during the investigation. In a successful conciliation, the Commission, the charging party and a respondent sign a written agreement providing full relief to the charging party and the respondent agrees to eliminate its discriminatory practices or policy.
LITIGATION	The Commission may authorize (in instances where conciliation has failed) the filing of a lawsuit against a respondent to obtain the appropriate relief.

and attorneys fees for prevailing plaintiffs. Thus, these changes will make discrimination potentially far more costly for employers, and argues for stronger preventative measures to be taken to avoid litigation.

The total of compensatory and punitive damages is limited according to the size of the employer (e.g., 15-100 employees, $50,000; 101-200 employees, $100,000; 201-500 employees, $200,000; and over 500 employees, $300,000). These amounts are available in addition to back pay, and any other amount previously available. The limit is per plaintiff, not per defendant; thus, cases with multiple plaintiffs present substantial exposure.

There is a "good faith" defense against claims for damages in an action brought under the Americans with Disabilities Act for employers that, in consultation with the employee, attempt to make a "reasonable accommodation" for the employee's disability.

The Supreme Court recently ruled that a victim of discrimination should not automatically lose a civil rights lawsuit if the employer later discovers the worker lied to get the job or otherwise violated a company policy that would have resulted in termination if discovered while employed. Basically, such a worker will not be eligible for reinstatement or recovery for any damages from the date the "after acquired" evidence is obtained.

While most litigation is brought against an employer, individuals who may be in a supervisory capacity are frequently named as defendants. There are tactical reasons for this including the need for separate counsel and raising the stakes to encourage an eventual settlement with the employer.[1] It is clear that

---

1. Title VII and several other statutes have been interpreted by the Supreme Court as not imposing personal liability on supervisors. The Court's reasoning was that if Congress intended to exclude small businesses, those with less than 15 employees, it could not have intended to hold supervisors liable.

both the Family and Medical Leave Act and the Fair Labor Standards Act are intended to cover individuals such as supervisors because the statute extends employer status "to any person who acts, directly or indirectly, in the interest of an employer to any of the employees of such employer."

In the case of the anti-discriminations laws, Title VII, the ADA, the Equal Pay Act, and the Age Discrimination in Employment Act, the Supreme Court in a 1999 ruling made it difficult for employees to be able to collect punitive damages against their employers. In a narrow 5-4 decision, the Court decided that a company which has made "good faith efforts" to comply with the civil rights laws cannot be required to pay punitive damages for the discriminatory actions of managers who violate company policy. In effect, in the punitive damages context, an employer may not be vicariously liable for the discriminatory employment decisions of managerial agents where these decisions are contrary to the employer's good faith efforts to comply with the various laws.

Retaliation

Title VII of the Civil Rights Act of 1964, the Age Discrimination in Employment Act, the Americans with Disabilities Act and the Equal Pay Act prohibit retaliation by an employer because an individual has engaged in protected activity, which is defined as:

1. Opposing a practice made unlawful by one of the employment discrimination statutes (the "opposition clause"); or

2. Filing a charge, testifying, assisting, or participating in any manner in an investigation, proceeding, or hearing under the applicable statue (the "participation clause").

The EEOC has a strong policy of protecting the process by ensuring that individuals who oppose unlawful employment discrimination, participate in employment discrimination proceedings, or otherwise assert their rights under the laws enforced by the Commission are protected against retaliation. Voluntary compliance with and effective enforcement of the anti-discrimination statutes depend in large part on the initiative and willingness of individuals to oppose employment practices that they reasonably believe to be unlawful and to file charges of discrimination. If retaliation against those who engage in such activities were permitted to go unremedied, it would have a chilling effect upon the willingness of individuals to speak out against employment discrimination or to participate in the EEOC's administrative process or other employment discrimination proceedings.

The Commission can sue for temporary or preliminary relief before completing its processing of a retaliation charge if the charging party or the Commission will likely suffer irreparable harm because of the retaliation. Compensatory and punitive damages are also available to those who have suffered retaliation.

1. Basis For Filing A Charge

A charging party who alleges retaliation need not also allege that he was treated differently because of race, religion, sex, national origin, age, or disability. A charging party who alleges retaliation in violation of the ADA need not be a qualified individual with a disability. Similarly, a charging party who alleges retaliation for opposing discrimination against persons in a protected age group need not be a member of the protected age group in order to be protected. A charging party can challenge retaliation even if the retaliation occurred after their employment relationship ended.

A charging party can bring an ADA retaliation claim against an individual supervisor, as well as an employer. The ADA makes it unlawful for a "person" to retaliate against an individual for engaging in protected activity.

2. Elements of a Retaliation Claim

There are three essential elements to establishing a retaliation claim:

1) Opposition to discrimination or participation in covered proceedings;

2) Adverse action; and

3) A causal connection between the protected activity and the adverse action.

The Opposition Clause

Examples of Opposition include:

1) Threatening to file a charge or other formal complaint alleging discrimination.

2) Threatening to file a complaint with the Commission, a state fair employment practices agency, union, court, or any other entity that receives complaints relating to discrimination is a form of opposition.

3) Complaining to anyone about alleged discrimination against oneself or others.

4) Refusing to obey an order because of a reasonable belief that it is discriminatory.

5) Requesting reasonable accommodation or religious accommodation.

Although the opposition clause in the EEO statues is interpreted broadly, it does not protect every protest against job discrimination. The following principles apply:

1) The manner of opposition must be reasonable.

2) The opposition need only be based on reasonable and good faith belief.

3) Person claiming retaliation need not be the person who engaged in opposition.

4) Practices opposed need not have been engaged in by the named respondent.

For example, a violation would be found if a party refused to hire the charging party because it was aware that she opposed her previous employer's allegedly discriminatory practices.

Consider the following illustrations:

Example 1 – Complaining Party (CP) complains to her office manager that her supervisor failed to promote her because of her gender. (She believes that sex discrimination occurred because she was qualified for the promotion and the supervisor promoted a male instead.) CP has engaged in protected opposition regardless of whether the promotion decision was in fact discriminatory because she had a reasonable and good faith belief that discrimination occurred.

Example 2 – Same as above, except the job sought by CP was in accounting and required a CPA license, which CP lacked and the selectee had. CP knew that it was necessary to have a CP license to perform this job. CP has not engaged in protected opposition because she did not have a reasonable and good faith belief that she was rejected because of sex discrimination.

The Participation Clause

The anti-retaliation provisions make it unlawful to discriminate against any individual because that person has made a charge, testified, assisted, or participated in any manner in an investigation, proceeding, hearing, or litigation under Title VII, the ADEA, the EPA, or the ADA. This protection applies to individuals challenging employment discrimination under the statutes enforced by the EEOC in EEOC proceedings, in state administrative or court proceedings, as well as in federal court proceedings, and to individuals who testify or otherwise participate in such proceedings. Protection under the participation clause extends to those who file untimely charges.

5) Participation is protected regardless of whether the allegations in the original charge were valid or reasonable.

The anti-discrimination statutes do not limit or condition in any way the protection against retaliation for participating in the charge process. While the opposition clause applies only to those who protest practices that they reasonably and in good faith believe are unlawful, the participation clause applies to all individuals who participate in the statutory complaint process. Thus, courts have consistently held that a respondent is liable for retaliating against an individual for filing an EEOC charge regardless of the validity or reasonableness of the charge. To permit an employer to retaliate against a charging party based on its unilateral determination that the charge was unreasonable or otherwise unjustified would chill the rights of all individuals protected by the anti-discrimination statutes.

6) A person claiming retaliation need not be the person who engaged in participation.

For example, it would be unlawful for a respondent to retaliate against an employee because his or her spouse, who is also an employee, filed an EEOC charge.

7) The practices challenged in prior or pending statutory proceedings need not have been engaged in by the named respondent.

For example, a violation would be found if a respondent refused to hire the charging party because it was aware that she filed an EEOC charge against her former employer.

3. General types of adverse actions

Adverse action was defined by the Supreme Court in a June 2006 decision to be an action that a reasonable employee would find materially offensive, thereby dissuading a reasonable worker from making or supporting a discrimination claim as a result.

The statutory retaliation clauses prohibit any adverse treatment that is based on a retaliatory motive and is reasonably likely to deter the charging party or others from engaging in protected activity. Of course, petty slights and trivial annoyances are not actionable, as they are not likely to deter protected activity. More significant retaliatory treatment, however, can be challenged regardless of the level of actual harm or damage.

Retaliatory adverse actions include denial of promotion, refusal to hire, denial of job benefits, demotion, suspension, and discharge. Other types of adverse actions include threats, reprimands, negative evaluations, harassment, or other adverse treatment. Adverse actions can occur after the employment relationship between the charging party and respondent has ended.

Consider the following illustrations:

> Example 1 – Charging Party (CP) filed a charge alleging that he was racially harassed by his supervisor and co-workers. After learning about the charge, CP's manager asked two employees to keep CP under surveillance and report back about his activities. The surveillance constitutes

an "adverse action" that is likely to deter protected activity, and is unlawful if it was conducted because of CP's protected activity.

> Example 2 – CP filed a charge alleging that she was denied a promotion because of her gender. One week later, her supervisor invited a few employees out to lunch. CP believed that the reason he excluded her was because of her EEOC charge. Even if the supervisor chose not to invite CP because of her charge, this would not constitute unlawful retaliation because it is not reasonably likely to deter protected activity.

> Example 3 – Same as Example 2, except that CP's supervisor invites all employees in CP's unit to regular weekly lunches. The supervisor excluded CP from these lunches after she filed the sex discrimination charge. If CP was excluded because of her charge, this would constitute unlawful retaliation since it could reasonably deter CP or others from engaging in protected activity.

In order to establish unlawful retaliation, there must be proof that the respondent took an adverse action because the charging party engaged in protected activity. Proof of this retaliatory motive can be through direct or circumstantial evidence.

Post Employment Retaliation

The Supreme Court has stated that coverage of post-employment retaliation is consistent with the broader context of the statute and with the statutory purpose of maintaining unfettered access to the statute's remedial mechanisms. The Court's holding applies to each of the statutes enforced by the EEOC because of the similar language and common purpose of the anti-retaliation provisions.

Examples of post-employment retaliation include actions that are designed to interfere with the individual's prospects for employment, such as giving an unjustified negative job reference, refusing to provide a job reference, and informing an individual's prospective employer about the individual's protected activity. However, a negative job reference about an individual who engaged in protected activity does not constitute unlawful retaliation unless the reference was based on a retaliatory motive. The truthfulness of the information in the reference may serve as a defense unless there is proof of pretext, such as evidence that the former employer routinely declines to offer information about former employees, but violated that policy with regard to an individual who engaged in protected activity.

Retaliatory acts designed to interfere with an individual's prospects for employment are unlawful regardless of whether they cause a prospective employer to refrain from hiring the individual.

Recordkeeping

Under Title VII and the Americans with Disabilities Act (ADA), employers must retain all personnel or employment records made or kept by the employer for a period of one year from the date of the making of the record of the personnel action involved, whichever is later. However, if a charge of discrimination is filed, the records must be retained until the matter is finally resolved.

For the purposes of the Age Discrimination in Employment Act, employers must make and keep for three years payroll or other records for each employee that contain the employee's name, address, date of birth, occupation, rate of pay, and compensation earned each week.

Under the Equal Pay Act, employers must retain for three years all records kept in the regular course of business operations relating to the payment of wages, wage rates, job evaluations, job descriptions, merit systems, seniority systems, collective bargaining agreements, descriptions of practices, or other matters that describe or explain the basis for payment of any wage differential to employees of the opposite sex in the same establishment and which may be pertinent to a determination whether such differential is based on a .factor other than sex.

In the case of employers with 100 or more employees, there is an obligation to file an Employee Information Report (EEO-1) and keep a copy on file at the business location. Every employer is required to post an EEOC Poster in a conspicuous place so that employees and applicants for employment will be likely to see it.

Employers who are also federal contractors have additional compliance responsibilities administered by the Department of Labor's Federal Contract Compliance Programs. Contractors must keep records pertaining to hiring, assignment, promotion, demotion, applicant flow data, transfer, layoff, rates of pay, requests for reasonable accommodation, job advertisements and postings, tests and test results, and interview notes for a minimum of one year for employers with fewer than 150 employees and federal contracts of less than $150,000. Those with more employees and larger contracts must keep records for two years.

Family and Medical Leave Act 5

Legislative Purpose

In 1993, Congress passed the Family and Medical Leave Act (FMLA). The FMLA requires covered employers to allow eligible employees up to 12 weeks of unpaid leave during any 12-month period for medical reasons, for the birth or adoption of a child, or for the care of a child, spouse, or parent who has a serious health condition.

The enactment of the FMLA was predicated on the demands of the workplace and the needs of families. Many children and elderly have become dependent upon family members who are active in the workplace. When a family emergency arises, workers need reassurance that they will not be asked to choose between continuing their employment and meeting their personal and family obligations. At the same time, the law seeks to accommodate the legitimate interests of employers, and to minimize the potential for employment discrimination on the basis of sex, while promoting equal opportunity for men and women.

The FMLA is both intended and expected to benefit employers as well as their employees. A direct correlation exists between stability in the family and productivity in the workplace. The legislation's supporters believed that workers who can count on durable links to their jobs are able to make their own full commitments to their work and family.

Coverage

1. **Covered Employers** — The FMLA covers private employers with 50 or more employees. These employers must have 50 or more employees (part-time employees count for this purpose) for each working day during each of 20 or more calendar work weeks in either the current or the preceding calendar year. In the case of a public agency, or public or private elementary and secondary schools, coverage occurs without regard to the threshold that 50 employees are carried on the payroll each day for 20 or more weeks in a year; however, the requirement that there be 50 employees at a worksite or within 75 miles pertains. (This latter concept is explained later in this chapter.)

   One federal district court has held that supervisors are personally liable under the FMLA. The definition of an employer in the FMLA statute includes a person acting directly or indirectly in the interests of an employer. In addition, a U.S. Department of Labor regulation states that "individuals acting in the interest of the employer are individually liable under FMLA, like they are under the Fair Labor Standards Act."

2. **Eligible Employees** — The FMLA requires that an employee work for a covered employer and be employed by that employer for at least 12 months; have worked at least 1,250 hours in the 12-month

period immediately preceding any taking of leave; and be engaged at a worksite where 50 or more employees are employed by that employer within 75 miles of that worksite. The law is clear that the 12 months needed for coverage need not be consecutive. In order to establish whether the 1,250 hours have been worked, the principles of the Fair Labor Standards Act are used. The employer has the burden of proving that the worker has not worked the requisite hours. In the case of full-time teachers, regardless of the teaching level (e.g., primary, secondary, college, etc.), they are deemed to have met the 1,250-hour test.

The critical date for the application of these tests is as of the date of commencement of leave. An employer who receives a "need for FMLA leave" request must act within two business days or the employee will be deemed eligible. Once the employee is determined eligible in response to a notice of the need for a leave, the employee's eligibility is not affected by any subsequent change in the number of employees employed at or within 75 miles of the employee's worksite, for that particular leave request. Similarly, an employer may not terminate an employee's leave once started even if the employee count drops below 50.

The 75-mile distance is measured by surface miles, not as the crow flies, using surface transportation over public streets, roads, highways, and waterways, by the shortest route from the facility where the eligible employee needing leave is employed.

Circumstances That Require Granting Family or Medical Leave

Covered employers must grant requests for leave in the following situations:

1. For the birth and care of a newborn child;

2. For the placement of a child for adoption or foster care;

3. For the care of the employee's spouse, child, or parent with a serious health condition; and

4. For a serious health condition that makes the employee unable to perform the functions of the employee's job.

The law applies equally to male and female employees.

Defining a "Serious Health Condition"

A "serious health condition" means an illness, injury, impairment, or physical or mental condition that involves:

1. Inpatient care (i.e., an overnight stay) in a medical care facility which would include any period of incapacity during which work, school, or regular daily activities are restricted due to the serious health condition, treatment, or convalescence arising out of the inpatient care; or

2. Continuing treatment of a serious health condition by a health care provider. Continuing treatment includes any one or more of the following conditions:

    a. A period of incapacity for more than three consecutive calendar days, and any subsequent treatment or period of incapacity relating to the same condition, that also involves:

        i. Two or more treatments by a health care provider; or

        ii. One treatment by a health care provider with a continuing regimen of treatments under the supervision of that provider.

    b. Any period of incapacity due to pregnancy or for prenatal care.

c. A period of incapacity on account of a chronic serious health condition that:

   i. Requires periodic visits for treatment by a health care provider;

   ii. Continues over an extended period of time; and

   iii. May cause episodic rather than a continuing period of incapacity (i.e., asthma, diabetes, epilepsy, etc.).

d. A period of incapacity which is permanent or long term due to a condition for which treatment may not be effective (e.g., Alzheimer's, a severe stroke, or the terminal stages of a disease).

e. Any period of absence to receive multiple treatments including restorative surgery that is likely to result in a period of incapacity of more than three consecutive calendar days (e.g., chemotherapy, radiation, etc.).

Determining How Much Leave an Employee Is Entitled To

The FMLA provides that an eligible employee is entitled to a total of 12 work weeks of leave during any 12-month period. The actual year may be based on the calendar year, any fixed 12-month "leave year," the 12-month period measured forward from the date any employee's first FMLA leave begins, or a "rolling" 12-month period measured backward from the date an employee uses any FMLA leave. To illustrate this last option, assume an employee has taken eight weeks of leave during the past 12 months; therefore, an additional four weeks of leave could be taken.

An employer can choose any option so long as it is consistently and uniformly applied to all employees. If a change is made, then employees are to be given 60 days' notice, and under no circumstance may a new method be implemented in order to avoid the law's leave requirements. There is, however, one exception to this rule involving an employer with operations in a number of states. If one state mandates that family leave be taken by using a certain 12-month period, it is permissible to use a different method in all other states other than the one with the mandate.

1. **Intermittent Leave** — When one takes leave in separate periods of time, rather than in one continuous period of time, it is called intermittent leave. A reduced leave schedule is a leave schedule that reduces an employee's usual number of working days or hours per workweek or hours per workday.

   After the birth or placement of a child for adoption or foster care, an employee may take leave intermittently or on a reduced leave schedule only if the employer agrees. The employer's consent is not necessary when there is a serious health condition in connection with the birth of a child or if the newborn child has a serious health condition.

   Examples of intermittent leave would include leave taken on an occasional basis for medical appointments, or leave taken several days at a time spread over a period of six months, such as for chemotherapy treatment. A pregnant employee may take leave intermittently for prenatal examinations or for her own condition, such as for periods of severe morning sickness. An example of an employee taking leave on a reduced leave schedule is an employee who is recovering from a serious health condition and is not strong enough to work a full-time schedule.

   There is no limit on the size of an increment of leave when an employee takes intermittent leave or leave on a reduced leave schedule. However, an employer may limit leave increments to the shortest period of time that the employer's payroll system uses to account for absences or use of leave, provided it is one hour or less. For example, an employee might take two hours off for a medical appointment, or might work a reduced day of four hours over a period of several weeks while recuperating from an illness.

2. **Intermittent Leave/Alternative Position** — The employer may require the employee to transfer temporarily, during the period of intermittent or reduced leave, to an available alternative position for which the employee is qualified and which better accommodates recurring periods of leave than does the employee's regular position.

The alternative position must have equivalent pay and benefits.

An employer may not transfer the employee to an alternative position in order to discourage the employee from taking leave or otherwise work a hardship on the employee.

When an employee, who is taking leave intermittently or is working on a reduced leave schedule and has been transferred to an alternative position, no longer needs to continue on leave and is able to return to full-time work, the employee must be placed in the same or equivalent job as the one left when the leave commenced.

3. **Calculating Intermittent Leave** — When an employee takes leave on an intermittent schedule, only the amount of leave actually taken may be counted toward the 12 weeks of leave to which an employee is entitled. For example, if an employee who normally works five days a week takes off one day, the employee would use one-fifth of a week of FMLA leave. Similarly, if a full-time

employee who normally works eight-hour days works four-hour days under a reduced leave schedule, the employee would use one-half week of FMLA leave each week.

Where an employee normally works a part-time schedule or variable hours, the amount of leave to which an employee is entitled is determined on a pro rata or proportional basis by comparing the new schedule with the employee's normal schedule. For example, if an employee who normally works 30 hours per week works only 20 hours a week under a reduced leave schedule, the employee's 10 hours of leave would constitute one-third of a week of FMLA leave for each week the employee works the reduced leave schedule.

If an employer has made a permanent or long-term change in the employee's schedule (for reasons other than FMLA, and prior to the notice of need for FMLA leave), the hours worked under the new schedule are to be used for making this calculation.

If an employee's schedule varies from week to week, a weekly average of the hours worked over the 12 weeks prior to the beginning of the leave period would be used for calculating the employee's normal work week.

FMLA Leave – Paid or Unpaid

As a general proposition, FMLA leave is unpaid. Paid vacation or personal leave, including leave earned or accrued under plans allowing "paid time off," may be substituted, at either the employee's or the employer's option, for any qualified FMLA leave. If neither the employee nor the employer elects to substitute paid leave for unpaid FMLA leave, the employee will remain entitled to all the paid leave which is earned or accrued under the terms of the employer's plan.

Substitution of paid sick/medical leave may be elected to the extent the circumstances meet the employer's usual requirements for the use of sick/medical leave. An employer is not required to allow substitution of paid sick or medical leave for unpaid FMLA leave "in any situation" where the employer's uniform policy would not normally allow such paid leave. An employee, therefore, has a right to substitute paid medical/sick leave to care for a seriously ill family member only if the employer's leave plan allows paid leave to be used for that purpose. Similarly, an employee does not have a right to substitute paid medical/sick leave for a serious health condition which is not covered by the employer's leave plan.

Informing Employees of Their FMLA Rights

1. **Posting Requirements** – Every employer covered by the FMLA is required to post and keep posted on its premises, in conspicuous places where employees are employed, whether or not it has any "eligible" employees, a notice explaining the Act's provisions, and providing information concerning the procedures for filing complaints of violations of the Act with the Wage and Hour Division.

   An employer that fails to post the required notice cannot take any adverse action against an employee, including denying FMLA leave, for failing to furnish the employer with advance notice of a need to take FMLA leave.

   Where an employer's workforce is composed of a significant portion of workers who are not literate in English, the employer shall be responsible for providing a notice in a language in which the employees are literate.

2. **Employee Handbook** – If an employer provides an employee handbook to all employees that describes the employer's policies regarding leave, wages, attendance, and similar matters, the handbook must incorporate information on FMLA rights and responsibilities, and the employer's policies regarding the FMLA.

3. **No Employee Handbook** – If an employer does not have a handbook describing employee benefits and leave provisions, the employer shall provide written guidance to an employee concerning all the employee's rights and obligations under the FMLA. This notice shall be provided to employees each time a request is made for FMLA leave. Employers may duplicate and provide the employee a copy of a notice contained in the Appendix — "Employer Responses to Employee Request for Family or Medical Leave."

   The employer shall also provide the employee with written notice detailing the specific expectations and obligations of the employee and explaining any consequences of a failure to meet these obligations. The written notice must be provided to the employee in a language in which the employee is literate. Such specific notice must include, as appropriate:

   a. that the leave will be counted against the employee's annual FMLA leave entitlement;

   b. any requirements for the employee to furnish medical certification of a serious health condition and the consequences of failing to do so;

   c. the employee's right to substitute paid leave and whether the employer will require the substitution of paid leave, and the conditions related to any substitution;

d. any requirement for the employee to make any premium payments to maintain health benefits and the arrangements for making such payments and the possible consequences of failure to make such payments on a timely basis (i.e., the circumstances under which coverage may lapse);

e. any requirement for the employee to present a fitness-for-duty certificate to be restored to employment;

f. the employee's status as a "key employee" and the potential consequence that restoration may be denied following FMLA leave, explaining the conditions required for such denial;

g. the employee's right to restoration to the same or an equivalent job upon return from leave; and

h. the employee's potential liability for payment of health insurance premiums paid by the employer during the employee's unpaid FMLA leave if the employee fails to return to work after taking the leave.

The written notice must be provided to the employee no less often than the first time in each six-month period that an employee gives notice for the need for FMLA leave (if FMLA leave is taken during the six-month period). The notice shall be given within a reasonable time after notice of the need for leave is given by the employee, generally within one or two business days, if feasible. If leave has already begun, the notice should be mailed to the employee's address of record.

The Elements of an Employee's Notice for FMLA Leave

1. **30 Days' Notice** – An employee must provide the employer at least 30 days' advance notice before FMLA leave is to begin if the need for the leave is foreseeable based on an expected birth, placement for adoption or foster care, or planned medical treatment for a serious health condition of the employee or of a family member. If 30 days' notice is not practicable, because of lack of knowledge of approximately when the leave will be required to begin, a change in circumstances, or a medical emergency, notice must be given as soon as practicable. For example, an employee's health condition may require leave to commence earlier than anticipated before the birth of a child. Similarly, little opportunity for notice may be given before placement or adoption. Whether the leave is to be continuous, taken intermittently, or on a reduced schedule basis, notice need only be given one time, but the employee shall advise the employer as soon as practicable if dates of scheduled leave change or are extended, or were initially unknown.

"As soon as practicable" means as soon as both possible and practical, taking into account all of the facts and circumstances in the individual case. The Department of Labor regulations and cases interpreting them indicate that the employee need not specifically request an FMLA leave. If the employee gives notice to his employer that his leave may be covered, it is the burden of the employer to adequately investigate to determine whether an FMLA leave is available.

For foreseeable leave, when it is not possible to give as much as 30 days' notice, "as soon as practicable" ordinarily would mean at least verbal notification to the employer within one or two business days of when the need for leave becomes known to the employee.

2. **Verbal Notice** – An employee shall provide at least verbal notice sufficient to make the employer aware that the employee needs FMLA-qualifying leave and the anticipated timing and duration of the leave. The employee need not expressly assert rights under the FMLA or even mention the FMLA, but may state only that leave is needed for an expected birth or adoption, for example. The employer should inquire further if it is necessary to have more information about whether FMLA leave is being sought by the employee. In the case of medical conditions, the employer may find it necessary to inquire further to determine if the leave is because of a serious health condition and may request medical certification to support the need for such leave.

3. **Scheduling Medical Treatments** – When planning medical treatment, the employee must consult with the employer and make a reasonable effort to schedule the leave so as not to unduly disrupt the employer's operations, subject to the approval of the health care provider. Employees are ordinarily expected to consult with their employers prior to scheduling treatment in order to work out a treatment schedule which best suits the needs of both the employer and the employee. If an employee who provides notice of the need to take FMLA leave on an intermittent basis for planned medical treatment neglects to consult with the employer to make a reasonable attempt to arrange the schedule of treatments so as not to unduly disrupt the employer's operations, the employer may initiate discussions with the employee and require the employee to attempt to make such arrangements subject to the approval of the health care provider.

4. **Intermittent Leave** – In the case of intermittent leave or leave on a reduced leave schedule which is medically necessary, an employee shall advise the employer, upon request, of the reasons why the intermittent reduced leave schedule is necessary. The employee and employer shall attempt to work out a schedule which meets the employee's needs without unduly disrupting the employer's operations, subject to the approval of the health care provider.

5. **Unforeseeable Need for Leave** – When the approximate timing of the leave is not foreseeable, an employee should give notice to the employer of the need for FMLA leave as soon as practicable. It is expected that an employee will give notice to the employer within no more than one or two working days of learning of the need for leave, except in extraordinary circumstances where such notice is not feasible. In the case of a medical emergency requiring leave because of an employee's own serious health condition or to care for a family member with a serious health condition, written advance notice pursuant to an employer's internal rules and procedures may not be required when FMLA leave is involved.

The employee should provide notice to the employer either in person or by telephone, e-mail, facsimile, or other electronic means. Notice may be given by the employee's spokesperson (e.g., spouse, adult family member, or other responsible party) if the employee is unable to do so personally. The employee need not expressly assert rights under the FMLA or even mention the FMLA, but may state only that leave is needed. The employer will be expected to obtain any additional required information through informal means. The employee or spokesperson will be expected to provide more information when it can readily be accomplished as a practical matter, taking into consideration the exigencies of the situation.

6. **Employer's Right if Employee Fails to Provide the Required Data** – An employer may waive employees' FMLA notice obligations or the employer's own internal rules on leave notice requirements.

If an employee fails to give 30 days' notice for foreseeable leave with no reasonable excuse for the delay, the employer may delay the FMLA leave until at least 30 days after the date the employee provides notice to the employer of the need for FMLA leave.

In all cases, in order for the onset of an employee's FMLA leave to be delayed due to lack of required notice, it must be clear that the employee had actual notice of the FMLA notice requirements. This condition would be satisfied by the employer's proper posting of the required notice at the worksite where the employee is employed.

Medical Certification

The Department of Labor has provided a medical certification form for use by health care providers. A copy of the "Certification of Health Care Provider" is contained in the Appendix. Use of this form will meet certification requirements.

An employer may require an employee to provide medical certification. In those circumstances, an employer must give written notice of a requirement for medical certification each time a certification is required. An employer's oral request to an employee to furnish any subsequent medical certification is sufficient.

When the leave is foreseeable and at least 30 days' notice has been provided, the employee

should provide the medical certification before the leave begins. When this is not possible, the employee must provide the requested certification to the employer within the time frame requested by the employer (which must allow at least 15 calendar days after the employer's request), unless it is not practicable under the particular circumstances to do so despite the employee's diligent, good faith efforts.

In most cases, when the employer requests that an employee furnish certification from a health care provider, it should be given to the employer at the time the employee gives notice of the need for leave or within two business days thereafter, or, in the case of unforeseen leave, within two business days after the leave commences. The employer may request certification at a later date if the employer later has a reason to question the appropriateness of the leave or its duration.

At the time the employer requests certification, the employer must also advise an employee of the anticipated consequences of an employee's failure to provide adequate certification. The employer shall advise an employee whenever the employer finds a certification incomplete and provide the employee a reasonable opportunity to cure any such deficiency.

If an employee submits a complete certification signed by the employee's health care provider, the employer may not request additional information from the provider. However, a health care provider representing the employer may contact the employee's health care provider, with the employee's permission, for the purposes of clarification and authenticity of the medical certification.

An employer who has reason to doubt the validity of a medical certification may require the employee to obtain a second opinion at the employer's expense. Pending receipt of the second (or third) medical opinion, the employee is provisionally entitled to thc benefits of the Act, including maintenance of group health benefits. If the certifications do not ultimately establish the employee's entitlement to FMLA leave, the leave shall not be designated as FMLA leave and may be treated as paid or unpaid leave under the employer's established leave policies. The employer is permitted to designate the health care provider to furnish the second opinion, but the selected health care provider may not be employed on a regular basis by the employer.

If the opinions of the employee's and the employer's designated health care provider differ, the employer may require the employee to obtain certification from a third health care provider, again at the employer's expense. This third opinion shall be final and binding.

Employee Rights on Return to Work

On return from FMLA leave, an employee is entitled to be reinstated to the same position the employee held when leave commenced, or to an equivalent position with equivalent benefits, pay, and other terms and conditions of employment. An employee is entitled to such reinstatement even if the employee has been replaced or the position has been restructured to accommodate the employee's absence.

If the employee is unable to perform an essential function of the position because of a physical or mental condition, including the continuation of a serious health condition, the employee has no right to restoration to another position under the FMLA. However, the employer's obligations may be governed by the Americans with Disabilities Act (see Chapter 7 for a discussion of the ADA). An equivalent position is one that is virtually identical to the employee's former position in terms of pay, benefits, and working conditions, including privileges, perquisites, and status. It must involve the same or substantially similar duties and responsibilities, which must entail substantially equivalent skill, effort, responsibility, and authority.

With respect to pension and other retirement plans, any period of unpaid FMLA leave shall not be treated as, or counted toward, a break in service for purposes of vesting and eligibility to participate.

Denying a "Key" Employee's Right to Reinstatement

A "key employee" is a salaried FMLA-eligible employee who is among the highest paid 10 percent of all the employees employed by the employer within 75 miles of the employee's worksite.

In order to deny restoration to a key employee, an employer must determine that the restoration of the employee to employment will cause "substantial and grievous economic injury" to the operations of the employer, not whether the absence of the employee will cause such substantial and grievous injury.

A precise test cannot be set for the level of hardship or injury to the employer which must be sustained. If the reinstatement of a "key employee" threatens the economic viability of the firm, that would constitute "substantial and grievous economic injury." A lesser injury which causes substantial, long-term economic injury would also be sufficient. Minor inconveniences and costs that the employer would experience in the normal course of doing business would certainly not constitute "substantial and grievous economic injury."

An employer who believes that reinstatement may be denied to a key employee must give written notice to the employee at the time the employee gives notice of the need for FMLA leave (or when FMLA leave commences, if earlier) that he or she qualifies as a key employee. At the same time, the employer must also fully inform the employee of the potential consequences with respect to reinstatement and maintenance of health benefits if the employer should determine that substantial and grievous economic injury to the employer's operations will result if the employee is reinstated from FMLA leave. An employer who fails to provide such timely notice will lose its right to deny restoration even if substantial and grievous economic injury will result from reinstatement.

After notice to a "key" employee has been given that substantial and grievous economic injury will result if the employee is reinstated to employment, that employee is still entitled to request reinstatement at the end of the leave period even if the employee did not return to work in response to the employer's notice. The employer must then again determine whether there will be substantial and grievous economic injury from reinstatement, based on the facts at that time. If it is determined that substantial and grievous economic injury will result, the employer shall notify the employee in writing (in person or by certified mail) of the denial of restoration.

FMLA Enforcement

Employees who believe their rights under the FMLA have been violated can either: (1) file, or have another person file on his or her behalf, a complaint with the Secretary of Labor; or (2) file a private lawsuit.

If the employee files a private lawsuit, it must be filed within two years after the last action which the employee contends was in violation of the Act, or three years if the violation was willful.

If an employer has violated one or more provisions of FMLA, and if justified by the facts of a particular case, an employee may receive one or more of the following: wages, employment benefits, or other compensation denied or lost to such employee by reason of the violation; or, where no such tangible loss has occurred, such as when FMLA leave was unlawfully denied, any actual monetary loss sustained by the employee as a direct result of the violation, such as the cost of providing care, up to a sum equal to 12 weeks of wages for the employee. A court may award liquidation damages unless such amount is reduced by the court because the violation was in good faith and the employer had reasonable grounds for believing the employer had not violated the Act. When appropriate, the employee may also obtain appropriate equitable relief such as employment, reinstatement, and promotion. When the employer is found in violation, the employee may recover a reasonable attorney's fee, reasonable expert witness fees, and other costs of the action from the employer, in addition to any judgment awarded by the court.

FMLA Recordkeeping Requirements

The FMLA provides that employers shall preserve records in accordance with the recordkeeping requirements of the Fair Labor Standards Act and the FMLA regulations. FMLA also authorizes the Department of Labor (DOL) to require any employer to submit books or records not more than once during any 12-month period unless the Department has reasonable cause to believe a violation of the FMLA exists or the DOL is investigating a complaint. The regulations establish no requirement for the submission of any records unless specifically requested by a Department official.

No particular order or form of records is required. However, employers must keep the records specified by these regulations for no less than three years and make them available for inspection by representatives of the Department of Labor upon request.

Records must disclose the following:

1. Basic payroll and identifying employee data, including name, address, and occupation; rate or basis of pay and terms of compensation; daily and weekly hours worked per pay period; additions to or deductions from wages; and total compensation paid.

2. Dates FMLA leave is taken by FMLA-eligible employees (e.g., available from time records, requests for leave, etc., if so designated). Leave must be designated in records as FMLA leave; leave so designated may not include leave required under state law or an employer plan which is not also covered by FMLA.

3. If FMLA leave is taken by eligible employees in increments of less than one full day, the hours of the leave.

4. Copies of employee notices of leave furnished to the employer under FMLA, if in writing, and copies of all general and specific written notices given to employees as required under FMLA. Copies may be maintained in employee personnel files.

5. Any documents (including written and electronic records) describing employee benefits or employer policies and practices regarding the taking of paid and unpaid leaves.

6. Prepayments of employee benefits.

7. Records of any dispute between the employer and an eligible employee regarding designation of leave as FMLA leave, including any written statement from the employer or employee of the reasons for the designation and for the disagreement.

Covered employers with no eligible employees must maintain the payroll records. Covered employers in a joint employment situation must keep all the records required with respect to any primary employees, and must keep the payroll records only for secondary employees.

If FMLA-eligible employees are not subject to FLSA's recordkeeping regulations for purposes of minimum wage or overtime compliance, an employer need not keep a record of actual hours worked, provided that:

1. Eligibility for FMLA leave is presumed for any employee who has been employed for at least 12 months; and

2. With respect to employees who take FMLA leave intermittently or on a reduced leave schedule, the employer and employee agree on the employee's normal schedule or average hours worked each week and reduce their agreement to a written record.

Records and documents relating to medical certifications, recertifications, or medical histories of employees or employees' family members, created for purposes of FMLA, shall be maintained as confidential medical records in separate files/records from the usual personnel files, and if the Americans with Disabilities Act (ADA) is also applicable, such records shall be maintained in conformance with ADA confidentiality requirements.

FMLA's Effect on Other Federal and State Laws

Nothing in the FMLA modifies or affects any federal or state law prohibiting discrimination on the basis of race, religion, color, national origin, sex, age, or disability (e.g., Title VII of the Civil Rights Act of 1964, as amended by the Pregnancy Discrimination Act). FMLA's legislative history explains that FMLA is not intended to modify or affect the Rehabilitation Act of 1973 or the Americans with Disabilities Act of 1990. Thus, the leave provisions of the FMLA are wholly distinct from the reasonable accommodation obligations of employers covered under the ADA. The purpose of the

FMLA is to make leave available to eligible employees and employers within its coverage, and not to limit already existing rights and protection.

Nothing in FMLA supersedes any provision of state or local law that provides greater family or medical leave rights than those provided by FMLA. The FMLA poster is to be prominently displayed in the workplace.

Frequently Asked Questions
Relating to the Family and Medical Leave Act

Q. How much leave am I entitled to under FMLA?

A. If you are an "eligible" employee, you are entitled to 12 weeks of leave for certain family and medical reasons during a 12-month period.

Q. How is the 12-month period calculated under FMLA?

A. Employers may select one of four options for determining the 12-month period:

- the calendar year;

- any fixed 12-month "leave year" such as a fiscal year, a year required by State law, or a year starting on the employee's "anniversary" date;

- the 12-month period measured forward from the date any employee's first FMLA leave begins; or

- a "rolling" 12-month period measured backward from the date an employee uses FMLA leave.

Q. Does the law guarantee paid time off?

A. No. The FMLA only required unpaid leave. However, the law permits an employee to elect, or the employer to require the employee, to use accrued paid leave, such as vacation or sick leave, for some or all of the FMLA leave period. When paid leave is substituted for unpaid FMLA leave, it may be counted against the 12-week FMLA leave entitlement if the employee is properly notified of the designation when the leave begins.

Q. Does workers' compensation leave count against an employee's FMLA leave entitlement?

A. It can. FMLA leave and workers' compensation leave can run together, provided the reason for the absence is due to a qualifying serious illness or injury and the employer properly notifies the employee in writing that the leave will be counted as FMLA leave.

Q. Can the employer count leave taken due to pregnancy complications against the 12 weeks of FMLA leave for the birth and care of my child?

A. Yes. An eligible employee is entitled to a total of 12 weeks of FMLA leave in a 12-month period. If the employee has to use some of that leave for another reason, including a difficult pregnancy, it may be counted as part of the 12-week FMLA leave entitlement.

FAQs – Family and Medical Leave Act ^(continued)

Q. Can the employer count time on maternity leave or pregnancy disability leaves as FMLA leave?

A. Yes. Pregnancy disability leave or maternity leave for the birth of a child would be considered qualifying FMLA leave for a serious health condition and may be counted in the 12 weeks of leave so long as the employer properly notifies the employee in writing of the designation.

Q. If an employer fails to tell employees that the leave is FMLA leave, can the employer count the time they have already been off against the 12 weeks of FMLA leave?

A. In most situations, the employer cannot count leave as FMLA leave retroactively. Remember, the employee must be notified in writing that an absence is being designated as FMLA leave. If the employer was not aware of the reason for the leave, leave may be designated as FMLA leave retroactively only while the leave is in progress or within two business days of the employee's return to work.

Q. Who is considered an immediate "family member" for purposes of taking FMLA leave?

A. An employee's spouse, children (son or daughter), and parents are immediate family members for purposes of FMLA. The term "parent" does not include a parent "in-law." The terms son or daughter do not include individuals age 18 or over unless they are "incapable of self-care" because of a mental or physical disability that limits one or more of the "major life activities" as those terms are defined in regulations issued by the Equal Employment Opportunity Commission (EEOC) under the Americans With Disabilities Act (ADA).

Q. May I take FMLA leave for visits to a therapist, if my doctor prescribes the therapy?

A. Yes. FMLA permits you to take leave to receive "continuing treatment by a health care provider," which can include recurring absences for therapy treatments such as those ordered by a doctor for physical therapy after a hospital stay, or for treatment of severe arthritis.

Q. Which employees are eligible to take FMLA leave?

A. Employees are eligible to take FMLA leave if they have worked for their employer for at least 12 months, and have worked for at least 1,250 hours over the previous 12 months, and work at a location where at least 50 employees are employed by the employer within 75 miles.

Q. Do the 12 months of service with the employer have to be continuous or consecutive?

A. No. The 12 months do not have to be continuous or consecutive; all time worked for the employer is counted.

Q. Do the 1,250 hours include paid leave time or other absences from work?

A. No. The 1,250 hours include only those hours actually worked for the employer. Paid leave and unpaid leave, including FMLA leave, are not included.

FAQs – Family and Medical Leave Act ^(continued)

Q. How do I determine if I have worked 1,250 hours in a 12-month period?

A. Your individual record of hours worked would be used to determine whether 1,250 hours had been worked in the 12 months prior to the commencement of FMLA leave. As a rule of thumb, the following may be helpful for estimating whether this test for eligibility has been met:

- 24 hours worked in each of the 52 weeks of the year; or

- over 104 hours worked in each of the 12 months of the year; or

- 40 hours worked per week for more than 31 weeks (over seven months) of the year.

Q. Do I have to give my employer my medical records for leave due to a serious health condition?

A. No. You do not have to provide medical records. The employer may, however, request that, for any leave taken due to a serious health condition, you provide a medical certification confirming that a serious health condition exists. (See the Appendix for a sample certification form.)

Q. Can my employer require me to return to work before I exhaust my leave?

A. Subject to certain limitations, your employer may deny the continuation of FMLA leave due to a serious health condition if you fail to fulfill any obligations to provide supporting medical certification. The employer may not, however, require you to return to work early by offering you a light duty assignment.

Q. Are there any restrictions on how I spend my time while on leave?

A. Employers with established policies regarding outside employment while on paid or unpaid leave may uniformly apply those policies to employees on FMLA leave. Otherwise, the employer may not restrict your activities. The protections of FMLA will not, however, cover situations where the reason for leave no longer exists, where the employee has not provided required notices or certifications, or where the employee has misrepresented the reason for leave.

Q. Can my employer make inquiries about my leave during my absence?

A. Yes, but only to you. Your employer may ask you questions to confirm whether the leave needed or being taken qualifies for FMLA purposes, any may require periodic reports on your status and intent to return to work after leave. Also, if the employer wishes to obtain another opinion, you may be required to obtain additional medical certification at the employer's expense, or rectification during a period of FMLA leave. The employer may have a health care provider representing the employer contact your health care provider, with your permission, to clarify information in the medical certification or to confirm that it was provided by the health care provider. The inquiry may not seek additional information regarding your health condition or that of a family member.

Q. Can my employer refuse to grant me FMLA leave?

A. If you are an "eligible" employee who has met FMLA's notice and certification requirements (and you have not exhausted your FMLA leave entitlement for the year), you may not be denied FMLA leave.

FAQs – Family and Medical Leave Act ^(continued)

Q. Will I lose my job if I take FMLA leave?

    A. Generally, no. It is unlawful for any employer to interfere with or restrain or deny the exercise of any right provided under this law. Employers cannot use the taking of FMLA leave as a negative factor in employment actions, such as hiring, promotions or disciplinary actions; nor can FMLA leave be counted under "no fault" attendance policies. Under limited circumstances, an employer may deny reinstatement to work - but not the use of FMLA leave - to certain highly-paid, salaried ("key") employees.

Q. Are there other circumstances in which my employer can deny me FMLA leave or reinstatement to my job?

    A. In addition to denying reinstatement in certain circumstances to "key" employees, employers are not required to continue FMLA benefits or reinstate employees who would have been laid off or otherwise had their employment terminated had they continued to work during the FMLA leave period as, for example, due to a general layoff.

Employees who give unequivocal notice that they do not intent to return to work lose their entitlement to FMLA leave.

Employees who are unable to return to work and have exhausted their 12 weeks of FMLA leave in the designated "12 month period" no longer have FMLA protections of leave or job restoration.

Under certain circumstances, employers who advise employees experiencing a serious health condition that they will require a medical certificate of fitness for duty to return to work may deny reinstatement of an employee who fails to provide the certification, or may delay reinstatement until the certification is submitted.

Q. Can my employer fire me for complaining about a violation of FMLA?

    A. No. Nor can the employer take any other adverse employment action on this basis. It is unlawful for any employer to discharge or otherwise discriminate against an employee for opposing a practice made unlawful under FMLA.

Q. Does an employer have to pay bonuses to employees who have been on FMLA leave?

    A. The FMLA requires that employees be restored to the same or an equivalent position. If an employee was eligible for a bonus before taking FMLA leave, the employee would be eligible for the bonus upon returning to work. The FMLA leave may not be counted against the employee. For example, if an employer offers a perfect attendance bonus and the employee has not missed any time prior to taking FMLA leave, the employee would still be eligible for the bonus upon returning from FMLA leave.

On the other hand, FMLA does not require that employees on FMLA leave be allowed to accrue benefits or seniority. For example, an employee on FMLA leave might not have sufficient sales to qualify for a bonus. The employer is not required to make any special accommodation for this employee because of FMLA. The employer must, of course, treat an employee who has used FMLA leave at least as well as other employees on paid and unpaid leave (as appropriate) are treated.

FAQs – Family and Medical Leave Act ^(continued)

Q. What employees are to be counted?

A. Any employee whose name appears on the employer's payroll will be considered employed each working day of the calendar week, and must be counted whether or not any compensation is received for the week. However, the FMLA applies only to employees who are employed within any state of the United States, the District of Columbia, or any territory possession of the United States.

Employees on paid or unpaid leave, including FMLA leave, leaves of absence, disciplinary suspension, etc., are counted as long as the employer has a reasonable expectation that the employee will later return to active employment. If there is no employer/employee relationship (as when an employee is laid off, whether temporarily or permanently) such individual is not counted. Part-time employees, like full-time employees, are considered to be employed each working day of the calendar week, as long as they are maintained on the payroll.

Employees jointly employed by two employers must be counted by both employers, whether or not maintained on one of the employer's payroll, in determining employer coverage and employee eligibility. For example, an employer who jointly employs 15 workers from a leasing or temporary help agency and 40 permanent workers is covered by FMLA. An employee on leave who is working for a secondary employer is considered employed by the secondary employer, and must be counted for coverage and eligibility purposes, as long as the employer has a reasonable expectation that the employee will return to employment with that employer.

Q. What are the rules covering joint employment?

A. In joint employment relationships, only the primary employer is responsible for giving required notices to its employees, providing FMLA leave, and maintenance of health benefits. Factors considered in determining which is the "primary" employer include authority/responsibility to hire and fire, assign/place the employee, make payroll, and provide employment benefits. For employees of temporary help or leasing agencies, for example, the placement agency most commonly would be the primary employer.

Q. What is a "public agency"?

A. All public agencies are covered by the FMLA regardless of the number of employees; they are not subject to the coverage threshold of 50 employees carried on the payroll each day for 20 or more weeks in a year. However, employees of public agencies must meet all of the requirements of eligibility, including the requirement that the employer (e.g., state) employ 50 employees at the worksite or within 75 miles.

Q. What federal agencies are covered?

A. Most employees of the government of the United States including the postal service are covered. The U.S. Government constitutes a single employer for purposes of determining employee eligibility. These employees must meet all of the requirements for eligibility, including the requirement that the federal government employ 50 employees at the worksite or within 75 miles.

FAQs – Family and Medical Leave Act ^(continued)

Q. What happens if the number of employees drops below 50?

A. Once an employee is determined eligible in response to notice of the need for leave, the employee's eligibility is not affected by any subsequent change in the number of employees employed at or within 75 miles of the employee's worksite, for that specific notice of the need for leave. Similarly, an employer may not terminate employee leave that has already started if the employee count drops below 50.

Q. What factors determine the worksite that is constantly shifting?

A. An employee's worksite under the FMLA will ordinarily be the site the employee reports to or, if none, from which the employee's work is assigned.

For employees with no fixed worksite, such as construction workers, transportation workers (e.g., truck drivers, seamen, pilots), salespersons, etc., the "worksite" is the site to which they are assigned as their home-base or to which they report.

Q. Can an employer take action against an employee for substance abuse?

A. Yes. When an employer has an established policy, applied in a non-discriminatory manner, that has been communicated to all employees, that provides under certain circumstances that an employee may be terminated for substance abuse, an employee may be terminated whether or not one is presently taking FMLA leave. An employee may take FMLA leave to care for an immediate family member who is receiving treatment for substance abuse. The employer, however, may not take action against an employee who is providing care for an immediate family member receiving treatment for substance abuse.

Q. What kinds of treatment are covered by FMLA?

A. Treatment does not include routine physical examinations, eye examinations, or dental examinations. A regimen of continuing treatment that includes the taking of over-the-counter medications such as aspirin, antihistamines, salves, or bed-rest, drinking fluids, exercise, and other similar activities that can be initiated without a visit to a health care provider, is not, by itself, sufficient to constitute a regimen of continuing treatment for purposes of FMLA leave.

Ordinarily, unless complications arise, the common cold, flu, ear aches, upset stomach, minor ulcers, headaches other than migraine, routine dental or orthodontia problems, periodontal disease, etc., are examples of conditions that do not meet the definition of a serious health condition and do not qualify for FMLA leave.

Q. Are there situations of incapacity where there is no treatment lasting longer than three days, but where FMLA coverage still occurs?

A. Yes. For example, an employee with asthma may be unable to report for work due to onset of an asthma attack or because the employee's health care provider has advised the employee to stay home when the pollen count exceeds a certain level. An employee who is pregnant may be unable to report to work because of severe morning sickness.

FAQs – Family and Medical Leave Act [(continued)]

Q. What does it mean that an employee is "needed to care for" a family member?

A. The medical certification provision that an employee is "needed to care for" a family member encompasses both physical and psychological care. It includes situations where, for example, because of a serious health condition, the family member is unable to care for his or her own basic medical, hygienic, or nutritional needs or safety, or is unable to transport himself or herself to the doctor, etc. The term also includes providing psychological comfort and reassurance which would be beneficial to a child, spouse, or parent with a serious health condition who is receiving inpatient or home care.

Q. Who is a "health care provider"?

A. A doctor of medicine or osteopathy, podiatrist, dentist, clinical psychologist, optometrist, and a chiropractor authorized to practice in the State; nurse practitioners and nurse-midwives who are authorized to practice under state law; or a Christian Science practitioner.

Q. During an FMLA leave week, a holiday occurs, resulting in the employer being closed. Does this still constitute a week?

A. Yes. The fact that a holiday may occur within the week taken as FMLA leave has no effect; the week is counted as a week of FMLA leave. However, if for some reason the employer's business activity has temporarily ceased and employees generally are not expected to report for work for one or more weeks (e.g., a school closing two weeks for Christmas/New Year holiday or the summer vacation or an employer closing the plant for retooling or repairs), the days the employer's activities have ceased do not count against the employee's FMLA leave entitlement.

Q. If leave is taken for the birth of a child, when must the leave be concluded?

A. An employee's entitlement to leave for a birth or placement for adoption or foster care expires at the end of the 12-month period beginning on the date of the birth or placement, unless state law allows, or the employer permits, leave to be taken for a longer period. Any such FMLA leave must be concluded within this one-year period.

Q. How much leave may a husband and wife take if they are employed by the same employer?

A. A husband and wife eligible for FMLA leave and employed by the same covered employer may be limited to a combined total of 12 weeks of leave during any 12-month period.

Q. If a holiday occurs during FMLA leave does the employer have to pay the employee on leave?

A. An employee's entitlement to benefits other than group health benefits during a period of FMLA leave (e.g., holiday pay) is determined by the employer's established policy for providing such benefits when the employee is on other forms of leave (paid or unpaid, as appropriate).

Q. Is an employee entitled to benefits while using FMLA leave?

A. During any FMLA leave, an employer must maintain the employee's coverage under any group health plan on the same conditions as coverage would have been provided if the employee had been continuously employed during the entire leave period.

Therefore, any share of group health plan premiums which had been paid by the employee prior to FMLA leave must continue to be paid by the employee during the FMLA leave period.

FAQs – Family and Medical Leave Act [(continued)]

However, an employer may recover its share of health plan premiums during a period of unpaid FMLA leave from an employee if the employee fails to return to work after the employee's FMLA leave entitlement has been exhausted or expires, in most circumstances.

Q. Are there any limitations on an employer's obligation to reinstate an employee?

A. An employee has no greater right to reinstatement or to other benefits and conditions of employment than if the employee had been continuously employed during the FMLA leave period. An employer must be able to show that an employee would not otherwise have been employed at the time reinstatement is requested in order to deny restoration to employment. For example, if an employee is laid off during the course of taking FMLA leave and employment is terminated, the employer's responsibility to continue FMLA leave, maintain group health plan benefits, and restore the employee, cease at the time the employee is laid off.

Q. Under what circumstances may an employer require that an employee submit a medical certification that the employee is able (or unable) to return to work (i.e., a "fitness-for-duty" report)?

A. As a condition of restoring an employee whose FMLA leave was occasioned by the employee's own serious health condition that made the employee unable to perform, an employer may have a uniformly applied policy or practice that requires all similarly situated employees (i.e., same occupation, same serious health condition) who take leave for such conditions to obtain and present certification from the employee's health care provider that the employee is able to resume work.

Q. What special rules apply to employees of schools?

A. Certain special rules apply to employees of "local educational agencies," including public school boards and elementary and secondary schools under their jurisdiction, and private elementary and secondary schools. The special rules do not apply to other kinds of educational institutions, such as colleges and universities, trade schools, and preschools.

Educational institutions are covered by the FMLA, but the Act's 50-employee coverage test does not apply. The usual requirements for employees to be "eligible" do apply, however, including employment at a worksite where at least 50 employees are employed within 75 miles. For example, employees of a rural school would not be eligible for FMLA leave if the school has fewer than 50 employees, and there are no other schools under the jurisdiction of the same employer (usually, a school board) within 75 miles.

There are special rules for instructional employees that affect their rights to take intermittent leave or leave near the end of an academic term.

Sexual Harassment in the Workplace

6

Sexual Harassment Overview

There has been dramatic growth in the number of sexual harassment complaints that have been filed in recent years, and there is no reason to believe that this trend will abate. When it enacted Title VII in 1964, Congress did not define sexual harassment as a form of discrimination or even mention the term in the statute or the legislative history.

In 1980 the EEOC issued guidelines declaring sexual harassment a form of sex discrimination in violation of Title VII, establishing criteria for determining when unwelcome conduct of a sexual nature constitutes sexual harassment, defining the circumstances under which an employer may be held liable, and suggesting affirmative steps an employer should take to prevent sexual harassment. The flood of litigation on this subject commenced in 1986, when for the first time, the Supreme Court construed the Title VII prohibitions against sex discrimination to include sexual harassment.

Because Title VII does not proscribe all conduct of a sexual nature in the workplace, it is crucial to understand the concept of sexual harassment. Sexual harassment is defined as unwelcome sexual conduct that is a term or condition of employment. The EEOC Guidelines define two types of sexual harassment: "quid pro quo" and "hostile environment." "Quid pro Quo" harassment occurs when submission to or rejection of such conduct by an individual is used as the basis for employment decisions affect such individual. "Hostile environment" harassment includes unwelcome sexual conduct that unreasonably interferes with an individual's job performance or creates an "intimidating, hostile, or offensive working environment," even if it leads to no tangible or economic job consequences.

Although "quid pro quo" and "hostile environment" harassment are theoretically distinct claims, the line between the two is not always clear and the two forms of harassment often occur together. For example, an employee's tangible job conditions are affected when a sexually hostile work environment results in her constructive discharge. Similarly, a supervisor who makes sexual advances toward a subordinate employee may communicate an implicit threat to adversely affect his or her job status if one does not comply. "Hostile environment" harassment may acquire characteristics of "quid pro quo" harassment if the offending supervisor abuses his or her authority over employment decisions to force the victim to endure or participate in the sexual conduct. Sexual harassment may culminate in a retaliatory discharge if a victim tells his or her employer that that he or she will no longer submit to the harassment, and is then fired in retaliation for this protest. In these circumstances it would be appropriate to conclude that both harassment and retaliation in violation of Title VII have occurred.

Sexual Harassment Defined by the Supreme Court

1. **1986 *Meritor Savings Bank* Case.** In this landmark decision, a unanimous Supreme

Court held that Title VII accords employees the right to work in an environment free from discriminatory intimidation, ridicule, and insult. "Without question, when a supervisor sexually harasses a subordinate because of the subordinate's sex, that supervisor 'discriminates' on the basis of sex." The Court found actionable two distinct kinds of sexual harassment: "unwelcome sexual advances, requests for sexual favors, and other verbal or physical conduct of a sexual nature" directly linked to the grant or denial of an economic quid pro quo, and such conduct that has "the purpose or effect of unreasonably interfering with an individual's work performance or creating an intimidating, hostile, or offensive working environment.

2. **1993 *Harris* Case.** In 1993, the Supreme Court further clarified the harassment standard by explaining that two requirements must be satisfied:

    a. The conduct must "create an objectively hostile or abusive" work environment, in other words, an environment that a reasonable person would find hostile or abusive; and

    b. The victim must "subjectively perceive the environment to be abusive" in order for the conduct to have altered the conditions of the victim's employment.

    The Court was saying that requiring a tangible, psychological injury was too high of a standard, and a "conduct that is merely offensive", standard would be too low. In effect, the Court stated that offensive conduct did not have to be so severe as to lead to a nervous breakdown in order to qualify as hostile environment harassment. In an effort to explain the Court decision, EEOC has advised that the appropriate standard for determining whether hostile environment harassment has occurred is the "reasonable person" standard.

However, a reasonable person is one with the perspective of the victim. Thus, if a woman is the victim of alleged sexual harassment, then a determination of whether sexual harassment did in fact occur will be based on consideration of a reasonable person in her position. Petty slights suffered by the hypersensitive do not amount to hostile environment harassment.

3. **1998 *Oncale* Case.** For the first time the Supreme Court had to decide if a sexual harassment suit was valid if the harasser and the harassed employee were of the same sex. In a unanimous decision the Court concluded that "nothing in Title VII necessarily bars a claim of discrimination 'because of ...sex' merely because the plaintiff and the defendant are of the same sex." The Court expressed concern that its ruling would expand Title VII into a general civility code, and went on to explain that Title VII sexual harassment claims would not reach genuine but innocuous differences in the ways men and women routinely interact with members of the same sex and of the opposite sex. "The prohibition of harassment on the basis of sex requires neither asexuality nor androgyny in the workplace; it forbids only behavior so objectively offensive as to alter the 'conditions' of the victim's employment. We have always regarded that requirement as crucial, and as sufficient to ensure that courts and juries do not mistake ordinary socializing in the workplace—such as male-on-male horseplay or intersexual flirtation—for discriminatory 'conditions of employment.'" The Court provided an excellent illustration of its rationale with this following example:

    "In same-sex (as in all) harassment cases, that inquiry requires careful consideration of the social context in which particular behavior occurs and is experienced by its target.

A professional football player's working environment is not severely or pervasively abusive, for example, if the coach smacks him on the buttocks as he heads onto the field – even if the same behavior would reasonably be experienced as abusive by the coach's secretary (male or female) back at the office. The real social impact of workplace behavior often depends on a constellation of surrounding circumstances, expectations, and relationships which are not fully captured by a simple recitation of the words used or the physical acts performed. Common sense, and an appropriate sensitivity to social context, will enable courts and juries to distinguish between simple teasing or roughhousing among members of the same sex, and conduct which a reasonable person in the plaintiff's position would find severely hostile or abusive."

4. **1998 *Burlington* Case.** In this case the Court addressed the issue whether an employee who refuses the unwelcome and threatening sexual advances of a supervisor, but suffers no adverse, tangible job consequences, can recover under Title VII against the employer without showing that employer was negligent or otherwise at fault for the supervisor's actions.

In examining this hostile environment sexual harassment claim, the Court articulated a new bright line test:

"An employer is subject to vicarious liability to a victimized employee for an actionable hostile environment created by a supervisor with immediate (or successively higher) authority over the employee. When no tangible employment action is taken, a defending employer may raise an affirmative defense to liability or damages, subject to proof by a preponderance of the evidence. The defense comprises two necessary elements: (1) that the employer exercised reasonable care to prevent and correct promptly any sexually harassing behavior, and (2) that the plaintiff employee unreasonably failed to take advantage of any preventive or corrective opportunities provided by the employer or to avoid harm otherwise. While proof that an employer had promulgated an anti-harassment policy with complaint procedure is not necessary in every instance as a matter of law, the need for a stated policy suitable to the employment circumstances may appropriately be addressed in any case when litigating the first element of the defense. And while proof that an employee failed to fulfill the corresponding obligation of reasonable care to avoid harm is not limited to showing any unreasonable failure to use any complaint procedure provided by the employer, a demonstration of such failure will normally suffice to satisfy the employer's burden under the second element of the defense. No affirmative defense is available, however, when the supervisor's harassment culminates in a tangible employment action, such as discharge, demotion, or undesirable reassignment (e.g., "Quid Pro Quo" harassment)."

5. **1998 *Faragher* Case.** This case, decided at the same time as the *Burlington* case, had a fact pattern similar to *Burlington* except in this instance the employer did not disseminate its sexual harassment grievance procedures to its employees.

After restating the *Burlington* rule, the court went on to add this additional element. "Under such circumstances, we hold as a matter of law that the defendant could not be found to have exercised reasonable care to prevent the supervisors' harassing conduct. Unlike the employer of a small work force, who might expect that sufficient care to prevent tortious behavior could be exercised informally, those responsible for defendant's operations could not reasonably have thought that precautions against hostile environments in any one of many departments in far flung locations could be effective without communication of some formal policy against harassment, with a sensible complaint procedure."

Determining Whether Sexual Conduct Is Unwelcome

Sexual harassment is "unwelcome... verbal or physical conduct of a sexual nature." Because sexual attraction may often play a role in the day-to-day social exchange between employees, the distinction between invited, uninvited-but-welcome, offensive-but-tolerated, and flatly rejected sexual advances may well be difficult to discern. But this distinction is essential because sexual conduct becomes unlawful only when it is unwelcome. The challenged conduct must be unwelcome in the sense that the employee did not solicit or incite it, and in the sense that the employee regarded the conduct as undesirable or offensive.

When confronted with conflicting evidence as to welcomeness, the Commission looks at the record as a whole and at the totality of circumstances evaluating each situation on a case-by-case basis. When there is some indication of welcomeness or when the credibility of the parties is at issue, the charging party's claim will be considerably strengthened if s/he made a contemporaneous

complaint or protest. Particularly when the alleged harasser may have some reason (e.g., prior consensual relationship) to believe that the advances will be welcomed, it is important for the victim to communicate that the conduct is unwelcome. Generally, victims are well-advised to assert their right to a workplace free from sexual harassment. This may stop the harassment before it becomes more serious. A contemporaneous complaint or protest may also provide persuasive evidence that the sexual harassment in fact occurred as alleged. Thus, in investigating sexual harassment charges, it is important to develop detailed evidence of the circumstances and nature of any such complaints or protests, whether to the alleged harasser, higher management, co-workers or others.

While a complaint or protest is helpful to charging party's case, it is not a necessary element of the claim. Indeed, the Commission recognizes that victims may fear repercussions from complaining about the harassment and that such fear may explain a delay in opposing the conduct. If the victim failed to complain or delayed in complaining, the investigation must ascertain why. The relevance of whether the victim has complained varies depending upon the nature of the sexual advances and the context in which the alleged incidents occurred.

The Supreme Court has made clear that voluntary submission to sexual conduct will not necessarily defeat a claim of sexual harassment. The correct inquiry is whether the employee by his or her conduct indicated that the alleged sexual advances were unwelcome. Thus, acquiescence in sexual conduct at the workplace may not mean that the conduct is welcome to the individual.

In some cases the courts and the Commission have considered whether the complainant welcomed the sexual conduct by acting in a sexually aggressive manner, using sexually-oriented language, or soliciting the sexual conduct. Conversely, occasional use of sexually explicit language does not necessarily negate a claim that sexual conduct was unwelcome. Although a charging party's use of sexual terms or off-color jokes may suggest that sexual comments by others in that situation were not unwelcome, more extreme and abusive or persistent comments or a physical assault will not be excused, nor would "quid pro quo" harassment be allowed. In other words, to rely on the victim's conduct as evidence of welcomeness, the conduct must be at the same level as the alleged harassing conduct.

Any past conduct of the charging party that is offered to show "welcomeness" must relate to the alleged harasser. In other words, the conduct must be verbal or nonverbal form of communication between the victim and the harasser. Thus, evidence concerning a charging party's general character and past behavior toward others has limited, if any, probative value and does not substitute for a careful examination of his or her behavior toward the alleged harasser.

A more difficult situation occurs when an employee first willingly participates in conduct of a sexual nature but then ceases to participate and claims that any continued sexual conduct has created a hostile work environment. Here the employee has the burden of showing that any further sexual conduct is unwelcome, work-related harassment. The employee must clearly communicate to the alleged harasser that that his or her conduct is no longer welcome. If the conduct still continues, his or her failure to bring the matter to the attention of higher management or the EEOC is evidence, though not dispositive, that any continued conduct is, in fact, welcome or unrelated to work. In any case, however, one's refusal to submit to the sexual conduct cannot be the basis for denying an employment benefit or opportunity; that would constituted a "quid pro quo" violation.

Evaluating Evidence of Harassment

The Commission recognizes that sexual conduct may be private and unacknowledged, with no eyewitnesses. Even sexual conduct that occurs openly in the workplace may appear to be consensual. Thus the resolution of a sexual harassment claim often depends on the credibility of the parties. The investigator should question the charging party and the alleged harasser in detail. The Commission's investigation also should search thoroughly for corroborative evidence of any nature. Supervisory and managerial employees, as well as co-workers, should be asked about their knowledge of the alleged harassment.

In appropriate cases, the Commission may make a finding of harassment based solely on the credibility of the victim's allegation. As with any other charge of discrimination, a victim's account must be sufficiently detailed and internally consistent so as to be plausible, and lack of corroborative evidence where such evidence logically should exist would undermine the allegation. By the same token, a general denial by the alleged harasser will carry little weight when it is contradicted by other evidence.

Of course, the Commission recognizes that a charging party may not be able to identify witnesses to the alleged conduct itself. But testimony may be obtained from persons who observed the charging party's demeanor immediately after an alleged incident of harassment. Persons with whom she discussed the incident, such as co-workers, a doctor or a counselor, should be interviewed. Other employees should be asked if they noticed changes in charging party's behavior at work or in the alleged harasser's treatment of charging party. As stated earlier, a contemporaneous complaint by the victim would be persuasive evidence both that the conduct occurred and that it was unwelcome. So too is evidence that other employees were sexually harassed by the same person. The investigator should determine whether the employer was aware of any other instances of harassment and, if so, what the response was.

If the investigation exhausts all possibilities for obtaining corroborative evidence, but finds none, the Commission may make a cause finding based solely on a reasoned decision to credit the charging party's testimony.

Determining a "Hostile Environment"

For sexual harassment to violate Title VII, it must be sufficiently severe or pervasive alter the conditions of (the victim's) employment and create an abusive working environment.

Since "hostile environment" harassment takes a variety of forms, many factors may affect this determination, including: (1) whether the conduct was verbal or physical, or both; (2) how frequently it was repeated; (3) whether the conduct was hostile and patently offensive; (4) whether the alleged harasser was a co-worker or a supervisor, (5) whether the others joined in perpetrating the harassment; and (6) whether the harassment was directed at more than one individual.

In determining whether unwelcome sexual conduct rises to the level of a "hostile environment" in violation of Title VII, the central inquiry is whether the conduct "unreasonably interfer(es) with an individual's work performance" or creates "an intimidating, hostile or offensive working environment." Thus, sexual flirtation or innuendo, even vulgar language that is trivial or merely annoying, would probably not establish a hostile environment.

1. **Standard for Evaluating Harassment** – In determining whether harassment is sufficiently severe or pervasive to create a hostile

environment, the harasser's conduct should be evaluated from the objective standpoint of a "reasonable person." Title VII does not serve as a vehicle for vindicating the petty slights suffered by the hypersensitive. Thus, if the challenged conduct would not substantially affect the work environment of a reasonable person, no violation should be found. A "reasonable person" standard also should be applied to be more basic determination of whether challenged conduct is of a sexual nature. Thus, if a reasonable person would not consider the co-worker's invitations as sexual in nature, then no violation would be found.

This objective standard should not be applied in a vacuum, however. Consideration should be given to the context in which the alleged harassment took place. A trier of fact must "adopt the perspective of a reasonable person's reaction to a similar environment under similar or like circumstances."

The reasonable person standard should consider the victim's perspective and not stereotyped notions of acceptable behavior. For example, the Commission believes that a workplace in which sexual slurs, displays of "girlie" pictures, and other offensive conduct abound can constitute a hostile work environment even if many people deem it to be harmless or insignificant.

2. **Isolated Instances of Harassment** – Unless the conduct is quite severe, a single incident or several isolated incidents of offensive sexual conduct or remarks generally do not create an abusive environment. Mere utterance of an ethnic or racial epithet which engenders offensive feelings in an employee would not affect the conditions of employment to a sufficiently significant degree to violate Title VII. A "hostile environment" claim generally requires a showing of a pattern of offensive conduct. In contrast, in "quid pro quo" cases a single sexual advance may

constitute harassment if it is linked to the granting or denial of employment benefits.

A single, unusually severe incident of harassment may be sufficient to constitute a Title VII violation; the more severe the harassment, the less need to show a repetitive series of incidents. Thus, there is an inverse relationship between the concepts of severe or pervasive; the more severe the conduct, the less pervasive it has to be and vice versa. This is particularly true when the harassment is physical.

The Commission will presume that the unwelcome, intentional touching of a charging party's intimate body areas is sufficiently offensive to alter the condition of her working environment and constitute a violation of Title VII. More so than in the case of verbal advances or remarks, a single unwelcome physical advance can seriously poison the victim's working environment. If an employee's supervisor sexually touches an employee, the Commission normally would find a violation. In such situations, it is the employer's burden to demonstrate that the unwelcome conduct was not sufficiently severe to create a hostile work environment.

When the victim is the target of both verbal and non-intimate physical conduct, the hostility of the environment is exacerbated and a violation is more likely to be found. Similarly, incidents of sexual harassment directed at other employees in addition to the charging party are relevant to a showing of hostile work environment.

3. **Non-Physical Harassment** – When the alleged harassment consists of verbal conduct, the investigator should ascertain the nature, frequency, context, and intended target of the remarks.

Questions to be explored might include:

-   Did the alleged harasser single out the charging party?
-   Did the charging party participate?

-   What was the relationship between the charging party and the alleged harasser(s)?
-   Were the remarks hostile and derogatory?

No one factor alone determines whether particular conduct violates Title VII. As the guidelines emphasize, the Commission will evaluate the totality of the circumstances. In general, a woman does not forfeit her right to be free from sexual harassment by choosing to work in an atmosphere that has traditionally included vulgar, anti-female language.

4. **Constructive Discharge** – Claims of "hostile environment" sexual harassment often are coupled with claims of constructive discharge. It is the position of the Commission and a majority of courts that an employer is liable for constructive discharge when it imposes intolerable working conditions in violation of Title VII when those conditions foreseeably would compel a reasonable employee to quit, whether or not the employer specifically intended to force the victim's resignation.

Vicarious Employer Liability for Unlawful Harassment by Supervisors

As previously discussed, the Supreme Court made clear that employers are subject to vicarious liability for unlawful harassment by supervisors. The standard of liability set forth in these decisions is premised on two principles: 1) an employer is responsible for the acts of its supervisors, and 2) employers should be encouraged to prevent harassment and employees should be encouraged to avoid or limit the harm from harassment. In order to accommodate these principles, the Court held that an employer is always liable for a supervisor's harassment if it culminates in a tangible employment action. However, if it does not, the employer may be able to avoid liability or limit damages by establishing an affirmative defense that includes two necessary elements:

- the employer exercised reasonable care to prevent and correct promptly any harassing behavior, and

- the employee unreasonably failed to take advantage of any preventive or corrective opportunities provided by the employer or to avoid harm otherwise.

An employer is subject to vicarious liability for unlawful harassment if the harassment was committed by a supervisor with immediate (or successively higher) authority over the employee. Thus, it is critical to determine whether the person who engaged in unlawful harassment had supervisory authority over the complainant.

The federal employment discrimination statutes do not contain or define the term "supervisor." The statutes make employers liable for the discriminatory acts of their "agents," and true supervisors are agents of their employers. However, agency principles "may not be transferable in all their particulars" to the federal employment discrimination statutes. The determination of whether an individual has sufficient authority to qualify as a "supervisor" for purposes of vicarious liability cannot be resolved by a purely mechanical application of agency law. Rather, the purposes of the anti-discrimination statutes and the reasoning of the Supreme Court decisions on harassment must be considered.

The Supreme Court reasoned that vicarious liability for supervisor harassment is appropriate because supervisors are aided in such misconduct by the authority that the employers delegated to them. Therefore, that authority must be of a sufficient magnitude so as to assist the harasser explicitly or implicitly in

carrying out the harassment. The determination as to whether a harasser had such authority is based on his or her job function rather than job title (e.g., "team leader") and must be based on the specific facts.

In some circumstances, an employer may be subject to vicarious liability for harassment by a supervisor who does not have actual authority over the employee. Such a result is appropriate if the employee reasonably believed that the harasser had such power. The employee might have such a belief because, for example, the chains of command are unclear. Alternatively, the employee might reasonably believe that a harasser with broad delegated powers has the ability to significantly influence employment decisions affecting him or her even if the harasser is outside the employee's chain of command.

Harassment by Supervisor that Results in a Tangible Employment Action

An employer is always liable for sexual harassment by a supervisor that culminates in a tangible employment action. No affirmative defense is available in such cases. The Supreme Court recognized that this result is appropriate because an employer acts through its supervisors, and a supervisor's undertaking of a tangible employment action constitutes an act of the employer.

A tangible employment action is a significant change in employment status. Unfulfilled threats are insufficient. Characteristics of a tangible employment action are:

1. A tangible employment action is the means by which the supervisor brings the official power of the enterprise to bear on subordinates, as demonstrated by the following:

- it requires an official act of the enterprise;

- it usually is documented in official company records;

- it may be subject to review by higher level supervisors; and

- it often requires the formal approval of the enterprise and use of its internal processes.

2. A tangible employment action usually inflicts direct economic harm.

3. A tangible employment action, in most instances, can only be caused by a supervisor or other person acting with the authority of the company.

   Examples of tangible employment actions include:

   - hiring and firing;

   - promotion and failure to promote;

   - demotion;

   - undesirable reassignment;

   - a decision causing a significant change in benefits;

   - compensation decisions; and

   - work assignment.

When harassment culminates in a tangible employment action, the employer cannot raise the affirmative defense. This sort of claim is analyzed like any other case in which a challenged employment action is alleged to be discriminatory. If the employer produces evidence of a nondiscriminatory explanation for the tangible employment action, a determination must be made whether that explanation is a pretext designed to hide a discriminatory motive.

Harassment by Supervisor that Does Not Result in a Tangible Employment Action

When harassment by a supervisor creates an unlawful hostile environment but does not result in a tangible employment action, the employer can raise an affirmative defense to liability or damages, which it must prove by a preponderance of the evidence. The defense consists of two necessary elements:

(a) the employer exercised reasonable care to prevent and correct promptly any harassment; and

(b) the employee unreasonably failed to take advantage of any preventive or corrective opportunities provided by the employer or to avoid harm otherwise.

If an employer can prove that it discharged its duty of reasonable care and that the employee could have avoided all of the harm but unreasonably failed to do so, the employer will avoid all liability for unlawful harassment. For example, if an employee was subjected to a pattern of disability-based harassment that created an unlawful hostile environment, but the employee unreasonably failed to complain to management before she suffered emotional harm and the employer exercised reasonable care to prevent and promptly correct the harassment, then the employer will avoid all liability.

If an employer cannot prove that it discharged its duty of reasonable care and that the employee unreasonably failed to avoid the harm, the employer will be liable. For example, if unlawful harassment by a supervisor occurred and the employer failed to exercise reasonable care to prevent it, the employer will be liable even if the employee unreasonably failed to complain to management or even if the employer took prompt and appropriate corrective action when it gained notice.

Harassment is the only type of discrimination carried out by a supervisor for which an employer can avoid liability, and that limitation must be construed narrowly. The employer will be shielded from liability for harassment by a supervisor only if it proves that it exercised reasonable care in preventing and correcting the harassment and that the employee unreasonably failed to avoid all of the harm. If both parties exercise reasonable care, the defense will fail.

Affirmative Defense: Employer's Duty to Exercise Reasonable Care

The first prong of the affirmative defense requires a showing by the employer that it undertook reasonable care to prevent and promptly correct harassment. Such reasonable care generally requires an employer to establish, disseminate, and enforce an anti-harassment policy and complaint procedure and to take other reasonable steps to prevent and correct harassment.

The steps described below are not mandatory requirements, whether or not an employer can prove that it exercised reasonable care depends on the particular factual circumstances and, in some cases, the nature of the employer's workforce. Small employers may be able to effectively prevent and correct harassment through informal means, while larger employers may have to institute more formal mechanisms.

There are no "safe harbors" for employers based on the written content of policies and procedures. Even the best policy and complaint procedure will not alone satisfy the burden of proving reasonable care if, in the particular circumstances of a claim, the employer failed to implement its process effectively. If, for example, the employer has an adequate policy and complaint procedure and properly responded to an employee's complaint of harassment, but

management ignored previous complaints by other employees about the same harasser, then the employer has not exercised reasonable care in preventing the harassment. Similarly, if the employer has an adequate policy and complaint procedure but an official failed to carry out his or her responsibility to conduct an effective investigation of a harassment complaint, the employer has not discharged its duty to exercise reasonable care. Alternatively, lack of a formal policy and complaint procedure will not defeat the defense if the employer exercised sufficient care through other means.

Affirmative Defense: Employee's Duty to Exercise Reasonable Care

The second prong of the affirmative defense requires a showing by the employer that the aggrieved employee unreasonably failed to take advantage of any preventive or corrective opportunities provided by the employer or to avoid harm otherwise.

This element of the defense arises from the general theory that a victim has a duty to use such means as are reasonable under the circumstances to avoid or minimize the damages that result from violations of the statute. Thus an employer who exercised reasonable care is not liable for unlawful harassment if the aggrieved employee could have avoided all of the actionable harm. If some but not all of the harm could have been avoided, then an award of damages will be mitigated accordingly.

A complaint by an employee does not automatically defeat the employer's affirmative defense. If, for example, the employee provided no information to support his or her allegation, gave untruthful information, or otherwise failed to cooperate in the investigation, the complaint would not qualify as an effort to avoid harm. Furthermore, if the employee unreasonably delayed complaining, and an earlier complaint could have reduced the harm, then the affirmative defense could operate to reduce damages.

Proof that the employee unreasonably failed to use any complaint procedure provided by the employer will normally satisfy the employer's burden. However, it is important to emphasize that an employee who failed to complain does not carry a burden of providing the reasonableness of that decision. Rather, the burden lies with the employer to prove that the employee's failure to complain was unreasonable.

1. **Failure to Complain** – A determination as to whether an employee unreasonably failed to complain or otherwise avoid harm depends on the particular circumstances and information available to the employee at that time. An employee should not necessarily be expected to complain to management immediately after the first or second incident of relatively minor harassment. Workplaces need not become battlegrounds where every minor, unwelcome remark based on race, sex, or another protected category triggers a complaint and investigation. An employee might reasonably ignore a small number of incidents, hoping that the harassment will stop without resort to the complaint process. The employee may directly say to the harasser that s/he wants the misconduct to stop, and then wait to see if that is effective in ending the harassment before complaining to management. If the harassment persists, however, further delay in complaining might be found unreasonable.

There might be other reasonable explanations for an employee's delay in complaining or failure to utilize the employer's complaint process. For example, the employee might have had reason to believe that:

- using the complaint mechanism entailed a risk of retaliation;

- there were obstacles to complaints; and

- the complaint mechanism was not effective.

To establish the second prong of the affirmative defense, the employer must prove that the belief or perception underlying the employee's failure to complain was unreasonable.

a. Risk of Retaliation. An employer cannot establish that an employee unreasonably failed to use its complaint procedure if that employee reasonably feared retaliation. Surveys have shown that employees who are subjected to harassment frequently do not complain to management due to fear of retaliation. To assure employees that such a fear is unwarranted, the employer must clearly communicate and enforce a policy that no employee will be retaliated against for complaining of harassment.

b. Obstacles to Complaints. An employee's failure to use the employer's complaint procedure would be reasonable if that failure was based on unnecessary obstacles to complaints. For example, if the process entailed undue expense by the employee, inaccessible points of contact for making complaints, or unnecessarily intimidating or burdensome requirements, failure to invoke it on such a basis would be reasonable.

An employee's failure to participate in a mandatory mediation or other alternative dispute resolution process also does not does not constitute unreasonable failure to avoid harm. While an employee can be expected to cooperate in the employer's investigation by providing relevant information, an employee can never be required to waive rights, either substantive or procedural, as an element of his or her exercise of reasonable care.

Nor must an employee have to try to resolve the matter with the harasser as an element of exercising due care.

c. Perception That Complaint Process Was Ineffective. An employer cannot establish the second prong of the defense based on the employee's failure to complain if that failure was based on a reasonable belief that the process was ineffective. For example, an employee would have a reasonable basis to believe that the complaint process is ineffective if the procedure required the employee to complain initially to the harassing supervisor. Such a reasonable basis also would be found if he or she was aware of instances in which coworkers' complaints failed to stop harassment. One way to increase employees' confidence in the efficacy of the complaint process would be for the employer to release general information to employees about corrective and disciplinary measures undertaken to stop harassment.

2. **Other Efforts to Avoid Harm** – Generally, an employer can prove the second prong of the affirmative defense if the employee unreasonably failed to utilize its complaint process. However, such proof will not establish the defense if the employee made other efforts to avoid harm.

For example, a prompt complaint by the employee to the EEOC or a state fair employment practices agency while the harassment is ongoing could qualify as such an effort. A union grievance could also qualify as an effort to avoid harm. Similarly, a staffing firm worker who is harassed at the client's workplace might report the harassment either to the staffing firm or to the client, reasonably expecting that either would act to correct the problem. Thus the worker's failure to complain to one of those

entities would not bar him or her from subsequently bringing a claim against it.

With these and any other efforts to avoid harm, the timing of the complaint could affect liability or damages. If the employee could have avoided some of the harm by complaining earlier, then damages would be mitigated accordingly.

Harassment by "Alter Ego" of Employer

An employer is liable for unlawful harassment whenever the harasser is of a sufficiently high rank to fall "within that class... who may be treated as the organization's proxy." In such circumstances, the official's unlawful harassment is imputed automatically to the employer. Thus the employer cannot raise the affirmative defense, even if the harassment did not result in a tangible employment action (e.g., president, owner, partner or corporate officer).

EEOC Recommended Anti-Harassment Policy and Complaint Procedure

It generally is necessary for employers to establish, publicize, and enforce anti-harassment policies and complaint procedures. As the Supreme Court stated, "Title VII is designed to encourage the creation of anti-harassment policies and effective grievance mechanisms." While the Court noted that this "is not necessary in every instance as a matter of law," failure to do so will make it difficult for an employer to prove that it exercised reasonable care to prevent and correct harassment.

An employer should provide every employee with a copy of the policy and complaint procedure, and redistribute it periodically. The policy and complaint procedure should be written in a way that will be understood by all employees in the employer's workforce. Other measures to ensure effective dissemination of the policy and complaint procedure include posting them in central locations and incorporating them into employee handbooks. If feasible, the employer should provide training to all employees to ensure that they understand their rights and responsibilities.

An anti-harassment policy and complaint procedure should contain, at a minimum, the following elements:

- A clear explanation of prohibited conduct;

- Assurance that employees who make complaints of harassment or provide information related to such complaints will be protected against retaliation;

- A clearly described complaint process that provides accessible avenues of complaint;

- Assurance that the employer will protect the confidentiality of harassment complaints to the extent possible;

- A complaint process that provides a prompt, thorough, and impartial investigation; and

- Assurance that the employer will take immediate and appropriate corrective action when it determines that harassment has occurred.

Reasonable Avenues of Complaint

The complaint procedure should provide accessible and alternative points of contact for the initial complaint. A complaint process is not effective if employees are always required to complain first to their supervisors about alleged harassment, since the supervisor may be a harasser. Moreover, reasonable care in preventing and correcting harassment

requires an employer to instruct all supervisors to report complaints of harassment to appropriate officials.

It is advisable for an employer to designate at least one official outside an employee's chain of command to take complaints of harassment. For example, if the employer has an office of human resources, one or more officials in that office could be authorized to take complaints. Allowing an employee to bypass his or her chain of command provides additional assurance that the complaint will be handled in an impartial manner, since an employee who reports harassment by his or her supervisor may feel that officials within the chain of command will more readily believe the supervisor's version of events.

It also is important for an employer's anti-harassment policy and complaint procedure to contain information about the time frames for filing charges of unlawful harassment with the EEOC or state fair employment practice agencies and to explain that the deadline runs from the last date of unlawful harassment, not from the date that the complaint to the employer is resolved. While a prompt complaint process should make it feasible for an employee to delay deciding whether to file a charge until the complaint to the employer is resolved, he or she is not required to do so.

Confidentiality

An employer should make clear to employees that it will protect the confidentiality of harassment allegations to the extent possible. An employer cannot guarantee complete confidentiality, since it cannot conduct an effective investigation without revealing certain information to the alleged harasser and potential witnesses. However, information about the allegation of harassment should be shared only with those who need to know about it. Records relating to harassment complaints should be kept confidential on the same basis.

A conflict between an employee's desire for confidentiality and the employer's duty to investigate may arise if an employee informs a supervisor about alleged harassment, but asks him or her to keep the matter confidential and take no action. Inaction by the supervisor in such circumstances could lead to employer liability. While it may seem reasonable to let the employee determine whether to pursue a complaint, the employer must discharge its duty to prevent and correct harassment. One mechanism to help avoid such conflicts would be for the employer to set up an informational phone line which employees can use to discuss questions or concerns about harassment on an anonymous basis.

Effective Investigative Process

An employer should set up a mechanism for a prompt, thorough, and impartial investigation into alleged harassment. As soon as management learns about alleged harassment, it should determine whether a detailed fact-finding investigation is necessary. For example, if the alleged harasser does not deny the accusation, there would be no need to interview witnesses, and the employer could immediately determine appropriate corrective action.

Prohibition Against Harassment

An employer's policy should make clear that it will not tolerate harassment based on sex (with or without sexual conduct), race, color, religion, national origin, age, disability, and protected activity (i.e., opposition to prohibited discrimination or participation in the statutory complaint process). This prohibition should cover harassment by anyone in the workplace - supervisors, co-workers, or non-employees. Employers should convey the seriousness of the prohibition. One way to do that is for the mandate

to "come from the top," i.e., be communicated to the employees from upper management.

The policy should encourage employees to report harassment before it becomes severe or pervasive. While isolated incidents of harassment generally do not violate federal law, a pattern of such incidents may be unlawful. Therefore, to discharge its duty of preventive care, the employer must make clear to employees that it will stop harassment before it rises to the level of a violation of federal law.

Protection Against Retaliation

An employer should make clear that it will not tolerate adverse treatment of employees because they report harassment or provide information related to such complaints. An anti-harassment policy and complaint procedure will not be effective without such an assurance.

Employers should undertake whatever measures are necessary to ensure that retaliation does not occur. For example, when management investigates a complaint of harassment, the official who interviews the parties and witnesses should remind these individuals about the prohibition against retaliation. Management also should scrutinize employment decisions affecting the complainant and witnesses during and after the investigation to ensure that such decisions are not based on retaliatory motives.

Effective Complaint Process

An employer's harassment complaint procedure should be designed to encourage victims to come forward. To that end, it should clearly explain the process and ensure that there are no unreasonable obstacles to complaints. A complaint procedure should not be rigid, since that could defeat the goal of preventing and correcting harassment. When an employee complains to management about alleged harassment, the employer is obligated to investigate the allegation regardless of whether it conforms to a particular format or is made in writing.

If a fact-finding investigation is necessary, it should be launched immediately. The amount of time that it will take to complete the investigation will depend on the particular circumstances. If, for example, multiple individuals were allegedly harassed, then it will take longer to interview the parties and witnesses.

It may be necessary to undertake intermediate measures before completing the investigation to ensure that further harassment does not occur. Examples of such measures are making scheduling changes so as to avoid contact between the parties; transferring the alleged harasser; or placing the alleged harasser on non-disciplinary leave with or without pay pending the conclusion of the investigation. The complainant should not be involuntarily transferred or otherwise burdened, since such measures could constitute unlawful retaliation.

The employer should ensure that the individual who conducts the investigation will objectively gather and consider the relevant facts. The alleged harasser should not have supervisory authority over the individual who conducts the investigation and should not have any direct or indirect control over the investigation. Whoever conducts the investigation should be well-trained in the skills that are required for interviewing witnesses and evaluating credibility.

Assurance of Immediate and Appropriate Corrective Action

An employer should make clear that it will undertake immediate and appropriate corrective action, including discipline, whenever it determines that harassment has occurred in violation of the employer's policy. Management should inform both parties about these measures.

Remedial measures should be designed to stop the harassment, correct its effects on the employee, and ensure that the harassment does not recur. These remedial measures need not be those that the employee requests or prefers, as long as they are effective.

In determining disciplinary measures, management should keep in mind that the employer could be found liable if the harassment does not stop. At the same time, management may have concerns that overly punitive measures may subject the employer to claims such as wrongful discharge, and may simply be inappropriate.

To balance the competing concerns, disciplinary measures should be proportional to the seriousness of the offense. If the harassment was minor, such as a small number of "off-color" remarks by an individual with no prior history of similar misconduct, then counseling and an oral or written warning might be all that is necessary. On the other hand, if the harassment was severe or persistent, then suspension or discharge may be appropriate.

Remedial measures should not adversely affect the complainant. Thus, for example, if it is necessary to separate the parties, then the harasser should be transferred (unless the complainant prefers otherwise). Remedial responses that penalize the complainant could constitute unlawful retaliation and are not effective in correcting the harassment. Remedial measures also should correct the effects of the harassment. Such measures should be designed to put the employee in the position s/he would have been in had the misconduct not occurred.

Examples of Measures to Stop the Harassment and Ensure that it Does Not Recur

- oral or written warning or reprimand;
- transfer or reassignment;
- demotion;
- reduction of wages;

- suspension;

- discharge;

- training or counseling of harasser to ensure that s/he understands why his or her conduct violated the employer's anti-harassment policy; and

- monitoring of and/or self reporting by the harasser to ensure that harassment stops.

Examples of Measures to Correct the Effects of the Harassment

- restoration any leave time taken because of the harassment;

- expungement of negative evaluation(s) in employee's personnel file that arose from the harassment;

- reinstatement;

- apology by the harasser;

- monitoring treatment of employee to ensure that s/he is not subjected to retaliation by the harasser or others in the work place because of the complaint; and

- correction of any other harm caused by the harassment (e.g., compensation for losses).

Other Preventive and Corrective Measures

An employer's responsibility to exercise reasonable care to prevent and correct harassment is not limited to implementing an anti-harassment policy and complaint procedure. In creating the affirmative defense, the Supreme Court stated, "the employer has a greater opportunity to guard against misconduct by supervisors than by common workers; employers have greater opportunity and incentive to screen them, train them, and monitor their performance."

An employer's duty to exercise due care includes instructing all of its supervisors and managers to address or report to appropriate officials complaints of harassment regardless of whether they are officially designated to take complaints and regardless of whether a complaint was framed in a way that conforms to the organization's particular complaint procedures. For example, if an employee files an EEOC charge alleging unlawful harassment, the employer should launch an internal investigation even if the employee did not complain to management through its internal complaint process.

Furthermore, due care requires management to correct harassment regardless of whether an employee files an internal complaint, if the conduct is inappropriate. For example, if there are areas in the workplace with graffiti containing racial or sexual epithets, management should eliminate the graffiti and not wait for an internal complaint.

An employer should ensure that its supervisors and managers understand their responsibilities under the organization's anti-harassment policy and complaint procedure. Periodic training of those individuals can help achieve that result. Such training should explain the types of conduct that violate the employer's anti-harassment policy; the seriousness of the policy; the responsibilities of supervisors and managers when they learn of alleged harassment; the obligation to lead by example; the importance of reporting complaints promptly and to the right people; how to ensure complainants do not walk away frustrated; and the prohibition against retaliation.

An employer should keep track of its supervisors' and managers' conduct to make sure that they carry out their responsibilities under the organization's anti-harassment program. For example, an employer could include such compliance in formal evaluations.

Reasonable preventive measures include screening applicants for supervisory jobs to see if any have a record of engaging in harassment. If so, it may be necessary for the employer to reject a candidate on that basis or to take additional steps to prevent harassment by that individual.

Finally, it is advisable for an employer to keep records of all complaints of harassment. Without such records, the employer could be unaware of a pattern of harassment by the same individual. Such a pattern would be relevant to credibility assessments and disciplinary measures.

Conducting an Investigation of Sexual Harassment

A sexual harassment investigation should be prompt, reasonable and thorough. Some guideposts for this aspect include the following:

- **Promptness** – an investigation must be commenced within 24-48 hours (excluding non-business days), and if not done in this time frame, there should be documentation setting forth an important reason as to why it did not.

EEOC Examples of Sexual Harassment

1. **Consensual Relationships** — Complainant alleges that she lost a promotion for which she was qualified because the co-worker who obtained the promotion was engaged in a sexual relationship with their supervisor. The EEOC's investigation discloses that the relationship at issue was consensual and that the supervisor has never subjected complainant's co-worker or any other employees to unwelcome sexual advances. The Commission would find no violation of Title VII in these circumstances, because men and women were equally disadvantaged by the supervisor's conduct for reasons other than their genders. Even if complainant is genuinely offended by the supervisor's conduct, she has no Title VII claim.

2. **Coerced Sexual Favoritism** — Same as above, except the relationship at issue was not consensual. Instead, complainant's supervisor regularly harassed the co-worker in front of other employees, demanded sexual favors as a condition for her promotion, and then audibly boasted about his "conquest." In these circumstances, complainant may be able to establish a violation of Title VII by showing that in order to have obtained the promotion, it would have been necessary to grant sexual favors. In addition, she and other qualified men and women would have standing to challenge the favoritism on the basis that they were injured as a result of the discrimination leveled against their co-worker.

3. **Hostile Environment and Widespread Favoritism** — Same as example 1, except that complainant's supervisor and other management personnel regularly solicited sexual favors from subordinate employees and offered job opportunities to those who complied. Some of those employees willingly consented to the sexual requests and in turn received promotions and awards. Others consented because they recognized that their opportunities for advancement would otherwise be limited. Complainant, who did not welcome this conduct, was not approached for sexual favors. However, she and other female and male co-workers may be able to establish that the conduct created a hostile work environment. She can also claim that by their conduct, the managers communicated to all female employees that they can obtain job benefits only by acquiescing in sexual conduct.

- **Thoroughness** – prepare in advance, carefully select the investigator, and outline your investigative plan to keep focused. Make sure all relevant witnesses are interviewed.

- **Neutrality** – identify and collect all potential evidentiary items and interview witnesses.

- **Accuracy** – keep accurate records and consider having interviewees, including the complainant if willing, sign off on notes taken.

- **Focus** – manifest a commitment to the investigation by keeping to the purpose of the investigation and not to stray beyond that required by business necessity.

- **Confidentiality** – to the extent possible, discuss the investigation only with those who need to know.

- **Ethical restraint** – keep the investigation within the parameters of relevance and the alleged misconduct.

- **Documentation** – take good, detailed notes, avoid using a tape recorder because of the "chilling effect" it will have on witnesses. Consider writing a report.

- **Corrective action** – the maximum reasonable under the circumstances to show the resolve of the employer to have a healthy working environment.

- **Procedure** – Make sure the terms of all policies, manuals, handbooks, collective bargaining agreements or employment contracts are followed.

As to whom should conduct the investigation, there are four obvious choices: the employer or his or her designated representative, in-house counsel (if available), an outside attorney, or a specialist in the field. The critical consideration is the severity of the alleged harassment.

In general, the more severe the harassment, the more an employer would benefit from using professionals to conduct the investigation involving serious conduct, that, if substantiated, would result in severe discipline or termination. Do not select anyone who may have a real or perceived conflict of interest or bias, or may be accused of such.

Credibility Determinations

If there are conflicting versions of relevant events, the employer will have to weigh each party's credibility. Credibility assessments can be critical in determining whether the alleged harassment in fact occurred. Factors to consider include:

- **Inherent plausibility:** Is the testimony believable on its face? Does it make sense?

- **Demeanor:** Did the person seem to be telling the truth or lying?

- **Motive to falsify:** Did the person have a reason to lie?

- **Corroboration:** Is there witness testimony (such as testimony by eyewitnesses, people who saw the person soon after the alleged incidents, or people who discussed the incidents with him or her at around the time that they occurred) or physical evidence (such as written documentation, e-mails, or telephone records) that corroborates the party's testimony?

- **Past record:** Did the alleged harasser have a history of similar behavior in the past?

Suggested Questions
to Ask Parties and Witnesses

Questions to Ask the Complainant:

- Who, what, when, where, and how: Who committed the alleged harassment? What exactly occurred or was said? When did it occur and is it still ongoing? Where did it occur? How often did it occur?

- How did you react? What response(s) did you make when the incident(s) occurred or afterwards?

- How did the harassment affect you? Has your job been affected in any way?

- Are there any persons who have relevant information? Was anyone present when the alleged harassment occurred? Did you tell anyone about it? Did anyone see you immediately after episodes of alleged harassment?

- Did the person who harassed you harass anyone else? Do you know whether anyone complained about harassment by that person?

- Are there any notes, physical evidence, or other documentation regarding the incident(s)?

- How would you like to see the situation resolved?

- Do you know of any other relevant information?

Questions to Ask the Alleged Harasser:

- What is your response to the allegations?

- If the harasser claims that the allegations are false, ask why the complainant might lie.

- Are there any persons who have relevant information?

- Are there any notes, physical evidence, or other documentation regarding the incident(s)?

- Do you know of any other relevant information?

Questions to Ask Third Parties:

- What did you see or hear? When did this occur? Describe the alleged harasser's behavior toward the complainant and toward others in the workplace.

- What did the complainant tell you? When did s/he tell you this?

- Do you know of any other relevant information?

- Are there other persons who have relevant information?

Americans with Disabilities Act 7

Legislative Purpose

In 1990, Congress approved the Americans with Disabilities Act (ADA), and immediately it was hailed as landmark legislation that would help to end discrimination in the workplace against individuals with disabilities and bring these individuals into the economic and social mainstream of American life. It has been estimated that nearly one in five Americans has one or more physical or mental disabilities.

The legislation has four major titles: Employment, Public Services (e.g., public transportation), Telecommunications, Public Accommodations, and Services Operated by Private Entities. This book addresses only the provisions set forth in the Employment title.

Coverage

The law covers both private and public sector employers who have 15 or more full-time employees (e.g., individuals who work more than 20 hours per week) for each working day in each of 20 or more calendar weeks in the current or preceding calendar year. It is enforced by the Equal Employment Opportunity Commission (EEOC).

The Rehabilitation Act of 1973, on which ADA is patterned, is the other primary federal law which prohibits disability discrimination in three discrete employment settings:

1. Section 501 of the Rehabilitation Act prohibits federal executive branch agencies, including the U.S. Postal Service and the Postal Rate Commission, from discriminating against qualified individuals with disabilities. It requires executive branch agencies to take affirmative action in the hiring, placing, and advancing of individuals with disabilities.

2. Section 503 of the Rehabilitation Act requires private sector contractors and subcontractors who have contracts with the federal government for $10,000 or more annually to take affirmative action to employ, and to advance in employment, qualified individuals with disabilities.

3. Section 504 prohibits private sector recipients of federal financial assistance from discriminating against qualified individuals with disabilities in employment and in their programs and activities.

The Department of Labor, Office of Federal Contract Compliance Programs enforces the Rehabilitation Act of 1973.

Disability Defined

The ADA prohibits discrimination in all employment practices, including job application procedures, hiring, firing, advancement, compensation, training, and other terms, conditions, and privileges of employment. It applies to recruitment, advertising, tenure, layoff, leave, fringe benefits, and all other employment-related activities.

Employment discrimination is prohibited against "qualified individuals with disabilities."

Persons discriminated against because they have a known association or relationship with a disabled individual also are protected. The ADA defines an "individual with a disability" as a person who has a physical or mental impairment that substantially limits that person's major life activities, who has a record of such an impairment, or who is regarded as having such an impairment.

An impairment is a physiological disorder affecting one or more of a number of body systems or a mental or psychological disorder. The following are not considered impairments: environmental, cultural, and economic disadvantage; homosexuality and bisexuality; normal pregnancy; a broken leg; physical characteristics; common personality traits; or normal deviations in height, weight, or strength. The impairment must affect a major life activity. The EEOC regulations define this as caring for oneself, performing manual tasks, walking, seeing, hearing, speaking, breathing, learning, and working. Other examples of major life activities include sitting, standing, lifting, and mental and emotional processes such as thinking, concentrating and interacting with others.

Once there is evidence of an impairment that affects a major life activity, it must be shown to be substantially limiting. The EEOC offers these examples:

a. An impairment is substantially limiting if it prohibits or significantly restricts an individual's ability to perform a major life activity as compared to the ability of the average person in the general population to perform the same activity.

b. The determination of whether an impairment substantially limits a major life activity depends on the nature and severity of the impairment, the duration or expected duration of the impairment, and the permanency or long-term impact of the impairment.

c. An impairment substantially limits an individual's ability to work if it prevents or significantly restricts the individual from working.

d. Although very short-term temporary restrictions generally are not substantially limiting, an impairment does not have to be permanent to rise to the level of a disability. Temporary impairments that take significantly longer than normal to heal, long-term impairments, or potentially long-term impairments of indefinite duration may be disabilities if they are severe.

e. Chronic or episodic disorders that are substantially limiting when active or have a high likelihood of recurrence in substantially limiting forms may be disabilities.

f. An individual who has two or more impairments that are not substantially limiting by themselves but that together substantially limit one or more major life activities has a disability.

An individual is deemed to have a "record" of a substantially limiting impairment where there is a history of a substantially limiting impairment or where the individual has been misclassified as having a substantially limiting impairment. An individual is regarded as having a substantially limiting impairment if he or she has: (1) an impairment that does not substantially limit major life activities but is treated by an employer as having such a limitation; (2) an impairment that substantially limits major life activities only as a result of the attitudes of others toward such impairment; or (3) has no impairment but is treated by an employer as having a substantially limiting impairment that disqualifies or significantly restricts an individual from working.

In 1999, the Supreme Court resolved one of the controversial issues surrounding the definition of a disability by ruling that people with physical impairments who can function normally with remedial action as when they wear their glasses or take medication generally cannot be considered disabled, and therefore are outside the law's protection from employment discrimination. In explaining the split decision, the majority opinion found that a "disability exists only where an impairment 'substantially limits' a major life activity, not where it 'might,' 'could,' or 'would' be substantially limiting if mitigating measures were not taken." Thus, a person with a corrected impairment still has the impairment, but if the impairment is corrected it does not substantially limit a major life activity.

A five year review by the EEOC of the impairments most often cited in complaints filed at the agency include the following:

Back impairments	18.2%
Emotional/psychiatric impairments	12.7%
Neurological impairments	11.3%
Extremities	9.0%
Heart impairments	4.1%
Diabetes	3.6%
Substance abuse	3.3%
Hearing impairments	2.9%
Vision impairments	2.6%
Blood disorders and HIV	2.6%
Cancer	2.3%
Asthma	1.7%

Mental Illness – Psychiatric or Emotional Illness

In 1997, the EEOC issued guidelines advising employers that they: (1) may not discriminate against qualified workers with mental illness; (2) may not ask job applicants if they have a history of mental illness; and (3) must take reasonable steps to accommodate employees with psychiatric or emotional problems. The guidelines reemphasize that even where

accommodation is required, employers are not required to do so if it would result in lowering standards for performance. Additionally, the guidelines remind employers that they are not obligated to make an accommodation if doing so would impose an undue hardship on the operation. Cost is a factor that may be considered.

Examples of accommodation include: allowing extra time off from work, altering work schedules or assignments, and making physical changes in the workplace (e.g., room dividers, partitions or other soundproofing or visual barriers between work spaces to help employees who have difficult concentrating because of mental illness). For example, a person with schizophrenia might be unusually sensitive to noise and visual distractions in the workplace.

In certain instances, an employer may be required to provide a temporary job coach to assist in the training of a qualified individual with a disability. Where an employee takes antidepressants that cause extreme grogginess and lack of alertness in the morning an employer may need to change the employee's work schedule.

The EEOC identified special problems with certain mental disabilities including major depression, manic depression, schizophrenia, obsessive-compulsive disorder and personality disorders. The guidelines alert employers to the possibility that traits normally regarded as undesirable – chronic lateness, poor judgment, hostility to co-workers or supervisors – may be linked to these mental impairments.

The EEOC guidelines state that employers may not ask on job applications whether prospective employees have a history of mental illness or whether they have been treated or hospitalized for such illness.

After making a job offer, an employer may require a medical examination, including a psychiatric examination, if the company requires all newly hired employees in the same job category to have such examinations. However, if the employer uses the results to screen out a person because of a disability, the employer must prove that the exclusionary criteria are job-related and consistent with business necessity.

Employees need not use any "magic words" to request an accommodation. If an employee asks for time off because he or she is "stressed or depressed," that is enough to put the employer on notice that the worker is requesting a reasonable accommodation. If the worker's need is not obvious to the employer, the latter may ask for documentation from a doctor, to show that the employee has a psychiatric disability requiring time off.

All information on psychiatric disabilities must be kept confidential on separate forms and in separate medical files. If other employees ask questions about a co-worker who seems to be receiving preferential treatment, the employer must not disclose any medical information. For example, the employer may not tell employees that a worker has a disorder requiring a reasonable accommodation, but may explain that the company is "acting for legitimate business reasons or in compliance with Federal law."

Qualified Individual With a Disability

A qualified individual with a disability is a person who meets legitimate skill, experience, education, or other requirements of an employment position that he or she holds or seeks, and who can perform the "essential functions" of the position with or without reasonable accommodation. Requiring the ability to perform "essential" functions assures that an individual will not be considered unqualified simply because of inability to

perform marginal or incidental job functions. If the individual is qualified to perform essential job functions except for limitations caused by a disability, the employer must consider whether the individual could perform these functions with a reasonable accommodation. If a written job description has been prepared in advance of advertising or interviewing applicants for a job, this will be considered as evidence, although not necessarily conclusive evidence, of the essential functions of the job. For a description of enforcement and penalties, refer to Chapter 4, EEOC Enforcement Procedures and Penalties.

Reasonable Accommodation

The Americans with Disabilities Act requires a covered employer to provide reasonable accommodation for individuals with disabilities, unless it would cause undue hardship. A reasonable accommodation is any change in the work environment or in the way a job is performed that enables a person with a disability to enjoy equal employment opportunities. There are three categories of "reasonable accommodations":

- changes to a job application process;
- changes to the work environment, or to the way a job is usually done; and
- changes that enable an employee with a disability to enjoy equal benefits and privileges of employment (e.g. training).

Although many individuals with disabilities can apply for and perform jobs without any reasonable accommodations, workplace barriers may keep others from performing jobs which they could do with some form of accommodation. These barriers may be physical obstacles (such as inaccessible facilities or equipment), or they may be procedures or rules (such as policies concerning when work is performed, when breaks are taken, or how job tasks are performed). Reasonable accommodation removes workplace barriers for individuals with disabilities.

The accommodation process focuses on the needs of a particular individual in performing a particular job because of a physical or mental impairment. A problem-solving approach should be used to identify the particular tasks or aspects of the work environment that limit performance and to identify possible accommodations that will result in a meaningful equal opportunity for the individual with a disability.

To illustrate this provision, consider a job requiring the use of a computer, the essential function of which is the ability to access, input and retrieve information from the computer. It is not essential that the person be able to use the keyboard or visually read the computer screen, if providing adaptive equipment or software would enable the person with the disability – for example, impaired vision or limited hand control – to control the computer and access the information. The relevant question would be whether the acquisition of the adaptive equipment would be a reasonable accommodation, given the factors to be considered in making that determination.

Another example of reasonable accommodation may involve the work schedule or assignments. Part-time or modified work schedules can provide useful accommodation. Some people with disabilities are denied employment opportunities because they cannot work a standard schedule. For example, persons who need medical treatment may benefit from flexible or adjusted work schedules. A person with epilepsy may require constant shifts rather than rotation from day to night shifts. Other persons who may require modified work schedules are persons with mobility impairments who depend on a public transportation system that is not currently fully accessible.

There is no obligation to create a position for an applicant who is not qualified for the position sought. Employers are not required to lower quality or quantity standards in order to make an accommodation, nor are they obligated to provide personal use items such as glasses or hearing aids.

The decision as to the appropriate accommodation must be based on the particular facts of each case. In selecting the particular type of reasonable accommodation to provide, the principal test is that of effectiveness; i.e., whether the accommodation will enable the person with a disability to do the job in question. An employer is not required to make an accommodation if it would impose an "undue hardship" on the operation of the employer's business.

In 1999, the Supreme Court decided a case involving reasonable accommodation in favor of an employee who sought to come back to work after a stroke and requested extra time and training. The employer denied the accommodation request because the employee had applied for and received disability benefits under the Social Security Act because he was deemed "totally disabled." The employer, relying on this fact and previous lower court rulings, asserted the employee could not bring a discrimination suit in these circumstances. The Court ruled that while the two federal laws appeared divergent, they do not inherently conflict. The Social Security program made broad determinations without making a finely tuned examination of an individual's situation. For example, it does not normally inquire into the question whether employees who cannot work without accommodations can return to work if their special needs are addressed. As a result of this ruling, employers have to consider an accommodation request notwithstanding the individual's past receipt of disability benefits. Similarly, those who have a debilitating condition and move in and out of being able to work may pursue Social Security benefits, and not be presumptively denied accommodation under the ADA.

ADA Employee Classification Flow Chart

The flow chart below shows the process for analyzing whether an employee is protected by the ADA:

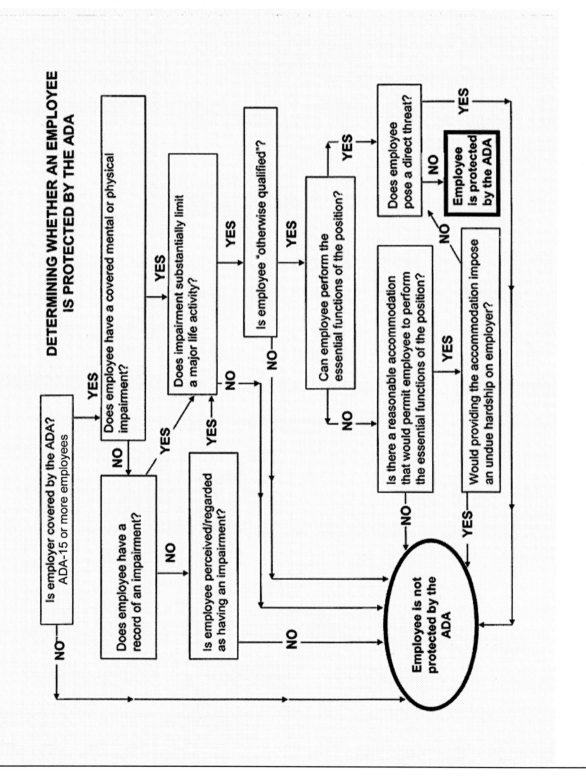

Frequently Asked Questions
Relating to Reasonable Accommodation and Undue Hardship

Q. How must an individual request a reasonable accommodation?

A. The individual must let the employer know that s/he needs an adjustment or change at work for a reason related to a medical condition. An individual may use "plain English" and need not mention the ADA or use the phrase "reasonable accommodation." Requests for reasonable accommodation do not need to be in writing, though an employer may choose to write a memorandum or letter confirming the request.

Q. What must an employer do after receiving a request for reasonable accommodation?

A. When the disability and/or the need for accommodation is not obvious, the employer may ask the individual for reasonable documentation about his/her disability and functional limitations.

The employer and the individual with a disability should engage in an informal process to clarify what the individual needs and identify the appropriate reasonable accommodation. The employer may ask the individual questions that will enable it to make an informed decision about the request. This includes asking what type of reasonable accommodation is needed.

There are extensive public and private resources to help employers and individuals with disabilities who are not familiar with possible accommodations.

Q. Must an employer provide the reasonable accommodation that the individual wants?

A. The employer may choose among reasonable accommodations as long as the chosen accommodation is effective (i.e., it removes the workplace barrier at issue). The employer may offer alternative suggestions for reasonable accommodations to remove the workplace barrier in question. If there are two possible reasonable accommodations, and one costs more or is more difficult to provide, the employer may choose the one that is less expensive or easier to provide, as long as it is effective.

Q. How quickly must an employer respond to a request for reasonable accommodation?

A. An employer should respond promptly to a request for reasonable accommodation. If the employer and the individual with a disability need to engage in an interactive process, it too should proceed as quickly as possible. Similarly, the employer should act promptly to provide the reasonable accommodation.

Q. Is restructuring a job a reasonable accommodation?

A. Yes. This includes: (1) shifting responsibility to other employees for minor job tasks that an employee is unable to perform because of a disability and (2) altering when and/or how a job task is performed. If an employee is unable to perform a minor job task because of a disability, an employer can require the employee to perform a different minor job function in its place.

Q. Is providing leave necessitated by an employee's disability a form of reasonable accommodation?

A. Yes, absent undue hardship, providing unpaid leave is a form of reasonable accommodation. However, an employer does not have to provide more paid leave than it provides to other employees.

FAQs – Reasonable Accommodation and Undue Hardship [(continued)]

Q. May an employer apply a "no-fault" leave policy, under which employees are automatically terminated after they have been on leave for a certain period of time, to an employee with a disability who needs additional leave?

A. If an employee with a disability needs additional unpaid leave as a reasonable accommodation, the employer must provide the employee with the additional leave even if it has a "no-fault" policy. An employer, however, does not need to provide leave if: (1) it can provide an effective accommodation that allows the person to keep working, or (2) it can show that granting additional leave would cause an undue hardship.

Q. When an employee requests leave as a reasonable accommodation, may an employer provide accommodation that requires him/her to remain on the job instead?

A. Yes, if the employer's proposed reasonable accommodation would be effective and eliminate the need for leave. Accordingly, an employer may reallocate minor job tasks or provide a temporary transfer instead of leave, so long as the employee can still address his/her medical needs.

Q. Is a modified or part-time schedule reasonable accommodation?

A. Yes, absent undue hardship. A modified schedule may involve adjusting arrival or departure times, providing periodic breaks, altering when certain job tasks are performed, allowing an employee to use accrued paid leave, or providing additional unpaid leave.

Q. Is it a reasonable accommodation to modify a workplace policy because of an employee's disability?

A. Yes. For example, granting an employee time off from work or an adjusted work schedule as a reasonable accommodation may involve modifying leave or attendance procedures or policies. However, reasonable accommodation only requires that the employer modify the policy for an employee with a disability. The employer may continue to apply the policy to all other employees.

Q. Does an employer have to reassign an employee who can no longer perform his/her job because of a disability to a vacant position?

A. Yes, unless the employer can show that it would be an undue hardship. The following criteria apply to reassignment:

An employee must be "qualified" for the new position. This means that s/he: (1) satisfies the skill, experience, education, and other job-related requirements of the position, and (2) can perform the primary job tasks of the new position, with or without reasonable accommodation. The employer does not have to assist the employee to become qualified.

An employer does not have to bump other employees or create a position. Nor does an employer have to promote the employee.

Reassignment should be to a position that is equal in pay and status to the position that the employee held, or to one that is as close as possible in terms of pay and status if an equivalent position is not vacant.

FAQs – Reasonable Accommodation and Undue Hardship [(continued)]

Q. Does a reasonable accommodation include changing a person's supervisor?

A. No. The ADA may, however, require that supervisory methods, such as the method of communicating assignments, be altered as a form of reasonable accommodation.

Q. Are there certain things that are not considered reasonable accommodations and are therefore not required?

A. An employer does not have to eliminate a primary job responsibility.

- An employer is not required to lower production standards that are applied to all employees, though it may have to provide reasonable accommodation to enable an employee with a disability to meet them.

- An employer does not have to provide personal use items, such as a prosthetic limb, a wheelchair, eyeglasses, hearing aids, or similar devices.

- An employer never has to excuse a violation of a uniformly applied conduct rule that is job-related and consistent with business necessity. This means, for example, that an employer never has to tolerate or excuse violence, threats of violence, stealing, or destruction of property. An employer may discipline an employee with a disability for engaging in such misconduct if it would impose the same discipline on an employee without a disability.

Q. Must an employer modify the work hours of an employee with a disability if doing so would prevent other employees from performing their jobs?

A. No. If modifying one employee's work hours (or granting leave) would prevent other employees from doing their jobs, then the significant disruption to the operations of the employer constitutes an undue hardship.

Q. Can an employer deny a request for leave when an employee cannot provide a fixed date of return?

A. In some situations, an employee may be able to provide only an appropriate date of return because treatment and recuperation do not always permit exact timetables. If an employer is able to show that the lack of a fixed return date imposes an undue hardship, then it can deny the leave. Undue hardship could result if the employer can neither plan for the employee's return nor permanently fill the position. In other situations, an employer may be able to be flexible.

The format for these questions and answers is based upon information contained in the EEOC's *Enforcement Guidance on Reasonable Accommodation and Undue Hardship Under the ADA.*

Undue Hardship

An employer is not required to make an accommodation if it imposes an undue hardship. The term "undue hardship" is defined as an action requiring significant difficulty or expense; i.e., an action that is unduly costly, extensive, substantial, or disruptive, or that will fundamentally alter the nature of the program.

In determining whether a particular accommodation would impose an undue hardship on the operation of the entity – i.e., require significant difficulty or expense – factors to be considered include: (1) the nature and cost of the accommodation need under the ADA; (2) the overall financial resources of the facility or facilities involved in the provision of the reasonable accommodation, the number of persons employed at such facility, the effect on expenses and resources, or the impact otherwise of such accommodation upon the operation of the facility; (3) the overall financial resources of the employer; the overall size of the entity with respect to the number of its employees; the number, type, and location of its facilities; and, (4) the type of operation or operations of the covered entity, including the composition, structure, and functions of the work force; the geographic separateness, administrative, or fiscal relationship of the facility or facilities if under the employer's control.

What is apparent is that Congress intended that the weight given to each factor in making the determination as to whether a reasonable accommodation nonetheless constitutes an "undue hardship" will vary depending on the facts of a particular situation and turns on both the nature and cost of the accommodation in relation to the employer's resources and operations. In illustrating this point, the legislative history contains the example of a small day-care center that might not be required to expend more than a nominal sum, such as that necessary to equip a telephone for

Sources for Information on Assistive Devices

1. State offices of the Division of Rehabilitation Services.

2. Job Accommodation Network (JAN). Provides free information on job accommodations and the employability of people with disabilities. The network is based at West Virginia University in Morgantown, WV. Call (800) 526-7234 or see JAN's World Wide Web site, http://www.jan.wvu.edu.

3. ABLEDATA. This electronic database of information on assistive technology and rehabilitation equipment is run by the U.S. Department of Education. Information specialists conduct product searches for callers at no charge. Users may search an extensive World Wide Web site for fact sheets and products. On-site assistance is available by appointment. Call (800) 227-0216 or see ABLEDATA's World Wide Web site, http://www.abledata.com.

4. President's Committee on Employment of People with Disabilities. Provides general information about the ADA, employment issues and accommodation. Call (202) 376-6200 or see the Committee's World Wide Web site, http://www.pcepd.com.

5. Regional Disability and Business Technical Assistance Centers. Ten federally funded centers across the United States provide information, training and technical assistance to businesses and government on all aspects of the ADA. Call (800) 949-4232.

use by a secretary with impaired hearing, but a large school district might be required to make available a teacher's aide to a blind applicant for a teaching job.

If cost is an issue, an employer should determine whether funding is available from an outside source, such as a state rehabilitation agency, to pay for all or part of the accommodation. In addition, the employer should determine whether

Practical Advice on ADA Compliance

1. Remember that the law contemplates an interactive process between the employee and employer following a request for a job accommodation because of a health condition.

2. The focus of the conversation should initially be on the job performance, and the employer should be asking how he/she can help the employee perform.

3. If a simple answer to the problem is not evident, then it is proper to determine if the employee has a disability that is covered by law.

4. Once the employer has determined that the ADA covers this situation, then the next line of inquiry should be how the company can effectively make an accommodation (e.g., a hand truck, allowing more breaks for medication, restructuring a job, etc.) The key is what is effective, not necessarily what the employee wants.

5. The employer should contact resources such as those in the section entitled Sources for Information on Assistive Devices, that have solid information and experience counseling employers with similar questions. Indeed, if the matter ends in litigation, all these efforts will go a long way toward mitigating damages or successfully defending a lawsuit.

6. Courts have taken a dim view of employees who have not cooperated during this interactive process. Some courts have ruled that employees who have not cooperated have lost their right to a reasonable accommodation.

7. As is the rule in personnel matters, employers must document every step along the way. It is simply the case that documentation is the most effective way of minimizing the impact of employee lawsuits over alleged violations in the workplace.

it is eligible for certain tax credits or deductions to offset the cost of the accommodation. In fact, the EEOC guidance on this subject suggests that to the extent that a portion of the cost of an accommodation causes undue hardship, the employer should ask the individual with a disability if s/he will pay the difference.

An employer cannot claim undue hardship based on employees' or customers' fears or prejudices, or because providing a reasonable accommodation might have a negative impact on employee morale. Employers, however, may claim undue hardship where a reasonable accommodation would be unduly disruptive to other employees' ability to work or violate a seniority system.

Job Analysis

All hiring decisions and performance evaluations should be made on objective criteria. An employer needs to know for each job the qualifications needed to perform it, and needs to develop objective interview questions and objectively evaluate an employee's performance.

Job analysis provides an objective basis for hiring, evaluating, training, accommodating, and supervising persons with disabilities, as well as improving the efficiency of any organization. It is a logical process to determine (1) purpose – the reason for the job, (2) essential functions – the job duties which are critical or fundamental to the performance of the job, (3) job setting – the work station and conditions where the essential functions are performed, and (4) job qualifications – the minimal skills an individual must possess to perform the essential functions. A job analysis describes the job, not the person who performs it.

The recent Supreme Court cases involving a corrected impairment (e.g. glasses, hypertension medicine, etc.) make clear that an employer is free to decide that physical characteristics

How to Conduct a Job Analysis

The following questions can help analyze each job in any organization.

PURPOSE

1. What are the particular contributions of the job toward the accomplishment of the overall objective of the unit or organization?

ESSENTIAL FUNCTIONS

1. What three or four activities actually constitute the job? Is each really necessary? (For example, a secretary types, files, answers the phone, takes dictation.)

2. What is the relationship between each task? Is there a special sequence which the tasks must follow?

3. Do the tasks necessitate sitting, standing, crawling, walking, climbing, running, stooping, kneeling, lifting, carrying, digging, writing, operating, pushing, pulling, fingering, talking, listening, interpreting, analyzing, seeing, coordinating, etc.?

4. How many other employees are available to perform the job function? Can the performance of that job function be distributed among any other employees?

5. How much time is spent on the job performing each particular function? Are the less frequently performed tasks as important to job success as those done more frequently?

6. Would removing a function fundamentally alter the job?

7. What happens if a task is not completed on time?

JOB SETTING

1. Location – Where are the essential functions of the job carried out?

2. Organization – How is the work organized for maximum safety and efficiency? How do workers obtain necessary equipment and materials?

3. Movement – What movement is required of employees to accomplish the essential functions of the job?

4. Conditions – What are the physical conditions of the job setting (hot, cold, damp, inside, outside, underground, wet, humid, dry, air-conditioned, dirty, greasy, noisy, sudden temperature changes, etc.)? What are the social conditions of the job (works alone, works around others, works with the public, works under close supervision, works under minimal supervision, works under deadlines, etc.)?

WORKER QUALIFICATIONS

1. What are the physical requirements (lifting, driving, cleaning, etc.)?

2. What are the general skills needed for the job (ability to read, write, add, etc.)?

3. What specific training is necessary? Can it be obtained on the job?

4. What previous experience, if any, can replace or be substituted for the specific training requirements?

HOW TO USE THE JOB ANALYSIS

Once the job analysis has been completed, one is in a better position to:

1. Develop objective, job-related interview questions.

2. Write current and accurate job descriptions. Job descriptions should be updated on a regular basis and a job analysis done if any factors outlined above have to be altered.

3. Perform objective performance appraisals.

4. Determine if accommodations can assist a person with a disability to perform the job.

5. Conduct personnel functions in a non-discriminatory manner.

or medical conditions do not rise to levels of an impairment, such as one's height, build, or singing voice. Similarly, it is clear that employers are free to decide that some limiting, but not substantially limiting, impairments may make some individuals less suited for a job than others. Of course, state employment laws may define disability in broader terms than the ADA.

Job Description Defense

The ADA provides that, in the event of a discrimination charge, consideration be given to the employer's judgment as to what functions of a job are essential. In this connection, if an employer has prepared a written description before advertising or interviewing applicants for the job, this description will be considered

Some Suggestions for Communicating with Persons with Disabilities

1. When talking with a person with a disability, speak directly to that person rather than through a companion or sign language interpreter who may be present.

2. When introduced to a person with a disability, it is appropriate to offer to shake hands. People with limited hand use or who wear an artificial limb can usually shake hands. (Shaking hands with the left hand is an acceptable greeting.)

3. When meeting a person with a visual impairment, always identify yourself and others who may be with you. When conversing in a group, remember to identify the person to whom you are speaking.

4. If you offer assistance, wait until the offer is accepted. Then listen to or ask for instructions.

5. Treat adults as adults. Address people who have disabilities by their first names only when extending that same familiarity to others. (Never patronize people who use wheelchairs by patting them on the head or shoulder.)

6. Leaning or hanging on a person's wheelchair is similar to leaning or hanging on a person and is generally considered annoying. The chair is part of the personal body space of the person who uses it.

7. Listen attentively when you are talking with a person who has difficulty speaking. Be patient and wait for the person to finish, rather than correcting or speaking for the person. If necessary, ask short questions that require short answers, a nod or a shake of the head. Never pretend to understand if you are having difficulty doing so. Instead, repeat what you have understood and allow the person to respond. The response will clue in and guide your understanding.

8. When speaking with a person in a wheelchair or a person who uses crutches, place yourself at eye level in front of the person to facilitate the conversation.

9. To get the attention of a person who is hearing-impaired, tap the person on the shoulder or wave your hand. Look directly at the person and speak clearly, slowly, and expressively to establish if the person can read your lips. Not all people with a hearing impairment can lip-read. For those who do lip-read, be sensitive to their needs by placing yourself facing the light source and keeping hands, cigarettes, and food away from your mouth when speaking.

10. Relax. Don't be embarrassed if you innocently happen to use inappropriate, but accepted, common expressions such as "See you later," or "Did you hear about this," that seem to relate to the person's disability.

evidence of the essential function of the job. Naturally, the written description will not be dispositive, but it will be a beginning point for the factfinder's evaluation and could prevent a court or jury from substituting its judgment for the employer's. In order to comply with the law, the job description must be current and well detailed, and should be based upon the job analysis suggestions provided in this Chapter.

Employment Testing and Job Selection

Under the law, discrimination on an adverse impact basis includes using qualification standards, employment tests, or other selection criteria that screen out or tend to screen out an individual with a disability or a class of individuals with disabilities unless the standard, test, or other selection criteria is shown to be job-related for the position in question, and is consistent with business necessity.

Discrimination includes failing to select and administer tests so as best to ensure that, when the test is administered to an applicant or employee with a disability that impairs sensory, manual, or speaking skills, the test results accurately reflect the individual's job skills, aptitude, or whatever other factor the test purports to measure. The employer must ensure than any test used does not, instead, measure the individual's impaired sensory, manual, or speaking skills (except where those skills are the factors that the test purports to measure).

Pre-Employment Disability-Related Questions

Under the Americans with Disabilities Act of 1990 (ADA), an employer may ask disability-related questions only after the applicant has been given a conditional job offer.

Under the law, an employer may not ask disability-related questions until after it makes a conditional job offer to the applicant. This

helps ensure that an applicant's possible hidden disability (including a prior history of a disability) is not considered before the employer evaluates an applicant's non-medical qualifications. An employer may not ask disability-related questions pre-offer even if it intends to look at the answers or results only at the post-offer stage.

Although employers may not ask disability-related questions or require medical examinations at the pre-offer stage, they may do a wide variety of things to evaluate whether an applicant is qualified for the job, including the following:

- Employers may ask about an applicant's ability to perform specific job functions. For example, an employer may state the physical requirements of a job (such as the ability to lift a certain amount of weight, or the ability to climb ladders), and ask if an applicant can satisfy these requirements.

- Employers may ask about an applicant's non-medical qualifications and skills, such as the applicant's education, work history, and required certifications and licenses.

- Employers may ask applicants to describe or demonstrate how they would perform job tasks.

Once a conditional job offer is made, the employer may ask disability-related questions as long as this is done for all entering employees in that job category. If the employer rejects the applicant after a disability-related question, and a charge is filed, investigators will closely scrutinize whether the rejection was based on the results of that question.

If the question screens out an individual because of a disability, the employer must demonstrate that the reason for the rejection is "job-related and consistent with business necessity."

In addition, if the individual is screened out for safety reasons, the employer must demonstrate that the individual poses a "direct threat." This means that the individual poses a significant risk of substantial harm to him/herself or others, and that the risk cannot be reduced below the direct threat level through reasonable accommodation.

For questions relating to drug/alcohol use, please refer to Chapter 13 for an explanation of an employer's right to make such inquiries.

Medical Examination

Under the Americans with Disabilities Act of 1990, an employer may require a medical examination of an applicant only after the applicant has been given a conditional job offer.

A "medical examination" is a procedure or test that seeks information about an individual's physical or mental impairment or health.

At the pre-offer stage, an employer cannot require examinations that seek information about physical or mental impairments or health. It is not always easy to determine whether something is a medical examination. The following factors are helpful in determining whether a procedure or test is medical:

- Is it administered by a health care professional or someone trained by a health care professional?

- Are the results interpreted by a health care professional or someone trained by a health care professional?

- Is it designed to reveal an impairment or physical or mental health?

- Is the employer trying to determine the applicant's physical or mental health or impairments?

- Is it invasive (for example, does it require the drawing of blood, urine, or breath)?

- Does it measure an applicant's performance of a task, or does it measure the applicant's physiological responses to performing the task?

- Is it normally given in a medical setting (for example, a health care professional's office)?

- Is medical equipment used?

In many cases, a combination of factors will be relevant in determining whether a procedure or test is a medical examination. In some cases, one factor may be enough to determine that a procedure or test is medical.

Post Offer Activities

After making a job offer to an applicant, an employer may ask disability-related questions and perform medical examinations. The job offer may be conditioned on the answers to post offer disability-related questions or the results of medical examinations.

At the "post offer" stage, an employer may ask about an individual's workers' compensation history, prior sick leave usage, illnesses/diseases/impairments, and general physical and mental health. Disability-related questions and medical examinations at the post offer stage do not have to be related to the job.

If an employer asks post offer disability-related questions, or requires post offer medical examinations, it must make sure that all entering cmployees in the same job category must be subjected to the examination/inquiry, regardless of disability.

Medical Confidentiality

An employer must keep any medical information on applicants or employees confidential, with the following limited exceptions:

- Supervisors and managers may be told about necessary restrictions on the work or duties of the employee and about necessary accommodations;

- First aid and safety personnel may be told if the disability might require emergency treatment;

- Government officials investigating compliance with the ADA must be given relevant information on request;

- Employers may give information to state workers' compensation offices, state second injury funds, or workers' compensation insurance carriers in accordance with state workers' compensation laws; and

- Employers may use the information for insurance purposes.

Examples of Permissible/Impermissible Disability-Related Questions

Diabetes – An individual with diabetes applying for a receptionist position voluntarily discloses that she will need periodic breaks to take medication. The employer may ask the applicant questions about the reasonable accommodation such as how often she will need breaks, and how long the breaks must be. Of course, the employer may not ask any questions about the underlying physical condition.

Visual Impairment – An applicant with a severe visual impairment applies for a job involving computer work. The employer may ask whether he will need reasonable accommodation to perform the functions of the job. If the applicant answers "no," the employer may not ask additional questions about reasonable accommodation (although, of course, the employer could ask the applicant to describe or demonstrate performance). If the applicant says that he will need accommodation, the employer may ask questions about the type of required accommodation such as, "What will you need?" If the applicant says he needs software that increases the size of text on the computer screen, the employer may ask questions such as, "Who makes that software?" "Do you need a particular brand?" or "Is that software compatible with our computers?" However, the employer *may not* ask questions about the applicant's underlying condition. In addition, the employer *may not* ask reasonable accommodation questions that are unrelated to job functions such as, "Will you need reasonable accommodation to get to the cafeteria?"

Absentee Record – An employer may ask an applicant, "How many Mondays or Fridays were you absent last year on leave other than approved vacation leave?"

However, at the pre-offer stage, an employer may not ask how many days an applicant was sick, because these questions relate directly to the severity of an individual's impairments. Therefore, these questions are likely to elicit information about a disability.

Workers' Compensation – An employer may not ask applicants about job-related injuries or workers' compensation history. These questions relate directly to the severity of an applicant's impairments. Therefore, these questions are likely to elicit information about disability.

Physical Impairment – An employer may ask questions about an applicant's impairments. If the particular question is not likely to elicit information about whether the applicant has a disability, it is permissible. It is important to remember that not all impairments will be disabilities; an impairment is a disability only if it substantially limits a major life activity. So, an employer may ask an applicant with a broken leg how she broke her leg. Since a broken leg normally is a temporary condition which does not rise to the level of a disability, this question is not likely to disclose whether the applicant has a disability. But, such questions as "Do you expect the leg to heal normally?" or "Do your bones break easily?" would be disability-related. Certainly, an employer may not ask a broad question about impairments that is likely to elicit information about disability, such as, "What impairments do you have?"

Medical information must be collected and maintained on separate forms and in separate medical files. An employer should not place any medically-related material in an employee's non-medical personnel file. If an employer wants to put a document in a personnel file, and that document happens to contain some medical information, the employer must simply remove the medical information from the document before putting it in the personnel file. An employer must keep medical information confidential even if someone is no longer an applicant or is no longer an employee.

Threat to Safety Defense

The ADA permits employers to impose as a qualification standard that an individual "not pose a direct threat to the health or safety of other individuals in the workplace." In the case of a legal challenge, the employer would have the onus of proving that the engagement of a disabled individual poses a direct threat to health or safety.

The EEOC has defined "direct threat" in a highly circumscribed manner; therefore, an employer should rely on the defense with caution and careful evaluation of the actual requirements

Examples of What Is/Is Not a Medical Examination

Example 1 – An employer requires applicants to lift a 30-pound box and carry it 20 feet. This is not a medical examination; it is just a test of whether the applicant can perform this task. But, if the employer takes the applicant's blood pressure or heart rate after the lifting and carrying, the test would be a medical examination because it is measuring the applicant's physiological response to lifting and carrying, as opposed to the applicant's ability to lift and carry.

Example 2 – A psychological test is designed to reveal mental illness, but a particular employer says it does not give the test to disclose mental illness (for example, the employer says it uses the test to disclose just tastes and habits). But, the test also is interpreted by a psychologist, and is routinely used in a clinical setting to provide evidence that would lead to a diagnosis of a mental disorder or impairment (for example, whether an applicant has paranoid tendencies, or is depressed). Under these facts, this test is a medical examination.

Example 3 – An employer may require applicants to take physical agility tests. A physical agility test, in which an applicant demonstrates the ability to perform actual or simulated job tasks, is not a medical examination under the ADA. Thus, if a police department tests officer applicants' ability to run through an obstacle course designed to simulate a suspect chase in an urban setting, the test is not a medical examination.

Example 4 – A messenger service tests applicants' ability to run one mile in 15 minutes. At the end of the run, the employer takes the applicants' blood pressure and heart rate. Measuring the applicants' physiological responses makes this a medical examination.

Example 5 – An employer may ask an applicant to provide medical certification that one can safely perform a physical agility or physical fitness test. Although an employer cannot ask disability-related questions, it may give the applicant a description of the agility or fitness test and ask the applicant to have a private physician simply state whether one can safely perform the test.

of a job and the nature of an individual's disability. Conjecture, prejudice, speculation, or fear cannot support this defense.

"Direct threat" means a significant risk of substantial harm to the health or safety of the individual or others that cannot be eliminated or reduced by reasonable accommodation. The determination that an individual poses a "direct threat" shall be based on an individualized assessment of the individual's present ability to safely perform the essential functions of the job. This assessment shall be based on a reasonable medical judgment that relies on the most current medical knowledge and/or on the best available objective evidence. In determining whether an individual would pose a "direct threat," the factors to be considered include:

1. The duration of the risk;

2. The nature and severity of the potential harm;

3. The likelihood that the potential harm will occur; and

4. The imminence of the potential harm.

Enforcement and Recordkeeping

Please refer to Chapter 4 for an expanded treatment of the enforcement and recordkeeping requirements of the EEOC, which is the federal agency responsible for administering the ADA.

Age Discrimination 8

Legislative Purpose

In 1967, Congress passed the Age Discrimination in Employment Act (ADEA) to prohibit discrimination in employment because of age in such matters as hiring, job retention, compensation, and other terms, conditions, and privileges of employment. The ADEA establishes as a matter of basic civil rights that people should be treated in employment on the basis of their individual ability to perform a job rather than on the basis of stereotypes about age. Indeed, the ADEA has created a new awareness concerning discrimination against the elderly and has spurred a great deal of academic research which concludes that chronological age alone is an unreliable indicator of ability to perform a job. The law is enforced by the Equal Employment Opportunity Commission.

Coverage

The law prohibits employers with 20 or more employees, public employers, employment agencies serving such employers, and labor organizations with 24 or more members from discriminating against persons over the age of 40 on the basis of their job. The operative language of the statute makes it unlawful for an employer to:

1. Fail or refuse to hire or to discharge any individual or to discriminate against an individual with respect to compensation, terms, conditions, or privileges of employment because of age;

2. Limit, segregate, or classify employees in any way which would deprive or tend to deprive any individual of employment opportunities, or otherwise adversely affect his or her status as an employee because of age; or

3. Reduce the wage rate of any employees in order to comply with the Act.

To establish a prima facie case of age discrimination, an employee or applicant must prove that they were: (i) a member of the protected class; (ii) suffered an adverse employment action; and (iii) the adverse employment was motivated by age. In proving a causal connection, an employee or applicant typically show they were qualified but a younger, less qualified individual received the opportunity denied them.

In 1996, the U.S. Supreme Court ruled that employees are not required to show they were replaced by someone outside the above-40 age group protected by the ADEA in order to establish a prima facie case of age bias. The replacement by someone "substantially" younger than the plaintiff, whether or not that person is 40 or older, will suffice to establish the requirement that the adverse employment occurred under circumstances suggesting discrimination and shift the burden of proof to the defendant. The Court stated, "the fact that one person in the protected class has lost out to another person in the protected class is thus irrelevant, so long as he has lost out because of his age."

In 1996, the Sixth Circuit Court of Appeals applied the hostile-environment doctrine in an ADEA action. Previously, the EEOC had taken the position that this kind of claim is cognizable under the ADEA. For a hostile work environment claim to be established, the Court indicated the following elements must be present:

1. The employee must be 40 years old or older;

2. The employee must be subject to harassment based on age;

3. The harassment must unreasonably interfere with the employee's work performance or create an objectively intimidating, hostile, or offensive work based environment; and

4. The employer must be responsible for the conduct which created these conditions.

Some Practical Advice

Two traditional trouble spots for employers are "help wanted" advertisements and job application forms. The EEOC regulations provide some useful guidance:

1. **"Help Wanted" Ads** – When "help wanted" notices or advertisements contain terms such as "age 25 to 35," "young," "college student," "recent college graduate," "boy," "girl," or other phrases of a similar nature, such a term or phrase deters the employment of older persons and their usage is a violation of the Act, unless one of the exceptions applies. Such phrases as "age 40 to 50," "age over 65," "retired person," or "supplement your pension" discriminate against others within the protected group and, therefore, are prohibited unless one of the exceptions applies. (The "exceptions" are explained in subsequent sections of this chapter.)

2. **Employment Applications** – A request on the part of an employer for information such as "Date of Birth" or "State Age" on

an employment application form is not, in itself, a violation of the Act.[1] But because the request that an applicant state his or her age may tend to deter older applicants or otherwise indicate discrimination based on age, employment application forms which request such information will be closely scrutinized to assure that the request is for a permissible purpose. The EEOC recommends that an application form contain language to the following effect:

> *"The Age Discrimination in Employment Act of 1967 prohibits discrimination on the basis of age with respect to individuals who are over 40 years of age."*

The term "employment application," refers to all written inquiries about employment or applications for employment or promotion including resumes or other summaries of the applicant's background. [Due to the different definitions of age discrimination under the various state anti-discrimination statutes, addition of such a statement alone could prove to be confusing and problematic.]

Many reported cases involve inappropriate comments which relate to age. Comments may be direct references to age such as you "can't teach an old dog new tricks", "we need some new or young blood in here" or "we need to get rid of some dead wood". There is also a substantial amount of litigation based on what can be described as indirect or code words for being too old. For example, the word "overqualified" in conversations with applicants in the protected age group has been ruled to be such a code word. Indeed, one appeals court found that the use of the word by itself is enough to deny summary judgment and justify a trial on the issue of age discrimination. Therefore, it is sound practice to avoid telling

---

1. Keep in mind that various state anti-discrimination statutes may make such pre-employment inquiries illegal. Further, answers to pre-employment inquiries concerning age prevent an employer defending against an ADEA claim from asserting lack of knowledge as to the applicant's age.

job applicants that they are overqualified. Often times, certain characteristics highly correlated to age and conversation concerning those characteristics can be evidence of age discrimination. An example is the high correlation between salary and age, particularly in a seniority based compensation system. Comments to an employee indicating he was not hired or selected for layoff because he is too "highly compensated," can create age discrimination issues.

Exemptions

There are certain situations which are exempt from the ADEA. They are the following:

1. When age is a bona fide job qualification reasonably necessary to the normal operation of a particular business; e.g., modeling clothes for teenagers. This exemption is very limited in scope and application. The employer asserting this defense has the burden of showing that the age limit is reasonably necessary.

2. When the differentiation is based on reasonable factors other than age, such as the use of stringent physical requirements necessitated by the nature of the work, ADEA prohibitions do not apply.

3. When differentiations are based on the terms of a bona fide seniority system or any bona fide employee benefit plan, such as a retirement, pension, or insurance plan, the actions are exempt from the ADEA. No employee benefit plan, however, can excuse the failure to hire any individual, and no such seniority system or employee benefit plan shall require or permit the involuntary retirement of an individual upon reaching any specific age. The mandatory retirement prohibition applies to all new and existing seniority systems and employer benefit plans. Therefore, any system or plan provision requiring or permitting

involuntary retirement is unlawful, regardless of whether the provision was part of an agreement entered into prior to the 1967 Act or the subsequent amendments.

4. Another exception to the prohibition on mandatory retirement at any age covers state and local governments with mandatory retirement ages for firefighters and law enforcement officers.

5. When an individual has, for a two-year period prior to retirement, been employed in a bona fide executive or high policy-making position, and is entitled to an immediate, nonforfeitable, annual retirement benefit from a pension, profit-sharing, savings, or deferred compensation plan which equals at least $44,000, then compulsory retirement at 65 is not prohibited. Therefore, an employee within the exemption can lawfully be forced to retire on account of age at age 65 or above. The "executive" position does not apply to middle-management employees who exercise substantial executive authority over a significant number of employees and a large volume of business. The term "high policy-making position" is likewise expected to have limited application. It is limited to those who are not "executive" but whose position and responsibility are such that they play a significant role in the development of corporate policy and effectively recommend implementing actions.

6. When there is a bona fide apprenticeship program, which has been traditionally limited to training younger persons for skilled employment, the ADEA prohibitions do not apply.

New Benefit Equivalence Provisions

Amendments to the Age Discrimination in Employment Act require that employees 65 and older be entitled to coverage under any group health plans offered to employees under age 65 under the same terms and conditions. For example, any employee age 65 or older must be offered spousal coverage, if employees under the age of 65 are offered such coverage. Further, each employee in the age group of 65 or older must be offered the opportunity to elect any group health plan offered by the employer. With this group, employers have an additional obligation to explain how Medicare coverage complements the employer's plans.

Older Workers Protection Act

In 1990, Congress passed the Older Workers Benefit Protection Act amending ADEA in two important respects. The law makes clear that discrimination on the basis of age, in virtually all forms of employee benefits, is unlawful. In addition, the law set forth certain requirements in order to ensure that older workers are not coerced or manipulated into waiving their rights to seek legal relief under the ADEA.

1. **Employee Benefits** — The new law clarifies and restores one of the original purposes of the ADEA, the eradication of age discrimination in employee benefits. The law overturns both the reasoning and holding of a 1989 Supreme Court case, *Public Employees Retirement System of Ohio v. Betts*, in which the Court permitted arbitrary age discrimination in employee benefit plans.

   The amendment reaffirmed what is known as the "equal benefit or equal cost principle" which ensures that productive older workers, an ever-growing segment of the labor force, are not discouraged from remaining actively employed. Employers invoking this defense are required to either provide equal benefits to, or incur equal cost for benefits on behalf of, all employees. For example, if a $100 contribution purchases

$50,000 of life insurance coverage for an employee age 35 and only $25,000 worth of life insurance coverage for an employee age 60, that difference in coverage can be lawful if certain requirements are met. Congress has made clear that employers bear the burden of proving this defense.

The law does recognize a few limited exceptions to this "equal benefit or equal cost" requirement. One involves defined benefit pension plans, in which case there is a safe harbor provided for three specified practices. Another exception involves instances in which there is benefit coordination (e.g., retirement health benefits and severance pay). Finally, in the case of early retirement incentive plans, the law will allow them provided they are truly voluntary, are made available for a reasonable period of time, and do not result in arbitrary age discrimination.

Employees eligible for early retirement incentive plans must be given sufficient time to consider their option, particularly in circumstances when no previous retirement counseling has been provided. Eligible employees must be provided complete and accurate information regarding the benefits available under the plan. If subsequent layoffs or terminations are contemplated or discussed, employees should be advised of the criteria by which those decisions will be made. The critical question involving an allegation of involuntary retirement is whether, under the circumstances, a reasonable person would have concluded that there was no choice but to accept the offer.

2. **Waiver of Rights** – Congress expressly provided that waivers may be valid and enforceable under the ADEA so long as the waiver is "knowing and voluntary."

The ADEA provides, as part of the minimum requirements for a knowing and voluntary waiver, that:

> "the waiver is part of an agreement between the individual and the employer that is written in a manner calculated to be understood by such individual, or by the average individual eligible to participate."

In 1998, the EEOC provided guidelines concerning the minimum requirements necessary in order to demonstrate that a waiver is knowing and voluntary on how

How to Draft a Waiver

1. Waiver agreements must be drafted in plain language geared to the level of understanding of the individual party to the agreement or individuals eligible to participate. Employers should take into account such factors as the level of comprehension and education of typical participants.

   Consideration of these factors usually will require the limitation or elimination of technical jargon and of long, complex sentences.

2. The waiver agreement must not have the effect of misleading, misinforming, or failing to inform participants and affected individuals. Any advantages or disadvantages described shall be presented without either exaggerating the benefits or minimizing the limitations.

3. The exit incentive or other employment termination programs offered should be conveyed "in writing in a manner calculated to be understood by the average participant."

4. The waiver should specifically refer to rights or claims under the Age Discrimination in Employment Act (ADEA) by name in connection with the waiver.

5. The individual must be "advised in writing to consult with an attorney prior to executing the agreement."

6. The waiver of future rights or claims that may arise following the execution of a waiver is prohibited. However, the ADEA does not bar the enforcement of agreements to perform future employment-related actions such as the employee's agreement to retire or otherwise terminate employment at a future date.

7. A waiver may not be considered knowing and voluntary unless, at a minimum, the individual waives rights or claims only in exchange for consideration in addition to anything of value to which the individual already is entitled in absence of a waiver.

8. An employer is not required to give a person age 40 or older a greater amount of consideration for the waiver than is given to a person under the age of 40, solely because of that person's membership in the protected class under the ADEA.

9. A waiver may not be considered knowing and voluntary unless, at a minimum, (i) the individual is given a period of at least 21 days within which to consider the agreement; or (ii) if a waiver is requested in connection with an exit incentive or other employment termination program offered to a group or class of employees, the individual is given a period of at least 45 days within which to consider the agreement. (The term "exit incentive or other employment termination program" includes both voluntary and involuntary programs.)

How to Draft a Waiver (continued)

10. A waiver may not be considered knowing and voluntary unless, at a minimum, the agreement provides that for a period of at least 7 days following the execution of such agreement, the individual may revoke the agreement, and the agreement shall not become effective or enforceable until the revocation period has expired. The 7 day revocation period cannot be shortened by the parties, by agreement or otherwise.

11. The 21 or 45 day period runs from the date of the employer's final offer. Material changes to the final offer restart the running of the 21 or 45 day period and, conversely, non-material changes to the final offer do not restart the running of the 21 or 45 day period. The parties may agree, however, that changes, whether material or immaterial, do not restart the running of the 21 or 45 day period.

12. An employee may sign a release prior to the end of the 21 or 45 day time period, thereby commencing the mandatory 7 days revocation period. This is permissible as long as the employee's decision to accept such shortening of time is knowing and voluntary and is not induced by the employer through fraud, misrepresentation, or threat to withdraw or alter the offer prior to the expiration of the 21 or 45 day time period, the employer may expedite the processing of the consideration provided in exchange for the waiver.

13. If the waiver is requested in connection with an exit incentive or other employment termination program, there is an additional requirement to provide the employee with enough information regarding the program to allow an informed choice as to whether or not to sign a waiver agreement. Employers must disclose to the employee presented with the waiver request, the job titles and ages of employees affected by a program in an easy-to-understand format that compares them to unaffected employees in the same job classification. Presumably, this will provide affected employees with enough information, and adequate time to consult with an attorney, in order to decide if they want to sign a waiver agreement. The rule prohibits employers from supplying age-related information in bands broader than one year (for example, describing a group as "age 20 to 30"). Finally, an employer seeking to establish the validity of a waiver agreement has the burden of proving that it was knowingly and voluntarily executed. The required information must be given to each person in the decisional unit who is asked to sign a waiver agreement.

---

to prepare a waiver. Highlights of the guidelines are summarized below:

In circumstances where there is a challenge to the waiver by a plaintiff who retains monies paid in exchange for the waiver, the Supreme Court has ruled that this does not amount to a ratification when the waiver did not otherwise meet the "knowing and voluntary" standard. In other words, the employee is not required to tender back the money in order to challenge a waiver as being invalid under the ADEA. The EEOC has issued regulations that restate this Supreme Court ruling. The regulation expressly states that an individual may retain severance benefits, even if he or she subsequently challenges the validity of the waiver under the ADEA. The EEOC considers any covenant not to sue or any action taken which adversely affect any individual's right to challenge a waiver as invalid under the ADEA. The regulations do permit, however, in appropriate circumstances, that an employer may assert a setoff claim against an employee who recovers damages in a subsequent lawsuit. The restitution, however, cannot be greater than the amount paid to the employee. Finally, the EEOC rules require an employer to honor its agreement with other employees, even when the validity of a waiver is successfully challenged by an employee.

Defending the Age Discrimination Lawsuit

In observing employment litigation trends over the years in an economy that has experienced considerable downsizing, the ADEA is often the "statute of choice" for either unfair termination or improper selection in a reduction in force situation. If one is within the protected age group, and the safe harbor of "seniority" was not the sole reason for selection for termination, those over 40 years of age often seek redress under the ADEA.

Since an aggrieved party can fairly easily assert a claim merely by showing that termination was on account "of age," the burden of proof is then on the employer to prove otherwise. Often times, a new supervisor or a tighter economy result in the performance of long term employees, once acceptable, no longer being adequate. These cases present unique challenges and must be carefully handled. It is important that there is ample documentation in the personnel file regarding that individual's performance (e.g., evaluations, reprimands, etc.), opportunities to improve and the need for improvement. In a reduction in force, the relevant statistics of the population eligible for selection and the relevant statistics of those actually selected should be reviewed and analyzed before any decisions are made.

For additional insights on handling terminations, refer to "Termination: A Planned Event" and "How To Handle a Termination" in Chapter 16, Human Resource Management/The Basics.

Recordkeeping

There is no precise order or form for the required records for ADEA compliance. The following information is required to be kept for three years:

1. Employee's Name
2. Address
3. Date of Birth
4. Occupation
5. Rate of Pay
6. Compensation Earned Each Week

The following information must be kept for one year from the date of the personnel action to which any records relate:

1. Job applications, resumes, or any other form of employment inquiry that was submitted to the employer in response to an advertisement or other notice of existing or anticipated job openings, including records pertaining to the failure or refusal to hire any individual;

2. Promotion, demotion, transfer, selection for training, layoff, recall, or discharge of any employee;

3. Job orders submitted by the employer to an employment agency or labor organization for recruitment of personnel for job openings;

4. Test papers completed by applicants or candidates for any position which disclose the results of any employer-administered aptitude or other employment test considered by the employer in connection with any personnel action;

5. The results of any physical examination where such examination is considered by the employer in connection with any personnel action; and

6. Any advertisements or notices to the public or to employees relating to job

openings, promotions, training programs, or opportunities for overtime work.

Finally, there are two further special requirements concerning benefit plans and application forms:

1. Every employer must keep on file any employee benefit plan such as pension and insurance plans, as well as copies of any seniority systems and merit systems which are in writing, for the full period the plan or system is in effect, and for at least one year after its termination. If the plan or system is not in writing, a memorandum fully outlining the terms of such plan or system and the manner in which it has been communicated to the affected employees, together with notations relating to any changes or revisions, must be kept on file for a like period.

2. Application forms and other pre-employment records of applicants for positions which are, and are known by applicants to be, of a temporary nature, must be kept for a period of 90 days from the date of the personnel action to which the record relates.

Enforcement and Remedies

For a full description of enforcement and remedies, please refer to Chapter 4 (EEOC Enforcement Procedures), which describes the EEOC Compliance Program.

Occupational Safety and Health 9

Legislative Purpose

In 1970, Congress passed landmark legislation establishing the Occupational Safety and Health Administration (OSHA) within the Department of Labor. The Act's purpose was to:

1. Encourage employers and employees to reduce workplace hazards and implement new or improved existing safety and health programs;

2. Provide for research in occupational safety and health and develop innovative ways of dealing with occupational safety and health problems;

3. Establish "separate but dependent responsibilities and rights" for employers and employees for the achievement of better safety and health conditions;

4. Maintain a reporting and recordkeeping system to monitor job-related injuries and illnesses;

5. Develop mandatory job safety and health standards; and

6. Provide for the development, analysis, evaluation, and approval of state occupational safety and health programs.

Coverage

In general, compliance with OSHA workplace standards and regulations extends to every employer of the 50 states and the District of Columbia, and all territories under federal jurisdiction. The Act defines an "employer" as "any person engaged in a business affecting commerce who has employees." This broad definition encompasses virtually all business enterprises. There are several exceptions, however, which are not covered by the Act (e.g., self-employed individuals, farms on which only immediate family members of the owner are employed, and workplaces already protected by other federal agencies or laws, such as mines).

Workplace Standards

The Occupational Safety and Health Act requires that all employers "shall furnish a place of employment which is free from recognized hazards that are causing or are likely to cause death or serious physical harm to their employees." To carry out this statutory requirement, OSHA is authorized to issue legally enforceable workplace safety standards, such as limitations on worker exposure to hazardous chemicals and maximum workplace noise levels.

OSHA can begin the standards-setting procedure on its own initiative or upon petition from other parties, such as employers or labor organizations, the federal National Institute for Occupational Safety and Health, or even interested individuals. Once OSHA determines that there is a need to propose, amend, or delete a workplace standard, the agency will publish its intentions in the Federal Register. This notice will include the rationale for the regulation and provide an opportunity (usually 60 days) for affected organizations and individuals to comment on the proposal. Often, public hearings are held to solicit additional information. Following the close of the comment period, OSHA evaluates all information and makes a determination as whether to issue a final standard. OSHA also has the option of deciding that no standard or amendment is required. In certain limited circumstances, OSHA may set emergency safety standards which can take effect immediately, but the agency must first conclude that workers are in "grave danger."

OSHA workplace standards fall into four major categories: general industry, construction, agriculture and maritime. All employers are responsible for complying with the OSHA regulations affecting their particular businesses.

OSHA Hazard Communication Standard

More and more substances in today's workplace are being viewed as hazardous – and not necessarily life threatening, although they may be. In fact, OSHA estimates there are some 575,000 existing chemical products in the workplace. OSHA also estimates 32 million workers are potentially exposed to one or more chemical hazards.

As a result, all employers covered by OSHA must comply with OSHA's Hazard Communication Standard. While some states also require employers to disclose to employees the use of hazardous chemicals, the Hazard Communication Standard is broader in scope and preempts state law, where applicable. Given the broad scope of the rule, and the fact that it requires employers to undertake certain affirmative action to educate and train workers, it is important that every employer become familiar with the basic rule.

Purpose – To ensure that the hazards of all chemicals produced or imported by chemical manufacturers or importers are evaluated and that information concerning their hazards is transmitted to affected employers and employees. This transmittal of information is to be accomplished by means of comprehensive hazard communication programs, which are to include container labeling and other forms of warning, material safety data sheets, and employee training.

Scope and Application – Requires all chemical manufacturers or importers to assess the hazards of chemicals which they produce or import. Employers are then responsible for informing their employees about the hazardous materials to which they are exposed.

A chemical is considered hazardous if it:

1. Is on the OSHA Z list;

2. Is listed in the "Threshold Limit Values for Chemical Substances and Physical Agents in the Work Environment," American Conference of Governmental Industrial Hygienists;

3. Is a carcinogen;

4. Is a physical hazard because it is a combustible liquid; compressed gas; explosive; flammable; organic peroxide; oxidizer, pyrophoric; unstable (reactive); water reactive; or

5. Is a health hazard because of the existence of statistically significant and scientifically valid evidence that exposure to the chemical can cause acute or chronic adverse health effects.

Written Hazard Communication Program – Employers must develop and put into practice a written hazard communication program for their workplaces which describes their procedures for using material safety data sheets, labels and other forms of warning, and employee information and training. The written program should also contain a list of the hazardous chemicals known to be present, the methods of safety training for non-routine tasks where chemicals are involved, and the methods for insuring that independent contractors are properly trained.

Labels and Other Forms of Warning – The chemical manufacturer, importer, or distributor must ensure that each container of hazardous chemicals is labeled, tagged, or marked with: (i) the identity of the hazardous chemical(s) (this identity should correspond with the name on the material safety data sheet); (ii) an appropriate hazard warning; and (iii) the name and address of the chemical manufacturer, importer, or other responsible party. The employer must ensure that labels or other forms of warning are legible, in English, and prominently displayed on the container, or readily available in the work area throughout each work shift.

Material Safety Data Sheets (MSDS's) – Chemical manufacturers and importers must develop or obtain an MSDS for each hazardous chemical which they use, and must ensure that copies of the required MSDS's are readily accessible during each work shift to employees when they are in their work area(s), and make them available, upon request, to designated representatives of the employees and to OSHA officials.

OSHA has updated its rules for providing employee access to MSDS's and clarifies the issue of electronic access to MSDS's, stating that employers may provide MSDS's to employees through computers, microfiche machines, the Internet, CD-ROM and fax machines.

Employers using electronic means must ensure that: (i) reliable devices are readily accessible in the workplace at all times; (ii) that workers are trained in the use of these devices, including specific software; (iii) that there is an adequate back-up system in the event of the failure of that system, such as power outages or on-line access delays; and (iv) that the system is part of the overall hazard communication program of the workplace. Additionally, employees must be able to access hard copies of the MSDS's and, in medical emergencies, employers must be immediately able to provide copies of MSDS's to medical personnel.

Employee Information and Training — Each employee who routinely works with any hazardous chemical must be trained regarding:

- the physical and health hazards of the chemicals in the work area;

- methods and observations that may be used to detect the presence or release of a hazardous chemical in the work area;

- the protective measures available, including specific safety procedures, appropriate work practices, emergency procedures, and personal protective equipment to be used; and

- the details of the employer's hazard communication program, including an explanation of the labeling and MSDS's.

Work Environment Issues

Physical working conditions are becoming increasingly important to employees. Since the enactment of the Occupational Safety and Health Act (OSHA), workplace safety has been widely publicized. Therefore, employee information concerning hazardous working conditions should be solicited and, if legitimate, acted upon. Safety on the job should be encouraged and rewarded.

Apart from safety, employers must consider other physical aspects of the working environment to make it as conducive to productivity and employee morale as possible. If practicable, facilities such as cafeterias, lunch rooms, vending machines, break areas and lounges should be made available. In addition, keeping these areas clean and properly maintained demonstrates appropriate consideration and respect for the employees' general well-being and safety.

Restricting Smoking in the Workplace – Increasingly, state laws require workplaces to be free of tobacco smoke. Some employers have taken it even further by attempting to not hire smokers or make them pay more for insurance.

A non-smoking policy that is limited to the workplace should withstand a legal challenge based upon discrimination. However, there are many state laws that protect employees from discrimination for off duty conduct including the use of consumable products. Management often rationalizes the benefits of a smoke-free workforce by pointing to increased productivity and decreased health care claims. In a unionized setting, smoking policies may be a mandatory subject of bargaining and not susceptible to unilateral implementation.

Recent data reveal that smokers have an absenteeism rate 33 to 45 percent greater than that of nonsmokers, use medical systems 25 percent more than nonsmokers, and are significantly more likely to experience disability and premature death. The smoking habits of employees reportedly cost industry some $12.8 billion annually.

The Environmental Protection Agency and the U.S. Surgeon General have concluded that environmental tobacco smoke is a major contributor of particulate indoor air pollution. Thus, the Federal government proposes that "employers and employees should ensure that the act of smoking does not expose nonsmokers to environmental tobacco smoke, by restricting smoking to separately ventilated areas or banning smoking from buildings."

Video Display Terminals – There has been considerable media attention given to VDT health and safety issues. Employers, therefore, can anticipate some questions from employees on such subjects as physical discomfort, eye fatigue, radiation, etc. VDT's present no known health or safety risks to users, when they are ergonomically well designed and used in suitable work environments.

The Workplace Inspection

OSHA's considerable authority to regulate working conditions is enhanced by the agency's power to conduct workplace inspections and impose citations and penalties for workplace conditions which violate OSHA regulations.

Obviously, not all of the estimated six million businesses covered by the Occupational Safety and Health Act can be inspected on a regular basis. OSHA, therefore, has established a system of priorities which targets a business for inspection.

"Imminent danger situations" are given top priority. An imminent danger situation is defined as "any condition where there is reasonable certainty that a danger exists that can be expected to cause harm to employees."

Second priority is given to investigation of "fatalities" and "catastrophes" resulting in hospitalization of five or more employees. These situations must be reported to OSHA by the employer within 48 hours, and inspections are made to determine if OSHA standards were violated and to avoid recurrence of similar accidents.

Third priority is given to employee complaints of alleged violation of standards or of unsafe or unhealthful working conditions. The law gives each employee the right to request an OSHA inspection when the employee feels in imminent danger from a hazard or when that individual feels that there is a violation of an OSHA standard that threatens physical harm.

Finally, OSHA pursues programmed inspections aimed at specific high-hazard industries, occupations, or health substances. Industries are selected for inspection on the basis of factors such as the death, injury, or illness incidence rates, and employee exposure to toxic substances.

In 1998, Congress enacted a law that prohibits OSHA officials from evaluating enforcement staff based upon the number of citations given or penalties assessed. Thus, prior practices which included the imposition of quotas or goals with regard to enforcement activities are no longer permitted.

General Inspections

OSHA responds to complaints based upon the immediacy of the risk of injury or illness. An inspection will be conducted if reasonable grounds are established to conclude that physical harm or imminent danger is a possibility. If OSHA decides an inspection is not needed, it will still notify the employer of the possible violation and necessary corrective action. The employer who receives such a letter and fails to respond or take corrective action may be subject to an on-site inspection.

OSHA will inspect only in cases of "imminent danger." However, OSHA will send a letter to the employer outlining the nature of the complaint and requesting that any potentially hazardous situation be corrected. OSHA may contact the complainant to ensure that corrective measures have been taken.

Inspection Exemptions

Workplaces with 10 or fewer employees will be exempted from generally scheduled safety inspections if they are in an industry that has a lost workday occupation injury rate lower than 3.6 cases per 100 workers, the national average injury rate for the private sector for 1984. This is the most recent period for which such data has been reported by the Bureau of Labor Statistics.

To compute your "Lost Workday Injury Rate":

1. From the OSHA Form 300, "Log and Summary of Occupational Injuries and Illnesses," count the number of injuries involving lost workdays (column 2).

2. Determine the number of hours all employees actually worked during the year, using payroll or other time records. All employees include salaried and sales forces. The "hours worked" figure should not include any non-worked time even though paid, such as vacation, sick leave, holiday, etc. The lost workday rate may be computed from the following formula:

$$\frac{\text{Number of Lost Workday Injuries} \times 2,000}{\substack{\text{Total Hours Worked By All Employees} \\ \text{During Period Covered}}}$$

$$= \text{Lost Workday Rate}$$

Self-Inspection Checklist

An OSHA Self-Inspection Checklist
recommended by the agency is reproduced below:

	OK	Action Needed		OK	Action Needed
1. Is the required OSHA workplace poster displayed in your place of business as required where all employees are likely to see it?	☐	☐	8. Are all electrical cords strung so they do not hang on pipes, nails, hooks, etc.?	☐	☐
2. Are you aware of the requirement to report all workplace fatalities and any serious accidents (where five or more are hospitalized) to a federal or state OSHA office within 48 hours?	☐	☐	9. Is there no evidence of fraying on any electrical cords?	☐	☐
			10. Are metallic cable and conduit systems properly grounded?	☐	☐
			11. Are switches mounted in clean, tightly closed boxes?	☐	☐
3. Are workplace injury and illness records being kept as required by OSHA?	☐	☐	12. Are all exits visible and unobstructed?	☐	☐
4. Are you aware that the OSHA annual summary of workplace injuries and illnesses must be posted by February 1st and must remain posted until March 1st?	☐	☐	13. Are all exits marked with a readily visible sign that is properly illuminated?	☐	☐
			14. Are there sufficient exits to ensure prompt escape in case of emergency?	☐	☐
5. Are you aware that employers with 10 or fewer employees are exempt from the OSHA recordkeeping requirements, unless they are part of an official Bureau of Labor Standards or state survey and have received specific instructions to keep records?	☐	☐	15. Are portable fire extinguishers provided in adequate number and type?	☐	☐
			16. Are fire extinguishers recharged regularly and properly noted on the inspection tag?	☐	☐
			17. Are fire extinguishers mounted in readily accessible locations?	☐	☐
6. Do all employees know what to do in emergencies?	☐	☐	18. Are NO SMOKING signs prominently posted in areas containing combustibles and flammables?	☐	☐
7. Are emergency telephone numbers posted?	☐	☐	19. Are waste receptacles provided and are they emptied regularly?	☐	☐

Self-Inspection Checklist (continued)

	OK	Action Needed		OK	Action Needed
20. Are stairways in good condition with standard railing provided for every flight having four or more risers?	☐	☐	24. Are hand tools and other equipment regularly inspected for safe condition?	☐	☐
21. Are portable wood ladders and metal ladders adequate for their purpose, in good condition, and provided with secure footing?	☐	☐	25. Are approved safety cans or other acceptable containers used for handling and dispensing flammable liquids?	☐	☐
22. Are all machines or operations that expose operators or other employees to rotating parts, pinch points, flying chips, particles, or sparks adequately guarded?	☐	☐	26. Are your first-aid supplies adequate for the potential injuries in your workplace?	☐	☐
			27. Are hard hats provided and worn where any danger of falling objects exists?	☐	☐
23. Are mechanical power transmission belts and pinch points guarded?	☐	☐	28. Are protective goggles or glasses provided and worn where there is any danger of flying particles or splashing of corrosive materials?	☐	☐

What the OSHA Inspector Will Do

Upon arriving at a worksite, an OSHA compliance officer will display official credentials and will ask to meet with the employer's representative.

Normally, the OSHA health inspector meets with an employer representative and an employee representative in an "opening conference" to discuss procedures for the inspection. When it is not practical to hold a joint employer-employee conference, separate conferences will be held. OSHA will, on request, provide written summaries of each conference.

If the inspector feels that it is necessary to observe workplace conditions without delay, the opening conference can be kept brief and, if appropriate, can be continued later.

In most cases, the inspector reviews the employer's records on health problems, noise or ventilation monitoring, and use of hazardous materials before beginning the inspection. This helps the inspector identify probable health hazards.

Next, the inspector makes a "walkaround" inspection, looking for signs of health hazards. Danger signals include:

- eye irritation
- strong odors
- visible dust or fumes in the air
- excessive noise
- spilled or leaking chemicals
- use of substances which are known to be dangerous even when handled properly.

After identifying possible hazards, the OSHA inspector takes measurements and samples, using a number of instruments to determine the levels of noise, dust, chemical vapors, and other hazards.

It may be necessary to attach some of these instruments to the workers in order to make proper measurements. Some sampling must be done over an entire shift, while other samples can be taken in a few minutes.

Some other things the inspector will look for include the following:

- Has the employer made use of engineering controls (changes in the physical work environment) or administrative controls (changes in work procedures) to reduce health hazards?

- If personal protective devices (such as respirators) are being used, are they effective in controlling the hazard involved? Are they properly fitted to the workers and properly maintained? Have workers been trained in their use?

- Are areas for eating, washing, and resting being kept isolated from work areas where there are hazardous substances?

The inspector gathers information about the employer's efforts to provide a healthy workplace, including the following:

- Monitoring of health hazards. Does the employer have qualified personnel and the right equipment to keep track of the levels of hazardous substances?

- Medical program. Does the employer provide regular medical examinations, if required, as a way of identifying health problems?

- Education and training. Does the employer conduct a training program on hazards and their control, and on emergency procedures? Are workers participating in the program?

At the end of the inspection, the inspector meets with the employer and employee representatives in a "closing conference" to discuss hazards which have been found.

If it is not practical to hold a joint conference, separate conferences will be held, and OSHA will provide written summaries, on request.

It may be necessary to send the test samples for laboratory analysis, which may take time to be analyzed. When the results are available, second conferences will be held.

Sampling results will be provided to a workers' representative.

During the closing conference, an employee representative can describe what hazards exist, what should be done to correct them, and how long it should take. The employee representative also can provide facts about the history of health and safety conditions at the workplace.

Any citation issued must be posted by the employer at or near the place where each violation occurred. Employees then have the right to:

- help check to be sure the employer corrects hazards within the deadlines OSHA sets,

- appeal those hazard correction deadlines,

- give the employee's side of the story, if the employer appeals OSHA actions.

Consultation Assistance

Consultation assistance is available to employers who want help in establishing and maintaining a safe and healthful workplace. The service is provided at no cost to the employer. No penalties are proposed and no citations are issued for hazards identified by the consultant. The service is provided to the employer with the assurance that neither his or her name, the firm nor any information about the workplace will not be routinely reported to OSHA enforcement staff.

Besides helping employers identify and correct specific hazards, consultation can include assistance in developing and implementing effective workplace safety and health programs with emphasis on the prevention of worker injuries and illnesses. Such comprehensive consultation assistance includes an appraisal of all mechanical systems, physical work practices, environmental hazards of the workplace, and all aspects of the employer's present job safety and health program. Employers may also receive training and education services, as well as limited assistance away from the worksite.

Primarily targeted for smaller employers with more hazardous operations, the consultation service is delivered by state government agencies employing professional safety consultants and health consultants. All consultation services are provided at the request of an employer. When delivered at the worksite, consultation assistance includes an opening conference with the employer to explain the ground rules for consultation, a walk through the workplace to identify any specific hazards and to examine those aspects of the employer's safety and health program which relate to the scope of the visit, and a closing conference followed by a written report to the employer of the consultant's findings and recommendations.

Possible violations of OSHA standards will not be reported to OSHA enforcement staff unless the employer fails or refuses to eliminate or control worker exposure to any identified serious hazard or imminent danger situation. In such unusual circumstances, OSHA may investigate and begin enforcement action.

Employers who receive a comprehensive consultation visit and demonstrate exemplary achievements in workplace safety and health through the abatement of all identified hazards, and who develop and implement an excellent

safety and health program, may request participation in OSHA's SHARP program. SHARP is an acronym for "Safety and Health Achievement Recognition Program." Employers who are accepted into SHARP may receive an exemption from programmed inspections (not compliant or accident investigation inspections) for a period of one year.

OSHA-Approved State Programs

The federal OSHA law encourages states to develop and operate, under OSHA guidance, state job safety and health plans.

When all development steps concerning resources, procedures, and other requirements have been completed and approved, OSHA certifies that a state has the legal, administrative, and enforcement means necessary to operate effectively. This action renders no judgment on how well or how poorly a state is actually operating its program but merely attests to the structural completeness of its program. After this certification, there is a period of at least one year to determine if a state is effectively providing safety and health protection. If it is found that the state is operating at least as effectively as federal OSHA, and other requirements including compliance staffing levels are met, final approval of the plan may be granted, and federal authority will cease in those areas over which the state has jurisdiction.

There are currently 25 state plan states – 23 cover the private and public (state and local government) sectors and two cover the public sector only (Connecticut and New York):

Alaska	New York
Arizona	North Carolina
California	Oregon
Connecticut	Puerto Rico
Hawaii	South Carolina
Indiana	Tennessee

Iowa	Utah
Kentucky	Vermont
Maryland	Virgin Islands
Michigan	Virginia
Minnesota	Washington
Nevada	Wyoming
New Mexico	

In 1998, Congress enacted a new law which mandates that OSHA establish and support cooperative agreements with the states to facilitate on-site consultations outside the scope of normal OSHA enforcement activity. Once a voluntary inspection occurs, a workplace may not be visited again by OSHA inspectors for a one-year period.

Recordkeeping and Reporting

With certain exceptions (listed below), employers of 10 or more workers must maintain records of occupational injuries and illnesses as they occur. Records must be maintained for each business establishment, defined as "a single physical location where business is conducted or where services are performed." Recordkeeping forms are kept on a calendar year basis. These forms are not sent to OSHA or any other agency. Rather, they must be kept for a minimum of five years and be available for inspection by representatives of OSHA, the Department of Health and Human Services, the Bureau of Labor Statistics, and certain designated state agencies. Two forms are necessary to fulfill the recordkeeping requirements. Employers must post a notice in a conspicuous place, and in states operating under an OSHA-approved plan, the equivalent state poster.

OSHA No. 300 – Log and Summary of Occupational Injuries and Illnesses. Each recordable occupational injury and illness must be logged on this form within six working days from the time the employer learns of it. If the log is prepared at a central location by automatic data processing equipment, a copy current to within 45 calendar days must be present at all times in the establishment. A substitute for the OSHA No. 300 is acceptable if it is as detailed, easily readable, and as understandable as the OSHA No. 300.

The OSHA No. 300 must be completed for the calendar year and then conspicuously posted for the entire month of February of the following year. A copy of OSHA No. 300 is provided in the Appendix.

OSHA No. 301 – Supplemental Record of Occupational Injuries and Illnesses. The form OSHA No. 301 contains much more detail about each injury or illness. It also must be completed within six working days from the time the employer learns of the work-related injury or illness. A substitute for the OSHA No. 301 (such as insurance or workers' compensation) may be used if it contains all required information. A copy of OSHA Form 301 is provided in the Appendix.

In addition, many specific OSHA workplace standards have additional recordkeeping and reporting obligations.

An occupational injury is an injury such as a cut, fracture, sprain, or amputation which results from a work-related accident or from exposure involving a single incident in the work environment. An occupational illness is any abnormal condition or disorder, other than one resulting from an occupational injury, caused by exposure to environmental factors associated with employment. Included are acute and chronic illnesses which may be caused by inhalation, absorption, ingestion, or direct contact with toxic substances or harmful agents.

Occupational injuries must be recorded if they result in one or more lost workdays; restriction of work or motion; loss of consciousness;

medical treatment (other than first aid); transfer to another job; or death.

If an on-the-job accident occurs which results in the death of an employee or in the hospitalization of five or more workers, all employers, regardless of the number of employees, are required to report the accident in detail to the nearest OSHA Regional Office.

OSHA has exempted certain types of businesses from maintaining the annual record of occupational injuries and illnesses because of their low incidence of workplace mishaps. Types of businesses exempted from the recordkeeping requirements are:

1. Retail trade, except for general merchandise, food, building materials, and garden supply retailers;

2. Real estate, insurance, and finance establishments; and

3. Service, except for hotels and other lodging places, repair facilities, amusement and recreational services, and health services.

OSHA Citations and Penalties

Citations – After the OSHA compliance officer reports findings, the area director determines what citations, if any, will be issued, and what penalties, if any, will be proposed. Citations inform the employer and employees of the regulations and standards alleged to have been violated and of the proposed length of time set for their abatement. The employer will receive citations and notices of proposed penalties by certified mail. The employer must post a copy of each citation, at or near the place the violations occurred, for three days or until the violation is abated, whichever is longer.

Penalties – Under the OSHA law, there are various types of violations that may be cited and penalties that may be proposed. Among the prominent ones are:

1. **Other-Than-Serious Violation** – A violation that has a direct relationship to job safety and health, but probably would not cause death or serious physical harm. A proposed penalty of up to $7,000 for each violation is discretionary. A penalty for an other-than-serious violation may be adjusted downward by as much as 80 percent, depending on the employer's good faith (demonstrated efforts to comply with the Act), history of previous violations and size of business. When the adjusted penalty amounts to less than $60, no penalty is proposed.

2. **Serious Violation** – A violation where there is substantial probability that death or serious physical harm could result and that the employer knew, or should have known, of the hazard. A mandatory penalty of up to $7,000 for each violation is proposed. A penalty for a serious violation may be adjusted downward, based on the employer's good faith, history of previous violations, the gravity of the alleged violation, and size of business.

3. **Willful Violation** – A violation that the employer intentionally and knowingly commits. The employer either knows that the activity constitutes a violation, or is aware that a hazardous condition existed and made no reasonable effort to eliminate it. Penalties of up to $70,000 may be proposed for each willful violation, with a minimum penalty of $5,000 for each violation. A proposed penalty for a willful violation may be adjusted downward, depending on the size of the business and its history of previous violations. Usually, no credit is given for good faith. If an employer is convicted of a willful violation of a standard that has resulted in the death of an employee, the offense is punishable by a court-imposed fine or by imprisonment for up to six months, or both. A fine of up to $250,000 for an individual, or $5,000,000

for a corporation, may be imposed for a criminal conviction.

OSHA's penalty reduction plan is based on employer size, creating four distinct categories:

- Employers with 10 or fewer employees would be eligible for an 80 percent penalty reduction;

- Employers with 11 to 30 employees, a 60 percent reduction;

- Employers with 31 to 100 employees, a 40 percent reduction; and

- Employers with 101 to 250 workers, a 20 percent reduction.

Appeals Process

When issued a citation or notice of a proposed penalty, an employer may request an informal meeting with OSHA's area director to discuss the case. Employee representatives may be invited to attend the meeting. The area director is authorized to enter into settlement agreements that revise citations and penalties to avoid prolonged legal disputes.

1. **Petition for Modification or Abatement** – Upon receiving a citation, the employer must correct the cited hazard by the prescribed date unless it contests the citation or abatement date.

   The written petition should specify all steps taken to achieve compliance, the additional time needed to achieve complete compliance, the reasons such additional

Most Frequently Cited OSHA Violations

Standard	Subject
Hazard Communication/General Industry	Written Program
Hazard Communication/General Industry	Information, Training
Machine Guarding	Guarding Methods
Fall Protection	Unprotected Sides and Edges
Head Protection	Protective Helmets
Recordkeeping	OSHA Log
Abrasive Wheel Machinery	Guard Adjustment
Safety Training	Worker Instruction
Excavations	Protective System
Lockout/Tagout	Energy Control Program

Source: Occupational Safety and Health Administration 1997 Data

time is needed, all temporary steps being taken to safeguard employees against the cited hazard during the intervening period, that a copy of the petition was posted in a conspicuous place at or near each place where a violation occurred, and that the employee representative (if there is one) received a copy of the petition.

2. **Notice of Contest** – If the employer decides to contest either the citation, the time set for abatement, or the proposed penalty, the employer has 15 working days from the time the citation and proposed penalty are received in which to notify the OSHA area director of its decision in writing. An orally expressed disagreement will not suffice. This written notification is called a "Notice of Contest" and must contain certain information. A copy of the Notice of Contest must be given to the employee's authorized representative.

The written Notice of Contest results in the case being sent to the Occupational Safety and Health Review Commission (OSHRC). The Commission is an independent agency not associated with OSHA or the Department of Labor. The Commission assigns the case to an administrative law judge.

Employer Responsibilities & Rights under OSHA

Employers have certain responsibilities and rights under the Occupational Safety and Health Act of 1970. The following checklist provides a review of some of those obligations. Employers must:

- Meet their general duty responsibility to provide a workplace free from recognized hazards that are causing or are likely to cause death or serious physical harm to employees, and comply with standards, rules, and regulations issued under the Act.

- Be familiar with mandatory OSHA standards and make copies available to employees for review upon requests.

- Inform all employees about OSHA.

- Examine workplace conditions to make sure they conform to applicable standard.

- Minimize or reduce hazards.

- Make sure employees have and use safe tools and equipment (including appropriate personal protective equipment) and that such equipment is properly maintained.

- Use color codes, posters, labels, or signs when needed to warn employees of potential hazards.

- Establish or update operating procedures and communicate them so that employees follow safety and health requirements.

- Provide medical examinations when required by OSHA standards.

- Provide training required by OSHA standards (e.g., hazard communication, lead, etc.).

- Report to the nearest OSHA office within 48 hours any fatal accident or one that results in the hospitalization of five or more employees.

- Keep OSHA-required records of work-related injuries and illnesses, and post a copy of the totals from the last page of OSHA No. 200 during the entire month of February of each year. (This applies to employers with 11 or more employees.)

Employer Responsibilities & Rights under OSHA [(continued)]

- Post, at a prominent location within the workplace, the OSHA poster informing employees of their rights and responsibilities. (In states operating OSHA-approved job safety and health programs, the state's equivalent poster may be required.)

- Provide employees, former employees, and their representatives access to the Log and Summary of Occupational Injuries and Illnesses (OSHA No. 200) at a reasonable time and in a reasonable manner.

- Provide access to employee medical records and exposure records to employees or their authorized representatives.

- Cooperate with OSHA compliance officer by furnishing names of authorized employee representatives who may be asked to accompany the compliance officer during an inspection. (If none, the compliance officer will consult with a reasonable number of employees concerning safety and health in the workplace.)

- Not discriminate against employees who properly exercise their rights under the Act (e.g., file safety or health grievance).

- Not retaliate for such activities in any way such as through firing, demotion, taking away seniority or other earned benefits, transferring the worker to an undesirable job or shift, or threatening or harassing the worker.

- Post OSHA citations at or near the worksite involved. Each citation, or copy thereof, must remain posted until the violation has been abated, or for three working days, whichever is longer.

- Abate cited violations within the prescribed period.

- Seek advice and off-site consultation, as needed, by writing, calling, or visiting the nearest OSHA office. (OSHA will not inspect merely because an employer requests assistance.)

- Be active in your industry association's involvement in job safety and health.

- Request and receive proper identification of the OSHA compliance officer prior to inspection.

- Be advised by the compliance officer of the reason for an inspection.

- Have an opening and closing conference with the compliance officer.

- Accompany the compliance officer on the inspection.

- File a Notice of Contest with the OSHA area director within 15 working days of receipt of a notice of citation and proposed penalty.

- Apply to OSHA for a temporary variance from a standard if unable to comply because of the unavailability of materials, equipment, or personnel needed to make necessary changes within the required time.

- Apply to OSHA for a permanent variance from a standard if you can furnish proof that your facilities or method of operations provide employee protection at least as effective as the one required by the standard.

- Take an active role in developing safety and health standards through participation in OSHA Standards Advisory Committees and recognized standards-setting organizations.

National Labor Relations Act: Unfair Labor Practices, Union Organizing, and the Collective Bargaining Process

10

Introduction

The purpose of this chapter is to familiarize employers, in very general terms, with the major aspects of dealing with unions. These include: (i) conduct by employers or unions that constitutes unfair labor practices; (ii) organizing (how it is that the employees in a workforce become represented by a union); (iii) the process of collective bargaining once employees are represented by a union; (iv) deferral of an unfair labor practice to arbitration; and (v) issues involving the discipline of bargaining unit employees.

Background and Overview of the National Labor Relations Act

Originally passed in 1935, the National Labor Relations Act ("NLRA" or the "Wagner Act") was the first major piece of legislation which provided a protected environment in which unions could develop.

The NLRA established an independent federal agency, the National Labor Relations Board ("NLRB"), which has jurisdiction over all private sector employers affecting interstate commerce. The NLRB consists of 5 members, appointed by the President. Its functions are to adjudicate unfair labor practice cases, to determine the proper employee units for representation (the "appropriate bargaining unit") and to oversee elections. The task of

investigating and prosecuting unfair labor practices belongs to the General Counsel, who is also appointed by the President. However, much of the responsibility for supervising elections and investigating unfair labor practices is delegated to local regional offices throughout the country.

The basic purpose of the NLRA is to provide employees with the right to engage in concerted activity and bargain collectively with their employer over terms and conditions of employment. These rights apply to all employees, except those in managerial, supervisory, or confidential positions. This means that unionization is not limited to hourly, manufacturing employees, but extends to all types of employees – clerical, technical and professional employees – so long as they do not have managerial, supervisory or confidential responsibilities.

The heart of the NLRA, and much of federal labor law, derives from two sections of the statute, Sections 7 and 8. Section 7 of the NLRA provides that:

> Employees shall have the right to [1] self organization, to form, join, or assist labor organizations, [2] to bargain collectively through representatives of their own choosing, and [3] to engage in other concerted activities for the purpose of collective bargaining or other mutual , aid or protection. . . .

In 1947, in an attempt to bring some balance the statute, the words "… or to refrain from any and all activities" were added to Section 7.

Unfair Labor Practices

After describing in Section 7 what employees may do, or refuse to do, Congress set forth in Section 8 what employers and unions <u>cannot</u> do. Section 8(a) provides that it shall be an Unfair Labor Practice ("ULP") for an employer:

(1) to interfere with or restrain employees in the exercise of their Section 7 rights;

(2) to dominate or interfere with the formation or administration of a labor organization, or to contribute financial or other support to it;

(3) to discriminate against any applicant or employee for the purpose of encouraging or discouraging membership in a labor organization;

(4) to discharge or otherwise discriminate against an employee because he has filed charges or given testimony in an NLRB proceeding, and

(5) to refuse to bargain with the certified representative of the employees.

For example, if an employer improperly refuses to recognize a union, withdraws recognition, makes unilateral changes in the terms and conditions of employment, refuses to provide relevant information, bargains in bad faith, discriminates or retaliates against employees engaged in protected concerted activity, the union, or in some cases an individual employee, either represented or unrepresented, may file a ULP.[1] Engaging in prohibited conduct during an organizational campaign,

such as spying on employees involved in union meetings, interrogating employees concerning their support for a union, making threats or promises, permits the union to file ULP charges alleging a violation of §8(a)(1) for interfering with employees' right to organize. If an employer refuses to hire an individual or discharges an employee because of support for a union, then it can expect a charge alleging a violation of §8(a)(3). Less common types of prohibited conduct include alleged violations of §8(a)(2), for creating a so-called "company union", and alleged violations of §8(a)(4), for retaliating against an employee for initiating or participating in a Board proceeding.

Section 8(b)(1) through (7) sets forth the list of ULP's that may be committed by unions. It is illegal for a union to:

(1) restrain employees in the exercise of their Section 7 rights;

(2) cause or attempt to cause an employer to discriminate against an employee or discriminate against an employee with respect to union membership;

(3) refuse to bargain collectively;

(4) engage in certain secondary boycotts or strike activity;

(5) charge excessive or discriminatory fees;

(6) attempt to extract money, or other value, for services not performed; or

(7) engage in illegal picketing.

Unfair Labor Practice Procedure[2]

The NLRA includes an elaborate procedure for enforcing the unfair labor practices in Section 8. An aggrieved employee, employer,

---

1. The same conduct may also constitute grounds for filing an objection to the results of an election.

2. The Board has published the NLRB Case Handling Manual, which sets forth, in detail, the policies and procedures implemented by the Board with respect to unfair labor practices, representation proceedings, compliance proceedings, etc. Online: http://www.nlrb.gov/nlrb/legal/manuals/chm1.asp

or union may file a charge with the Regional Office of the NLRB (the "Charging Party") within 6 months of the commission of the unfair labor practice. NLRA §10(b). An NLRB Field Examiner will then conduct an investigation into the allegations. Following this preliminary investigation, the NLRB Regional Director will decide whether to issue a complaint. If a complaint is issued and the parties do not agree on a resolution, the matter will proceed to a hearing before an NLRB administrative law judge ("ALJ"). At trial, the General Counsel will act as prosecutor against the respondent. After this administrative trial and the filing of post hearing briefs, the ALJ will render his or her decision. The Board is not bound by the ALJ's findings, but often adopts them, and after considering the case, sometimes after oral argument, it will enter a final order either dismissing the complaint or awarding affirmative relief. The Board's decision can be appealed to the federal court of appeals.

The NLRB has broad remedial authority. It may order the reinstatement of employees with back pay and benefits, modify terms of employment that were imposed unlawfully, reopen closed or transferred operations, and, in some cases, order the employer to bargain collectively with the union.[3]

Unfair Labor Practice Impact in a Strike Situation

Before concluding this brief overview of ULP procedures under the NLRA, a discussion about an employer's duties and obligations during a strike is warranted. A strike is a concerted refusal to work by employees and is, therefore, protected by Section 7 of the NLRA.

Where employees are represented by a union, however, the right to strike is often prohibited, as a matter of contract, by a no-strike clause. Typically, such a clause will provide that the union will not engage in or support any work stoppages, picketing or slowdowns during the term of the collective bargaining agreement, and the employer agrees not to lock out any of the employees while the contract is in effect. Strikes, therefore, typically occur either when the parties are unable to agree to a first contract or when an existing contract has expired and no new agreement is reached.

In understanding the employer's rights and obligations in a strike situation, it is essential to distinguish between "economic" strikes and strikes that are caused or prolonged by an employer's unfair labor practices. Economic strikers may be permanently replaced and, even if they unconditionally offer to return to work, the employer is not required to discharge the replacements and reinstate the strikers. In other words, the strikers offering to return must wait for openings to occur within the replacement workforce before they are entitled to reinstatement.

Unfair labor practice strikers, on the other hand, are entitled to reinstatement and back pay as soon as they make an unconditional offer to return to work, regardless of whether any permanent replacements were hired. It should also be noted that an economic strike can be converted into an unfair labor practice strike. For example, a strike may begin as an economic strike because the employees are not satisfied with the final contract offer. However, if the employer were to discharge a member of the union's bargaining committee because of his or her union activity or commit some other unfair labor practice during the course of the strike, the strike could then become an unfair

---

3. In the case of election objections, the NLRB may order an employer to bargain with the union without an election or contrary to the employees' rejection of the union in the election.

labor practice strike and the striking workers could no longer be permanently replaced.

Union Organizing

The focus of this part of the chapter is on union organizing and the role of the NLRA to insure the fairness of representation elections. This emphasis is appropriate in light of the aggressive campaign planned by organized labor to step up its union organizing efforts with the aim of reversing the trend of dwindling union membership in the U.S. Thus, the information given here will be especially useful to those employers who are presently non-union.

Bargaining Unit

The NLRA gives employees the right to form or attempt to form a union among employees of a company, join a union whether the union is recognized by the employer or not, and assist a union to organize the employees of an employer.

The group of employees that a union represents is known as a bargaining unit. To obtain representation over a group of employees, the unit sought must be deemed "appropriate" for the purposes of bargaining. The NLRB is primarily responsible for determining the appropriateness of a bargaining unit. The underlying concept the NLRB has historically used in determining appropriateness of a unit is "community of interest" (i.e., those employees who share similar terms and conditions of employment). Some of the criteria considered in making unit determinations are similar wages and benefits, working conditions, employee transfers and interchange, supervisors, integration of work product, and geographical location. It should also be noted that a unit may be deemed "appropriate" even if it is not the most appropriate unit.

The National Labor Relations Act provides that a representative chosen by "the majority of employees in a unit appropriate for such purposes" is to be the "exclusive" representative for all employees of such a unit. The structure and operation of a particular employer's operation will be critical in ascertaining the appropriateness of a bargaining unit. The NLRB focus will be directed toward the nature of the management and administration. To the extent that the components of an employer's business are administratively and functionally integrated, there is greater likelihood that the NLRB will examine not only the particular facility but also the history of bargaining by other employers in the industry.

A brief listing of some common types of bargaining units follows:

1. Production and Maintenance Units. This is the kind of unit usually found in manufacturing facilities and is favored by the NLRB in industrial and similar establishments. Plant clerical employees who work with production are ordinarily included in production and maintenance units.

2. Craft Units. Craft units are composed of a distinct and homogeneous group of skilled craftsmen, working as such, together with their apprentices and/or helpers.

3. Technical Units. These are composed of employees whose work is of a technical nature. These employees are involved with the use of specialized training, ordinarily obtained either in colleges or in technical schools.

4. Department Units. The NLRA sanctions a subdivision of a plant unit. Although these employees lack the skills of craftsmen, they may be treated as separate units.

5. Office Clerical Units. The NLRB has consistently held that the interests of office clerical employees are different from those of other employees.

6. Guards. While the NLRA permits guards to be organized, it will not require an employer to recognize a unit which includes guard and non-guard employees.

7. Single vs. Multi-Plant Units. The NLRB relies upon the presumption that one plant of a multi-plant operation may be an appropriate unit.

A unit must have at least 2 members and may cover employees in one or more plants of the same employer. In some industries in which employers are grouped together in voluntary associations, a unit may include employees of two or more employers in any number of locations.

It should be noted that a bargaining unit can include only persons who are "employees" within the meaning of the NLRA. The law excludes certain individuals, such as agricultural laborers, independent contractors, supervisors, and persons in managerial positions, from the meaning of "employees." None of these individuals can be included in a bargaining unit. In addition, the NLRB, as a matter of policy, excludes from bargaining units employees who act in a confidential capacity to an employer's labor relations officials.

Basic Union Organizing Techniques

Authorization Cards – The union's major aim, through the initial steps of an organizing campaign, is to obtain signed authorization cards. There are two basic kinds of authorization cards – pure and dual purpose. "Pure" cards designate the union as the signer's exclusive bargaining representative. The "dual purpose" card carries both the exclusive bargaining representative designation and a request for an election.

Certification – Although a union may become the designated bargaining agent for a company's employees through the employer's voluntary recognition, unions generally try to obtain certification from the NLRB. Certification provides the union with several advantages. For example, unless there are unusual circumstances, an employer is required to bargain with a certified union for at least one year. Furthermore, any petition which results in an election, whether filed by the employees, the employer, or another union, will bar another union from attempting certification for one year.

Filing Petitions

A representation case is initiated by filing a petition for an election with one of the NLRB's regional offices.

A union files an "RC-Certification of Representation" petition. The petition must be accompanied by documentary proof (usually authorization cards) showing that at least 30 percent of the employees in the proposed bargaining unit support the petition. The proof submitted by the petitioning union is held in strict confidence by the NLRB. The Board is solely responsible for evaluating the sufficiency and validity of a union's showing of interest. An employer may question the validity of a showing of interest by alleging, for example, that the authorization cards were obtained by fraud. The Regional Director will investigate the charges and administratively determine, without a hearing, whether the employee's allegations are true.

An employer may also file a petition with the NLRB, referred to as an "RM-Representation" (Employer Petition). An RM petition may be filed only after a union has made a demand upon the employer to be recognized as the employees' bargaining representative. When the employer files the election petition, no showing of interest is required.

After a petition is filed, an NLRB representative will investigate the matter to determine if a question concerning representation exists which warrants holding an election. The investigation will center around such issues as whether the union is a *bona fide* labor organization, whether the NLRB has jurisdiction over the employer, whether a contract exists which would bar an election, whether certain employees are eligible to vote and whether the designated bargaining unit is an appropriate one.

Initial Correspondence

Initial NLRB correspondence with the employer will include a request that the employer post a "Notice to Employees" concerning union and employer conduct while the representation question is being resolved. This posting is purely voluntary and is not required under the Board's rules. Employers are also requested at that time to submit to the NLRB:

1. A payroll list covering the employees in the proposed bargaining unit, as of the date of the petition. This list is used to check the union's showing of interest and should not be confused with the *Excelsior* list described later in this chapter;

2. Data indicating the nature of the employer's business and the volume of the operations for jurisdictional purposes; and

3. A position statement on the appropriateness of the unit and whether the employer is willing to consent to an election.

Included in the initial correspondence are several other NLRB forms which inform the Board as to whether the employer will be represented by counsel, a designation of a representative for the purposes of receiving service of documents and a brief statement of representation procedures.

Hearings

At the time the petition is filed, the NLRB will usually schedule a formal hearing for the purpose of resolving any election issues that cannot be resolved informally. Generally, the parties' informal discussions will deal with such questions as the appropriateness of the unit, which employees are eligible to vote, voting hours, and the place, time and date of the election. In most cases, the parties will be able to resolve a good number of these issues through a negotiated stipulation. If they cannot, a fact-finding hearing will be held.

If a hearing is necessary, the Regional Director will serve a notice of hearing on all interested parties. Technically, representation hearings are supposed to be non-adversarial, investigatory proceedings. The NLRB agent assigned to the case will most likely preside as hearing officer and evidence will be presented by the parties concerning the issues in dispute. The hearing is open to the public. A verbatim transcript of the hearing is made by an official reporter of the NLRB. Any party has the right to appear in person, by counsel, or by other representative.

After the hearing is closed, the parties may submit briefs to the Regional Director on any or all of the questions raised. The hearing officer also submits a report to the Regional Director. It consists of an analysis of the issues presented at the hearing and a summary of the evidence. The Regional Director will then issue a decision; in rare instances the Director may transfer a particularly complex or novel case to the Board in Washington, D.C.

The Regional Director's decision will set forth findings of fact and conclusions of law, and include either a direction for an election or an order dismissing the petition. Review of the Regional Director's decision by the NLRB in Washington, D.C., is procedurally available, but it is not available as a matter of right and most requests for review are denied.

Consent Agreements

A hearing will not be necessary, of course, if the parties are able to resolve their differences. In such an event, they will enter into a formal consent agreement which provides for holding a representation election. There are two different kinds of such agreements: one is called an "Agreement for Consent Election" (Consent), and the other is called a "Stipulation for Certification upon Consent Election" (Stipulation).

Both agreements provide for the wording on the ballot, a payroll period eligibility date, hours and place of the election, and description of the appropriate bargaining unit. The Consent, however, vests final authority with the Regional Director (with limited review by the Board in Washington, D.C.) to investigate and rule upon challenged ballots and objections to the conduct of the election. The Stipulation, by contrast, provides that the Board in Washington, D.C., shall determine all election questions, including challenges and objections to the conduct of the election. Even where there is a Stipulation, however, the Regional Director will investigate a dispute for the Board and may issue a report and recommendations with respect to the disposition of the issues in question. In either case, the election will be supervised by the NLRB's regional office.

Excelsior List

Within seven days after the direction of an election or the execution of an election agreement, the employer must furnish the NLRB with an alphabetical list, by last name, of the employees eligible to vote and their home addresses. This list, known as the *Excelsior* list, is then made available to the union for use during its election campaign. An election may not be held sooner than 10 days after the *Excelsior* list

is received, and failure to timely furnish the list is grounds for setting aside an election.

Notice of Election

Unlike the original "Notice to Employees," the official "Notice of Election" must be posted before the election. This notice includes details of the upcoming election and a facsimile of the official ballot. It is intended to inform all eligible voters about the details of the election. Failure to post these notices properly may be sufficient grounds for setting aside an election.

Campaign Strategies

With respect to union tactics, their traditional method was to simply stand at a plant gate and pass out leaflets. In the last 10 years, however, unions have become a lot more sophisticated in their campaign techniques.

Today, union campaigns typically are conducted in secret until the petition is filed. They often begin with selection of an organizing committee which initiates one-on-one contact and informal polling of employees for local "gripes" to give the union some specific issues around which to rally people. Extensive use of telephone trees and meetings in employee homes is also very common. Finally, unions have not abandoned the use of ordinary letters and leaflets to communicate their standard themes. These themes include getting respect from management, job security, seniority rights, protection of existing benefits (such as insurance), changes in work rules, union democracy, improved safety and other working conditions, and, of course, better wages and benefits for the bargaining unit.

With respect to the employer's campaign, the first point to make is that employees have the legal right to actively oppose a unionization effort. In fact, if an employer has any hope of winning the election, it is essential that it take a strong position on the issues and conduct a carefully orchestrated and comprehensive campaign. As noted earlier, most unions will not file a petition unless it has signed authorization cards from at least 50% of the unit employees. In some cases, they will seek to have cards from as many as 90% of the employees. This means that most election campaigns are, initially, an uphill battle for employers because unions do not file a petition and commit the time and resources necessary for a full-blown campaign unless they have been fairly successful in obtaining authorization cards and believe they have a good chance of winning.

However, even where 90% of the employees have signed cards, the election can be won. People sign cards for a variety of reasons including simple curiosity about the union, because a friend did, or because they wanted to get the organizer off their back. Employees must be told that even if they signed a card, they are not required to vote in favor of the union.

Once an employer becomes aware of the existence of union organizing activity, numerous complex NLRB rules and regulations come into effect. Employers must be aware of these rules and campaign in a manner which avoids the commission of violations of the Act. This is a specialized area of the law which requires competent legal counsel. Whatever your decision with respect to a unionization effort, it is critical to understand the employer's rights and options. Knowing that a union organizing campaign is underway, many employers opposed to unionization, in frustration, strike out blindly in an attempt to communicate with their employees or take action against those considered to be union activists. Such conduct, in addition to being unlawful, may actually enhance the union's efforts.

Before reacting to a union organizing effort, employers must determine the issues or problems which may have induced employees to seek a union. The first step is to determine what these problems are and how they arose. Employers will need to assess their entire employee relations posture, and review the employer's personnel policies, wage and benefit structure, and employee benefit plans to isolate which specific issues gave rise to the union organizational campaign. Contrary to a popularly expressed belief, employers are generally unionized because the employees have sought a union, not because the union has "targeted" the employer.

Management actions in response to union activity will be closely scrutinized by the union and its followers and may become the subject of ULP's. As noted, this is an area where complex rules and regulations are in effect. Employers must know these rules before attempting to communicate with employees. For example, even innocent employer inquiries of employees may be characterized as "interrogations" and thus may be violative of the Act. Normal administration of discipline may be challenged as "retaliatory measures" against employees who are known to be sympathetic to the union. Changes in wages and benefits, or even discussions regarding changes, may be interpreted as election "inducements" and "promises of benefit." Employers must be cognizant of these restrictions and ensure that no statements are made that could be interpreted as interfering with the Section 7 rights of the employees.

Top management representatives should hold meetings with all supervisors to outline the mechanics and procedures of a union organizing drive and to explain the NLRB rules governing supervisors' conduct. Employers should explain to supervisors that there are rules to be followed, but that compliance is not difficult once the restrictions are understood. More importantly, supervisors should realize that they have a vital stake in preventing the union activity from gaining momentum and that they will play an active role in the employer's efforts to communicate "the other side of the story" to employees. Supervisors are part of management and are the key link between top management and its employees. Without their enthusiastic acceptance of the employer's decision to oppose the union and their assistance, responding effectively to a union drive will be extremely difficult, if not impossible. Communication between management and front line supervisors regarding their vital role in the employer's campaign may be critical to the final election results.

By the time the petition has been filed, the union's strength is usually at its peak. At this point, however, employees have heard "only one side of the story." A campaign typically highlights the negative consequences of unionization, as well as the putting the employer's past record in the best possible light.

One of the first steps should be to hold group and individual meetings with all supervisory personnel. Because supervisors are the employer's agents, and the employer is responsible for their statements and conduct, the NLRB ground rules and restrictions must be explained at the outset. They must be educated in the "Do's and Don'ts." In addition, supervisor input is needed to determine what issues gave rise to the employees' perception that they need a union.

Once the proper bargaining unit has been determined, a date will be set for an election. Generally, the pre-election period is five to six weeks. With the advice of labor counsel, a week-by-week "game plan" should then be developed and take into account: a) the positive aspects of employment with the employer, including existing benefits; b) the lack of need for a union in the organization; c) information and data responding to the issues that have been identified as giving rise to the employees' initial interest in the union; and d) the negative aspects of unionism, such as union

dues and fines, the loss of individual freedom to the employees, risk of strikes, realities of the collective bargaining process, the decline in unionization in general and the realities of union finances.

Management should develop and/or strengthen its method of communicating with the employees. Information should be provided through a variety of means including group meetings, handouts, and follow-up mailings. The main spokesperson on behalf of the employer in large group meetings should be an official who can credibly present the employer's views and speak authoritatively on the employer's behalf.

Supervisors should be aware of the employer's position on issues in the campaign. Supervisors should reiterate the employer's views to the employees on a daily basis. In addition, supervisors can provide invaluable employee feedback to be used in determining the effectiveness of the employer's efforts to communicate with the employees.

While employers should not hesitate to present forceful arguments against unionization, and in favor of the employer, the following conduct is prohibited and could result in a bargaining order even if a majority of the employees vote "no" to a union:

1) promises (express or implied)
2) threats (express or implied)
3) interrogation
4) surveillance
5) discrimination against union advocates

Careful attention must be paid to these prohibitions. Because the line between legitimate persuasion and unlawful conduct is often finely drawn, all employer communications must be carefully reviewed and screened in advance. The employer's objectives in communicating with the employees can be accomplished without needlessly violating the Act. Employers do not give up their right to free speech during union drives, but they must be prepared to defend and document what they have said. Although frivolous unfair labor practice charges cannot be prevented, the risk of having charges filed is reduced significantly by carefully following the rules.

After the election, either party may file objections to conduct which they believe may have improperly affected the results of the election. For example, conduct which would constitute a ULP or illegal electioneering can form the basis of an objection.

Finally, at the risk of stating the obvious, it is worth noting that the best way to avoid organizational activity among a workforce is to develop personnel policies and procedures which treat employees positively, fairly, and openly at all times. A clean, safe working environment, competitive pay rates and benefits for the type of work and geographic area of the employment and a system of listening to and communicating with employees are all essential to successful union avoidance.

A method of handling employee complaints should be formal and workable. Merely maintaining an "open door" policy – or claiming to maintain an "open door" policy – is probably not sufficient. Genuine concern and respect for the interests of employees must be communicated and demonstrated to them.

A current employee handbook should be in place which informs employees about the employer: what employees are entitled to and what is expected of them along with disciplinary rules, equal employment policies, no solicitation[4]

---

4. Issues concerning the use of employer e-mail systems for union solicitation and distribution are emerging and complex. Policies concerning solicitation and distribution, company e-mail and the practices permitted should be carefully reviewed prior to the commencement of any union organizing activity in order to prohibit the employer's system from becoming a useful tool for union organizing.

and no distribution rules, and procedures by which their complaints can be communicated and addressed.

Misleading Campaign Propaganda

The NLRB's position on regulating campaign propaganda has fluctuated over the years. Therefore, any employer statement or action during an election campaign should be carefully examined to determine if it meets the Board's standards.

Under current NLRB rules, the Board will not probe into the veracity of campaign statements, but will intervene if a party has used forged documents, thereby preventing the voters from recognizing the material as propaganda.

The Board's fluctuating rules on the veracity of campaign statements is limited to determining whether an election should be overturned as a result of alleged misrepresentations. It will, however, continue to enforce a different set of rules against threats of reprisal, promises of benefits, and other prohibited practices.

Threats of Reprisal, Promises of Benefits, and Other Prohibited Practices

Section 8(c) of the National Labor Relations Act expressly prohibits an employer from making any statement that threatens employees or promises them benefits. Threats or promises by an employer are considered an illegal inducement to vote against union representation.

Although direct threats are clearly impermissible, the employer is confronted with a dilemma when he wishes to emphasize some of the detrimental economic consequences of union representation. On the one hand, this is the kind of information an employee who is about to make an important decision should have. On the other hand, it may be regarded as a threat of reprisal for a pro-union vote. Several years ago, the Supreme Court tried to establish some guidelines for evaluating employer statements concerning adverse consequence of unionization.

The employer must be prepared to demonstrate that the stated consequences of any such prediction (1) are probable and (2) are based on economic considerations alone. The employee must be left with the impression that the employer's comment is not based on anti-union feelings which may result in retaliation if the union wins. This framework necessitates that an employer use care in formulating any statement about the economic consequences of unionization.

Just as threats of reprisals cannot be made, neither can promises or grants of benefits be allowed. A promise or grant may be unconditional – that is, not tied to a vote against the union – but may still be regarded as improper if it appears to be related to the union campaign and/or there is not a valid business reason for it. Therefore, if an employer can establish a bona fide business reason for increasing benefits at the time in question, such as past practice, the grant of benefits or announcement of a change in benefits will be permissible.

Union Election Campaign "TIPS"

Visits to Employees' Homes – Although union representatives may visit employees' homes and speak to them about the election, an employer may not do so.

Appeals to Racial Prejudice – The standard used by the Board in evaluating racially oriented statements in the context of an election campaign is whether the party making the statement truthfully sets forth the other party's position on racial matters. Any inflammatory or irrelevant statements are prohibited.

Duplication of NLRB Ballot and Other Official Documents – One of the strictest Board election campaign policies is that parties are not permitted to reproduce copies of the official ballot. Any tampering with a facsimile ballot is regarded as grounds for setting an election aside, regardless of the motive or effect of the action. This rule is not limited to ballots only. It applies to all official NLRB election documents.

Discrimination – Discrimination against union supporters is prohibited by the National Labor Relations Act. Employers must be careful, therefore, in dealing with union ring leaders and supporters. Any action taken against them which could be construed as discriminatory could lead to an unfair labor practice charge. Before an employer takes any action against a known union supporter, the nondiscriminatory basis for such action should be firmly established. Even where there are obvious nondiscriminatory reasons for the employer's actions, the NLRB will find that the company has engaged in unlawful discrimination if any part of the decision was motivated by anti-union sentiment.

Interrogation – Employees may not be interrogated by the employer as to their own, or their fellow employee's, feelings concerning the union. Further, employers may not solicit grievances in an attempt to destroy union support.

Surveillance – Surveillance of employees engaged in union activity is forbidden by the NLRB. It is immaterial whether the surveillance is conducted by the employer, supervisors, employees, or outsiders. Furthermore, there may be a violation even if the surveillance is apparent rather than actual.

Peerless Plywood Rule – Under the Board's holding in the *Peerless Plywood* case, an employer is forbidden from delivering a captive audience address within the 24 hours immediately preceding the beginning of an election. Other forms of campaigning within the 24-hour period are permissible, for example, if employee attendance is voluntary or communication is one-on-one.

Union Election Campaign "TIPS" (continued)

Campaigning Within the Voting Area – An election can be set aside if a party engages in electioneering near a polling place. This rule applies to employers and unions equally. The Board agent will indicate an area within which no campaigning may occur. The rule is so strictly enforced that conversations with voters in the restricted area, by either employer or union representatives, are sufficient to set aside an election.

The foregoing is only a summary of some of the campaign conduct that may invalidate an election. The admonition to the employer is to be cautious regarding conduct during a campaign since even harmless and unintentional actions may have serious legal consequences.

Supervisors must be trained in the "Do's" and "Don'ts" early in a campaign. They must be taught not to engage in "TIPS" or "PITS"— no threats, interrogation, promises or surveillance.

The Election

The election itself is conducted by an NLRB agent. Election observers will be designated by the parties involved to represent the company and the union during the election. Under Board policy, the observers must be nonsupervisory employees.

The NLRB agent will instruct the observers about their duties – identifying voters, checking names against the Excelsior list, challenging individuals if necessary, and assisting in counting the ballots. If an employee is ineligible to vote, he or she must be challenged when asking for a ballot. The NLRB agent will then permit the challenged employee to vote, but the ballot will be placed in an envelope and sealed, its status to be determined later, if necessary. Once a ballot makes its way into the ballot box, it may not be challenged. If a prospective voter is not on the eligibility list, the NLRB agent should automatically challenge that individual.

Tally of Ballots and Certification on Conduct of Election

As soon as the polls close, the NLRB agent will count the ballots. To win representation rights, the union must receive a majority, 50% plus one, of the votes cast.

The NLRB agent, after counting the ballots, will prepare two documents. One is a "Tally of Ballots" showing the results of the count and a statement that the tabulation was accurate. The Tally will be signed and a copy will be served on both parties. He or she will also prepare a "Certification on Conduct of Election" to be signed by the parties' observers. The Certification states that the election was conducted fairly and the secrecy of the ballot was preserved. If there is any question about the way in which the election was conducted, the Certification should not be signed. However, signing the Certification does not preclude a party from thereafter filing objections.

Finally, if the number of challenged ballots is sufficient to affect the results of the election, then the eligibility of the challenged voters will have to be resolved before the outcome can be determined.

Objections

Within seven days after the "Tally of the Ballots" has been prepared, any objections to the election must be filed with the Regional Director, with copies served to the other parties. Objections may be based on the manner in which the election was held, or based on conduct which affected the results of the election. If the objections are sustained, the election will be set aside and a new one will be conducted.

The Regional Director has the authority to conduct an investigation into the objections. If substantial factual issues exist, a hearing is ordered. After completion of the investigation, the procedure for reviewing the Regional Director's actions depends upon whether the election was a directed election, a Stipulation, or a Consent. Essentially, the Board or the Regional Director will resolve the objections and/or challenges. In either case, a decision will be rendered overruling the objections and certifying the results, or sustaining the objections, in whole or part, and setting the election aside.

If the union wins the election, the NLRB will certify it as the bargaining representative for the employees in the designated appropriate bargaining unit. There is no direct court review of the NLRB's representation determination. The employer may, however, refuse to bargain with the union, thereby committing an unfair labor practice which can then be reviewed by a United States Circuit Court.

If, on the other hand, the union loses the election, the NLRB will issue a "Certification of Results," legally precluding another election in that bargaining unit for a one-year period. If the Union withdraws the petition before the election is held, another petition may be filed after six months.

Collective Bargaining Process

The Obligation to Bargain – Assuming the union wins the election and is certified as the collective bargaining representative for the employees in the unit, the employer now has a duty to bargain collectively with the union. A failure to do so will constitute an unfair labor practice under §8(a)(5) of the NLRA. The union has a corresponding duty to bargain in good faith and if it fails to do so, it will be in violation of §8(b)(3) of the NLRA.

Elements of the Obligation to Bargain – The NLRA requires the parties "to meet at reasonable times and confer in good faith with respect to… the negotiation of an agreement." The Act does not require that the parties reach an agreement, but only that they negotiate in good faith with the view of reaching an agreement. In other words, they must negotiate with the purpose of trying to reach an agreement.

Since an intent to avoid reaching agreement is seldom announced by a party, it is usually inferred from the totality of the circumstances including conduct at and away from the bargaining table. In determining whether an employer has bargained "hard", which is lawful, or engaged in bad faith or "surface" bargaining, which is unlawful, the NLRB will consider many factors including positions taken at the bargaining table, the nature of the proposals, the making of counterproposals, willingness to reach agreement on some issues and the conduct of the parties away from the table.

Mandatory Versus Permissive Subjects – One of the most basic questions concerns the nature of the subjects over which the employer has a duty to bargain. The language of the statute directs the parties to "confer in good faith" with respect to wages, hours, and other terms and conditions of employment." From this, the NLRB and federal courts have developed three categories of subjects for bargaining – mandatory, permissive and illegal.

The legal duty to bargain is limited to mandatory subjects of bargaining; those integral to earnings and working conditions. The clearest examples of which are wages, holidays, pensions, vacations, insurance, and other employee benefits. With respect to permissive subjects of bargaining, there is no obligation to bargain over them. The parties are free to bargain or not bargain. Examples of permissive subjects include internal union or employer affairs, issues involving employees not covered by the Act (e.g., supervisors) or the identity of the parties' negotiators. Illegal subjects, as expected, are off limits and the parties are forbidden from bargaining over them. For example, proposing there will be no federal or state withholdings taken from employee paychecks would be an illegal subject of bargaining.

The Board and the courts have taken a somewhat broad view of what constitutes a mandatory subject under the vague statutory reference to "other terms and conditions of employment." For example, the Supreme Court has held that subjects which "vitally affect" employees are mandatory subjects of bargaining even though they may relate to conditions outside the bargaining unit. If these conditions have a substantial impact on the unit employees, then the employer may have a duty to negotiate with the union over them. The Court has also declared that industry practices are "highly relevant" in determining whether a subject is mandatory or permissive. Even the employer's unilateral approval of a supplier's increase in cafeteria and vending food prices has violated 8(a)(1).

The Court has developed a balancing test for determining whether there is a duty to bargain over certain fundamental business decisions such as partial shutdowns. The balancing is between the benefits to the collective bargaining process and the employer's need for unencumbered decision making in certain areas affecting its business. If the subject is amenable to resolution through the collective bargaining process, such as a decision to relocate certain work due to high labor costs, the balancing test will weigh in favor of it being a mandatory subject. The reason is that the union might be willing to make some concessions that would alleviate or remove the economic reasons for the move. On the other hand, if the decision is driven by forces that cannot be influenced by

the union, such as a relocation in order to be closer to a major customer, the balancing test will weigh against mandatory bargaining.

Three important principles about the duty to bargain are derived from the distinction between mandatory and permissive subjects:

(1) A party has a statutory obligation to bargain only with regard to mandatory bargaining subjects. Conversely, a party may refuse to bargain over a permissive bargaining subject.

(2) Bargaining to the point of impasse or deadlock over a permissive subject is treated as an automatic violation of Section 8(a)(5) because it is, in effect, an attempt to force a party to bargain over a permissive subject.

(3) A unilateral change in what would be a mandatory subject of bargaining usually violates Section 8(a)(5). Conversely, an employer does not usually violate Section 8(a)(5) by unilaterally changing a permissive bargaining subject.

Therefore, bargaining strategy, as well as many business decisions, often depend on whether the subjects involved are mandatory or permissive. If management refuses to discuss a subject on the ground that it is not a mandatory subject, and the Board disagrees, the employer will have violated the Act.

"Surface" bargaining refers to a situation where management does not bargain in good faith with the intent to reach a labor agreement, but instead has an unlawful purpose to frustrate agreement and create an impasse. When management meets with the union and goes through the motions of bargaining but intends all along to avoid an agreement, this constitutes unlawful surface bargaining in violation of Section (a)(5) of the NLRA.

To understand the motives an employer might have for actually avoiding a negotiated agreement, we need to remember the consequences of reaching an impasse. If the parties become dead-locked over one or more major issues, then they have reached an impasse in bargaining. Once a lawful impasse is reached, management has the right to unilaterally implement all or part of its offer.

The union can respond either by calling a strike or by continuing to work under the implemented terms. Not only does the employer achieve its ultimate objective by implementing the terms it is seeking, but the union is placed in a very difficult position which could lead to a loss of majority support among the employees. If the union calls a strike, the employees must go without pay for an indefinite period and run the risk of being permanently replaced.

On the other hand, if the union fails to call a strike and the employees continue working at the employer's implemented terms, it would constitute a fairly dramatic demonstration of the union's weakness and the employer's strength. Either way, the employees may begin to lose confidence in their bargaining representative. This is particularly true in a first contract situation after the union has been made a number of campaign promises about changes it will achieve and, as a result, been certified as the exclusive bargaining representative of the unit.

Thus, if management sets out to develop a strategy that will "break the union," one obvious course is to reach an impasse in bargaining and unilaterally implement the terms of its final offer. Such an anti-union motive is, of course, prohibited by the NLRA.

It is important to note that while the employer has a duty to bargain in good faith, the law does not require it to reach agreement on any particular issue, to withdraw any of its proposals, or to accept any union proposal. Thus, there is no presumption of bad faith merely because the parties reached an impasse in bargaining.

The term "surface bargaining" refers to an employer's attempt to give the superficial appearance of good faith by meeting with the union and engaging in a dialogue in order to cover up its desire to frustrate rather than achieve a mutually acceptable agreement. The key point to bear in mind is that anytime an employer takes particularly difficult positions in bargaining that eventually lead to an impasse and perhaps a strike, the situation is ripe for §8(a)(5) charges alleging that the employer deliberately engaged in bad faith, surface bargaining. As always, careful planning and preparation can greatly reduce the risk of later being found to have violated the Act.

When management begins to formulate its objectives for upcoming negotiations, it can anticipate the degree of resistance it is likely to face at the bargaining table. For example, concessionary bargaining will clearly meet with staunch opposition from the union. Thus, whenever management determines that there is a substantial possibility that negotiations will break down, it should conduct bargaining in a way that consciously seeks to avoid a finding of unlawful surface bargaining. In order to do this, it is helpful to know what factors the Board looks at in resolving surface bargaining charges.

The Board examines a variety of factors to determine whether the employer had a lawful intent. There are at least seven recognized indicia of surface bargaining:

1. delaying tactics;

2. unreasonable bargaining demands;

3. unilateral changes in mandatory subjects of bargaining;

4. efforts to bypass the union;

5. failure to designate an agent with sufficient bargaining authority;

6. withdrawal of already agreed-upon provisions; and

7. arbitrary scheduling of meetings

In addition, the Board places great emphasis on whether: (1) the procedural requirements of Section 8(d) to meet at reasonable times and places are satisfied; (2) the employer justified and explained its proposals, including whether it provided information sought by the union; (3) the employer evidenced flexibility in its bargaining position by responding to the union's concerns, offering compromises, or agreeing on particular issues; and (4) the employer's conduct away from the table evidenced an attempt to reach an agreement, including the presence or absence of other unfair labor practices. The Board is reluctant to infer overall bad faith where the employer was flexible and modified its position in bargaining. On the other hand, where the employer exhibits little or no movement and refuses to agree on any issues, the Board is far more likely to find unlawful surface bargaining.

Thus, in order to minimize the risk of liability for unlawful surface bargaining, employers should meet promptly upon request or by mutual agreement at reasonable times and places. They should study the union's proposals and explain why they are either acceptable or unacceptable, make counterproposals, demonstrate flexibility in their bargaining positions by responding to the union's concerns. They should avoid proposals that may be viewed as unreasonably harsh (e.g., open shop, no just-cause requirement for discipline, no grievance procedure, promotion, layoff, or recall without regard to seniority, etc.), justify and explain the employer's proposals, and above all, reach agreement on as many issues as possible before reaching impasse on remaining issues. If there is some other evidence of bad faith, such as employer statements reflecting an unlawful motive, then the Board may conclude that engaging in the above conduct was nothing more than a "sophisticated pretense." In the absence of other evidence, however, following the above guidelines will greatly reduce the risk of a finding of surface bargaining.

Duty to Furnish Information

During Bargaining – Another major aspect of the duty to bargain is the employer's obligation to supply the union with requested information. The basic rule is that the union has the right to all information that is potentially relevant to the performance of its function as bargaining representative. For example, when an employer claims an "inability to pay," it makes its financial condition relevant and, therefore, if requested, must disclose information to substantiate its claim. In other words, if an employer claims during bargaining that it cannot afford to pay the union's demands or that the Company is operating at a loss, then the employer will have a duty to "open its books" to the union.

Although this principle has been well established for decades, Board precedent provides little guidance on the question of just what type of financial material must be turned over. The U.S. Supreme Court has stated that an employer is obligated to present "some sort of proof" to substantiate its claim. The type and extent of disclosure required depends on the circumstances of the case. Employers may not, however, limit the information disclosed to just those fragments which satisfy management's own view of the issues. In cases involving a claim of inability to pay wage increases demanded, employers have been required to disclose profit and loss statements, and to disclose gross profits.

The union will not be entitled to such sensitive information as executive salaries and detailed breakdowns of operating expenses unless it can show a special need for this information. On the other hand, if the union demonstrates its need for specific information, it is unlawful to refuse to comply.

Even clearly relevant information need not be disclosed in precisely the form requested by the union. Generally, if management can demonstrate undue burden, legitimate business need for confidentiality, or justifiable fear of harassment of employees, requested information may be withheld, or presented in an alternative, reasonable and useful manner. The Board and the courts have stated that a union is not entitled to conduct a "fishing expedition" into the employer's records, and a remedy may be fashioned which accommodates an employer's legitimate interests.

The courts have also recognized that an employer is entitled to regulate access to sensitive financial data if the limitations are necessary to avoid disclosure of such information to competitors or third parties. The test is a balancing of each party's need, with consideration given to alternative methods of substantiation. Thus, if management raises bona fide objections to the union's request for information, and offers an alternative method of substantiation, the union must rely on more than general assertions of relevance to establish its right to more specific information.

Thus, before the employer decides to justify its bargaining positions based on poor financial performance, it should be prepared to disclose, if requested, documentation to substantiate such claims. The data may include profit and loss statements, gross profits, and similar aggregate financial information. Unless the union can show a special need, however, the employer need not disclose confidential or highly sensitive information such as officers' salaries or details that may assist a competitor. If faced with such a request, the employer should explain its concerns, inquire as to why the union needs this specific information, and offer other responsive information as an alternative.

There are a few other points that should be kept in mind about the duty to disclose financial information that is relevant to bargaining. First, it is critical to recognize that any statements made at the bargaining table can have specific legal consequences. In particular, any statements about the financial performance of the employer should be avoided and/or carefully considered in advance.

Another point to keep in mind is that employers are only obligated to provide information that is specifically requested by the union. Nothing should be volunteered unless material is being used affirmatively to persuade the union to accept the employer's proposals.

Aside from financial information following a claim of inability to pay, there is a host of information that is relevant to the terms and conditions of employment which must be provided in response to a request from the union. This information includes lists of employees and their job classifications, wages, overtime, seniority, vacation benefits, accrued paid time off, accrued pension benefits, etc., as well as the cost to the employer of various benefits such as health insurance premiums. The basic rule is that information relevant to the terms and conditions of employment must be provided.

The best way to handle a specific information request during bargaining is to respond across the table and in writing that the employer will consider the specific request and respond within a reasonable period of time (e.g., before the next scheduled bargaining session or within 2 weeks). The Board recognizes that an employer must be given a reasonable opportunity to evaluate and respond to a request for information before it can be found to have unlawfully refused to provide the information.

Grievance Handling/Other Information Requests – The duty to supply information applies not only during contract negotiations, but also during the life of a currently existing agreement. Indeed, in a variety of contexts, the Board has found a violation where an employer refused to supply the union with information needed for the proper enforcement and administration of the contract. The Board will also find a violation if the employer refuses to supply information concerning the implementation of changes which have an effect on the wages, seniority, and promotional rights of employees.

A common demand for information during the term of a contract concerns information pertaining to grievances. The union's access to adequate information concerning grievances enables the union to make a considered judgment about the strength of its claim, to eliminate non-meritorious claims at an early stage in the grievance process, and, if necessary, to prepare for arbitration.

An employer's duty to provide information relative to a grievance does not cease when the union files a demand for arbitration. In order to enable a union to process a grievance, employers have been required to provide information concerning employees' names, addresses, dates of hire, social security numbers, telephone numbers, wage and benefit data, job titles, age, sex, work rules and job descriptions, statistical data, job site locations, starting and quitting times, information in the personnel files of non-bargaining-unit employees, subcontracting information and wage and benefit information on temporary employees hired through an employment agency.

NLRB Deferral of an Unfair Labor Practice Charge to Arbitration

In many situations, acts by an employer may give rise to allegations of violations of both the labor agreement and the rights guaranteed by the NLRA. Typical examples of such overlapping claims include the following:

1. a union claim that the discipline or discharge of an employee violated both the "just cause" clause of the contract and Section 8(a)(3) which prohibits discrimination based on an employee's support for the union;

2. a union claim that an employer's unilateral change in working conditions violated both the duty to bargain under Section 8(a)(5) and a provision of the contract; and

3. a union claim that the employer's refusal to provide requested information for grievance handling violated its duty to bargain, where the employer's defense is that the union contractually waived any right to the information.

In cases involving overlapping contract and NLRA claims, the employer may be able to successfully defend against the ULP charge by asserting that the matter has already been arbitrated, or, if not, an arbitration concerning the matter is currently pending, or if a grievance has not yet been filed, that the employer is willing to submit the dispute to an arbitrator rather than submit it to the formal NLRB procedure.

The NLRB has established certain policies for determining when deferral to arbitration is appropriate. Different standards for deferral apply depending on whether

1. the unfair labor practice issues have already been considered and determined by an arbitrator ("post-arbitral deferral" under the Board's *Spielberg* Doctrine);

2. an arbitration proceeding is currently pending in which the issues are being considered ("pending arbitral deferral" under the Board's *Dubo* Doctrine); or

3. the arbitration process has not yet been invoked ("pre-arbitral deferral" under the Board's *Collyer* Doctrine).

Post-Arbitral Deferral – First, let's take a look at the Board's standards for deferral in the post-arbitral setting. The NLRB has announced that it would defer to an arbitrator's decision concerning the subject of an unfair labor practice if four conditions are met:

1. the unfair labor practice issue has been presented to and considered by the arbitrator;

2. the arbitral proceedings appear to have been fair and regular;

3. all parties to the arbitral proceedings agreed to be bound; and

4. the decision of the arbitrator is not clearly repugnant to the purpose and policies of the Act.

Unless something strange took place during the arbitration hearing or either party attempted to improperly influence the selection of the arbitrator or his decision; the second requirement of fair and regular proceedings will normally be satisfied. Similarly, the third requirement that both parties agreed to be bound is typically satisfied by the grievance and arbitration clause of the labor agreement.

With respect to the first requirement, that the arbitrator adequately considered the unfair labor practice issue, explicit consideration of the statutory issue is not necessary. Rather, if the contractual issue is factually parallel to the unfair labor practice issue, and the arbitrator was presented generally with the facts relevant to resolving the unfair labor practice, then deferral to the arbitrator's decision will be appropriate as long as the decision does not clearly conflict with the policies of the National Labor Relations Act.

Pre-Arbitral Deferral – The Board has also announced that it is willing to defer ULP determinations to an arbitrator even before any grievance has been filed. Such pre-arbitral deferral is only appropriate if the following conditions are met:

1. the unfair labor practice dispute arose within the context of a long and productive collective bargaining relationship and there is no claim of anti-union animus;

2. the parties have agreed to a contract clause that provides for binding arbitration over a broad range of disputes including the current unfair labor practice disputes; and

3. the contract and its meaning are central to the dispute.

Assuming the grievance is filed in time or the employer agrees to permit a late-filing, pre-arbitral deferral under the Board's *Collyer* Doctrine will be appropriate whenever the contract and its meaning are central to the unfair labor practice issues. Whether this third requirement is satisfied depends upon both the nature of the alleged ULP and the express provisions of the labor agreement.

The Board has held that certain types of cases are more amenable to resolution through the Board's procedures than deferral to arbitration. These exceptions to the *Collyer* Doctrine include questions of representation, accretion, appropriate unit, compliance with a previous Board order, definition of mandatory subjects of bargaining, contests between rival unions, and a refusal to provide relevant information. As to other contractual disputes, including allegations of unilateral action, the Board will generally defer.

Discipline of Bargaining Unit Employees

Discrimination/Retaliation – As indicated earlier, Section 8(a)(3) of the NLRA makes it an unfair labor practice to discriminate against any applicant or employee for the purpose of encouraging or discouraging membership in a labor organization, and Section 8(a)(4) prohibits retaliation against an employee because he has filed charges or given testimony in an NLRB proceeding. With respect to the discipline of bargaining unit employees, there are three key points to keep in mind.

First, employers should be particularly attuned to utilizing progressive discipline for significant acts of misconduct before discharging an employee who is a representative or outspoken advocate of the union. This does not mean, however, that these employees are entitled to favorable treatment. They are subject to the same disciplinary measures that other employees have received for similar acts of misconduct.

Second, during pre-employment interviews, employers should follow a strict policy against asking applicants whether they have ever been in a union or whether they view unions favorably.

Third, when it comes to disciplining an employee who has participated in a Board proceeding, employers must pay close attention to timing. There is a strong presumption of retaliatory motive if an employee is disciplined or discharged shortly after he has filed charges or given testimony against the employer. Unless the employee is caught or admits some serious act of misconduct close in time to the proceeding, employers are best advised to wait before taking any disciplinary action for ongoing problems such as absenteeism or poor standards of performance. Even after waiting for some time, employers must be certain that the employee is treated in a manner that is consistent with the way that other employees have been treated for similar misconduct.

Weingarten Rights – There is one other unfair labor practice issue relating to employee discipline that deserves mention. In a 1975 case, the U.S. Supreme Court held that it is a violation of Section 8(a)(1) of the Act to deny an employee's request to have a union representative at an investigatory interview which the employee reasonably believes might result in disciplinary action. These rights are referred to as *Weingarten* rights.

The court concluded that the right to representation arises from the general language in Section 7 of the NLRA giving employees the right to engage in concerted activities for the purpose of collective bargaining "or other mutual aid or protection."

In order for *Weingarten* rights to apply, certain triggering conditions must be satisfied. First, the employee himself must ask to have a representative present at the investigatory interview. If no request is made, or if the representative makes the request instead of the employee, then the employer is not obligated to permit the representative's attendance. Furthermore, the employee's request must be directed to a management official who knows why the employee is being interviewed and is in a position to assess whether or not to grant the request. Thus, the Board has held that an employee's *Weingarten* rights did not arise when he directed his request for a representative to a different supervisor from the one who subsequently conducted the interview.

The second condition outlined by the Supreme Court was that the employee must reasonably believe that the interview will result in disciplinary action. The Board has consistently defined "reasonable belief" to be based upon objective standards. The Board will not probe an employee's subjective motivation, but rather will look to objective criteria, under all the circumstances of the case, to determine whether discipline could reasonably be expected. For example, the location of the interview is one such objective factor. An interview in a work area is less likely to result in discipline than one conducted in a private office. By the way, the *Weingarten* right does not apply to ordinary shop-floor conversations between an employee and a supervisor on subjects such as training or correction of work techniques.

A third condition is that the interview must be of an investigatory nature. Meetings held merely for the purpose of announcing predetermined discipline are not covered by *Weingarten*. If the employee seeks clarification of the discipline or the reasons for its imposition, the information may be provided without triggering the employee's right to a representative. If, however, the employer begins questioning the employee to obtain more information or an admission, regardless of the original purpose of the meeting, the employee has a right to a representative. Thus, an employer may transform a non-*Weingarten* meeting into a *Weingarten* investigative interview.

Once an appropriate request for representation has been made, the employer has one of 3 options: (1) it can grant the request and allow a representative to attend; or (2) discontinue the interview, complete the investigation and take appropriate disciplinary action without benefit of the interview; or (3) offer the employee the choice between continuing the interview without a representative or having no interview at all. The employer cannot discipline an employee for refusing to attend or for refusing to answer questions in an investigatory interview if the employee requested a representative. Similarly, if an employer ignores the employee's request, the employee may leave the interview without being subject to discipline for insubordination.

If the employee requests a representative, he has the right to consult with the representative prior to the interview. Furthermore, the employer must provide some indication of the matter under investigation in order to give the employee a meaningful opportunity to consult with his representative prior to the interview. The employer does not have to "reveal its case", the information it has obtained, or even the specifics of the misconduct to be discussed. A general statement as to the subject matter of the interview, which identifies to the employee and his representative the misconduct for which discipline may be imposed, is sufficient.

With respect to the identity of the representative, an employee may request that a union official or a co-employee attend a meeting as his representative. While an employee may request a particular individual, the request cannot interfere with legitimate employer prerogatives. For example, the employee cannot use his *Weingarten* rights to avoid or delay a disciplinary proceeding. It has been held that if no union official is immediately available, the employer can offer to allow a co-employee to attend and continue with the meeting. Furthermore, if the employee requests a specific individual and he is not available, the burden remains with the employee to ask for another representative.

Once an interview has begun, the representative may assist the employee by attempting to clarify the facts or suggest other employees who may have knowledge. The employer has the right, however, to insist that it is only interested in hearing the employee's own account of the matter under investigation. Thus, the employer may restrict the representative's role in order to prevent negotiation or adversarial confrontation, but it may not insist that the representative remain silent throughout the interview. *Weingarten* allows an employee to receive assistance from a representative and not just his presence.

The remedy for a *Weingarten* violation may include an order to retract any disciplinary action that was taken based on information unlawfully obtained during the interview. However, the Board has held that the remedy of reinstatement and backpay is inappropriate where the employee was discharged for just cause. Furthermore, if the discipline is based on information gathered from other sources, the Board will not upset the status quo, but instead will simply issue a cease and desist order instructing the employer to refrain from any future *Weingarten* violations.

Employee Health Insurance Laws 11

Introduction

Health care costs for employees and their dependents are a major concern for most employers. The soaring costs of health care have made it one of the central public policy issues of our time. As a result, bold initiatives that were once summarily dismissed are now receiving another look.

Employee insistence on an adequate health care program, the ever-rising cost of such benefits, and government's gradual shifting of these costs onto the employer sector of the economy have forced employers to rethink the traditional group insurance package. ERISA, COBRA, and other mandated benefit laws increase employer awareness of the direct relationship between employee wellness and "the bottom line" – all have brought attention to what, just a few years ago, was an area of the employer-employee relationship that was simply taken for granted. Therefore, employers have focused on plans which encourage prudent buying decisions, and which change buying habits for health care.

Historically, employees were insulated from the costs of their health care buying decision. The Health Research Institute has found, however, that unless the employee is paying at least 25 percent of the bill, there is no attention paid to the cost. Employers have developed a number of ways to shift premium costs to employees. For active employees, employers have:

- Required a straight percentage of premium cost to be shared by the employee. This approach is a simple and consistent hedge against future increases, but does not control a significant portion of the increased cost;

- Required a higher percentage of future increases or future increases that exceed a certain level;

- Required employees to pay a flat or capped amount;

- Required employees to pay a progressive percentage of premiums based on their wages or a percentage of their wages toward percentages;

- Frozen or deferred wages for use in paying premiums or traded off some other fringe benefit;

- Change plan design or type of plan;

- Changed carriers;

- Provided wellness incentives;

- Lengthened waiting periods (e.g., six months for individual coverage and twelve months for family coverage);

- Cutback on eligibility while employees are on Workers' Compensation or Disability; and

- Implemented two-tier programs for new hires in plan design and contributions.

In the past, employers were not very concerned about providing lifetime health insurance benefits to its retired employees. However, the cost of insurance, the burgeoning number of baby boomer retirees and their longer life expectancy is creating an unfunded liability of crisis proportion. If the benefit is not vested, it can be eliminated even for existing retirees.

Employers have taken the following actions to try to minimize the future, unfunded liability:

- Reserve the right to modify or eliminate the benefit in a summary plan description, the Plan and/or a collective bargaining agreement;

Health Care Cost Savings Checklist

☐ Identify doctors and hospitals that are more proficient and cost-effective and create a network around them.

☐ Provide incentives that encourage employees to make use of these medical services.

☐ Monitor, continually, medical services' quality and cost (e.g., one major company pays a greater percentage of the medical bill if the employee uses doctors and hospitals in the company's network).

☐ Design handbooks to inform employees how to use the health care system and how to encourage wiser consumer decisions by employees.

☐ To emphasize who is covering the cost, place the company's own name, in addition to the name of its insurance claims handler, on the checks with which it pays medical bills.

☐ Break out amounts spent on health care costs in the annual benefits summary.

☐ Use "health service advisors" to assist in cases of severe illness.

☐ Encourage wellness programs (annual physicals, mammary exams, smoking cessation programs).

☐ Explore using Health Savings Accounts.

☐ Encourage the use of generic drugs and establish a mail order prescription drug program for maintenance drugs.

- Offer to provide the same benefit as active employees receive (plan design and cost sharing are then not frozen);

- Limit eligibility (using years of service and other criteria); and

- Coordinate benefits with Medicare to ensure savings are achieved at age 65.

Other mechanisms for achieving cost-control include increasing deductibles, pre-admission testing (tests which can be performed before entering the hospital); changing the co-insurance percentage; outpatient surgery (many procedures once routinely performed in the hospital can now be done on an outpatient basis); audit programs (approximately 70-90 percent of all hospital bills have errors); generic drugs; health savings accounts or other consumer driven health plans; birthing centers; freestanding emergency medical centers; hospice care; and second-opinion surgery. Some forms of disincentive or "punishment for imprudent spending" include reducing benefits by 50 percent if there is no second opinion and not paying for weekend hospital pre-admission. Some employers have tried some noteworthy options other than shifting health care costs to employees.

COBRA — Legislative Purpose

A major provision of the Consolidated Omnibus Budget Reconciliation Act of 1986 (COBRA) allows for the extension of group insurance coverage on a self-pay basis to employees and/or their dependents who would otherwise lose their coverage.

Group health care plans providing "medical" benefits as defined in Internal Revenue Code Section 213, such as medical, dental, vision, and prescription drug plans (but not life insurance and disability benefit plans), are covered. Thus, not only group insurance plans, but self-insured plans, HMO's, and PPO's are included under the scope of COBRA. Eligible employees and/or dependents are entitled to continue their group health benefits for varying periods of time (typically eighteen months) by paying up to 102 percent of the current premium (including both employee and employer payments) or of the reasonable estimate of the self-insured plan cost.

In 1989, the COBRA law was amended to require employers to cover former employees whose medical condition kept them from immediately getting coverage under a new employer's plan. Thus, an individual may continue to pay for COBRA coverage even after becoming covered by another group plan if that plan excludes or limits the coverage of a preexisting condition. The continuation coverage is extended to 29 months, from 18 months, in the event a worker is disabled at the time of termination or the qualifying event occurs.

Suggestions for "Coping with COBRA"

1. All notices – initial and ongoing – should be sent Registered/Return Receipt Requested to verify notice in case of subsequent charges of notification not being made.

2. Enrollment forms for continuation coverage should identify eligibility and conditions of coverage.

3. The policy for premium payment and cancellation provisions for nonpayment of premiums should be clearly stated.

4. Tickler files should be maintained for:
   a. 180-day pre-continuation trigger notice for conversion application; and
   b. Notification to beneficiaries and/or administrator/insurer of the end of the continuation period for an individual.

5. Procedures should be adopted for updating beneficiary addresses – needed for premium overdue notices, plan revision information, etc.

6. The offer of continuation of benefits should be on an all-or-nothing basis (e.g., the beneficiary must continue dental and health, not dental only). This limits some effects of non-selection which would add to your benefit costs.

7. Require declination forms from those individuals indicating they do not wish to continue.

8. Notify claims personnel to screen for other sources of payment on providers' bills, then follow up to determine the potential ineligibility of the individual to continue on your plan.

9. Implement mandatory managed care plans to preclude inappropriate or excessive utilization patterns. Studies suggest that nonworking persons have higher utilization trends.

10. Create a system to log in and out all administrative notices and receipts.

11. Establish "premium" amounts (even if self-insured) prospectively; update annually.

12. If you terminate or lose employees shortly after hiring, determine the average time they are with your firm. Use this time period to set your plan eligibility date. This will cut down on benefit paperwork and also preclude a short-term employee from gaining significant coverage.

Coverage and Eligibility

Virtually every employer, private and public, with a group health plan as described above is included, except the federal government, District of Columbia, churches and synagogues, and employers with fewer than 20 employees.

Employees losing coverage on or after the effective date due either to termination of employment (for any reason except discharge for gross misconduct) or a reduction in hours of work, must be extended the continuation privilege. COBRA coverage must be offered military reservists and their families, unless an employer "voluntarily" maintains full coverage under a group health plan for these individuals and their families. Spouses and dependent children of covered employees are also eligible if they lose coverage on or after the effective date due to the employee's death, termination (other than for gross misconduct), reduced work hours, or becoming eligible for Medicare; divorce or legal separation from the employee; or ceasing to satisfy the plan's coverage requirements for dependent children.

Benefits and Duration

The individual has the right to continue the same coverages he or she had the day before the qualifying event as an ongoing participant or dependent in the plan, and no evidence of insurability can be required. Coverage on this self-pay basis can continue from the date coverage would have stopped for varying periods of time from 18 to 36 months. Coverage may be stopped if the employer terminates the plan, if the individual fails to pay the premium, if the individual becomes covered under another health care plan (regardless of the benefits included), or if the individual becomes eligible for Medicare. The employee must notify the plan administrator within 60 days of divorce, legal separation, or loss of dependent child status.

In 1998, the Supreme Court resolved a split among Circuit Courts, by deciding that an employer may not deny COBRA continuation coverage under its health plan to an otherwise eligible beneficiary because he is covered under another group health plan at the time he elects COBRA coverage. In this particular case, the individual who was terminated from his job, had concurrent coverage under his spouse's insurance; but nonetheless elected to continue under COBRA. When his former employer advised him six months after his election that he was not eligible for COBRA, he filed a lawsuit. The Supreme Court ruled that for his election of COBRA coverage to have been invalid he would have had to "first become" covered under his wife's policy after his termination. This plainly was not case, as he was already covered under her policy before his termination. Thus, he was entitled to continuation coverage.

Employees have to accept or reject continued coverage within a minimum of 60 days after notice, and pay the premium within 45 days after election of continued coverage.

Notification Requirements

The employer must give written notice to employees and spouses when the employer's plan year begins and compliance with COBRA becomes required. (See a "model" COBRA statement for employers' use in the Appendix.) An explanation of how COBRA applies must also be included in the employer's Summary Plan Description. Within 30 days of an employee's death or change in employment status, the employer must notify the plan administrator. Employees or "qualified beneficiaries" must notify the plan administrator when there is a divorce or legal separation or when the dependent has reached the contractual age limit.

The plan administrator has 14 days to notify the beneficiary of continuation rights (ensuring that the ex-spouse or dependent is aware of their options). The individual has 60 days to elect coverage and 45 more days to start paying the premium.

Penalties for Noncompliance

A private sector employer's failure to comply could result in the following:

1. Loss of a federal income tax deduction for the plan costs;

2. The cost of coverage for highly compensated employees would become taxable income to them;

3. The plan administrator and the plan fiduciary are liable for $100 per day personal damages for failure to give notice if requested to; and

4. Attorneys' fees and costs can be awarded for breach of fiduciary responsibility.

A public sector employer's penalty for noncompliance is injunctive relief.

The Health Insurance Portability and Accountability Act of 1996

The Health Insurance and Portability Act of 1996 (HIPAA) was signed into law on August 21, 1996. This law includes important new protections for an estimated 25 million Americans who move from one job to another, who are self-employed, or who have pre-existing

Frequently Asked Questions about Health Insurance Portability Law

Q. How will the new law help people who currently have health insurance through their employer and who want to change jobs?

A. Currently some plans do not cover pre-existing medical conditions. HIPAA limits this practice so that most plans cover an individual's pre-existing condition after 12 months. If at the time you change jobs you already have 12 months of continuous group health coverage, you will not have to start over with a new 12-month exclusion for any pre-existing conditions. Under HIPAA, your new employer will be required to give you credit for the length of time that you had continuous group health coverage.

Q. How does "crediting" for pre-existing conditions work under HIPAA?

A. You will receive credit for your previous coverage that occurred without a break in coverage of 63 days or more. However, any coverage occurring prior to a break in coverage of 63 days or more would not be credited against an exclusion period. To illustrate, suppose an individual had coverage for two years followed by a break in coverage for 70 days and then resumed coverage for eight months. That individual would only receive credit against any pre-existing condition exclusions for eight months of coverage; no credit would be given for the two years of coverage prior to the break of 63 days.

It is also important to remember that during any exclusion period you may be entitled to COBRA continuation coverage. "COBRA" is the name for a federal law that provides workers and their families the opportunity to purchase group health coverage through their employer's health plan for a limited period of time (generally 18, 29 or 36 months) if they lose coverage due to specified events including termination of employment, divorce or death. Workers in companies of 20 or more employees generally qualify for COBRA.

FAQs about Health Insurance Portability Law (continued)

Q. Can I receive credit for previous COBRA coverage?

A. Yes. Under HIPAA any period of time that you are receiving COBRA continuation coverage is counted as previous continuous health coverage as long as the coverage occurred without a break in coverage of 63 days or more. For example, if you were covered for five months by a previous health plan and then received seven months of COBRA continuation coverage, you would be entitled to receive credit for 12 months by your new group health plan.

Q. What is a "pre-existing condition"?

A. Under HIPAA a "pre-existing condition" is a condition for which medical advice, diagnosis, care or treatment was recommended or received within the six month period ending on the enrollment date in any new health plan. If you had a medical condition in the past, but have not received any medical advice, diagnosis, care or treatment within the six months prior to enrolling in the plan, your old condition is not a pre-existing condition for which an exclusion can be applied.

Q.   Are there "pre-existing conditions" that cannot be excluded from coverage?

A. Pre-existing condition exclusions cannot be applied to pregnancy, regardless of whether the woman had previous coverage. In addition, a pre-existing condition exclusion cannot be applied to a newborn or adopted child under age 18 as long as the child became covered under the health plan within 30 days of birth or adoption, provided they do not incur a subsequent 63 day or longer break in coverage.

Q. How will newly hired employees prove they had prior health coverage that should be credited?

A. Under HIPAA, providing information about an employee's prior health coverage is the responsibility of an employee's former employer, group health plan and/or the insurance company providing such coverage. HIPAA sets specific reporting and certification requirements for group health plans, insurance companies and HMO's. Certification statements detailing when the employee was covered under the plan must be provided to employees when they are no longer covered by the plan and when the employees' COBRA coverage ceases.

Q. What if I have trouble getting documentation from a prior employer?

A. Under HIPAA, insurers and group health plans are required to provide documentation to individuals that certifies any credible coverage they have earned. Insurers and group health plans that fail or refuse to provide such certification are subject to monetary penalties under HIPAA. HIPAA also requires that a process be established that will allow individuals to show they are entitled to credible coverage in situations where they cannot obtain a certification from an insurer or group health plan. It is important, therefore, for individuals to keep accurate records (e.g., pay stubs, copies of premium payments or other evidence of health care coverage) that can be used to establish periods of credible coverage in the event a certification cannot be obtained from an insurer or group health plan.

Q. If I change jobs am I guaranteed the same benefits that I have under my current plan?

A. No. When a person transfers from one plan to another, the benefits the person receives will be those provided under the new plan. Coverage under the new plan could be less or could be greater.

Q. Will I be covered immediately under my new employer's plan?

A. Not necessarily. Employers and insurance companies may set a waiting period before enrollees become eligible for benefits under the plan. HMO's may have an "affiliation period" during which an enrollee does not receive benefits and is not charged premiums. Affiliation periods may not last for more than two months and are only allowed for HMO's that do not use pre-existing condition exclusions.

FAQs about Health Insurance Portability Law ^(continued)

Q. Can I lose coverage if my health status changes?

A. Group health plans and issuers may not establish eligibility for enrollment based on your health status, medical condition (physical or mental), claims experience, receipt of health care, medical history, genetic information, evidence of insurability or disability. For example, you cannot be excluded or dropped from coverage the health plan offers just because you have a particular illness.

Although employers may establish limits or restrictions on benefits or coverage for similarly situated individuals under a plan, they may not require an individual to pay a premium or contribution which is greater than that for a similarly situated individual based on health status. They may also change plan benefits or covered service if they give participants notice of any "material reductions" within 60 days after the change is adopted.

Q. Does HIPAA require employers to offer health coverage or to provide specific benefits?

A. No. The provision of health coverage by an employer is still voluntary. HIPAA does not require specific benefits nor does it prohibit a plan from restricting the amount or nature of benefits for similarly situated individuals.

Q. What if my new employer does not provide health coverage?

A. There is no requirement for any employer to offer health insurance coverage. If your new employer does not offer health insurance, you may, if qualified, continue coverage under your previous employer's health plan under COBRA.

Q. What if I am unable to obtain group coverage?

A. You may have the option of obtaining coverage under an individual policy. HIPAA would guarantee access to individual insurance for those who:

- Have not had group coverage for at least 18 months.
- Did not have their group coverage terminated because of fraud or nonpayment of premiums.
- Are ineligible for COBRA or have exhausted their COBRA benefits; and
- Are not eligible for coverage under another group health plan.

The opportunity to buy an individual insurance policy is the same whether the individual is laid off, fired or quits his or her job. For information on individual insurance policies you should contact your State Insurance Commissioner's office or the Health Care Financing Administration.

Q. What if I cannot afford the premiums for health coverage?

A. HIPAA does not set premium rates but is does prohibit charging an individual more than similarly situated individuals in the same plan because of health status. Employers may offer premium discounts or rebates for participation in wellness or other health care promotions. In addition, many states limit insurance premiums and HIPAA does not pre-empt current or future state laws regulating the cost of insurance.

Q. If coverage under my health plan is provided through an HMO or an insurance policy of an insurance company licensed in my state, are there any state offices that I can contact if I have questions about my plan's insurance policy?

A. Yes. The State Insurance Commissioner's office can assist you in matters involving a group or individual health insurance policy offered by an insurance company licensed in your state. This includes managed care coverage offered by HMO's.

In addition, many states may limit insurance premiums and HIPAA does not pre-empt current or future state laws regulating the cost of insurance.

medical conditions. HIPAA's provisions place requirements on employer-sponsored group health plans, and insurance companies. The new law includes changes that:

- Protect many workers who change jobs or lose jobs by providing better access to health insurance coverage;

- Limit exclusions for pre-existing conditions;

- Prohibit discrimination against employees and dependents based on their health status;

- Guarantee renewability and availability of health coverage to certain employers and individuals; and

- Provide privacy and regulate the disclosure of medical data concerning employees.

The privacy regulations issued under the Health Insurance Portability and Accounting Act ("HIPAA") are designed to protect the privacy of individually identifiable health information. In doing so, these regulations impose significant restrictions and obligations on employers, both directly, as a covered entities, and indirectly, as a sponsor of health plans. Because the obligations imposed on employers vary based on the employer's involvement in the provision of group benefit plans and the health information received from group health plans, employers must ascertain how these regulations affect their organization and take steps to ensure compliance.

Who must comply with HIPAA's privacy regulations? HIPAA's privacy regulations apply to "covered entities", which includes health plans, health care clearinghouses, and health care providers who transmit health information in electronic form. Covered health plans include insured and self-insured hospital and medical benefit plans, some health flexible spending accounts, and employee assistance plans. Excepted from this general definition

are self-administered health plans with less than 50 participants.

HIPAA's privacy regulations also apply to "hybrid entities" -- entities whose primary business is not health care, but include components that qualify as a covered entity (e.g., a manufacturing company that has an on-site employee health services office may qualify as a hybrid entity). In these situations, the privacy regulations only apply to the health care component, but the organization is required to erect "firewalls" separating the covered entity from other components.

When employers provide benefits through a self-insured health plan, that plan is a "covered entity" and the employer is, therefore, a "hybrid entity" consisting of its business components that are not covered entities and its health plan component that is a covered entity. In such a hybrid entity, the business component may not receive individually identifiable health information from the health plan component, except in limited circumstances provided for in the regulations.

Employers who provide health coverage through a fully insured plan ("Employer Plan Sponsors") are neither covered, nor hybrid entities. Nonetheless, the health plan itself is a covered entity and HIPAA's privacy regulations impose limitations on the information Employer Plan Sponsors may obtain from the plan insurer.

What health information is protected by HIPAA's privacy regulations? HIPAA prohibits covered entities from using or disclosing an individual's "protected health information" ("PHI") unless specifically authorized by the individual or the HIPPA regulations. PHI includes virtually all "individually identifiable health information" that is transmitted or maintained by a covered entity, regardless of its form. "Individually identifiable health information" includes health information that relates to the past, present, or future physical or mental health or condition of an individual, including an individual's care or the payment for such care. To be protected as PHI, the health information must also identify the individual or there must be a reasonable basis to believe that the information could be used to identify the individual.

Health information that has been stripped of identifiers, such as name, birth date, phone number and social security number, does not constitute PHI and is not subject to the same restrictions on use and disclosure. The definition of PHI also excludes individually identifiable health information in education records covered by the Family Education Rights and Privacy Act ("FERPA") and employment records held by a covered entity in its role as an employer.

What limitations does HIPAA impose on the use and disclosure of PHI? Under the HIPAA privacy regulations, a covered entity generally may not use or disclose PHI, except: (1) for treatment, payment, or health care operations; (2) upon the individual's agreement in certain limited situations (after an opportunity to agree or object); (3) to the individual, subject to his or her rights under HIPAA; (4) as permitted or required by HIPAA; or (5) pursuant to an authorization from the individual.

Can a covered entity disclose an individual's PHI to an employer without the individual's authorization? A health plan may use and disclose PHI for treatment, payment, and health care operations without an individual's consent or authorization. However, to use and disclose PHI for any other reason, including employment-related determinations, a covered entity must obtain specific authorization from the individual describing who will have access to the PHI, when the access expires, and the individual's right to revoke the authorization.

This limitation will have a significant impact on employers since employers frequently obtain PHI for a wide variety of reasons, including pre-employment physicals, confirmation of the need for FMLA leave and reasonable accommodation, and drug and alcohol testing required by the U.S. Department of Transportation. While employers may continue to obtain PHI directly from their employees, under the privacy regulations covered entities, including health care providers, will no longer be able to disclose PHI directly to an employer for use in employment determinations without the applicant's/employee's authorization. Thus, a health care provider may not disclose the results of a pre-employment physical or fitness-for-duty examination without an employee's authorization. Similarly, an EAP that qualifies as a covered entity may not disclose its report to the employer without the employee's authorization to do so.

Importantly, HIPAA's privacy regulations do not prohibit an employer from requiring an employee to provide an authorization for a covered entity to disclose PHI to the employer. Therefore, an employer may require a job applicant to provide an authorization for the disclosure of the results of a pre-employment physical or require an employee to authorize the disclosure of alcohol and drug tests required by the U.S. Department of Transportation.

Responsibilities of Employers

The impact of HIPAA's privacy regulations on employers depends upon the employer's involvement in the provision of benefits and the information the employer receives as plan sponsor.

What are an employer's obligations under HIPAA if it provides benefits through a self-insured plan? An employer that self-insures its health plan is a "hybrid entity" and its health plan component is subject to the same HIPAA obligations as other covered entities. Specifically, the employer must ensure that the health plan component: (1) will not disclose PHI to any of the employer's other components;

(2) will not disclose PHI to business associates performing an activity or function on the plan's behalf, including claims administration, without obtaining "satisfactory assurances" that the business associate will appropriately safeguard the information; (3) will comply with HIPAA's individual privacy rights; and (4) will provide participants with notice of their rights with respect to their PHI as well as how the plan may use and disclose PHI.

The health plan component must also satisfy HIPAA's administrative requirements, including:

- Designating a qualified privacy official responsible for developing and implementing HIPAA-related policies and procedures, as well as a contact person to receive complaints about privacy (the privacy official may also serve as the contact person);

- Providing and documenting job-specific privacy awareness training for all workforce members who will have access to PHI;

- Implementing internal procedures to ensure that only those workforce members with a need to know use or access PHI;

- Establishing safeguards to protect the privacy of PHI from accidental or intentional use or disclosure in violation of HIPAA;

- Tracking all uses and disclosures of PHI;

- Creating a mechanism for receiving complaints from individuals regarding the plan's privacy practices; and

- Establishing a system of "appropriate sanctions" for workforce members who fail to comply with privacy and security policies and procedures, and a system for monitoring and evaluating such compliance.

What obligations does an employer have if it provides health coverage through a fully insured health plan? An employer who provides health benefits through a fully insured plan is not a "covered entity" under HIPAA and

is, therefore, not required to comply with most of the requirements HIPAA imposes on self-insured plans. Instead, the insurer of the health plan will generally be considered the covered entity and will be responsible for complying with the obligations imposed by HIPAA's privacy regulations.

Nonetheless, under ERISA, plan sponsors are deemed to be the plan administrators of their plans and are therefore fiduciaries of the plan. As fiduciaries, plan sponsors have an obligation to ensure that their plans are compliant with HIPAA. Therefore, Employer Plan Sponsors should seek assurances concerning HIPAA compliance from any third party administrators or insurance carriers involved in their plan.

HIPAA's privacy regulations also affect Employer Plan Sponsors by restricting and regulating the flow of health information from covered entities (i.e., the health plan) to noncovered entities (i.e., the plan sponsor). The specific requirements imposed on Employer Plan Sponsors depend on the information received by the plan sponsor. Therefore, Employer Plan Sponsors should examine how they handle health care information, whether this health care information constitutes PHI, and whether the Employer Plan Sponsor needs access to this information.

Employer Plan Sponsors Who Obtain PHI From Their Health Plan

Employers that self-administer a group health plan routinely obtain and use PHI. In addition, Employer Plan Sponsors may need health care information for a variety of reasons including setting premiums, modifying, amending, or terminating the plan, and determining plan design. While the privacy regulations do not absolutely prohibit a health plan from disclosing health care information to Employer Plan Sponsors, they impose some limitations and require the plan sponsor to take certain steps before such disclosure can occur.

The privacy regulations permit an Employer Plan Sponsor to use PHI for plan administration functions performed on behalf of the group health plan, including payment and health care operations, such as quality assurance, claims processing, auditing, and monitoring. However, the regulations prohibit an Employer Plan Sponsor from using PHI to modify, amend or terminate the plan, solicit bids from prospective insurers, for employment-related functions, or functions in connection with any other benefits or benefit plans. As discussed below, an Employer Plan Sponsor may use summary health information to amend or terminate the plan or to solicit bids from prospective insurers.

An Employer Plan Sponsor that obtains PHI from the plan must amend its plan document to include specific privacy requirements relating to PHI, agree to comply with the plan document, and make certain assurances. Specifically, the plan sponsor must amend plan documents to: (1) describe the permitted uses and disclosures of PHI; (2) specify that disclosure is permitted only upon receipt of a certification form the plan sponsor; and (3) provide adequate separation between the group health plan and the plan sponsor.

The plan sponsor that receives PHI must certify that it will:

- not use or further disclose or allow its agents to disclose PHI, except as permitted by the plan documents or as required by HIPAA;

- ensure that any subcontractors or agents to whom the plan sponsor provides PHI agree to the same restrictions;

- not use or disclose PHI for employment-related actions;

- report to the health plan any uses or disclosures inconsistent with these requirements;

- provide plan participants with access to their PHI, allow plan participants to amend incorrect data, and provide an accounting of disclosures;

- make documentation and internal practices relating to the use and disclosure of PHI available to the Department of Health and Human Services upon request;

- return or destroy all PHI that is no longer needed for the purpose it was obtained; and

- ensure adequate separation between the group health plan and the plan sponsor.

Employer Plan Sponsors Who Obtain Only Summary Health Information From The Health Plan

Employer Plan Sponsors can avoid the requirements discussed above by limiting the information it receives from the health plan to summary health information and enrollment/disenrollment information relating to the health plan. "Summary health information" is information that summarizes the claims history, claims expenses or types of claims by individuals enrolled in the health plan after certain individual identifiers have been removed. Summary health information may be disclosed by the health plan to the plan sponsor for the limited purposes of obtaining premium bids for health insurance coverage under the health plan and for amending or terminating the plan.

How does an employer limit its obligations under HIPAA's privacy regulations? If an employer provides benefits through a self-insured plan or otherwise receives PHI, HIPAA imposes significant obligations on the employer. An employer may avoid most HIPAA privacy requirements if it provides plan benefits through fully insured plans and receives no PHI.

What should an employer do to ensure it is in compliance with HIPAA's privacy regulations? In order to achieve compliance, employers should take these steps:

1. Determine if the organization or any employee benefit plans it provides is a covered entity under HIPAA.

2. Analyze the flow of health information and how that information is used and disclosed within the organization. How and why does the organization obtain PHI from employees and its benefit plans? How does the organization use PHI in administering the employment and plan relationship? What employees have access to PHI?

3. Analyze the flow of health information to, from, and within the employer's group health plan.

4. Examine whether information flow and documentation are consistent with HIPAA requirements.

5. Develop a plan to bring both the plan and the plan sponsor into HIPAA compliance.

6. Ascertain the HIPAA compliance status of business associates who deal with the plans or with insurance issuers or HMOs. Examine existing contracts with business associates and determine which need to be modified to bring the agreements into compliance with HIPAA.

7. Amend health plan documents to permit disclosure of PHI consistent with HIPAA's requirements.

8. Create privacy policies and procedures consistent with HIPAA's requirements.

What is the penalty for noncompliance? Neither HIPAA nor HIPAA's privacy regulations permit an individual employee to sue for violations of the privacy standards; however, HIPAA does provide both criminal and civil penalties for noncompliance. Failure to comply with HIPAA's privacy regulations can result in civil penalties of up to $100 per person per violation, with a cap of $25,000 per calendar year. Criminal penalties for violations include up to $250,000 in fines and possible imprisonment for up to 10 years.

The Newborns' and Mothers' Health Protection Act of 1996

The Newborns' and Mothers' Health Protection Act of 1996 (NMHPA) includes important new protection for mothers and their newborn children with regard to the length of hospital stays following the birth of a child.

Frequently Asked Questions
Relating to Pregnant Employee Insurance Rights

The insurance rights of pregnant women are the subject of Equal Employment Opportunity Commission guidelines. See Chapter 4 discussion of Pregnancy Discrimination Act.

Only Married Protected?
  Q. May an employer limit disability benefits for pregnancy-related conditions to married employees?
    A. No.

FAQs on Pregnant Employee Insurance Rights [(continued)]

All Female Workforce

Q. If an employer has an all-female workforce or job classification, must benefits be provided for pregnancy-related conditions?

A. Yes. If benefits are provided for other conditions, they must be also be provided for pregnancy-related conditions.

Income Maintenance

Q. For what length of time must an employer who provides income maintenance benefits for temporary disabilities provide such benefits for pregnancy-related disabilities?

A. Benefits should be provided for as long as the employee is unable to work for medical reasons unless some other limitation is set for all other temporary disabilities, in which case pregnancy-related disabilities should be treated the same as other temporary disabilities.

Long-Term Disability

Q. Must an employer who provides benefits for long-term or permanent disabilities provide such benefits for pregnancy-related conditions?

A. Yes. Benefits for long-term or permanent disabilities resulting from pregnancy-related conditions must be provided to the same extent that such benefits are provided for other conditions which result in long-term or permanent disability.

Fringe Benefits

Q. If an employer provides benefits to employees on leave, such as installment purchase disability insurance; payment of premium for health, life, or other insurance; or continued payments into pension, savings or profit-sharing plans, must the same benefits be provided for those on leave for pregnancy-related conditions?

A. Yes, the employer must provide the same benefits for those on leave for pregnancy-related conditions as for those on leave for other reasons.

Vacation

Q. Can an employee who is absent due to a pregnancy-related disability be required to exhaust vacation benefits before receiving sick leave pay or disability benefits?

A. No. If employees who are absent because of other disabilities causes receive sick leave pay or disability benefits without any requirement that they first exhaust vacation benefits, the employer cannot impose this requirement on an employee for a pregnancy-related cause.

FAQs on Pregnant Employee Insurance Rights [(continued)]

State Laws

Q. If state law requires an employer to provide disability insurance for a specified period before and after childbirth, does compliance with the state law fulfill the employer's obligation under the Pregnancy Discrimination Act?

A. Not necessarily. It is an employer's obligation to treat employees temporarily disabled by pregnancy in the same manner as employees affected by other temporary disabilities. Therefore, any restrictions imposed by state laws on benefits for pregnancy-related disabilities, but not for other disabilities, do not excuse the employer from treating the individuals in both groups of employees the same. If, for example, a state law requires an employer to pay a maximum of 26 weeks benefits for disabilities other than pregnancy-related ones, but only six weeks for pregnancy-related disabilities, the employer must provide benefits for the additional weeks to an employee disabled by pregnancy-related conditions, up to the maximum provided other disabled employees.

Public Employees

Q. If a state or local government provides its own employees income maintenance benefits for disabilities, may it provide different benefits for disabilities arising from pregnancy-related conditions than for disabilities arising from other conditions?

A. No. State and local governments, as employers, are subject to the Pregnancy Discrimination Act in the same way as private employers and must bring their employment practices and programs into compliance with the Act, including disability and health insurance programs.

Spouses of Male Employees

Q. Must an employer provide health insurance coverage for the medical expenses of pregnancy-related conditions of the spouses of male employees? Of the dependents of all employees?

A. Where an employer provides no coverage for dependents, the employer is not required to institute such coverage. However, if an employer's insurance program covers the medical expenses of spouses of female employees then it must equally cover the medical expenses of spouses of male employees, including those arising from pregnancy-related conditions. But the insurance does not have to cover the pregnancy-related conditions of non-spouse dependents as long as it excludes the pregnancy-related conditions of such non-spouse dependents of male and female employees equally.

Spouses

Q. Must an employer provide the same level of health insurance coverage for the pregnancy-related medical conditions of the spouses of male employees as it provides for its female employees?

A. No. It is not necessary to provide the same level of coverage for the pregnancy-related medical conditions of spouses of male employees.

Dependent Coverage

Q. May an employer offer optional dependent coverage which excludes pregnancy-related medical conditions or offers less coverage for pregnancy-related medical conditions where the total premium for the optional coverage is paid by the employee?

A. No. Pregnancy-related medical conditions must be treated the same as other medical conditions under any health or disability insurance or sick leave plan available in connection with employment, regardless of who pays the premiums.

FAQs on Pregnant Employee Insurance Rights [(continued)]

Insurance Protection

Q. Where an employer provides its employees a choice among several health insurance plans, must coverage for pregnancy-related conditions be offered in all of the plans?

A. Yes. Each of the plans must cover pregnancy-related conditions. For example, an employee with a single coverage policy cannot be forced to purchase a more expensive family coverage policy in order to receive coverage for her own pregnancy-related condition.

Medical Expenses

Q. On what basis should an employee be reimbursed for medical expenses arising from pregnancy, childbirth, or related conditions?

A. Pregnancy-related expenses should be reimbursed in the same manner as are expenses incurred for other medical conditions. Therefore, whether a plan reimburses the employees on a fixed basis, or on a percentage of a reasonable and customary charge basis, the same basis should be used for reimbursement of expenses incurred for pregnancy-related conditions. Furthermore, if medical costs for pregnancy-related conditions increase, reevaluation of the reimbursement level should be conducted in the same manner as are cost reevaluations of increases for other medical conditions. Coverage provided by a health insurance program for other conditions must be provided for pregnancy-related conditions. For example, if a plan provides major medical coverage, pregnancy-related conditions must be so covered. Similarly, if a plan covers the cost of a private room for other conditions, the plan must cover the cost of a private room for pregnancy-related conditions. Finally, where a health insurance plan covers office visits to physicians, pre-natal visits must be included in such coverage.

Insurance Protection

Q. May an employer limit payment of costs for pregnancy-related medical conditions to a specified dollar amount set forth in an insurance policy, collective bargaining agreement, or other statement of benefits to which an employee is entitled?

A. The amounts payable for the costs incurred for pregnancy-related conditions can be limited only to the same extent as are costs for other conditions. Maximum recoverable dollar amounts may be specified for pregnancy-related conditions if such amounts are similarly specified for these conditions, and so long as the specific amounts in all instances cover the same proportion of actual costs. If, in addition to the scheduled amount for other procedures, additional costs are paid for, either directly or indirectly, by the employer, such additional payments must also be paid for pregnancy-related procedures.

Deductible

Q. May an employer impose a different deductible for payment of costs for pregnancy-related medical conditions than for costs of other medical conditions?

A. No. Neither an additional deductible, an increase in the usual deductible, nor a larger deductible can be imposed for coverage for pregnancy-related medical costs, whether as a condition for inclusion of pregnancy-related costs in the policy, or as payment of the costs when incurred. Thus, if pregnancy-related costs are the first incurred under the policy, the employee is required to pay only the same deductible as would otherwise be required had other medical costs been the first incurred. Once this deductible has been paid, no additional deductible can be required for other medical procedures. If the usual deductible has already been paid for other medical procedures, no additional deductible can be required when pregnancy-related costs are later incurred.

191

FAQs on Pregnant Employee Insurance Rights ^(continued)

Pre-Existing Condition

Q. If a health insurance plan excludes the payment of benefits for any conditions existing at the time the insured's coverage becomes effective (pre-existing condition clause), can benefits be denied for medical costs arising from a pregnancy existing at the time the coverage became effective?

A. Yes. However, such benefits cannot be denied unless the pre-existing condition clause also excludes benefits for other pre-existing conditions in the same way.

Insurance After Termination

Q. If an employer's insurance plan provides benefits after the insured's employment has ended (i.e., extended benefits) for costs connected with pregnancy and delivery where conception occurred while the insured was working for the employer, but not for the costs of any other medical conditions which began prior to termination of employment, may an employer (a) continue to pay these extended benefits for pregnancy-related medical conditions but not for other medical conditions, or (b) terminate these benefits for pregnancy-related conditions?

A. Where a health insurance plan currently provides extended benefits for other medical conditions on a less favorable basis than for pregnancy-related medical conditions, extended benefits must be provided for other medical conditions on the same basis as for pregnancy-related medical conditions. Therefore, an employer can neither continue to provide less benefits for other medical conditions nor reduce benefits currently paid for pregnancy-related medical conditions.

Extended Benefits Under Different Conditions

Q. Where an employer's health insurance plan currently requires total disability as a prerequisite for payment of extended benefits for other medical conditions but not for pregnancy-related costs, may the employer now require total disability for payments of benefits for pregnancy-related medical conditions as well?

A. Since extended benefits cannot be reduced in order to come into compliance with the Act, a more stringent prerequisite for payment of extended benefits for pregnancy-related medical conditions, such as a requirement for total disability, cannot be imposed. Thus, in this instance, in order to comply with the Act, the employer must treat other medical conditions as pregnancy-related conditions are treated.

Self-Insurance

Q. Can an employer self-insure benefits for pregnancy-related conditions if it does not self-insure benefits for other medical conditions?

A. Yes, so long as the benefits are the same. In measuring whether benefits are the same, factors other than the dollar coverage paid should be considered. Such factors include the range of choice of physicians and hospitals, and the processing and promptness of payment of claims.

Abortion

Q. Can an employer discharge, refuse to hire, or otherwise discriminate against a woman because she has had or is contemplating having an abortion?

A. No. An employer cannot discriminate in its employment practices against a woman who has had or is contemplating having an abortion.

FAQs on Pregnant Employee Insurance Rights (continued)

Abortion and Fringe Benefits

Q. Is an employer required to provide fringe benefits for abortions if fringe benefits are provided for other medical conditions?

A. All fringe benefits other than health insurance, such as sick leave, which are provided for other medical conditions, must be provided for abortions. Health insurance, however, need be provided for abortions only where the life of the woman would be endangered if the fetus were carried to term or where medical complications arise from an abortion.

Abortion and Complications

Q. If complications arise during the course of an abortion – for instance, excessive hemorrhaging – must an employer's health insurance plan cover the additional cost due to the complications of the abortion?

A. Yes. The plan is required to pay those additional costs attributable to the complications of the abortion. However, the employer is not required to pay for the abortion itself, except where the life of the mother would be endangered if the fetus were carried to term.

Abortion and Insurance

Q. May an employer elect to provide insurance coverage for abortions?

A. Yes. The Act specifically provides that an employer is not precluded from providing benefits for abortions whether directly or through a collective-bargaining agreement, but if an employer decides to cover the costs of abortion, the employer must do so in the same manner and to the same degree as other medical conditions.

Fetal Protection

Q. May an employer take fetal welfare into account in deciding whether to permit a pregnant or potentially pregnant woman to remain on a job?

A. No. Congress made clear that the decision to become pregnant or to work while being pregnant or capable of becoming pregnant was a decision for each individual woman to make for herself.

The requirements under NMHPA apply to group health plans, insurance companies and HMO's for plan years beginning on or after January 1, 1998. It is important, therefore, for you to review the terms of your health plan to find out when the changes required by NMHPA will affect you. NMHPA does not have a separate effective date for collectively bargained plans.

One of the most important changes provided under NMHPA relates to the amount of time a mother and newborn child can spend in the hospital in connection with the birth of a child. Under NMHPA, group health plans, insurance companies and health maintenance organizations (HMO's) offering health coverage for hospital stays in connection with the birth of a child must provide health coverage for a minimum period of time.

For example, NMHPA provides that coverage for a hospital stay following a normal vaginal delivery may generally not be limited to less than 48 hours for both the mother and newborn child. Health coverage for a hospital stay in connection with childbirth following a cesarean section may generally not be limited to less than 96 hours for both the mother and newborn child.

Please note, however, that NMHPA's requirements only apply to group health plans, insurance companies and HMO's that choose to provide insurance coverage for a hospital stay in connection with childbirth. NMHPA does not require group health plans, insurance companies or HMO's to provide coverage for hospital stays in connection with the birth of a child. It is important, therefore, to review your health care plan to understand if the changes in NMHPA affect you.

Indeed, NMHPA does not prevent a group health plan, insurance company or HMO from imposing deductibles, coinsurance, or other cost-sharing measures for health benefits relating to hospital stays in connection with childbirth as long as such cost-sharing measures are not greater than those imposed on any preceding portion of the hospital stay. For example, if you are required to pay a $50 co-payment for each day you spend in the hospital preceding childbirth you may not be charged a higher co-payment, or offered less benefits, for the time NMHPA allows you to spend in the hospital following childbirth (48 or 96 hours).

The Mental Health Parity Act of 1996

The Mental Health Parity Act of 1996 (MHPA) provides for parity in the application of limits to certain mental health benefits.

Under MHPA, group health plans, insurance companies and HMO's may not offer mental health benefits that are lower than any such limits for medical and surgical benefits, nor impose any lifetime limit on mental health benefits less than for medical and surgical benefits. However, the law does not mandate these entities provide mental health benefits.

There are two significant exemptions to these new rules. The mental health parity requirements do not apply to small employers who have between 2 and 50 employees or to any group health plan whose costs would increase one percent or more due to the application of these requirements.

The mental health parity requirements apply to group health plans for plan years beginning on or after January 1, 1998. At the present time there is a so-called "sunset" provision in the law requiring that these requirements will cease to apply to benefits for services furnished on or after September 30, 2001.

Workers' Compensation – Purpose

The basic tenet of workers' compensation laws is that employers are to provide compensation in the form of wage replacement and the cost of all reasonable and necessary hospital, surgical, and medical expenses, for all accidental injuries or illnesses and death arising out of and in the course of employment. In return, employees give up their right to sue their employer for damages resulting from injuries which they incur while working.

Each of the 50 states has its own workers' compensation law. In addition, there are federal laws, including the District of Columbia Workers' Compensation Act, the Federal Employee's Compensation Act, and the Longshoremen's and Harbor Workers' Compensation Act (covering both private and public employees in nationwide maritime work).

There are six basic objectives underlying workers' compensation laws:

1. Provide sure, prompt, and reasonable income and medical benefits to work accident victims, or income benefits to their dependents, regardless of fault;

2. Provide a single remedy and reduce court delays, costs, and workloads arising out of personal-injury litigation;

3. Relieve public and private charities of financial drains incident to uncompensated industrial accidents;

4. Eliminate payment of fees to lawyers and witnesses as well as time-consuming trials and appeals;

5. Encourage maximum employer interest in safety and rehabilitation through an appropriate experience-rating mechanism; and

6. Promote the frank and open study of causes of accidents (rather than concealment of fault), thereby reducing preventable accidents and human suffering.

Workers' Compensation Cost Control Suggestions

In every instance of an alleged work-related accident, injury, or illness, the employer should take the following steps to control costs:

1. Require prompt reporting of all accidents and injuries.

2. Conduct a prompt, thorough, and accurate investigation. Take whatever steps are necessary to avoid a recurrence of the accident or injury.

3. Set up a file for all of the information.

4. Critically evaluate all of the information gathered to be sure it supports the decision to pay or not to pay.

5. Update and review the file regularly, keeping in mind that to act reasonably does not necessarily mean the decision made will be upheld.

6. When in doubt, particularly as to questions of law or government agency procedure, the employer should confer with an attorney, insurance carrier, or service organization representative, and get their written opinions for the file.

   Note: Many employers rely on their insurance carrier to handle the entire claim. It takes a partnership, however, to really keep on top of every claim. The insurance carrier needs any and all information you can supply so the proper steps continue to be taken.

7. Provide safety training programs to prevent accidents. Approximately 85 percent of all work-related accidents are attributable to unsafe employee acts caused by a lack of worker knowledge or skill. Research has shown that employers pay an additional 5-10 percent on top of workers' compensation in hidden and indirect costs. The major hidden cost is lost productivity, including the lost production time of the injured worker and co-workers. Training and administrative costs are added when a replacement must be hired. Moreover, upon return to work, the injured worker may not be as productive as before the accident. There are also costs attached to an accident investigation.

8. Ensure appropriate rehabilitation so the injured worker can return to work quickly. Consider creating light duty assignments to assist in returning the injured worker to employment.

9. Demand sensible medical fee schedules. Consider cost containment programs.

10. Encourage simpler procedures and better communication of rights and benefits, plus teamwork between doctors, employers, and state regulatory agencies.

11. Support alternative methods for resolving legitimate disputes short of going to court.

12. Provide suitable alternative employment in the event a worker cannot return to his or her original job.

As with other runaway insurance cost issues, workers' compensation in many states is plagued by out-of-control costs, unnecessary litigation, and underfunded, understaffed state-administered agencies.

Coverage

Virtually every employer in the public and private sectors is covered. Employers are required to obtain insurance or prove financial ability to carry their own risk (self-insurance).

Six states require employers to participate in a monopolistic state fund. Thirteen states offer, as an alternative to private insurance companies, a competitive state fund. Twenty-eight states and the Longshoremen's Act authorize group self-insurance for smaller employers with similar risk characteristics who pool their risks and liabilities. Most states permit self-insurance for individual employers.

Occupational Diseases

All states now recognize responsibility for occupational diseases. Coverage extends to all diseases arising out of, and in the course of, employment. Most states do not provide compensation for a disease that is an "ordinary disease of life" or which is not "peculiar to or characteristic of the employee's occupation."

Benefits

Since workers' compensation is viewed as a beneficial system, it is liberally interpreted in favor of the intended beneficiary.

Medical benefits are usually provided without dollar or time limits, although many programs base maximum medical costs on a "reasonable and customary" test. Income replacement for lost work time is most often based on two-thirds of the employee's average earnings with some dollar maximum, such as the state's average weekly wage. Cash benefits may also be paid for specific physical impairments (e.g., permanent partial disabilities). The great majority of workers' compensation dollars are paid out for temporary total disability income replacement and permanent partial disabilities. Rehabilitation, both medical and vocational, is provided for those cases involving severe disabilities.

Loss Control and Prevention

A National Council on Compensation Insurance report on loss control and prevention advises:

"Insurers are no longer content to share the risk; they are committed to decreasing risks as well. The insurance specialties of loss control, risk control, and loss prevention are dedicated to the dual goals of reducing the chances that a loss will occur and minimizing the financial impact of losses which cannot be prevented…

"In the areas of workers' compensation, this means the establishment of a safe workplace. For greater safety in the workplace, it is necessary to increase the awareness of employers and employees that loss prevention and loss reduction prior to an accident are the most effective methods of minimizing injury and compensation costs. Safety awareness should not be limited to the workplace. A societal focus on safety as a 'cradle to grave' goal is highly recommended. Good safety habits should be universal, and not confined to the workplace. Further, employer involvement in safety issues must be sustained. An employer motivational campaign is essential to achieving a long-term commitment to safety…

"The initial minimization or prevention of injury should remain the primary focus of loss control. However, it also is essential to establish, through analysis of job hazards and incidents, procedures to reduce and eliminate the effects of incidents that do occur, to prevent recurrence and to establish return-to-work programs."

ADA and Health Insurance

The ADA imposes certain requirements in the area of health insurance:

1. Disability-based insurance variances are permitted only if an employer-provided health insurance plan is bona fide and if the distinctions are not being used as a subterfuge for purposes of evading the ADA;

2. Employment decisions concerning an individual with a disability cannot be

Frequently Asked Questions about Workers' Compensation and the ADA

Q. Suppose an employee is fully recovered from an occupational injury that resulted in a temporary back impairment. The employer fires the employee because it believes that, if he returns to his heavy labor job, he will severely injure his back and be totally incapacitated. Does the employee have a disability within the meaning of the ADA?

A. Yes. The employer regards the employee as having an impairment that disqualifies him from a class of jobs (heavy labor) and therefore is substantially limited in the major life activity of working.

Q. May an employer ask disability-related questions or require a medical examination of an employee either at the time the employee experiences an occupational injury or when the employee seeks to return to the job following such an injury?

A. Yes, in both instances as long as the disability-related questions or medical examinations are job-related and consistent with business necessity. The employer must reasonably believe that the occupational injury will impair the employee's ability to perform essential job functions or raises legitimate concerns about direct threat. However, the questions and examinations must not exceed the scope of the specific occupational injury and its effect on the employee's ability, with or without reasonable accommodation, to perform essential job functions or to work without posing a direct threat.

Q. May an employer refuse to return to work an employee with a disability-related occupational injury simply because of a workers' compensation determination that the employee has a "permanent disability" or is "totally disabled"?

A. No. Workers' compensation laws may utilize different standards for evaluating whether an individual has a disability, or whether the person is capable of working. Such a determination is never dispositive regarding an individual's ability to return to work, although it may provide relevant evidence regarding an employee's ability to perform the essential functions of the position in question or to return to work without posing a direct threat.

Q. Does the ADA require an employer to provide reasonable accommodation for an employee with an occupational injury who does not have a disability as defined by the ADA?

A. No.

Q. If an employer reserves light duty positions for employees with occupational injuries, does the ADA require it to consider reassigning an employee with a disability who is not occupationally injured to such positions as a reasonable accommodation?

A. Yes. If an employee with a disability who is not occupationally injured becomes unable to perform the essential functions of the employee's job, and there is no other effective accommodation available, the employer must reassign the employee to a vacant reserved light duty position as a reasonable accommodation if (1) the employee can perform its essential functions, with or without a reasonable accommodation; and (2) the reassignment would not impose an undue hardship. An employer does not prove undue hardship simply by showing that it would have no other vacant light duty positions available if an employee became injured on the job and needed light duty.

motivated by concerns about the impact of that individual's disability or because of concerns about the impact on the health plan of the disability of someone with whom that person has a relationship; and

3. Employees with disabilities must be accorded equal access to whatever health insurance the employer provides to employees without disabilities.

Where specific insurance term or provision is found to be a disability-based distinction, it is up to employers to prove:

1. The health insurance plan is either a bona fide insurance plan and is not inconsistent with applicable state law or is a bona fide self-insured plan; and

2. The disability-based distinction is not being used as a subterfuge to evade the purposes of the ADA.

Miscellaneous Laws Affecting the Workplace 12

Employee Polygraph Protection Act

A whole new area of potential employer liability for improper discharge involves the reliance on the results of polygraph examinations. To assist employers in understanding their rights and responsibilities, there is, in this and the following sections, an expanded explanation of the Employee Polygraph Protection Act. The law prohibits an employer from directly or indirectly requiring, requesting, suggesting, or causing any employee or prospective employee to take or submit to any lie detector test. Similarly, an employer may not inquire about the results of any previous tests taken at the direction of someone other than the current or prospective employer. Please note that state laws and collective bargaining agreements that are more restrictive, prevail over the federal law. Thus, if state law prohibits polygraph examinations, one need not read any further. The state prohibition is operative.

Further, an employer may not discharge, discipline, discriminate against in any manner, deny employment or promotion to, or threaten to take any such action against any employee or prospective employee who refuses, declines, or fails to take or submit to any lie detector test, or on the basis of any lie detector test results.

Every employer must post and maintain a Department of Labor poster in a conspicuous place for the benefit of employees.

Limited Exemption

The law bans the use of the polygraph to prescreen prospective employees of a private business, except for security firms and firms whose businesses are authorized to deal in controlled substances. Under extremely limited conditions, an employer may request an employee to submit to a polygraph test. A request may be made if:

1. The test is administered in connection with an ongoing investigation involving economic loss or injury to the employer's business, such as theft, embezzlement, misappropriation, or an act of unlawful industrial espionage or sabotage;

2. The employee had access to the property that is the subject of the investigation;

3. The employer has a reasonable suspicion that the employee was involved in the incident or activity under investigation; and

4. The employer executes a statement, provided to the examinee before the test, that:

    a. sets forth with particularity the specific incident or activity being investigated and the basis for testing particular employees,

    b. is signed by the person (other than the polygraph examiner) authorized to legally bind the employer,

    c. is retained by the employer for at least 3 years, and

d. contains at a minimum:

  i. an identification of the specific economic loss or injury to the business of the employer,

  ii. a statement indicating that the employee had access to the property that is the subject of the investigation, and

  iii. a statement describing the basis of the employer's reasonable suspicion that the employee was involved in the incident or activity under investigation.

Rights and Responsibilities

If a polygraph test is conducted under these limited circumstances, the law establishes further restrictions on employers and grants certain rights to the examinee.

The examinee is permitted to terminate the test at any time and may not be asked questions in a manner designed to degrade, or needlessly intrude. The examinee may not be asked any question concerning religious beliefs or affiliations; beliefs or opinions regarding racial matters; political beliefs or affiliations; any matter relating to sexual behavior; and, beliefs, affiliations, opinions, or lawful activities regarding unions or labor organizations.

The examiner cannot conduct the test if there is sufficient written evidence by a physician that the examinee is suffering from a medical or psychological condition or undergoing treatment that might cause abnormal responses during the actual testing phase.

Prior to the test, the employer must provide the examinee with reasonable written notice of the date, time, and location of the test. Also included in the statement must be a disclosure of the examinee's right to obtain and consult with legal counsel or an employee representative before each phase of the test.

The examinee must also be informed, in writing, of the nature and characteristics of the tests; whether other devices, including any device for recording or monitoring the conversation, will be used; or that the employer or the examinee may (with mutual knowledge) make a recording of the entire proceeding.

Further, prior to the test, the examinee must read and sign a written notice informing the examinee: that he or she cannot be required to take the test as a condition for employment; that any statement made during the test may constitute additional supporting evidence for the purposes of an adverse employment action; of limitations imposed under the law for use of the polygraph; and of the legal rights and remedies of the employer under the law.

The examinee must be provided the opportunity to review all questions to be asked during the test and must be informed of the right to terminate the test at any time. During the actual testing phase, the examiner may not ask the examinee any relevant question that was not presented in writing for review to the examinee before the test.

After the test, but before any adverse employment action, the employer must interview the examinee on the basis of the results of the test and provide the examinee with a written copy of any opinion or conclusion rendered as a result of the test and a copy of the questions asked during the test along with the corresponding charted responses.

Enforcement

If the employer fails to meet the conditions permitting limited use of the polygraph, the polygraph test will be considered in violation of the law. An employee cannot be discharged, disciplined, denied employment or promotion, or otherwise discriminated against in any manner as a result of one or more polygraph test charts or the refusal to take a polygraph test, without additional supporting evidence.

Any employer who violates any provision of the law may be assessed a civil penalty of not more than $10,000. The Secretary of Labor may determine the amount of the penalty and has the authority to issue subpoenas, make investigations and inspections, and require that necessary and appropriate records are kept. The Secretary may bring an action against employers who violate the statute.

An employee or job applicant may also sue the employer. The suit must be brought within three years of the alleged violation. The employer can be held liable for legal and equitable relief, including employment, reinstatement, promotion, and the payment of lost wages and benefits.

Polygraph Use – Some Advice

The complexity of the law reflects Congress's strong bias against polygraph use in the private sector. The immediate consequences arising out of the law have been a dramatic reduction in the use of polygraph examinations by private sector employers. Employers who wish to resort to using polygraphs should consult legal counsel for guidance.

Written psychological tests, or "pencil-and-papers," are not directly addressed by a specific federal law. However, they must satisfy the EEOC's Uniform Selection Guidelines criteria. If such tests have adverse impact, their validity as a reliable predictor of performance so as to show business necessity, must be established. These tests inquire into the applicant's attitudes toward personal behavior and work environment. This technique predicts future behavior based on the individual's attitudes and admissions of prior conduct. Pencil and paper integrity tests are formulated on the theory that dishonest and honest people do not think alike

and these differences will be revealed through their answers to the questions.

Wage Garnishments

The Consumer Credit Protection Act limits the amount of an employee's disposable earnings which may be garnished in any one week, as well as protects the employee's job so long as the garnishment results from a single indebtedness. Garnishment is the court procedure through which earnings of an individual are required to be withheld for the payment of any debt.

The employee's disposable earnings (i.e., that part of a person's pay remaining after the deduction from those earnings of any amounts required by law to be withheld) are that portion of his or her pay after deduction for any amount required by law. The maximum subject to garnishment in any workweek may not exceed the lesser of:

1. Twenty-five percent of the disposable earnings for that week; or

2. The amount by which disposable earnings exceed 30 times the prevailing federal minimum wage.

The Consumer Credit Protection Act is enforced by the Department of Labor's Wage and Hour Division unless a state, by prior agreement, has been specifically granted this responsibility. The federal government alone enforces the restrictions on job dismissal. Anyone who violates the discharge provision is subject to criminal prosecution.

Under the federal Welfare Reform Act (1996), all new hires will have to be reported to the state. The new hire information will be shared through a nationwide directory to be established by the federal government. New hire reports will have to be made within 20 days of a person being employed by a company using a W-4 Form or a form approved by the state. The state

Directory of New Hires is intended to allow the tracking down of "dead beat" parents who owe back child support.

Child Support Enforcement

The Federal/State Child Support Enforcement law's purposes are:

- to ensure that children are supported by their parents,

- to foster family responsibility, and

- to reduce the costs of welfare to the taxpayer.

To continue to deal with the national problem of financially abandoned children, the law was amended so as to strengthen state laws and increase efforts to develop strong enforcement techniques designed to regularly and reliably get the support money to the children for whom it is intended.

Today there is an automatic, mandatory wage withholding (i.e., withholding support payments without modification to the support order or a return to court) for all child support cases being enforced through the State Child Support Enforcement (CSE) program when the amount of past-due support equals one month's support payments (or at an earlier point at state option). All child support orders issued in a state must include a provision for wage withholding regardless of whether the petition for support was made by the state CSE agency or through a private attorney.

Frequently Asked Questions about Child Support

Q. How will an employer be informed to start withholding child support from an employee's wages?
A. An employer will receive a notice from the State Child Support Enforcement (CSE) withholding agency that tells when to begin, how much to deduct, and where to send the money.

Q. Will an employer have to tell the employee?
A. The employee will already have received notice of the forthcoming withholding action containing all the pertinent information, and will have been given a chance to contest any mistakes of fact believed to be in the notice.

Q. How long after an employer receives the notice does withholding begin?
A. Withholding is to begin no later than the first pay period that occurs 14 days after the mailing date of the notice, or on the date specified in the notice, whichever is earlier.

Q. Can an employer combine all of the deductions in a pay period and send one check to the withholding agency?
A. Yes. For each withholding agency an employer sends payments to, one check can be written for the total amount as long as there is an itemization of the amount withheld from each person and the date it was withheld.

Q. If employees are paid every two weeks, when does an employer have to send the payments to the withholding agency?
A. An employer has ten days to send all amounts to the withholding agency.

FAQs about Child Support ^(continued)

Q. Can an employer refuse to hire someone who has a withholding against his wages?

A. No. If an employer refuses to hire or if an employer disciplines or discharges an employee because of a wage withholding for child support, that employer is subject to a fine under state law.

Q. What are the consequences for the failure to withhold?

A. An employer will be liable for the full amount, as it accumulates from the date of the notice.

Q. How does an employer know when to stop the withholding?

A. The withholding remains in effect until the employer is notified by the withholding agency of any changes to the order.

Q. Does child support withholding apply to commissions?

A. Federal law requires that child support be withheld only from wages. The state is given the option, however, of applying withholding to other forms of income such as commissions, dividends, retirement benefits, and other types of compensation.

Q. Is there any limit to the amount that can be withheld?

A. The total amount allowed to be withheld from any employee's paycheck is limited to the amounts in the Consumer Credit Protection Act (CCPA) unless otherwise specified by State law. The limits provided in the CCPA are 50 percent of disposable earnings in the case of an absent parent who has a second family, and 60 percent if there is no second family. These limits are each increased by 5 percent (to 55 and 65) if payments are in arrears for a period equal to 12 weeks or more.

Q. If there is already a wage attachment against an employee, and a child support order comes in, the total deducted will be more than allowed under the law. What should the employer do in these circumstances?

A. By Federal law, withholding of child support takes priority over any other legal process carried out under state law against the same wages. This means that the child support withholding must be done first, then the deductions for other withholding orders can be made.

Q. If I receive a withholding notice from another state, am I required to honor it?

A. Some states have long arm statutes that allow them to request withholding directly from employers in other states. You should honor that request, just as you do one from your state. If you have questions, your state withholding agency will be able to assist you.

Q. What do I do when the employee leaves my employ?

A. You must notify the State Child Support Enforcement withholding agency promptly when the employee leaves, giving the employee's last known home address and new employer's name and address, if known.

Uniformed Services Employment and Reemployment Rights Act

In 1994, legislation called The Uniformed Services Employment and Reemployment Rights Act was enacted to strengthen and expand the reemployment rights of uniformed service members. The legislation constituted a major overhaul of the prior statute, which it replaced, and codified the nearly 50 years of case law surrounding the earlier statute. This law was further amended in 2005.

1. **"Service" Defined** – Service in the uniformed services means duty on a voluntary or involuntary basis in a uniformed service including:

   - active duty

   - active duty for training

   - initial active duty for training

   - inactive duty training

   - full-time National Guard duty

   - absence from work for an examination to determine a person's fitness for any of the above types of duty.

   Normally, the employee is obligated to give the employer advance notice of military service. There are, of course, situations where this may not be possible because of "military necessity." The employee's rights are protected for a period of five years of service.

2. **Reporting Back to Work** – Any returning member of a uniformed service who has been honorably discharged is entitled to reemployment rights. The returning employee who has been away is given a limited amount of time to return to work depending on the duration of a person's military service:

   a. Service of one to 30 days. The person must report on the first regularly scheduled work day that falls eight hours after a person returns home;

   b. Service of 31 to 180 days. The application for employment must be submitted no later than 14 days after completion of a person's service;

   c. Service of 181 or more days. An application for reemployment must be submitted no later than 90 days after completion of a person's military service; and

   d. Service-connected injury or illness. The reporting or application deadlines are extended for up to two years for persons who are hospitalized or convalescing because of service-connected illness or injury.

3. **"Escalator" position** – The reemployment position with the highest priority among the reemployment schemes reflects the "escalator" principle that has been a key concept in veteran reemployment legislation. In effect, each returning service member actually steps back onto the seniority escalator at the point the person would have occupied if that person had remained continuously employed. All benefits that would have been available to the service member, had there not been an interruption in employment, become the obligation of the employer. Accordingly, pay increases, vacations, pension rights based on length of service, etc., must be given to the service member upon return to the place of employment.

4. **Miscellaneous Provisions** – The federal law does not require pay during military leave. Note, however, that the Fair Labor Standards Act prohibits wage deductions from salaried employees for absences caused by temporary military leave. However, the regulations permit employers to offset any military pay received by an employee for a

particular workweek against the salary due for that week. The Act gives employees on military leave the right to use any vacation or similar leave with pay that they accrued prior to military service. The use of accrued vacation time is at the employees' option; employers cannot require the use of vacation time while on military leave.

Frequently Asked Questions about Service Personnel Rights

Q. Can an employer request that accrued vacation time be used for military service?

A. No. The law does not permit an employer to require that an employee use vacation time for military service.

Q. What about health benefits?

A. The new law provides for COBRA equivalent health benefit continuation for those who are away for military service. This is true, even if the employer would not otherwise be covered by COBRA, that is, someone with less than 20 employees. The person may elect to continue the health plan coverage for up to 18 months after the absence begins or for the period of service, whichever period is shorter.

Q. Who is covered by the law's anti-discrimination provisions?

A. The law's anti-discrimination coverage (e.g., hiring, promotion, reemployment, termination and benefits) applies to past members, current members, and persons who apply to be a member of any of the branches of the uniformed services.

Q. Who enforces the law?

A. The Department of Labor's Veterans' Employment and Training Service (VETS) investigates complaints and attempts to resolve them. Cases that remain unresolved can be referred to the Attorney General for court action, and individuals have the right to file suit.

Q. Does the law recognize any conditions which would lessen an individual's right to reemployment?

A. Yes. The law will excuse reemployment where the circumstances have changed so much that reemployment of the person would be impossible or unreasonable (e.g., a reduction in force that would have included the person seeking reemployment). Employers are excused from making efforts to qualify returning service members or from accommodating individuals with service-connected disabilities when doing so would be of such difficulty or expense as to cause "undue hardship" as that term is defined in the Americans with Disabilities Act.

5. **New USERRA Regulations** – On December 19, 2005, the U.S. Department of Labor ("DOL") published final regulations supposedly written in "plain English" to explain and clarify the Uniformed Services Employment and Reemployment Rights Act (USERRA, 38 U.S.C. §§ 4301-4334). The new regulations, located at 20 C.F.R. § 1002.1 et seq., went into effect on January 18, 2006. The DOL has also published a revised notice that informs employees of their rights and must be posted by the employer. USERRA protects employees against discrimination and retaliation by employers because of military service, ensures leaves from employment for up to 5 years of cumulative military service, establishes reemployment rights and protects certain benefits for those returning to work after completing their military obligations. The poster and regulations are available at the DOL web site, www.dol.gov.

The regulations are lengthy and complex. Below are some "highlights":

- Employees must give a verbal or written notice, reasonably in advance, of impending military service, once notice is given the employer is obligated to provide leave, but employees are not obligated at that time to indicate whether they intend to seek reemployment;

- Service members have the right to continue existing group health plan coverage on a self-pay basis for themselves and their dependents for the lesser of 24 months or the period of military service, and whether or not an employee elects to continue health coverage while serving, an employer is required to reinstate coverage upon a service member's reemployment;

- If returning within a specified time, service members must be treated as if continuously employed for the entire period of their military service for purposes of calculating pension benefits;

- An employer is not required to make contributions to pension or 401(k) plans during an employee's military leave, but must make up its contributions when the employee is reinstated;

- An employer must count the time spent on leave towards seniority and seniority-based benefits (including seniority benefits governed by statute, such as FMLA leave) but is generally not required to credit an employee for accrual of vacation or sick time during military leave unless given to employees on other types of leaves;

- Employers are prohibited from terminating employees returning from military service except "for cause" for one year after reemployment if the military service was for more than 180 days (a significant difference from other federal employment laws);

- A service member who properly returns from a qualified military leave must be reemployed into an "escalator position," i.e., the position the employee would have occupied with reasonable certainty had he or she remained in employment (if no escalation would have occurred or the person is not qualified to perform the escalated position, then reemployment is to the position the person held before military leave);

- The "escalator" principle also applies to the returning service member's rate of pay, that is, the total compensation package the employee would have received if he or she had remained on the job, including pay increases, differentials, step increases, merit increases or performance bonuses;

- The "escalator" principle may result in adverse consequences. For example, an employer may not be obligated to reinstate an employee who would have been laid off because of a reduction in force; and

- USERRA supersedes any state or local law and any agreement, contract or policy, which would reduce or limit any right or benefit provided under the Act.

Since September 11, 2001, over 500,000 National Guardsmen and Reservists have been called to active duty, and this number is expected to rise because of current U.S. conflicts. All employers, no matter their size or type of business, including foreign companies doing business in the U.S. and U.S. companies doing business overseas, must comply with the Act. Additionally, individual supervisors and managers who have control over employment opportunities may be personally liable as an "employer" under the Act. All employees, even temporary, part-time and seasonal employees, have some kind of protection under USERRA. Independent contractors, however, are not covered by USERRA.

Immigration Control – Verification of Employment

The Immigration Reform and Control Act *affects all employers*. It contains several provisions which require employers to institute procedures for verifying that a job applicant is authorized to be employed in the United States. It also establishes civil and criminal penalties for knowingly hiring, referring, recruiting, or retaining in employment "unauthorized aliens."

Frequently Asked Questions about Immigration Law

Q. Do citizens and nationals of the United States need to prove they are eligible to work?
A. Yes. While citizens and nationals of the United States are automatically eligible for employment, they too must present the required documents and complete an I-9 Form.

Q. Does an employer need to complete an I-9 for everyone who applies for a job?
A. No. An employer needs to complete I-9's only for people actually hired.

Q. If someone accepts a job but will not start work for a month, can an employer complete the I-9 when the employee accepts the job?
A. No. The law requires that an employer complete the I-9 only when the person actually begins working.

Q. Does an employer need to fill out an I-9 for independent contractors or their employees?
A. No. For example, if an employer contracts with a construction company to perform renovations, there is no obligation to complete I-9's for that company's employees. The construction company is responsible for completing I-9's for its own employees.

Q. What should an employer do if the person hired is unable to provide the required documents within three business days of the date employment begins?
A. If an employee is unable to present the required document or documents within three business days of the date employment begins, the employee must produce a receipt showing that he or she has applied for the document. In addition, the employee must present the actual document within 90 days of the hire.

FAQs about Immigration Law ^(continued)

Q. Can an employer terminate an employee who fails to produce the required documents within three business days?

A. Yes. An employer can terminate an employee who fails to produce the required document or documents, or a receipt for a document, within three business days of the date employment begins. However, an employer must apply these practices uniformly to all employees. If an employee has presented a receipt for a document, he or she must produce the actual document within 90 days of the date employment begins.

Q. What happens if an employer properly completes a Form I-9 and INS discovers that the employee is not actually authorized to work?

A. An employer cannot be charged with a verification violation, and will have a good faith defense against the imposition of employer sanctions penalties for knowingly hiring an unauthorized alien, where the following is done:

- Ensured that employees fully and properly completed Section 1 of the I-9 at the time employment began;
- Reviewed the required documents which should have reasonably appeared to have been genuine and to have related to the person presenting them;
- Fully and properly completed Section 2 of the I-9, and signed and dated the employer certification;
- Retained the I-9 for the required period of time; and
- Made the I-9 available upon request to a Federal government officer.

Q. What is an employer's responsibility concerning the authenticity of document(s) presented?

A. An employer must examine the document(s) and, if they reasonably appear on their face to be genuine and to relate to the person presenting them, accept them. To do otherwise could be an unfair immigration-related employment practice. If the document(s) do not reasonably appear on their face to be genuine or to relate to the person presenting them, an employer must not accept them.

Q. May an employer accept a photocopy of a document presented by an employee?

A. No. Employees must present original documents. The only exception is that an employee may present a certified copy of a birth certificate.

Q. What are the requirements for retaining the I-9?

A. An employer must retain the I-9 for 3 years after the date employment begins or 1 year after the date the person's employment is terminated, whichever is later.

Q. How can an employer avoid discrimination against certain employees while still complying with this law?

A. An employer can avoid discriminating against certain employees and still comply with the law by applying the employment eligibility verification procedures of this law to all newly hired employees and by hiring without respect to the national origin or citizenship status of those persons authorized to work in the United States. To request to see identity and employment eligibility documents only from persons of a particular origin or from persons who appear or sound foreign is a violation of the employer sanctions laws and may also be a violation of Title VII of the Civil Rights Act of 1964. An employer should not discharge present employees, refuse to hire new employees, or otherwise discriminate on the basis of foreign appearance, accent, language, or name.

FAQs about Immigration Law ^(continued)

Q. Do undocumented workers have workplace rights?

A. There is a trend in federal government policy to extend more and more protection to undocumented workers. They are covered by minimum wage laws and occupational safety laws. The National Labor Relations Board has ruled that employers who knowingly hire unauthorized workers are prohibited from firing them if they support unionization. The EEOC has declared that it will extend broad anti-discrimination rights to undocumented workers, saying, "The federal discrimination laws protect all employees in the United States, regardless of their citizenship or work eligibility. Employers may no more discriminate against unauthorized workers than they may discriminate against any other employees. EEOC will therefore assure that in its enforcement of the laws, unauthorized workers are protected to the same degree as all other workers." The EEOC will seek reinstatement for undocumented workers only when the individuals involved first obtained papers authorizing them to work in the United States. The Commission, however, will recommend back pay whether or not the immigrants had working papers.

All employers must verify that every new hire is either a U.S. citizen or authorized to work in the country. As a defense to a claim of violation, the employer should require of every new hire: birth or naturalization certificate; U.S. passport or an unexpired foreign passport authorizing U.S. employment; or a resident alien card containing the new hire's identification and U.S. employment authorization (the "green card"). In the absence of any of those, the employer should require two documents – Social Security card and driver's license or similar state identification. The employer should photocopy any such documents and keep them on file.

The Act also requires employers to state on Immigration and Naturalization Service Form I-9 (a copy is in the Appendix) that they have examined the necessary documents which show that the individual is not an unauthorized alien. The new hire must also attest on the verification form that he or she qualifies for employment. The verification forms must be retained for three years from the date of hire or one year from the date of termination, whichever is longer. There are civil penalties for violating these recordkeeping requirements.

Employment Eligibility Verification - Form I-9

The Immigration Reform and Control Act requires employers to verify both identity and eligibility for employment. In 1998, the Immigration and Naturalization Service issued new rules to streamline the verification process. A copy of the I-9 Form is in the Appendix.

1. **Eligible Documents** – The list of eligible documents has been nearly cut in half, it now includes:

   1. United States Passport

   2. Permanent Resident Card or Resident Alien Card (I-551)

   3. Foreign Passport with temporary I-551 stamp

   4. Temporary Resident Card (I-688)

   5. Employment authorization document (e.g., I-766; I-688B; I-699A)

   6. (For aliens authorized to work only for a specific employer) Foreign Passport with Form I-94 authorizing employment with this employer

7. Driver's License issued by a State or outlying possession

8. ID card issued by a State or outlying possession

9. Native American Tribal Document

10. (For Canadian aliens authorized to work only for a specific employer) Canadian Driver's License or ID card with a photograph

11. Social Security Account number card without employment restrictions

12. Native American Tribal Document

13. (For aliens authorized to work only for a specific employer) Form I-94 authorizing employment with this employer

2. **Receipts for Documents** – A person who is eligible to work, but is unable to provide a required document, may present a receipt. The person must attest that he or she is eligible for employment. An employer may not accept a receipt if the person indicates or the employer has actual or constructive knowledge that the person is not authorized to work. There are three kinds of acceptable receipts:

   (1) A person may present a receipt showing that they have applied for a replacement document. The person must present the required document within 90 days of the hire.

   (2) Immigration and Naturalization Service (INS) Arrival-Departure Record (Form I-94) may be treated as a receipt if it bears a "Temporary I-551" stamp or a refugee admission stamp. The temporary I-551 stamp may be accepted as a receipt for the Permanent Resident Card (Form I-551). The person must present Form I-551 within 180 days of the hire.

   (3) An INS Form I-94 bearing a refugee admission stamp may be accepted as

a receipt for either an Employment Authorization Document (Form I-766 or I-688B) or an unrestricted Social Security card. The person must present the required document within 90 days of the hire.

3. **Reverification** – Employers are responsible for reverifying the work authorization for a person if the Form I-9 indicates that the individual's employment authorization expires. Reverification must be completed no later than the date employment authorization expires. If the form used for reverification indicates that the individual's employment authorization expires, employers must again reverify no later than the expiration date.

WARN – Legislative Purpose

In 1988, Congress passed the Worker Adjustment and Retraining Act (WARN), commonly referred to as the "plant closing" law. This law applies to any type of business, not just a "plant," and the law covers layoffs as well as closing of facilities or businesses.

Coverage

Any employer who has 100 or more employees, excluding part-time employees, or has 100 or more employees who, in the aggregate, work at least 4,000 hours per week, exclusive of hours of overtime, is subject to the provisions of the law. Multi-site enterprises will be covered even if only one site is involved in a closing or layoff, if the entire enterprise under common control employs 100 or more employees.

A part-time employee is a worker who is employed for an average of fewer than 20 hours per week or who has been employed for fewer than six of the 12 months preceding the date on which notice is required.

Closings Requiring Notice

The law defines separate criteria for notification in the event of a business closing and a mass layoff. In the event of a business closing, employers are required to comply if the shutdown results in an employment loss during any 30-day period for 50 or more employees, excluding any part-time employees, at the site of the shutdown.

A closing is defined as the permanent or temporary shutdown of a single site of employment.

In the event of a "mass layoff" that is not a business closing, employers are required to comply if the layoff results in an employment loss at a single site during any 30-day period for at least 33 percent of the employees, but for no fewer than 50 employees (excluding part-time employees).

Temporary Employment

No notice is required if the closing is of a temporary facility or if the closing or layoff is the result of the completion of a particular project or undertaking, and the affected employees were hired with the understanding that their employment was limited to the duration of the facility or the project or undertaking.

Employees must clearly understand at the time of hire that their employment is temporary. Should questions arise, the burden of proof lies with the employer to show that the temporary nature of the project or facility was clearly communicated.

Employers in agriculture and construction frequently hire workers for harvesting, processing, or work on a particular building or project. Such work may be seasonal but recurring. Such work falls under the exemption if the workers understood at the time they were hired that their work was temporary. Giving written notice that a project is temporary will not convert permanent employment into temporary work.

Employment Loss

Both the closing and mass layoffs notices are triggered by "employment loss." Employment loss is termination of employment other than a discharge for cause, voluntary departure, or retirement. It is also a layoff exceeding six months or a reduction in hours of work of more than 50 percent during each month of any six-month period.

A layoff of more than six months which, at its outset, was announced to be a layoff of six months or less, shall be treated as an employment loss. If the extension beyond six months is caused by business circumstance (including unforeseeable changes in price or cost), not reasonably foreseeable at the time of the initial layoff, and notice is given at the time it becomes reasonably foreseeable that the extension beyond six months will be required, it will not result in liability.

When Notice Must Be Given

With certain exceptions, notice must be given at least 60 calendar days prior to any planned business closing or mass layoff. When all employees are not terminated on the same date, the date of the first individual termination with the statutory 30-day or 90-day period triggers the 60-day requirement. A worker's last day of employment is considered the date of the worker's layoff. The first and each subsequent group of terminees are entitled to a full 60 days' notice. In order for an employer to decide whether issuing a notice is required, the employer should consider the following.

An employer cannot order a business closing or mass layoff until the end of the 60-day period beginning with the written notice.

Mailing notice to an employee's last known address or inclusion of the notice in the employee's paycheck will be considered acceptable methods of fulfilling the employer's obligation to provide notice.

If notice is given directly to affected employees, it is to be written in language understandable to the employees and is to contain:

- A statement as to whether the planned action is expected to be permanent or temporary and, if the entire business is to be closed, a statement to that effect;

- The expected date when the business closing or mass layoff will commence and expected date the individual employee will be discharged;

- An indication of whether or not bumping rights exist; and

- The name and telephone number of a company official to contact for further information.

Under certain conditions, the notification periods may be reduced to less than 60 days (e.g., faltering company, natural disaster, and unforeseeable circumstances). For example, the Department of Labor regulations provide that no notice is required if the closure is "caused by business circumstances that were not reasonably foreseeable as of the time that notice would have been required." Thus, a principal client's sudden and unexpected termination of a major contract is deemed an unforeseeable business circumstance.

Sanctions

Employees are permitted to sue an employer for back pay and benefits under WARN. The operative time period for the calculation of back wages is the actual days that would have

been worked if the employer had not closed down or ordered a layoff. The amount may be reduced by the courts under certain conditions. The employer may also be liable for a civil penalty for failing to provide notice to the local government.

The U.S. Supreme Court has ruled that a local union has the authority to sue for damages on behalf of its members when an employer fails to give the required notice.

Privacy Issues in the Workplace

Several key laws, the Americans with Disabilities Act, the Family and Medical Leave Act, and the Occupational Safety and Health Act all require job applicant and employee medical records to be treated as confidential, and medical information files to be kept separate from personnel files. There is strict liability for unauthorized disclosure of information.

It is expected that Congress will add a new layer of rules imposing strict notice, access, correction and disclosure rules on all employers, even those already subject to the aforementioned medical confidentiality requirements. The Communications Decency Act of 1996 (CDA) imposes new requirements on employers whose telecommunication equipment creates the potential for liability.

The CDA extended the Communications Act of 1934 to cover all telecommunications equipment, not just the telephone, and made it a federal crime to use this equipment in ways to harass or annoy another party. Thus the average employee's access to a wide range of telecommunications equipment creates the potential for liability.

That CDA specifically prohibits the following:

1. Using telecommunications equipment to send a comment, request, proposal or image (i.e., a picture file) that is obscene, lewd or

lascivious with the intent to annoy, abuse, threaten, or harass the recipient or a third party, such as a co-worker.

2. Knowingly sending obscene images, communications, requests, etc., to a minor. Employers have a concern here because employees may seek to engage in this type of contact from office machines.

3. Using any telecommunications device to anonymously contact an individual with the intent to threaten, annoy or abuse the party that is contacted. This is an extension of an old prohibition against anonymous threatening phone calls. In the computer age, this includes anonymous faxes and e-mail messages.

4. Repeatedly calling an individual and hanging up (or letting the phone ring indefinitely) with the intent to harass the person receiving the call. This still only applies to the telephone.

5. Repeatedly using telecommunications equipment to contact another individual solely to harass that person. This prohibition extends protection from non-anonymous threatening calls to include faxes and e-mail, as well as any other system that could be used for this purpose.

The CDA provides for fines and prison terms for those who knowingly permit the use of equipment under their control for any of the above activities. The act, however, provides a broad indemnification from liability for employers who proactively develop and enforce proper policies.

A careful response to the CDA is warranted, and a well-developed and properly handled program will diminish the likelihood that violations will occur and will reduce the employer's liability for infractions beyond its control.

Workplace privacy is treated in more detail in Chapter 15.

Drug and Alcohol Abuse in the Workplace 13

Employers Have a Role in the "War" on Drugs

America has been waging a "war" on drugs. Illegal drugs – and the illegal use of legally manufactured drugs – continue to pose a growing threat to American society. Drugs are stronger, cheaper, more available, and, in some circles, more accepted than ever before.

The price tag is immense – in excess of $110 billion annually. Drug dependency and fatality rates are at record high levels.

The nexus of drug abuse to major crime and urban blight is well known. However, the relevance of drug abuse to the workplace is just now being fully recognized. The National Institute on Drug Abuse estimates that if every employee aged 18 to 40 were tested for drug use on any given day, anywhere from 14 percent to 25 percent would test positive.

Every community is affected by drug abuse. So is virtually every employer. Police officials alone cannot win the war on drugs. A concerted effort by the various segments of society is necessary – especially by schools and businesses.

Is there an employer role in preventing drug abuse? Yes. An effective employer program to prevent drug abuse is in the interests of both the community and the individual business. Such a program is not only humane, but cost-effective as well.

Furthermore, many people believe employers are best equipped to deter drug abuse because of the "power of the paycheck." If employees

and job applicants know that their jobs are contingent on their being "drug-free," they have a compelling incentive to get off, or stay off, drugs.

More and more businesses are recognizing and responding to the problems created by drug abuse in the United States. They recognize the enormity of our country's drug abuse problem, its costs economically and in human suffering and lives, and employers' responsibility to act firmly but fairly to combat drug abuse. The ultimate employer goals should be deterrence and rehabilitation. Ultimately, effective drug abuse prevention programs can save lives – and businesses.

How Drug Abuse Hurts Business

Perhaps drug abusers themselves tell the story most clearly. A study of drug abusers in rehabilitation resulted in admissions that:

- 75 percent had used drugs on the job
- 64 percent had experienced adverse job performance as a result of drug use
- 44 percent had sold drugs to co-workers
- 18 percent had stolen on the job to support their habits

The negative effects of drug abuse on the workplace include:

- lost productivity
- increased absenteeism
- increased on-the-job accidents

- increased medical insurance costs
- increased employee theft

An employee with drugs in his or her system is one-third less productive. That employee is 2.5 times more likely to have absences of eight days or more, 3.6 times more likely to injure himself or another person on the job, and 5 times more likely to file a workers' compensation claim. Drug-abusing workers also incur 300 percent higher medical insurance costs.

Employers also face other "hidden" costs of drug abuse, costs which are difficult to calculate but easy to recognize:

- Lower employee morale
- Compromised product integrity
- Decreased quality of customer service
- Increased absenteeism for the family members of drug users
- Increased destruction of company property
- Impaired judgment regarding day-to-day decisions affecting the company
- The introduction and influence of the criminal element in the workplace

The Elements of a Drug Abuse Prevention Program

Employer programs for drug abuse prevention have three major goals:

1. To keep drug abusers out of the workforce by screening job applicants;

2. To deter employees from developing a drug abuse problem; and

3. To rehabilitate employees who have a drug abuse problem.

Employers should keep in mind that this last goal – rehabilitation – is the ultimate and most

humane purpose of a drug abuse prevention program. Employers also should recognize that no testing at all is highly preferable to inaccurate testing.

An employer program for drug abuse prevention should include:

1. **Commitment** – It is essential that top management on a corporate-wide basis understand how comprehensive a drug abuse prevention program must be, and commit to that level of involvement.

2. **Analysis and Development** – Thoroughness is necessary. Analyze personnel, productivity, absenteeism, compensation claims, and safety and health records. Find out if your company has a drug problem significant enough to warrant a corporate response. Develop a formal, written company policy which includes whether and when drug testing will be performed, and what disciplinary actions are anticipated. Coordinate your company's policy – before implementation – with personnel, benefits, legal, medical, security, safety and health, and labor relations staff persons or outside counselors, and, if present, union representatives.

3. **Education and Training** – "Sell" your drug abuse prevention program to your employees. Communications regarding the company policy, the company's commitment, the dangers of drug abuse, and the availability of rehabilitation services or referral will encourage cooperation, give the program credibility, and prevent undue resentment or morale problems. Education may deter drug abuse as effectively as testing or disciplinary action. Training of supervisors is also critical, particularly regarding how to react to a workplace drug incident.

4. **Drug Testing** – Everyone is hurt by inaccuracies, misidentifications, or

unconfirmed tests. Commit the resources necessary to have a professional drug testing program. Strive to assure the integrity, accuracy, and fairness of the testing program in order to: (1) produce the most conclusive and useful test results; (2) minimize the intrusion on and discomfort of the individual; and (3) decrease legal vulnerability. Split the specimen taken for urinalysis into two samples so that a second confirming test can be performed using the same specimen if the first half of the specimen tests "positive" for the presence of drugs. These second tests, called "confirmation assays," should be performed using a different chemical process.

No disciplinary or job action should be taken unless both tests prove "positive." Take reasonable steps to preserve the confidentiality of employees' test results.

5. **Disciplinary Action** – Consistency is the key. Do not selectively enforce your company's drug abuse prevention program. Be prepared to make the same response for all employees, irrespective of their seniority and their value to the company. Document as fully as possible a relationship between drug use and declining performance. Dismiss chronic drug abuse cases who: (1) are unable or unwilling to rehabilitate; (2) present a significant safety or security risk; (3) are unable to perform their job responsibilities because of their illegal drug use; or (4) are engaged in criminal activities such as selling drugs.

6. **Rehabilitation** – Employee assistance programs (EAP's) best serve the ultimate goal of rehabilitation. Usually structured as an adjunct to company health care programs, EAP's generally include counseling, medical monitoring, treatment, retesting, and family support and reinforcement. EAP's can be effective, cost-effective, and good for employee morale. In the absence

of company-provided programs, referral to local counseling and treatment centers is an alternative. Suspension, rather than dismissal, for first-time cases is a humane policy which should be considered. However, a high level of accountability – with the requirement of strict adherence to the rehabilitation program and retesting – is entirely appropriate for employees in rehabilitation.

Guidelines to Prevent Liability for Drug Testing

Drug testing programs are not appropriate for all employers and may not be appropriate for most employers. But they can be an effective and integral part of an employer's drug abuse prevention program, and all employers should at least adopt an anti-drug abuse policy. Drug testing should be performed as accurately and fairly as is reasonably possible – or it should not be performed at all.

Employers are well-advised to stay current and in compliance with continuing legal and legislative developments in the field of drug abuse in the workplace.

No broad, federal legislation has received extensive consideration by Congress, thus far, regarding a private employer's ability to perform employee drug testing.

The Supreme Court, however, has given its approval to drug testing in two federal programs involving railroad industry workers and Customs Service drug-enforcement positions. The rulings are seen as the first of a series which will define the limit of testing under the Fourth Amendment's ban against "unreasonable searches." It should be noted that private-sector employees have no constitutional protection against testing; therefore, the court's decisions are not expected to materially affect testing in private industry.

Employers can minimize the legal risks of drug testing by taking appropriate steps:

1. **Contract with a reliable, professional drug testing service** – Businesses should contract with a service or use an in-house testing program which is staffed by well-trained and certified personnel who will follow acceptable professional procedures. Check out the service with medical professionals and other businesses. Ask for references. Make sure it has qualified professionals available to serve as expert witnesses if necessary.

2. **Assure that chain-of-custody is maintained for specimens** – Human error is the most common reason for inaccuracies in testing today. Maintaining chain-of-custody is vital in preventing tampering, substitution, misidentification, misplacement or problems of inadequate proof.

3. **Confirm "positive" tests before taking any job action** – As noted before, initial specimens should be split into two samples so that a second test can be performed using the initial specimen if the first half of that specimen tests "positive" for the presence of illegal drugs. The confirmatory assay should be conducted using a different chemical process. The most common initial screens use immunoassay techniques and are relatively simple and inexpensive. The most common confirmatory assays – gas chromatography/mass spectrometry, or high performance liquid chromatography – are more complex and expensive, but highly advisable from a legal standpoint. Employers should not take disciplinary action against employees – except in extraordinary circumstances – without the results of a confirmatory test.

4. **Enforce the company policy consistently** – Critical to employee acceptance of a company's drug abuse prevention program is even-handed enforcement. Perhaps even more important than what response an employer takes is that the same response be taken for each similar offense of company policy. Be prepared to take the same action when a "positive" test is confirmed for a long-term, highly placed employee as you do when it involves a newly hired employee whose performance is marginal.

5. **Maintain thorough, secure, and confidential records** – For both drug test results and reports on drug-related accidents or incidents, a secure and comprehensive documentation record should be established and maintained. The best legal defense to a challenge to disciplinary action based on drug abuse – and an important safeguard for innocent employees – is documentation. Equally important, employers should make reasonable efforts to observe employee expectations of privacy and confidentiality (1) as a sound employee relations policy, and (2) as a precaution against tort actions such as defamation and intentional infliction of emotional distress. Employers also should retain "positive" test samples as evidence for a reasonable period of time.

6. **Make sure reliable witnesses are present** – When confronting an employee suspected of being under the influence of drugs or involved in any drug-related incidents, make sure supervisors know what to do and what to say. It is especially important that supervisors do not act alone and that reliable witnesses are present.

7. **Document declining performance** – The safest legal policy for employers regarding disciplinary action is to document, as fully as possible, the relationship between the employee's declining performance and the employee's drug use.

8. **Request job applicant waivers of legal claims** – Employers, as a legal safeguard,

should consider requiring job applicants, at the time that the drug test is administered, to sign a consent to the test and possibly a waiver of legal rights of action against the employer. Such releases of employer liability permit both the test and the employer's right to act on the test's results. For the waiver to be valid, it must be knowingly and voluntarily given.

Of course, a critical first step for employers is the development of a formal written company policy and the effective and repeated communication of that policy to all employees. Common forms of communication which should be used include company bulletin boards, paycheck envelope inserts, and company newsletters. The policy needs to clearly communicate the employer's requirements and describe the consequences of a failure to consent to the test -- resignation.

To Test, or Not to Test ...

Six Reasons <u>Not</u> to Test for Drug Use

Why should an employer not implement a drug testing program in the workplace?

1. **To avoid morale problems** – Drug testing can upset even those employees most opposed to illegal drug use. It is, despite precautions, somewhat intrusive and somewhat of an invasion of privacy. Unless handled fairly and with full explanations, drug testing can create resentment in the workforce. This is particularly true when testing is random rather than for cause, reasonable suspicion or after a work-related accident.

2. **To avoid union grievances or union organizing** – Most unions actively oppose drug testing in the workplace. To attempt to implement drug testing may cause grievances and defeat or detract from other collective bargaining goals. In non-union workplaces, implementation of drug testing, particularly if handled inequitably, can provide the union organizer with a major issue to be used against the employer.

3. **To avoid an "overreaction"** – Employers may conclude that the best response is no response, or a prevention program without testing. A company may evaluate its situation and find that a drug abuse prevention program is unnecessary because: (1) it does not have a significant enough drug

Six Reasons to Test for Drug Use

Why should an employer implement a drug testing program in the workplace?

1. **To help the community** – By addressing the drug abuse problem effectively, employers "do their part" in addressing the needs of the community. All segments of society – government, schools, law enforcement, and businesses – must fight the war on drugs.

2. **To maintain productivity** – At this time of heightened national concern about the competitiveness of American business, can employers afford to carry significant numbers of employees who are one-third less productive because they have drugs in their systems?

3. **To protect employees and customers** – Safety and health are major employer concerns because of their moral and legal obligations to provide a workplace free of recognized hazards. In many occupations, workers on drugs present a clear and present danger to themselves, co-workers, and members of the public. Employers cannot and should not allow the safety and health of others to be jeopardized by drug abusers in the workplace.

Reasons **Not** to Test (continued)

abuse problem in its workforce to warrant a program; or (2) it is not the type of business that has safety, health, or security concerns which warrant efforts to assure a completely "drug-free" workforce.

4. **To avoid additional expenses** – Given the level of commitment necessary to maintain an effective drug abuse prevention program, employers also face a question of cost. Even if a business recognizes that it does have a drug abuse problem, it may not be able to afford a comprehensive program to address it. Development and implementation of a program is expensive. Drug testing, if done right, is expensive. Rehabilitation services are expensive. (Nonetheless, given the costs to employers of drug abuse, the more appropriate question may not be "can you afford a program?", but rather "can you afford not to have a program?")

5. **To avoid legal claims** – In our increasingly litigious society, employers face a plethora of legal claims, especially in the employee rights area. Even when an employer is legally "right" on the merits, the cost of litigation can be substantial. Some employers may see the implementation of a drug testing program as an invitation to legal challenges, and may avoid testing to avoid litigation. While it is agreed that an employer must be aware of state and local laws covering drug abuse and employment it is not clear that if drug testing is needed an employer should avoid it merely to minimize the risk of litigation.

6. **To observe privacy interests of employees** – An employer may feel that the legitimate individual rights and privacy interests of employees outweigh a company or societal interest in preventing drug abuse. However, most employers believe that while these interests are both valid and compelling, a balance must be struck with the legitimate, work related interests of the business.

Reasons to Test (continued)

4. **To contain health care costs** – American business, like American society in general, faces a crisis in health care costs. Drug users are not only more likely to injure others on the job, they also incur four times the medical expenses of the average employee. In order to contain medical costs and preserve an employer's ability to continue to provide comprehensive and affordable benefits for all employees, employers should limit the drug user's access to the workforce. Some state worker's compensation laws deny coverage if the injury resulted from the use of illicit drugs or alcohol. Taking advantage of these statutes is virtually impossible without testing.

5. **To deter drug abuse** – Contingency of employment is a powerful disincentive to illegal drug use. If drug users know a company makes "being drug-free" a condition of employment, they are more likely to refrain from illegal drug use or to apply for employment elsewhere. If you do not test, you will become the application process of choice for drug users.

6. **To rehabilitate employees** — The first step to rehabilitation is recognition of the problem. To the extent that drug testing uncovers drug dependency problems and forces people to face up to them, it can be constructive, humane, and even life-saving.

When to Test: Seven Options

When an employer decides to include drug testing in its drug abuse prevention program, it must decide under what conditions to test. The options of when and who to test include:

1. **Job applicant testing** – The drug screening of job applicants prior to employment is the most common employer drug testing practice, has the greatest deterrent effect, and is the most cost-effective – by keeping drug users out of the workforce, it helps avoid costly problems involving safety, productivity, and absenteeism.

2. **The testing of employees in safety-conscious jobs** – Jobs involving the safety, health, and security of the employee, his or her co-workers, and the public represent a compelling public interest and may warrant special employer precautions to assure that its workforce is "drug-free." Transportation, construction, and utility industries are common examples.

3. **Incident-driven drug testing** – Specific incidents may trigger employer suspicions of drug abuse and warrant drug testing. A medical emergency which appears to be drug-related, the observance of drugs or drug paraphernalia at an employee's desk or work station, or other evidence that an employee's behavior is influenced by drugs may prompt an incident-driven drug test.

4. **Post-accident investigation drug testing** – On-the-job accidents which may have involved human error often trigger drug testing of those employees involved. This is common, for example, in investigations of train or mass transit accidents.

5. **Retesting of employees during and after rehabilitation** – Employees who are, or have participated in, drug rehabilitation programs are commonly and appropriately retested for the presence of drugs in their systems. Continued employment is often predicated on an employee being successfully rehabilitated. Without random retesting, successful rehabilitation may be difficult to assure.

6. **Periodic drug testing with advance notice** – Scheduled in advance, usually as part of an annual employee physical, and uniformly administered, periodic testing is common for jobs involving stress, requiring physical endurance, or involving senior-level decision making.

7. **Random, unannounced drug tests** – Random testing without pre-notification is most likely to identify drug users. However, it also is most likely to create morale problems and trigger union grievances or employee legal claims. Employers should proceed with caution before selecting this option.

Job Applicants Versus Employees

There are several reasons why the testing of job applicants is much more common than the testing of incumbent employees:

1. Testing of job applicants is more legally defensible than the testing of employees for various reasons:

   a. There is no employer-employee relationship.

   b. There are no issues of job performance.

   c. Employers generally do have a right to make being "drug-free" a condition of employment prior to hiring.

   d. Job applicant testing is less likely to be of concern to union representatives than employee testing, and less likely to result in union-filed grievances.

2. Job denial for applicants, unlike employee dismissals, are not complicated by benefits, severance pay, or pension issues.

3. Job applicant testing is less likely to hurt employee morale than employee drug testing.

4. Job applicant testing, by keeping drug users out of the workforce, is cost-effective because it has a preventive impact on drug-related workplace problems. It also frees up limited employer resources so employers can provide more comprehensive rehabilitation programs for those employees who do develop drug abuse problems (since, presumably, there will be fewer problems due to application drug screening).

5. Job applicant testing is likely to have the greatest deterrent effect since it communicates a forceful and consistent anti-drug abuse policy at the outset of the new employees' careers.

Drug Testing and the Americans with Disabilities Act

With respect to drug testing, the ADA explicitly states that nothing in the law prohibits or restricts either drug testing or employment decisions taken on the basis of such drug tests. Therefore, an applicant who is tested and not hired because of a positive test result for illegal drugs, or an employee who is tested and is terminated because of a positive test result for illegal drugs, does not have a cause of action under the ADA. Thus, employers will not face litigation under the ADA on the part of current users of illegal drugs either for testing or for taking disciplinary action against such individuals based on such testing.

During the legislative debate on the ADA, an important principle was highlighted. The law recognizes the need to protect employers, workers, and the public from persons whose current illegal drug use impairs their ability to perform a job and whose employment could result in serious harm to the lives or property of others. At the same time, the law recognizes that treatment for those in the grips of substance abuse is not only the compassionate thing to do but an essential component of a comprehensive attack on drugs. Treatment can save the lives of individual abusers, and it can also return them to productive roles in society. This balance was achieved by providing protections against discrimination for recovered substance abusers and those in treatment or recovery who are no longer engaged in illegal drug use. Under the law, no one who seeks treatment and overcomes a drug abuse problem need fear discrimination because of past drug use.

Prior drug addiction is a covered disability under the ADA. However, an individual currently engaging in the illegal use of drugs is not protected under the ADA when an employer acts on the basis of such use. Although an employer may ask whether an applicant has illegally used drugs in the past (e.g., "Have you ever illegally used drugs?" or "Have you used cocaine in the past two years?"), an employer may not ask, at the pre-offer stage, about the extent of such prior use because this is likely to elicit information about a disability (i.e., drug addiction). Such inquiries are prohibited at the pre-offer stage.

Thus, an employer may not ask an applicant, at the pre-offer stage, questions such as "How often did you use illegal drugs in the past?"; "Have you ever been addicted to drugs?"; "Have you ever been treated for drug addiction?"; or "Have you ever been treated for drug abuse?"

On the other hand, asking about an applicant's arrest/conviction record (e.g., regarding illegal drug use, possession, and/or sale) would not be a prohibited medical question under the ADA. Such inquiries are not likely to elicit information as to whether an individual has a disability.

Transportation Industry Drug Testing Rules

In 1991, nearly 7 million "safety sensitive" employees in several transportation industries became subject to the Omnibus Transportation Employee Testing Act. Constructed on the premise that a transportation workplace free of drug and alcohol misuse is critical to the safety of the public, the law has given a major boost to those who argue the benefits of drug testing.

For the purpose of illustrating the coverage of the new law, the following references are from the *Federal Highway Administration's (Department of Transportation) Federal Motor Carrier Safety Regulations*, covering the rights and obligations of employers and drivers (employees) who operate a motor vehicle in interstate or intrastate commerce, including drivers who are independent contractors working under a lease agreement.

The federal regulations: (1) prohibit drivers from illegally using drugs or alcohol in conjunction with a driver's performance of driving and other safety-sensitive functions; (2) require the company to test drivers for the illegal use of drugs and alcohol; and (3) require the employer to notify drivers of its policies and procedures for complying with the federal regulations, as well as the rights and obligations of drivers under any independent company policies and procedures governing drug and alcohol use and testing.

Prohibited Acts – The following conduct by drivers is strictly prohibited: (i) using, being under the influence of, or possessing illegal drugs; (ii) using or being under the influence of legal drugs that are being used illegally; (iii) using or being under the influence of legal drugs whose use can adversely affect the ability of the driver to perform his or her job safely; (iv) selling, buying, soliciting to buy or sell, transporting, or possessing illegal drugs while on company time or property; (v) using alcohol within four (4) hours of driving or performing any other safety-sensitive function; (vi) using or being under the influence of alcohol at any time while performing any other safety-sensitive function; (vii) possessing any amount of alcohol (including possessing medications which contain alcohol) while on duty or driving unless the alcohol is manifested and being transported as part of the shipment; (viii) testing positive for drugs and/or alcohol; (ix) refusing to be tested for drugs and/or alcohol; (x) failing to submit to a drug and/or alcohol test as directed by the company; (xi) failing to stay in contact with the company and its medical review officer while awaiting the results of a drug test; (xii) violating any applicable federal and/or state requirement governing the use, possession, and/or purchase and/or sale of drugs or alcohol; (xiii) doing anything to obstruct the company's goals with respect to the prohibited use of drugs and alcohol.

The Tests:

1. *Mandatory Tests.* Drivers will be required to submit to a drug and/or alcohol test under the following conditions or times: (i) before a new driver is hired, or before an existing worker is transferred from a position which does not require driving to one that does; (ii) whenever the company has reasonable suspicion to believe that a driver has used drugs and/or alcohol in violation of federal regulations and/or the company's policy; (iii) following certain accidents; or (iv) on a random basis.

2. *Other Required Tests at a Company's Discretion.* Any driver who tests positive for drugs and/or alcohol, or who otherwise violates a drug or alcohol prohibition, can be prohibited from returning to duty until that driver has tested negative. Whether a company will permit a driver to return to duty, however, is at a company's discretion. The federal law also requires drivers diagnosed with drug and/or

alcohol problems to submit to random unannounced testing in the event such drivers are permitted to return to duty.

3. Whenever a driver is required to submit to a test, he or she will be expected to report for the test immediately.

The Drugs For Which A Driver Will Be Tested:

1. *At a minimum*. The federal rules require a driver to be tested for the following drugs:

   (i) marijuana;

   (ii) cocaine;

   (iii) amphetamines; and

   (iv) phencyclidine (PCP).

2. *Other*. In some instances, a company may test drivers for other drugs under applicable state law.

When A Test Result Will Be Considered Positive – If a driver's confirmed test result is positive, or if the driver refuses to be tested, the driver will be considered to have tested positive.

In the case of an alcohol test, a driver will always be considered to have tested positive if the confirmed alcohol concentration is 0.04 or greater.

Disciplinary Action – A driver who tests positive, refuses to be tested, or violates any of the federal drug and/or alcohol prohibitions is prohibited from driving to or performing any other safety-sensitive function and must be immediately removed from service. Drivers who test positive, refuse to be tested, or violate any federal drug and/or alcohol prohibitions are also subject to a fine and/or civil or criminal penalty.

Rehabilitation – The federal rules do not require companies to provide rehabilitation to drivers who test positive, refuse to be tested, or violate any other drug and/or alcohol prohibition.

For further information, interested employers should refer to the applicable DOT regulations.

Drug-Free Workplace Act

The Drug-Free Workplace Act of 1988 provides that federal contractors receiving awards of $25,000 or more must maintain a drug-free workplace. A contractor who fails to comply is subject to suspension of contract payments, and to contract termination, and could be barred from future federal contracts for up to five years. All federal procurement contracts exceeding $25,000 must now contain a clause in which the contractor undertakes to do the following:

• Publish a policy statement notifying employees that the unlawful manufacture, distribution, dispensation, possession, or use of a controlled substance is prohibited in the workplace, and specifying what actions will be taken against employees for violations of such prohibitions;

• Establish a program to inform employees of, among other things, the dangers of drug abuse in the workplace and the availability of drug counseling, rehabilitation, and employee assistance programs;

• Provide all employees working under the contract with a copy of the policy statement;

• Notify the employee in the policy statement that, as a condition of continued employment under the contract, the employee will abide by the statement and notify the employer if he or she is convicted of a criminal drug offense occurring in the workplace within five days after the conviction;

- Notify the contracting officer of an employee conviction within 10 days after the contractor learns of the conviction;

- Within 30 days after receiving notice of a conviction, impose a sanction on the convicted employee, up to and including termination, or require the employee to satisfactorily complete a drug rehabilitation program; and,

- Make a good faith effort to continue to maintain a drug-free workplace by meeting the requirements of the federal legislation.

Alcoholism and Employers

Alcohol abuse remains the most widespread and debilitating form of drug abuse in America and for American businesses.

Twelve million Americans are alcoholics, and another 90 million are "social drinkers" who have alcohol at least once a month.

While alcohol does not pose a danger to most people who drink it, it does remain a common and costly problem which adversely affects the workplace with:

- Increased absenteeism
- Reduced productivity
- Increased accident rates
- Increased health care costs

Frequently Asked Questions about the Drug-Free Workplace Act

Q. What is the minimum set of components for an employer program to meet the requirements of the Drug-Free Workplace Act?
A. Each employer must meet the specific requirements of the Act with a good faith effort, including having a policy statement and a drug awareness program. Neither the law nor the final rules require employers to establish an Employee Assistance Program (EAP), to conduct any drug testing, or to incorporate any particular component in an employer's program.

Q. What are examples of other possible components of an employer drug-free workplace program for contractors and grantees?
A. Here is a partial list of other possible components of an employer program. The list is provided for information only; there is no intention for the Federal Government to require any particular component.

Employee Education
Conduct education/outreach of employees/families via:
- Discussion groups on drug abuse/company policy
- Videotapes/pamphlets on drugs in workplace
- Brown bag lunch discussions
- Communication of available employee assistance
- Communication of available health benefits for drug/alcohol treatment

FAQs about the Drug-Free Workplace Act (continued)

Employee Assistance

- Establish an EAP
- Identify treatment resources
- Assemble resource file on providers of assistance
- Provide problem assessments
- Provide confidential counseling
- Provide referral to counseling and/or treatment
- Provide crisis intervention
- Establish hot-line
- Provide family support services
- Conduct follow-up during and after treatment
- Conduct evaluation of job performance pre- and post-program contact
- Review insurance coverage (to include outpatient as well as inpatient treatment)
- Institute mechanism to review employee complaints

Supervisory Training

Conduct management/supervisory/union training on:

- Drug abuse education
- Signs and symptoms of drug use
- Company policy on drug use
- Employee assistance resources
- How to deal with an employee suspected of drug use
- How and when to take disciplinary action

Drug Detection

Institute a program of drug testing of:

- All employees – testing of applicants or pre-employment; testing of employees based on reasonable suspicion, post-accident, during and after counseling and/or rehabilitation
- Employees in health and safety or national security sensitive positions – random unannounced testing

Increase security

Between 7 and 9 percent of all workers abuse alcohol – four times the abuse rate for marijuana.

Employers are unwise if they implement prevention and rehabilitation programs for drug abuse, but ignore alcohol abuse. The annual cost of alcohol abuse to business is nearly equivalent to that for drug abuse.

Employers need to address both problems – alcohol and drug abuse – in parallel programs which are humane and effective.

Alcoholism and the Americans with Disabilities Act

Under the Americans with Disabilities Act, alcoholism, unlike illegal drug use, is considered a disability. However, an employer may hold an employee who is an alcoholic to the same qualification standards for employment or job performance and behavior that the employer holds other employees, even if an unsatisfactory performance or behavior is related to the alcoholism of the employee. Thus, an employer under the reasonable accommodation provisions of the ADA does not have to provide a rehabilitation program or an opportunity for rehabilitation for any job applicant who is an alcoholic or for any current employee who is an alcoholic.

An employer may ask an applicant whether she/he drinks alcohol. However, at the pre-offer stage, an employer may not ask an applicant about whether she/he is an alcoholic, because alcoholism is a disability. In addition, an employer may not ask an applicant about how much alcohol she/he drinks because this inquiry is likely to elicit information about the existence, nature, or severity of a disability (i.e., alcoholism). Therefore, such inquiries are prohibited at the pre-offer stage.

For example, an employer may not, at the pre-offer stage, make inquiries such as, "How

Alcohol Control Program Checklist

☐ Provide policy statement affirming the belief that alcoholism is an illness that can be treated successfully in most cases. The employer must show a readiness to help those with drinking problems.

☐ Both employer and employees should jointly develop and administer the program.

☐ Make available information and education about the nature of alcohol so as to dispel myths.

☐ Middle management or, in larger companies, the first-level supervisor are the key individuals to insure implementation of an effective control program. These individuals are in daily contact with the largest part of the workforce and can most easily detect the signs of a person who needs help. They must be trained to recognize the signs of declining performance and how to approach the problem with an employee.

☐ Professional staff services must be chosen once a troubled employee is identified. There must be someone to whom the employee can be referred for diagnosis and assistance. The referral is usually to a doctor, but the function can also be performed by a nurse, psychologist, counselor, personnel worker, or other staff specialist. While these latter persons may be able to provide a counseling function, treatment should be left to physicians or hospitals.

☐ Early identification of the problem should be emphasized. An alcoholic will be masterful at developing rationales to deny the existence of a problem.

☐ There should be controls in place to be sure that ongoing efforts are not abandoned once an employee has been referred for assistance. Information should be gathered to review the progress made by employees who have been referred for aid.

☐ The records of people who voluntarily seek assistance should be maintained on a confidential basis. If employees know this will occur, they will be more likely to make effective use of the treatment program.

much alcohol do you drink per week?"; "Do you drink every day?"; "Do you drink alone?"; "Have you ever been treated for alcoholism?"; "Are you an alcoholic?"; or "Does alcohol interfere with your daily activities?"

Setting Up an Alcohol Abuse Prevention Program

Alcohol abuse is a major contributor to lost productivity in the workforce and growing health care costs. Employers who want to reduce costs from ineffective performance by impaired workers, accidents, lost time from work, and disability should consider the possible advantages of establishing an alcohol counseling program.

Any alcohol counseling program must be aggressive in its efforts to discover and control the problem. Early detection is important, as the employee must be persuaded to admit the problem exists, or the employer must take more coercive action by requiring the employee to straighten out work performance problems or face discharge. The initial step, then, is getting the employee some sort of professional help either through in-house referral or through staff employed by the firm.

Workplace Investigations 14

Introduction

Employers are often faced with the very difficult task of determining what actually occurred when one or more employees engage in possible misconduct in the workplace. While conducting investigations is not a core activity for most employers, today's decision makers, for many reasons including media exposure to sophisticated investigative techniques, expect a competent, thorough and unbiased investigation.

There may be many different goals to a workplace investigation – discharging a legal obligation to investigate, protecting victims, protecting assets, stopping illegal conduct, etc. While getting to the truth is usually the main goal, almost as important is getting there properly and avoiding exposure to any additional liability. There are inherent competing interests whenever a workplace investigation occurs. There is the need to obtain the necessary factual information in order to verify or dismiss the allegations. The competing interest is protecting and respecting employee privacy and other rights. There is the need for a thorough examination of the facts and circumstances and a competing need for immediate action and avoidance of a determination that the conduct has been condoned. There is the need for appropriate corrective or remedial action. This need raises just cause and due process concerns.

Achieving the objectives of an investigation and avoiding additional liability requires careful planning and skillful execution of the plan.

This chapter will highlight some important considerations to be kept in mind when an employer is faced with the need to investigate.

Characteristics of a Proper Investigation

The characteristics of a proper investigation will include:

- Selection of an appropriate investigator
- Promptness
- Open-mindedness
- Protection of participants from retaliation or reprisals
- Progression from open-ended questions to covering all of the specifics
- Thoroughness (all parties and potential witnesses are interviewed and all relevant work records and other documents are reviewed)
- Accuracy
- Minimal intrusiveness
- Maximum confidentiality
- Follow-up with the complainant
- Documentation (keeping in mind the possibility of discovery in a future lawsuit)
- A conclusion
- Remedial action if appropriate

Who Should Conduct the Investigation

Characteristics of a Good Investigator – In determining who should conduct the investigation, the nature of the conduct alleged, the persons accused and the persons available with the necessary level of training and experience must be considered. The investigator must be fair and impartial with respect to the issues and the parties. Common choices include human resources personnel, attorneys, outside consultants and law enforcement personnel. Here are some advantages and disadvantages of each choice:

1. ***Human Resources***
   a. Familiarity with employees
   b. Extensive knowledge of the employer's policies, practices and culture
   c. Openness of communications may be impeded (fear of retaliation)
   d. Cost advantage

2. ***Attorney***
   a. Aware of legal boundaries
   b. May or may not be a good investigator or interviewer
   c. May impede openness of communication (fear of legal liability or retaliation)
   d. May be unfamiliar with the employer's policies, practices and culture
   e. Loss of attorney-client privilege
   f. May be more useful as an overseer of the entire investigative process
   g. Cost disadvantage

3. ***Outside Consultant***
   a. May appear more objective and neutral than insiders, particularly if upper management is accused
   b. Less risk of confidentiality breach
   c. May be unfamiliar with the employer's policies, practices and culture
   d. Cost disadvantage

4. ***Law Enforcement Personnel***
   a. Must provide Miranda warnings and other constitutional protections (5th Amendment prohibition against self-incrimination, 4th Amendment protection against unreasonable searches, etc.)
   b. Loss of control of the investigation – arrests, public disclosure, etc.
   c. Lack of familiarity or interest in the employer's policies, practices and culture
   d. Delay
   e. Due to reasonable doubt standard of proof, may impose higher investigative standards than necessary
   f. Cost advantage

Whoever is selected to investigate, it should be someone who:

- Understands the purpose of the investigation

- Appreciates the legal and practical issues presented by the investigator

- Knows the employer's practices, policies and culture

- Has good interviewing skills

- Is credible, respected and impartial

- Would be effective as a witness

- Is able to maintain confidentiality

- Pays attention to detail, resolves inconsistencies, addresses all open issues and prepares good documentation

- Can execute the plan but is flexible enough to adapt to the twists and turns that arise during investigations

- Can weigh competing and conflicting information, make a recommendation to the decision maker and support it

Preparing For The Investigation

Once the need for an investigation and its goals have been identified and the investigator has been selected, it is now time to prepare the Investigation Plan. In developing a Plan, at a minimum, the employer should:

- Identify all potential witnesses
  - o Take the Complaint
    - Why, where, who, witnesses, documentation
    - Explain limited confidentiality
    - Explain no retaliation
    - Be objective, not judgmental
    - Communicate a realistic timetable
    - Do not promise complete confidentiality
    - Consider interim protective measures if necessary
    - Instill confidence in the process and assure them they make the correct choice in utilizing it
  - o Interview the Accused
    - Present the allegations
    - Allow opportunity for rebuttal
    - Observe and evaluate responses
    - Ask for reasons complaining party would have to lie
    - Advise of the possibility of discipline
    - Assure the accused no conclusions will be reached until the investigation is completed
    - Warn against retaliation

- Follow union contract and other special rules if accused is represented by a union
- Treat the accused with respect and dignity
- Perform follow-up interviews as needed
- Identify the documents to be reviewed
- Prepare the strategy to address the needs and goals of the investigation
- Interview the witnesses
  - o Prepare for the interviews
  - o Give thought to location of the interviews and timing
  - o Review witness personnel files
  - o Review other relevant documentation (e.g., emails, production records, reports, timesheets, expense reimbursement records, telephone records, etc.)
  - o Beware of motives and biases
- Establish a secure system of organizing and maintaining files and records
- Review the plan regularly and adapt it to meet any changes that arise
- Determine appropriate remedial action
  - o Do you have the whole story?
  - o Do the facts stand up?
  - o Was the investigation thorough?
  - o Was there a violation of the employer's policy?
  - o Was the conduct criminal?
  - o Administer appropriate discipline (consider the conduct, consider past practice, work rules, employee handbook, etc.)
  - o Does the punishment fit the crime?

- Communicate the result to the appropriate persons
  - o Follow-up with victim
  - o Report criminal conduct to the authorities
  - o Follow-up with witnesses as appropriate
- Prepare appropriate documentation
  - o Take copious notes
  - o Consider written statements or affidavits
  - o Consider recorded statements
  - o Maintain confidentiality safeguards

Perhaps the most frequent mistake committed by employers faced with a need to investigate is procrastination. Reasons for such are illness or absence of those involved, vacations, holidays, pressing work matters or the hope that if the information or allegations are ignored, they will somehow go away. Do not fall victim to any such beliefs.

Investigate promptly – it will show you took the matter seriously. Also, the trail will be fresh and memories will not have faded. Finally, striking while the iron is hot will not give the accused a chance to cover his or her tracks. You will have a better chance of getting straight answers and admissions.

Factors Used to Evaluate the Competency and Effectiveness of an Investigation

Juries and others, with the benefit of hindsight, look at several factors in evaluating the adequacy of an investigation. Often times, good plaintiff's lawyers will put the employer's investigation on trial in order to divert attention from their client's conduct. The report card of a good investigation contains passing grades in the following areas:

- Evidence of planning
- Devotion of sufficient skills and resources
- Promptness (but no rush to judgment)
- Thoroughness (all material witnesses were interviewed and documents reviewed)
- Fairness and Impartiality
- Accuracy
- Minimal Intrusion
- Maximum Confidentiality
- Adequate Documentation

Workplace Privacy 15

Introduction

Increasingly, employers are finding it more challenging to balance their need for information about their employees with employees' privacy rights. This conflict may first arise when an employer wants to perform a background check on a job applicant. It may also occur when the employer wishes to monitor employee communications or where an employee's off-duty activities create a potential conflict of interest. The challenge for employers is to protect their right to obtain necessary information, while establishing realistic employee privacy expectations and honoring any legally-protected privacy rights.

More and more employers are choosing to monitor employee communications and other personal activities. According to a 2005 survey by the Society for Human Resources Management and the Wall Street Journal, employers monitor employee activities for a variety of reasons, including:

- protection against computer viruses, hackers, and other intruders;

- quality assurance;

- evaluations of employee performance or productivity;

- protection of proprietary information;

- prevention of workplace violence;

- prevention of litigation (e.g., misconduct, workplace harassment).

When asked how their organization monitors employees, human resources professionals reported a range of activities by employers:

- over 40% read employee postal mail;

- almost 50% use cameras to monitor employee activities;

- more than half search employee desks and offices;

- 85% monitor employees' telephone use;

- more than 90% monitor employee computer use; and

- 96% perform reference or background checks on applicants for employment.

Before utilizing these strategies, however, employers should understand there are privacy protections employees enjoy under state and federal law and they must be properly balanced with the need for information.

Fair Credit Reporting Act

Under the Fair Credit Reporting Act ("FCRA"), employees also have certain rights regarding credit checks and general investigative background checks obtained from third parties. The FCRA governs the disclosure of "consumer reports," which includes information provided by consumer reporting agencies that address credit, character, general reputation, personal characteristics or mode of living. Although employers often fail to recognize that the

FCRA applies in the employment context, criminal background investigation reports and a credit histories generally fall within the FCRA's scope.

The FCRA requires employers to provide employees certain notices and disclosures before requesting a report, before taking any adverse action based on the report, and after taking adverse action based on the report. There are limited exceptions from these notice and disclosure requirements where the report concerns suspected employee misconduct, or compliance with federal, state, or local laws or regulations or preexisting written employer policies.

If the report falls within one of these exceptions, the statute requires only limited employee notice, but still restricts access to the report to individuals or organizations prescribed by statute.

Common Law Right to Privacy

Employees may have a common law right to privacy which gives the employee the right to be free from an "unreasonable intrusion" upon their privacy. The availability of this right varies from state to state. For example, a common law invasion of privacy cause of action has been recognized by the courts in Connecticut, but not in New York.

When considering whether an employee has proven a violation of a common law right to privacy, a court will generally ask three questions:

- Did the employee have a reasonable expectation of privacy?
- If so, did the employer have a legitimate business reason for monitoring, accessing or disclosing?
- Were the employer's actions reasonable under the circumstances?

However, employee consent to employer monitoring is a complete defense to common

law right to privacy claims, as an employee who gives consent no longer has a reasonable expectation of privacy. Also, an employer policy or conduct can destroy any reasonable expectation of privacy. For example, a policy permitting the employer to search of lockers, desks, packages, etc., under defined circumstances, would destroy any such expectation.

Electronic Communications Privacy Legislation

Another source of employee privacy rights is the federal "Electronic Communications Privacy Act" ("ECPA"). The ECPA prohibits intentional, unauthorized interception and access of wire, oral or electronic communications (including e-mail). This prohibition applies only to content of communication, not to the sender's or recipient's identities or the length of the communication. The ECPA generally applies to employers and provides employees a private cause of action, as well as punitive damages and attorneys' fees. Violators may also be subject to criminal sanctions.

Several ECPA exemptions may apply to employers, including an exemption for prior consent of one of the parties, and an exception for interception by an employer in the ordinary course of business.

State law may provide employees additional rights regarding privacy of electronic communications. For example, under New York Penal Law Section 250 ("Wiretapping Law"), monitoring, intercepting or accessing electronic communications without consent of one of the parties is a Class E felony.[1] Unlike the federal ECPA, New York's Wiretapping

---

1. Under this New York law, it would be lawful to install a hidden camera, for video purposes, in the workplace but unlawful to permit the audio function to, in effect, electronically eavesdrop on employee conversations.

Law provides no system provider or ordinary course exceptions. However, if an employer obtains consent of one of the parties, the employer is permitted to monitor, intercept, or access electronic communications.

So, for example, monitoring telephone calls for training or other purposes may fall within the ECPA's ordinary course of business exception and would be permissible under federal law, but would violate New York law, unless the employer had the prior consent of the employee. On the other hand, monitoring employees' personal calls without the employee's prior consent violates both the ECPA and New York's Wiretapping Law.

Consent is a defense to a common law right to privacy claim or to claims under the ECPA or some state statutes, such as the NY Wiretapping Law. Therefore, employers should obtain employee consent to intercept, monitor, access, and disclose, voice mail, telephone, e-mail, Internet, or computer files. Such consent can be express or implied.

Express consent exists when an employee consents to employer monitoring and access in writing. Employers may obtain express consent at the time of hire or at any time during employment. Employers who wish to obtain express consent from employees may circulate to current employees a consent form, which should be signed and returned to the employer. As new employees are hired, the employer should then obtain the same written consent by asking new employees to sign and return the consent form prior to beginning work.

Implied consent may be found where the employee did not provide written consent, but the facts and circumstances demonstrate employee consent. Several factors are considered in determining whether an employee has given implied consent, including whether:

- the employer has an established policy;

- employees had notice of the policy; and

- employees were informed the computer/ e-mail system is private and confidential.

To establish implied consent, employers should have a formal policy stating that use of the system constitutes consent and should provide a "pop-up" reminder to employees at log-in regarding waiver and the employer's rights to monitor, intercept, and access messages and files on its system.

Lawful Outside Political and Recreational Activities

Some thirteen states, including New York, prohibit discrimination against employees because of lawful, outside political or recreational activities. Under New York law, for example, an employee is protected from discrimination for engaging a variety of outside activities:

- political activities, such as running for public office, campaigning on behalf of a candidate, or participating in political fundraisers.

- recreational activities, such as sports, hobbies, television viewing, etc.

- use of legal products, such as tobacco or alcohol, when such use occurs during non-work hours, off-premises, and not on the employer's equipment.

New York's statute provides certain exceptions, which permit the employer to take action against an employee where, for example, the employee's outside activities create a material conflict of interest or violates an established substance abuse policy. Otherwise, the employee is protected from discrimination on the basis of his or her lawful off-duty activities.

Workplace Relationships

Close workplace relationships, romantic or platonic, can be a sensitive issue for employers and employees alike. Employees will likely view these types of relationships as private and therefore outside the scope of legitimate employer interest. On the other hand, employers should recognize that these relationships can give rise to several concerns, including:

- conflicts of interest,

- favoritism, and

- liability for sexual harassment.

Employers may address these concerns by taking individualized corrective action and by adopting policies concerning fraternization, nepotism, and sexual harassment. A non-fraternization policy prohibits employees from engaging in amorous or sexual behavior with one another, especially supervisors and their subordinates. A nepotism policy restricts employment of individuals who are related by blood or by marriage to a current employee of the organization.

Before implementing non-fraternization or nepotism policies, employers should consult with their employment counsel to ensure compliance with applicable state law. Employers who implement non-fraternization or nepotism policies must consistently enforce the policies against both male and female employees.

Workplace Privacy Tips for Employers

To summarize, employers should take appropriate steps to ensure they are appropriately respecting employees' privacy rights while preserving their own rights to monitor employee activities. To ensure that they are properly addressing privacy needs, employers should consider taking the following steps:

- Identify risks that may need to be reduced through monitoring or appropriate employer policies;

- Create, distribute and implement relevant policies and detail reasons for policy before it's implemented;

- Obtain employee consent for monitoring, accessing, and disclosing records;

- Only disclose private information where necessary and only on a "need to know" basis; and

- Consult with employment counsel regarding applicable state laws.

Human Resource Management–The Basics 16

Introduction

In this Chapter, we outline some of the effective strategies employers might consider in setting up their personnel policies. While the actual procedure may not be applicable to every employer, the principles are tried and tested and they can help employers create an effective workforce.

Hiring Procedures

Good personnel practice begins with the hiring process. All job applicants should be evaluated consistently as part of the interviewing process.

There are two issues that deserve additional explanation. One relates to pre-employment/ application form questions, and the other, to references.

Job Application Trouble Spots

Subject	Lawful	Unlawful
Age	Are you 18 years of age or older? If not, state your age. Do you have a work permit?	How old are you? What is your date of birth? What are the ages of your children, if any?
Arrest Record	Have you ever been convicted of a crime? (Give details)	Have you ever been arrested?
Disability	None	Do you have a disability? Have you ever been treated for any of the following diseases? Do you have now, or have you ever had, a drug or alcohol problem?
Marital Status	None	Do you wish to be addressed as Miss? Mrs.? Ms.? Are you married? Single? Divorced? Separated? Any information about one's spouse.
National Origin	None	Inquiry into applicant's lineage, ancestry, national origin, descent, parentage or nationality. Nationality of applicant's parents.
Race or Color	None	Complexion or color of skin. Coloring.
Sex	None	

Application Checklist (continued)

Subject	Lawful	Unlawful
Address or Duration of Residence	Applicant's place of residence. How long a resident of this state or city?	
Birthdate/ Birthplace	None	Requirements that applicant submit birth certificate, naturalization or baptismal record. Requirement that applicant produce proof of age in form of birth certificate or baptismal record.
Citizenship	Are you a citizen of the United States? If not a citizen of the United States, do you intend to become a citizen of the United States? If you are not a United States citizen, have you the legal right to remain permanently in the United States? Do you intend to remain permanently in the United States?	Of what country are you a citizen? Whether an applicant is naturalized or a native-born citizen; the date when the applicant acquired citizenship. Requirement that applicant produce naturalization papers or first papers. Whether applicant's parents are naturalized or native-born citizens of the United States; the date when such parents acquired citizenship.
Driver's License	Do you possess a valid driver's license?	Requirement that applicant produce a driver's license.
Education	Inquiry into applicant's academic, vocational, or professional education and the public and private schools attended.	
Experience	Inquiry into work experience.	
Language	Inquiry into languages applicant speaks or writes fluently.	What is your native language? Inquiry into how applicant acquired ability to read, write, or speak a foreign language.
Military Experience	Inquiry into applicant's military experience in the Armed Forces of the United States or in a State Militia. Inquiring into applicant's service in particular branch of United States Army, Navy, etc.	Inquiry into applicant's military experience other than in the Armed Forces of the United States or in a State Militia. Did you receive a discharge from the military in other than honorable circumstances?
Notice in Case of Emergency	None	Name and address of person to be notified in case of an accident or emergency.
Organizations	Inquiry into applicant's membership in organizations which the applicant considers relevant to his or her ability to perform the job.	List all clubs, societies, and lodges to which you belong.
Photograph	None	Requirement or option that applicant affix a photograph to employment form at any time before hiring.

Pre-Employment or Application Form Inquiries – New York is among the strictest states in regard to pre-employment inquiries, and that State's Human Rights Agency, the New York State Division of Human Rights, has issued the following guidelines on what is lawful and unlawful from both a state and federal viewpoint:

References – There are many employers who have been counseled to give only confirming facts that relate to dates of employment and title held, but nothing more. Indeed, when pressed with the question, "Would the individual be eligible for rehire?" many employers choose not to answer. The possible liability from defamation lawsuits brought by former employees who believe that their inability to land a position stems from an adverse job reference has had a chilling effect on references. As a rule, the employee claiming defamation must show that the employer's statement was false, given in malice and communicated to a third party. Although there are differences among the courts, malice refers to the making of a statement with the knowledge that the statement is false or with a serious doubt as to the statement's veracity. A limited reference policy avoids risk of defamation and provides a solution to the difficult reference request concerning a former employee who has or is suing you or is otherwise protected by an employment law. If an employer has a limited reference policy, it must be followed in all cases in order to be used as a shield when denying a reference concerning an employee who has engaged in some form of protected activity.

In 1997, the Supreme Court ruled that former employees can sue their previous employer over negative job references given in retaliation for bringing a claim of employment discrimination.

In 25 states (California, Oregon, Idaho, Florida, Louisiana, Georgia, South Carolina, Maine, Maryland, Michigan, Ohio, Wisconsin, Illinois, Indiana, Ohio, Oklahoma, Colorado, Utah, New Mexico, Arizona, South Dakota, Hawaii, Tennessee, Wyoming, and Kansas) laws have been passed to protect employers who provide good faith job references of former and current employees with varying degrees of protection against suits alleging defamation and other claims.

Supervisors need to be educated in the employer's policy concerning references as prospective employers will often call them instead of the human resources department. A strategy must be developed for handling difficult references which involve the possibility of future, foreseeable harm if knowledge concerning a former employee is not passed on.

If receiving a reference on a potential employee is going to be important to you, as it should be, then a waiver form should be signed by the job applicant to the effect that the individual authorizes a former employer "to provide any and all information contained in my personnel file to the prospective employer." Furthermore, the applicant should release that employer from any and all claims of liability arising out of the sharing of such information. The waiver release should be signed and dated. This will increase the chance that you will receive the information and also some defense to claims of negligent hiring.

Employment Policy — Employers should give job applicants a copy of the company's employment policy statement at the time of hire and prior to their joining the workforce. It also should be included in a firm's employee handbook and manual. Employers also may wish to have employees sign a copy of this statement. The signed and dated copy should be retained in the employee's personnel file.

Hiring Checklist

☐ Write a job description for the vacant position or review the old one, updating the duties required.

☐ Make a skills profile which lists the precise duties of the position and the skills needed to accomplish these duties in a minimally acceptable manner.

☐ Receive applications and evaluate them. Notify unqualified candidates. Rank qualified ones.

☐ Schedule interviews. Prepare specific open-ended questions which will help to determine whether the applicant will be able to accomplish the duties of the position.

☐ Discuss the duties, responsibilities, and skills required; and describe the wages, benefits, advancement opportunities, and other aspects of the job.

☐ Summarize the interviews in written reports and retain them in a file.

☐ Check the candidate's references. Check the requisite documents to determine whether the new hire is a U.S. citizen or has the proper authority to work in the U.S., and complete the INS Form I-9.

☐ Federal law prohibits the use of a polygraph to prescreen prospective employees in most situations.

Employee Handbooks

An Employee Handbook is one of the most common methods used by employers to communicate their personnel policies and benefit programs. It should set forth in detail the benefits, policies, and disciplinary rules of the company and should be updated periodically. An employee handbook cannot replace personal communication, but it is an effective means for informing your employees about vital information. It is safe to say that the advantages of a handbook far outweigh any potential drawbacks. Do not provide a copy to the employee until he has accepted employment. This can avoid claims that the employee quit a job and/or accepted a job in reliance on something in the handbook.

In recent years, there have been numerous court decisions which have held that employee handbooks can constitute a contract of employment. Accordingly, the common law right to dismiss at will has been carved out in certain jurisdictions. It would be advisable, therefore, to check on the status of the "employment at will" doctrine in your state. At the very least, the handbook should be explicit on this point of employment at will. Suggested language for the handbook follows:

"Employment is 'at will.' Employment can be terminated by either party, at any time, and for any reason. This includes termination with or without cause, and with or without notice.

"Any oral statements, promises, or assurances to the contrary are not binding on the employer and should not be relied upon by the employee or job applicant.

"Statements on the employment application, or in this handbook, training manuals, or other documents, do not constitute or imply an employment contract and should not be relied upon by the employee or job applicant under any circumstances as assuring continued employment or superseding the 'at will' employment policy."

Orientation for New Employees

After an individual has been hired, an orientation session with the employee should be held to discuss, in detail, the company's benefits and other personnel policies. If available, a copy of the company's Employee Handbook should be delivered at that time. First impressions are often lasting; therefore, a new employee's questions and concerns should be solicited and addressed, and he or she should be encouraged to discuss with the management any problems that may arise during employment with the company.

The new employee should also have a thorough orientation with his or her supervisor to become familiar with the job and working conditions. Again, the opportunity to establish effective communication channels should be stressed.

Employee Orientation Checklist

☐ Describe the company, its history, organization, and goals.

☐ Explain the duties and responsibilities of the position to the new employee and make clear what is expected. Furnish a written job description.

☐ Familiarize the employee with the firm's rules, compensation and benefits, frequency of employee appraisal reviews, advancement policies, and other pertinent information.

☐ Explain how the employee can find redress for a complaint.

☐ Introduce the new employee to co-workers and supervisory personnel.

☐ Furnish a copy of the Employee Handbook.

Communications

A company must ensure that employees are fully informed of benefits and policies as well as other matters of general interest.

The handbook could be supplemented by a regularly published company newsletter or other written forms of communications. Not only would the newsletter serve to update the handbook, it could also provide information on a variety of subjects of interest to employees and promote a sense of community. Similarly, a company bulletin board could serve as a means of communication for employees and employers. Both a bulletin board and a newsletter are useful devices for preventing misinformation or rumors from developing into crises.

Personal contact with employees is still the most simple and effective means of improving relations. Meetings with employees, both formal and informal, should be held periodically to explain policies and to listen to their concerns and suggestions. Such meetings will not only assure employees that the company cares, but also will afford management an opportunity to respond constructively to employee problems, and sympathetically to employee needs.

Communications Checklist

☐ Establish and maintain a communications program, including distribution of written material through the use of an Employee Handbook, periodic newsletters, and bulletin boards for informal notices.

☐ Train supervisors in methods of effective communication. They should serve as a very important link between management and workers.

☐ Solicit opinions from employees, and respond to questions and suggestions as soon as possible.

☐ Use orientation sessions and performance reviews as part of a communications program.

☐ Discuss the progress and goals of the firm with employees and explain any policy changes both formally and informally.

Child Care

While few employers provide child care or subsidize it, there is growing sentiment that employer-provided or employer-paid child care fosters a more productive work environment because the employee will be absent less and, when on the job, less distracted by child care problems.

For those employers who have offered such benefits, the prevailing rationale is that they provide an advantage to attract and retain quality employees, who care about the quality of their family life. The statistics on working mothers reveal that half of them return to work before their babies are a year old. Some 10 million children under the age of six need child care during some part of the day, and as many as 7 million children under age 13 are left unsupervised for some portion of the day. It is predicted that in the near future the number of mothers in the workforce will rise to 75 percent.

Bureau of Labor Statistics data establish that mothers of preschool children have an absence rate that is nearly twice as high as all other employee groups.

The single most popular child care benefit is a spending account. Where this is used, a set amount of money is deducted from the employee's paycheck for child care, the employee is later reimbursed upon submission of a receipt for child care, and the employee does not have to pay income tax on that amount. Neither is the FICA or FUTA tax assessed on amounts covered by employees' child care spending accounts.

Wages and Benefits

An employer must continually analyze and update its wage and benefits program. Data should be gathered concerning the wages and benefits offered locally (and nationally if relevant) for both union and non-union employees. This data should be evaluated and the company's relative position should be determined.

The company should also consider establishing a formal wage program based on merit and longevity. The factors involved in such a program should be outlined, in detail, both to employees and supervisors. The program should be flexible enough to permit general adjustments to the program when required by cost-of-living market conditions and/or competitive considerations.

Apart from wages, a comprehensive benefits program should also be established. It may consist of any or all of the following:

1. Holidays
2. Vacations
3. Sick Leave
4. Excused Absence for Emergencies
5. Insurance (life, accident, disability, medical, dental, and/or vision)
6. Pension
7. Profit Sharing
8. Bonus
9. Tuition Assistance
10. Parking or Travel Allowance
11. Medical and Personal Leave
12. Child Care Facility
13. Low Interest Loan Assistance
14. Jury Duty Pay
15. Funeral Leave

Job Advancement

A key ingredient to maintaining stable and effective personnel relations is assuring employees that there is real opportunity for personal advancement and growth. Thus, an employer must be continually aware of the employees' need for advancement; consequently, information concerning job openings should be publicized in the company newsletter or through some other job posting procedure.

Consistent with the desire to meet employee expectations for advancement, the company should inform its employees of its policies on promotion and transfer. The major policy considerations usually involved in any decision regarding promotion or transfer are seniority and ability. From a personnel relations standpoint, where ability is relatively equal, seniority should be considered in making the decision as to which employee will advance. This same consideration should be used in the event of a layoff or recall.

Performance Reviews

Performance reviews should be an integral part of the wage system. The review process is extremely important. It is not only a device for encouraging the employee who is doing a good job but also should be used to help an employee who is having difficulty. There should never be any surprises at a performance review. If the supervisor has been doing his or her job, the performance review should be only a formal confirmation of what the employee has already been told.

Employee Training

If the forecasts are correct, employers are facing a shortage of well-educated and well-trained workers to meet the nation's economic needs. There is an enormous challenge to employers to improve the nation's job-related learning system. If you are not spending 2 to 4 percent of payroll on training you are probably making an insufficient commitment.

Training is a good deal for employers because those who train end up with productivity increases more than twice as high as the wage increases that come with training. Unfortunately, the vast majority of American employees never

Performance Review Checklist

☐ Establish a date for a regular, timely, objective evaluation of the employee's performance.

☐ Document the appraisal with specific examples of acceptable or unacceptable performance by the employee. Gather examples throughout the year, do not do all evaluations the night before they are due.

☐ Emphasize positive comments where possible. Point out problem areas and possible solutions. Stress the attitude for achieving success and show how the employee can achieve it.

☐ Encourage the employee's comments on performance and discuss specific goals for the next review period. Outline methods of accomplishing these goals.

☐ Advise the employee of the date of the next appraisal, and place a summary of the performance review in the employee's personnel file. Employee should sign the file copy.

receive formal training that is provided and paid for by their employers.

In a study jointly conducted by the American Society for Training and Development and the Department of Labor, employers were urged to take the following steps:

• Create an institutional environment that encourages the proactive use of human resource development as a tool to encourage efficiencies, quality improvements, new applications, and innovations;

• Use selection and appraisal procedures that assess job-related training needs;

- Use reward systems that provide compensation based on skill;
- Build training-related, performance-based requirements into management and supervisory job descriptions and work objectives;
- Treat training as an investment with the same payoff as R&D; and
- Work together, sharing development and delivery costs of training materials, technologies, and basic research on applied learning among adults.

Disciplinary Rules

The maintenance of a consistent disciplinary policy is absolutely essential. There are two basic alternatives which should be considered. In the first, a company can publish disciplinary rules prescribing specific penalties for violations which may occur. The advantage of this system is that, by subjecting everyone to the same punishment for the same violation, it reduces charges of unfairness. The primary drawback, however, is that it reduces a company's flexibility to take into account extenuating circumstances. Furthermore, certain acts may not be clearly covered, resulting in confusion over which penalty is appropriate.

The second alternative is to have the supervisor recommend a specific disciplinary action and then, in order to ensure consistency, have another staff member review the matter before a final decision is made.

Regardless of which approach is selected, the company should also consider the possibility of establishing a formal grievance procedure, with a designated company official responsible for resolving disputes.

Termination: A Planned Event

The decision to discharge an employee should be carefully planned. It is not something to be left to spontaneity. Obviously, the degree of planning is much less necessary in those circumstances where the employee has committed crimes (i.e.

theft, assault, etc.) or serious infractions of an employer's work rules or policies.

In the vast majority of dismissals there should be a "paper trail" documenting the circumstances leading to the decision to terminate an individual. If it is insubordination, then the employee's personnel file should have a record of incidences. Signed periodic reviews should reflect earlier dissatisfaction.

If it is a matter of economics, then there should be a straightforward recitation of those facts (i.e. the loss of a major customer or a general business slowdown) and the reasons the employee was selected. What is important in these circumstances is to reveal the true basis for dismissal. There are many wrongful discharge suits that are brought to find the "real reasons" for termination, and some of these could have been avoided by forthrightly explaining the dismissal. Before making a termination decision, employers should:

- Review the timing of the termination;
- Review the employee's entire personnel file;
- Review all the events surrounding the termination;
- Verify the employee was adequately forewarned of the disciplinary consequences of his or her conduct;
- Make certain the rule/offense is reasonably related to business need;
- Review the investigative findings to ensure the investigation was fair and complete;
- Review the evidence of the employee's guilt to determine if "substantial evidence" exists to support the decision;
- Make sure the applicable rule, policy or criteria is being applied consistently;
- Verify that the punishment fits the offense; and
- Consider any protected status, anticipate potential claims and proceed in a manner which minimizes the risk.

The decision to hire or dismiss an employee is ultimately the employer's, but should be based on principles of fairness and respectful for dignity of the individual. If these two guideposts are followed, then there is greater certainty that a disgruntled former employee will not prevail in a wrongful discharge lawsuit.

How To Handle a Termination

The catalyst for a wrongful discharge claim often can be an inappropriately handled notice of termination – a notice that is poorly timed, poorly stated, and/or too publicly handled. A discharged employee who feels that he or she has been humiliated, lied to, or provoked, is much more likely to sue.

In some instances, the decision to dismiss may not be as critically important as how that decision is carried out.

Employers, therefore, should keep in mind the following recommendations regarding the elements of a termination:

Dismissal – Review all proposed dismissals at a centralized higher management level before they are implemented. Seek clearance from legal counsel. Standardize the methods used for termination. Do not vary in the application of company policies. Give the reasons for the discharge. Be honest, straightforward, and complete. Recognize that timing, tone, and confidentiality are important.

Severance Pay – Recognize the hardship and trauma which accompanies worker dislocations. When possible and appropriate, consider providing:

- a reasonable amount of notice prior to dismissal,
- a severance "package,"
- continuation of benefits for a reasonable time, and
- outplacement counseling.

Such practices help ease the transition for dismissed employees, help maintain the morale of employees continuing in the workforce, lessen the likelihood of legal challenges being filed, and help build a compelling case that the employer has acted fairly.

Avoiding Violence – If there is some reason to believe the employee may react violently, consider:

- The method of communication (e.g., suspension and termination by later letter);
- The location (e.g., conference room rather than an individual's office);
- The availability of security;
- Providing an adequate opportunity to be heard;
- Trying to preserve the employee's dignity; and
- Limiting subsequent access to the facility.

Releases from Liability – Releases and covenants not to sue should be considered standard procedures in finalizing severance agreements. By signing such agreements, employees forego specified legal remedies and waive their right to sue the employer over the dismissal – generally in return for enhanced severance pay or other benefits. Severance pay should not be disbursed without receipt by the employer of a signed and valid release agreement and covenant not to sue. However, it is important that employees be given a reasonable time to review and confer on the agreements, and that their decision be knowing, willing, and voluntary. Terms to be considered involve a release, benefits issues, confidentiality, non-admission clauses, reemployment ineligibility, opposition or non-opposition to unemployment insurance claims, mutuality of releases, responses to reference inquiries, severability issues, restrictive covenants, venue for enforcement of the agreement and non-disparagement clauses.

Personnel Practices to Avoid

- **Don't** give oral assurances of job security.

- **Don't** allow recruiters or job placement firms to speak for, or make promises on behalf of, your company.

- **Don't** promise annual or periodic performance evaluations.

- **Don't** overstate the significance of the completion of a "probationary" period.

- **Don't** allow supervisors or managers to base positive performance evaluations or appraisals on friendship, sympathy, the ability of an employee to qualify for a salary increase, or the hope that an employee's performance will improve.

- **Don't** allow recruiters, interviewers, or personnel staff to verbally discount or discredit company "at will" statements with such remarks as: "Don't worry about it, it's just a form everyone signs," "Layoffs never really occur," or "Just do your job and you won't be let go."

- **Don't** state on any document, or at any time, that discharge will only occur for "cause" or "just cause."

- **Don't** list in an employee handbook or company manual the reasons or grounds for termination, or if you do, make it clear that it is an illustrative list and not an exclusive list, by stating, "The following is a list of examples of dischargeable offenses …" or "… and for other reasons at the discretion of the company."

- **Don't** permit staff to discuss dismissals with employees who do not need to know. Such indiscretions could lead to a defamation action.

- **Don't** allow supervisors to provide inaccurately positive, or laudatory, letters of recommendation, or references, for discharged employees.

- **Don't** dispense severance pay without first receiving a properly executed release from liability.

Termination Checklist

- ☐ Know precisely why the employee is being dismissed; the grounds should be based, obviously, upon nondiscriminatory reasons.

- ☐ Once the decision is made, set a private appointment in your office to ensure control and privacy. Under no circumstances should the dismissal be done on the telephone or in a social setting.

- ☐ There is never a "good" time to dismiss, but an early Monday or Tuesday is preferred to a 5:00 p.m. on Friday. Emphasize that after a complete review of all relevant factors, the decision is final and irrevocable.

- ☐ Keep the meeting brief. Get the bad news across at the outset. Avoid platitudes.

- ☐ Let the dismissed employee have an opportunity to get his "side" across, without interruption. Keep control of the meeting, and in no way waver in your determination that the decision is final.

- ☐ Do not discuss the situation with any other employee.

- ☐ Have any final payroll checks, benefits, or vacation payments prepared in advance.

- ☐ Regardless of the reason for termination, be sure the employee understands his/her rights regarding employee benefits (e.g., group insurance continuation, pension plan electives, unemployment insurance).

- ☐ While most employees respond to a dismissal with shock and anger, it rarely reaches the level anticipated or feared by managers.

The Employment Contract Option

The threat of wrongful discharge litigation often inhibits employers in the development of their personnel programs and practices. One option for eliminating this influence on general personnel policies and yet limit potential liability in a particular situation, is an express employment contract.

Such express employment contracts require customization to address each particular employment relationship involved. Generally, these agreements specifically state the duration of employment and expressly limit the circumstances upon which employment can be terminated, by either party, prior to a certain date.

Express employment contracts may include provisions that permit dismissal "for cause,"

Guidelines for Limiting Employer Liability: What Employers Should Do

- Review and revise all written company policy statements, job application forms, employee handbooks, training manuals, performance evaluation forms, and the standard form letters offering or terminating employment. Repeat this re-evaluation and revision process periodically and as necessary.

- Establish a "paper trail" for all personnel actions. Generate documents and maintain comprehensive personnel files. Include documents regarding hiring and exit interviews, conferences, reprimands, warnings, probationary notices, performance evaluation, absenteeism records, commendations, and any evidence of remedial efforts. Record all oral admonitions. Assume the worst that disciplinary cases will lead to discharge and that discharge will lead to court. Do not create a paper trail that appears to be abnormal and was created, artificially, to support a particular dismissal or personnel action.

- Train and retrain interviewers, recruiters, supervisors, managers, and personnel staff. Make sure they know company policy. Make sure they know what to say, what not to say, and the importance of documentation and employee performance evaluations.

- Assure that employees are evaluated fairly, accurately, on time, and in accordance with company policy. Make sure supervisors and managers recognize the importance of candid, accurate evaluations.

- Require employees to sign and date key employment documents, and to acknowledge that they have read and understood the contents and importance of these documents.

- Consider establishing formal progressive disciplinary procedures. Recognize that progressive discipline can be a two-edged sword – if a company adheres to it effectively, it decreases the likelihood of legal claims and demonstrates fairness to potential jurors; if it is enforced inconsistently, it can trigger and sustain legal claims. It also tends to delay the dismissal process by implementing a multi-step process. It is not for all employers. However, progressive discipline which includes educating employees about the company's grounds for discharge, warnings that a lack of improvement will result in termination, and an internal level of appeal or review, can resolve potential problems, enhance employee morale, and ultimately save money.

Guidelines for Limiting Employer Liability (continued)

- Assure consistency of application for all company personnel policies. Even-handed enforcement with the same response taken for all similar cases is more likely to be accepted by employees and sustained by courts.

- Include appropriate disclaimers on company documents such as job application forms, employee handbooks, and company policy manuals. State explicitly that the information contained in such documents in intended only to inform and provide guidelines; it should not be considered a binding contract, terms and conditions of employment, or a promise or reassurance of continued employment.

- Consider including statements in these documents that employment is "at will" and can be terminated by either party, at any time, for any reason. The "plus" is that such language protects employers against all of the common law "wrongful discharge" claims, excluding the public policy exception. The "negative" is that such statements may hurt recruiting efforts.

- Make sure reliable witnesses, who are able to appear in court if necessary, are present during confrontations regarding incident-driven dismissals. Employee theft, destruction of company property, and sale of contraband are examples of situations where a quick employer response may be necessary and appropriate.

- Know the law, all of the law, as it pertains to personnel policies and employee dismissals. Keep abreast of legal and legislative developments. Stay current with relevant federal, state, and local laws. Retain outside counsel to periodically review your programs and policies. If it is determined that the company's position is legally vulnerable, then change that position.

- Consider all the circumstances before dismissing an employee. Look at the total picture to determine how significant the company's legal exposure could be. Be particularly sensitive regarding long-term employees or those that have engaged in protective activity or are members of a protected class.

---

invalidate the agreement at the discretion of the employer in the event of a company merger or acquisition, and specifically waive the contracting employee's access to grievance and arbitration procedures available to the employees. Perhaps most importantly, express employment contracts usually limit the remedies available for breach of contract. On the other hand, express employment contracts guarantee employment for a set period subject to those exceptions which are enumerated.

The disadvantages of express employment contracts are:

- greater administrative costs;

- reduced flexibility;

- inconvenience;

- a potential "chilling" effect on recruitment; and

- potential liabilities due to inadvertent omissions or unforeseen developments.

However, as the wave of wrongful discharge claims rise and judges demonstrate an increasing willingness to infer contractual protections for employees, express employment contracts are an alternative worth considering.

Human Resource Management – the Trends 17

Introduction

In this Chapter, we deal with some of the "hot button" topics and emerging trends in human resource management. The myriad subjects include: the growing contingent workforce, employee wellness programs, employment assistance programs, violence in the workplace, alternative dispute resolution, and diversity. These trends and their interaction with existing employment laws are a fascinating part of the emerging state of human resource management.

Contingent Workers

Contingent workers generally refer to those individuals who are outside an employer's "core" work force, such as those whose jobs are structured to last only a limited period of time, are sporadic, or differ in any way from the norm of regular, full-time employment. Known by a variety of names, ("temporaries," "part-timers," "casuals," non-regular") these individuals may be on the payroll or working for a staffing firm (e.g., temporary employment agency, a contract firm, staff leasing, etc.). Government data confirm that the contingent workforce is growing at a faster rate than the entire labor force.

Along with downsizing, outsourcing, subcontracting and temporary employment, part-time employment has been a major tool for employers in their attempts to keep compensation costs down. A recent study revealed both the major advantages and disadvantages of the contingent workforce as perceived by employers:

Advantages

Staffing flexibility	32%
Lower benefit costs	23%
"Instant staff"	16%
Cuts overall staffing costs	16%
Rapid availability	15%
Terminate without severance costs	14%
Future employment screen	13%
Access to skills not available	11%

Disadvantages

Lack of commitment	41%
Lack of skills	19%
High turnover	18%
Lower employee morale	12%
Difficult to integrate	10%
Higher costs	7%
Company security	5%

Because of a highly visible lawsuit that was decided by the Supreme Court in 1998 against Microsoft by holding that it's "independent contractors" were, in reality, regular employees, lawyers for temporary workers will be making similar claims and attempting to collect the millions in benefits they allege that they are owed.

The Equal Employment Opportunity Commission has published guidelines covering the application of employment discrimination laws it administers to staffing firms. The worker is a covered employee under the anti-discrimination statutes if the right to control the means and manner of work performance rests with the firm and/or its client rather than with the worker.

Once it is determined that a staffing firm worker is an "employee," the second question is who is the worker's employer. The staffing firm and/or its client will qualify as the employer if one or both businesses have the right to exercise control over the worker's employment. If both have control over the worker, then they are "joint employers."

A staffing firm is obligated, as an employer, to make job assignments in a nondiscriminatory manner. It also is obligated as an employment agency to make job referrals in a nondiscriminatory manner. The staffing firm's client is liable if it sets discriminatory criteria for the assignment of workers.

If the EEOC finds reasonable cause to believe that both a staffing firm and its client have engaged in unlawful discrimination, they are jointly and severally liable for back pay, front pay, and compensatory damages.

Employee Wellness Programs

Employers have seen that certain chronic disease problems among their employees are a result of poor lifestyle habits. Studies have shown that roughly 50 percent of large case costs could be mitigated substantially by improvement in four areas of wellness – smoking cessation, proper diet, regular exercise, and moderate consumption of alcohol.

To foster these improvements, the employer can offer wellness-oriented programs. These include on-site screening for major diseases and employer education programs aimed at informing employees about lifestyle choices which lead to optimum health. Employers who invest in these programs feel that the long-

term payoff will be a workforce with improved lifestyle habits, which will, in turn, lower health care costs.

An example of a wellness program used by one employer is based on simple flexibility stretching, for business and home. This program aims at the reported source of 50 percent of its workers' compensation claims and 25 percent of health claims – sprains and strains of the torso, with specific emphasis on the lower back. The cost of the program depends on the number of participants, but the company contends that it breaks down to approximately 2 percent of the monthly employee health care premium.

Employee Assistance Programs

A wide range of problems, not indirectly associated with a person's job function, can have an effect on that individual's job performance. Significant changes in any of the following areas can indicate that an employee is troubled:

- Low productivity
- Poor work quality
- Interpersonal conflicts with co-workers or customers/clients (e.g., inappropriately hostile, angry, withdrawn, or exhibiting inappropriate attitudes or behaviors)
- Excessive waste
- Excessive accidents/mistakes
- Excessive absenteeism (especially on Mondays)
- Poor judgment
- Reduced efficiency
- Disappearance from work
- Extending or not returning from lunch or other breaks
- Consistently missing deadlines
- Minimal contact with co-workers, especially supervisors

Typical problems employees can be expected to have include:

- Alcohol and/or drug dependency
- Family (which includes marital, children, extended families, parents, etc.)
- Financial
- Legal
- Work-related

In most instances, employees overcome such personal problems independently and the effect on job performance is negligible. In other instances, normal supervisory assistance either serves as motivation or guidance by which such problems can be resolved, thereby returning job performance back to an acceptable level. In some cases, however, neither the efforts of the employee or the supervisor have the desired effect and unsatisfactory job performance persists.

Many employers, recognizing that most human problems can be successfully treated if identified early and properly referred, are now offering an Employee Assistance Program (EAP). Such EAP's are designed to help employees resolve personal problems which may adversely affect their jobs or lives.

If employees are not performing their jobs they should be counseled or disciplined for the performance problems. Independent of that discipline, employees should be advised of the availability of EAP's. EAP services are normally available to employees on a voluntary, self-referral basis through an outside agency or by a supervisory referral. Resources through the EAP agency include professional counseling, doctors, and information resources to which employees may not have access or about which they may not be aware. Employers with EAP's should make it clear to employees that neither a request for treatment nor program participation will jeopardize the employee's job security or advancement opportunities.

Workplace Violence

The overwhelming number of violent crimes in the workplace are committed by outsiders. Notwithstanding this fact, there is a growing number of criminal attacks perpetrated by coworkers on each other. In fact, the Department of Justice estimates that nearly half of all criminal incidents in the workplace are not reported to police.

This serious issue deserves a zero-tolerance policy, even if high performing employees are involved. The EEOC has taken the position that the ADA does not prohibit an employer from addressing workplace violence even if the violent worker claims to have a mental disorder. Accommodating a worker with an emotional or psychiatric disability under the ADA does not mean ignoring misconduct.

Alternative Dispute Resolution

Mediation and arbitration, which are the best-known alternative dispute resolution techniques, consist of bringing in the help of outsiders to resolve an internal dispute. A mediator tries to facilitate an agreement which the parties themselves reach. In an arbitration, it is the arbitrator who imposes a settlement of a dispute.

The obvious attraction of these alternatives is their relative quickness and lower cost than formal litigation. In the final analysis, if they work properly they can boost morale by avoiding the potential embarrassment of a public trial. Most important, they introduce into the employment culture a dispute resolution process which relies heavily on direct communication by the parties. Often times, it is that lack of communication that actually leads to lawsuits.

One of the nation's leading experts in labor law suggests the following elements in setting up an ADR program.

Setting Up An ADR Program

If you want to set up an alternative dispute resolution (ADR) program at your company, you should consult an attorney. Here are some of the issues that must be considered:

1. Evaluate all the various models – open door policy, mediation, arbitration, peer review, and see what fits your culture and needs. Is the purpose to have a low cost alternative process or one to replace the legal system?

2. Develop a written ADR policy and insure that it appears in appropriate documents, including employment applications and employee handbooks.

3. Involve your senior managers in decisions related to the selection of an ADR and its terms.

4. Train and explain, so that managers and employees fully understand the rationale for the program and how it's going to work. It is critical that everyone buys in to the program.

5. Respond to complaints quickly, fairly, and effectively. Make sure the ADR program gains credibility.

6. Respect employee confidentiality except when there are compelling reasons not to do so. An employee's complaint of sexual harassment, for instance, ordinarily would require confronting the accused harasser with that complaint.

7. Prohibit retaliation against employees who utilize or support the ADR program and discipline any person who does retaliate.

8. Establish clear rules regarding costs of the selected program.

If mandatory arbitration is selected, there are a number of requirements the policy must meet in order to be binding on both sides. For example, employees must have the same relief that the employee would have if the employee went through the judicial system. In effect, an arbitrator should be able to impose punitive damages as well compensatory damages.

As noted earlier, the EEOC opposes binding-arbitration agreements; however, courts have consistently upheld most of them. Employment counsel should be consulted before embarking on an ADR program as the area is complex (see DiLorenzo, "Enforcing Employer-Employee Arbitration Agreements After Circuit City", 18 Fordham University Law Journal 27 (2001). A Due Process Protocol Study in 1995 suggested the following minimum considerations:

1. **Employee's right to counsel.** The employee should have the right to representation of the employee's own choosing.

2. **Employee's attorney fees.** The arbitrator should have the authority to award attorney's fees to prevailing employees in accordance with applicable law.

3. **Discovery.** Employees should have access to all relevant information, including conducting pre-hearing depositions.

4. **Roster of arbitrators.** The pool of arbitrators should be ethnically diverse and comprised of knowledgeable and independent male and female arbitrators experienced in workplace disputes.

5. **Remedies.** Arbitrators should have the authority to award the same relief that is available in court.

6. **Written award.** A written decision should summarize the issues and their resolutions.

7. **Arbitrator's compensation.** The parties should share the cost of the arbitrator in equitable proportions. It should be noted, however, that one federal appeals court takes the position that an employee who is seeking to enforce a statutory right cannot be required to pay any portion of the arbitrator's fee.

8. **Scope of review.** The award should be final and binding, with a limited scope of review. The precise standard need not be spelled out. The policy only needs to state that it is to be binding to the maximum extent permitted by law.

Diversity

Diversity is about acknowledging any difference that can impact the fair or equitable treatment of individuals in the workplace. It is all the ways we are similar and different which affect our interactions and performance. It has been empirically shown that on complex tasks, with equally skilled leadership, diverse teams will outperform teams that are not diverse.

In the employment arena where there are life-style differences, religious differences, etc., no one is asking for approval or disapproval. What is needed in the workplace is a level of acceptance and respectful treatment that allows for the degree of cooperation essential to get work done. Diversity in the workplace is related to equity, and should not be confused with equality. When a company treats its employees equally it negates their differences. When it treats it employees equitably, it recognizes their differences.

The National Association for Diversity Management is a non-profit, professional association organized to provide a forum for worldwide networking on the topic of workplace diversity. The web site (www.nadm. org) hosts a discussion list called the Global Diversity Forum, a database for consultants and a depository of images and other art that promote diversity.

"Glass Ceiling" Initiative

This curious term refers to the invisible, but nonetheless real barriers that may exist, resulting in women and minorities being kept out of higher level jobs. In 1995, the presidentially appointed Glass Ceiling Commission issued a report that found serious barriers to advancement continue to exist – such as persistent stereotyping, erroneous beliefs that "no qualified women or minorities are out there," or plain old fear of change.

The report noted that:

- 97 percent of senior managers in Fortune 500 companies and Fortune 1000 industrial companies are white; and

- 5 percent of senior managers in Fortune 200 industrial and service companies are women, virtually all of whom are white.

Employers can help shatter the glass ceiling, but it will take a concerted effort. Among the strategies suggested are the following:

1. Each employer should demonstrate that inclusion of minorities and women is a top priority.

2. Employers should emphasize the common needs of all employees for constructive performance appraisal, frequent feedback, coaching, and mentoring.

3. Employers should be held accountable for the development and advancement of minorities and women based on agreed-upon goals and timetables.

4. Employers should put a high priority on outreach and recruitment to attract qualified minorities and women. Leadership training and career development, mentoring and networks, and assessment and promotion enable them to advance.

Telecommuting Expands the Workplace

The technological advances, a near full-employment economy, serious traffic problems, technology developments, and life style changes have created explosive growth in the number of employees allowed to work at home. In a recent national survey, the number of workers who are telecommuting has surpassed 10 million, and is growing between 10-15 percent annually. While compliance issues involving telecommuting have not been prominent , there is nonetheless a real need for employer policy to reflect the various workplace laws.

Sample Telecommuting Policy

The purpose of this policy is to clarify issues involved in a telecommuting program sponsored for select employees. Please read this carefully and discuss with your supervisor.

1. The telecommuting program will continue as long as the results are satisfactory and it is mutually beneficial.

2. Employees considering telecommuting are volunteering for this program after having been given information about the program and the pros and cons of telecommuting. If an employee finds that telecommuting is not working and wants to return to the office work location, s/he should notify their supervisor immediately.

   Employees selected as telecommuters are being asked to commit to a minimum trial period of three months. We believe this is the least amount of time needed for the employee to learn how well telecommuting works for a particular position. If, however, the employee or employee's supervisor find that there are serious personal or work problems arising before three months are up, the employee will be able to return to the office.

3. It is possible that the program may be terminated at the discretion of management. If it is terminated, an employee will be asked to return to the office location. Also, if an employee's work performance suffers and the supervisor decides it will be in our best long-term interest to return to the office full-time, the employee will be expected to return to the office. If an employee chooses not to return on the expected date, this will be considered to be a voluntary resignation.

4. Telecommuting is not an employee benefit intended to be available to all employees at this time. As such, no employee is entitled to, or guaranteed the opportunity to, telecommute.

5. An employee's salary, job responsibilities, and benefits will not change because of telecommuting, except as they might have normally changed, e.g., regular salary reviews will occur as scheduled, and an employee will be entitled to any company-wide benefits changes that may be implemented. Employees telecommuting agree to comply with all existing job requirements as now are in effect in the office.

6. An hourly employee's total number of work hours are not expected to change while telecommuting, and an employee will be responsible for providing information for the weekly time sheet. In the event that an employee expects to work more than the standard number of hours, this must be discussed and approved in advance by the employees supervisor, just as any overtime scheduling would normally have to be approved.

7. The daily work schedule when telecommuting is subject to negotiation with and approval by the immediate supervisor. If an employee's job duties allow and the supervisor feels a change would not impair the employee's ability to be in contact with co-workers, flexible hours may be arranged. A supervisor may require that an employee work certain "core hours" and be accessible by telephone during those hours.

8. There may be times when an employee will be requested to come into the office. We will try to minimize unplanned office visits, but the telecommuting employee must recognize the need for office visits and agree to come in when requested.

   Similarly, there may be weeks when an employee will have to spend more time than planned (up to the full five days) in the office when the nature of the workload requires it. It will be the employee's responsibility to come into the office as requested during these times.

9. We will provide the necessary computer, modem, software, and other equipment needed for an employee to do their job. All of these items remain our property and must be returned upon request, in case of an extended illness, upon an employee's resignation or termination, or if the telecommuting program ends. When they are to be returned, the employee agrees to return all material or to allow us to arrange to pick them up from an employee's home.

Sample Telecommuting Policy ^(continued)

10. We will reimburse the employee for the cost of installation and monthly service on a telephone line to be installed for business use during the program. This is considered to be for our purposes only and not for an employee's personal use. We will reimburse the employee for all related business use of this telephone line when a reimbursement request is submitted. It will be the employee's responsibility to insure that no one else has access to the phone.

11. Office supplies as needed will be provided by us; out-of-pocket expenses for other supplies will not be reimbursed unless by prior approval of an employee's supervisor. Also, we will not reimburse for travel expenses to and from the office on days when an employee comes into the office, nor for any home-related expenses such as construction, renovations, heating/air conditioning, lighting, or electricity.

12. The computer, modem, software, and any other equipment or supplies provided are provided primarily for use on assignments. However, an employee can use these items for reasonable personal purposes as long as these do not create any conflict of interest with an employee's job. The equipment and software should not be used by other household members or anyone else.

13. The security of company property in an employee's home is as important as it is in the office. An employee will be expected to take reasonable precautions to protect the equipment from theft, damage, or misuse. The employee is required to contact their homeowner's insurance carrier to determine to what extent this property is covered under their homeowner's policy. If the property is NOT covered, the employee agrees to notify their supervisor and, if requested, take out additional coverage to cover employer's property.

14. The employee is responsible for weekly backup of the computer in case of any hard disk failure.

15. Any materials taken home should be kept in a designated work area at home and not be made accessible to others. In no case will an employee take proprietary or confidential materials home except with the approval of their supervisor.

16. We are interested in an employee's health and safety while working at home just as it is while working in the office. For this reason, an employee is required to maintain a separate, designated work area at home. We reserve the right to visit a home work area to see if it meets safety standards; such visits will be scheduled with at least 24 hours' advance notice.

    Any equipment provided should be placed where it is adequately supported and there is no danger of it falling. It should be connected to a properly-grounded electrical outlet and all wires kept out of walkways. If there are any questions about the adequacy/safety of a home work area, an employee must contact their supervisor immediately for resolution.

17. We will be responsible for any work-related injuries under the state's Workers Compensation laws, but this liability is limited to injuries resulting directly from work and only if the injury occurs in the designated work area. Any claims will be handled according to the normal procedure for Worker's Compensation claims.

18. Telecommuting is not to be viewed as a substitute for dependent care. We expect that an employee will make arrangements for child-care if needed. The company recognizes that one advantage of working at home is the opportunity to have more time with dependents, but it is an employee's responsibility to insure that they are fully able to complete work assignments on time.

19. It will be the employee's responsibility determine any income tax implications of maintaining a home office area. We will not provide tax guidance nor will the company assume any additional tax liabilities. Employees are encouraged to consult with a qualified tax professional to discuss income tax implications.

I have read and understand this agreement and accept its conditions.

EMPLOYEE SIGNATURE: _____ DATE: _____

Avoiding Common Employer Mistakes that Result in Employment-Related Litigation

18

Introduction

Santayana once said, "Those who cannot remember the past are condemned to relive it." Practicing employment lawyers are very much aware that employers often make the same, avoidable mistakes. Reviewing reported decisions and training supervisors and managers in the lessons to be learned from those cases can provide the ounce of prevention which is much more valuable than the pound of cure.

Mistakes to Avoid

Here are some common misconceptions that repeatedly translate into costly mistakes:

Mistake 1

As long as you have an Equal Employment Opportunity Policy somewhere in your employee handbook or posted in your break room, you do not have to worry about legal exposure for harassment or discrimination.

The Truth

Employers need comprehensive policies that prohibit unlawful harassment (sexual, sex, national origin, race, disability, age, religion) and other potential categories protected by state or local laws such as marital status, sexual orientation and criminal convictions. The policy needs to provide multiple avenues of complaint and a strong prohibition against retaliation. In addition, there needs to be a strong commitment to compliance from upper management. However, just having a policy is not enough. Employers must "walk the talk". Training in anti-discrimination principles and the employer's policy against retaliation needs to be provided to all supervisors, especially those who will handle complaints. An employer should consider training all employees.

Mistake 2

Place no limitation on employee use of company e-mail, voice mail and the internet.

The Truth

E-mails and internet misuse are often cited in discrimination and harassment lawsuits. Appropriate restrictions need to be put in place which prohibit inappropriate use and explain the limitations on personal use. A policy should reserve the right to monitor use to insure compliance and destroy any employee expectation of privacy. Employees need to be educated concerning the discoverability of e-mails in employment litigation. Consider conducting random audits and using discovered problems to correct inappropriate behavior. Finally, make sure whatever policy is adopted, is enforced.

Mistake 3

Do not give employees bad news about their performance until you fire them.

The Truth

Bad news needs to be communicated right away and as often as possible and appropriate. Such communication is an important method for improving behavior, but also avoids unrealistic employee expectations and provides needed documentation of unsatisfactory performance in order to defend any employer action. Obviously, evaluations must accurately relay bad news about conduct and performance. Evaluations should be:

(i) candid with criticism;

(ii) careful not to overemphasize criticism;

(iii) consistent, where appropriate, with other evaluations or explain why they are not;

(iv) based on specific examples, events or incidents and not "gut feelings"; and

(v) set forth a follow-up plan or method for coming up with one, if necessary.

In addition, negative feedback should be provided by e-mail, memos or letters. Progressive discipline (documented coaching or counseling, verbal warning, written warning or suspension) provides an opportunity, if successful, to correct the employee's behavior. If not, it provides an opportunity to memorialize the "bad news" and the fact that it was communicated to the employee.

Progressive discipline should communicate the employer's expectations, explain the action necessary to meet them and the consequences of failure. While employees understand a legitimate and reasonable response to non-performance or improper performance, they do not understand reprimands for performances or conduct that was routinely accepted in the past.

Progressive discipline also reinforces to co-employees the importance of following the rules and satisfies the need that 3 out of 4 jurors have that an employee must receive fair warning before being terminated.

Mistake 4

It's okay to apply a lesser penalty for a rule infraction if the employee in question is generally a nice person.

The Truth

In deciding on appropriate level of discipline, it is important to take into account various, relevant considerations. The punishment needs to fit the crime and in making that determination, the following considerations should be analyzed:

- The nature of the offense;
- The employee's prior record;
- Length of service;
- Extraordinary factors (mitigating or aggravating); and
- Past practice.

The "niceness" of the employee or lack thereof, must be ignored. It leads to a culture of favoritism, a lack of employer credibility and creates dangerous precedent which may have to be followed in the future. The focus needs to be on the objective facts, the behavior and its impact on the workforce and the workplace. Subjective feelings concerning "niceness" are irrelevant.

Mistake 5

Your employees are employed "at will" and so you can fire them whenever you feel like it.

The Truth

The existence of the many federal and state statutes offer some form of protection to virtually every employee in your workforce. If employees are taken for granted and treated as disposable assets, "at the will" or whim of the "master", they will turn to a union, plaintiff's attorney or the courts for real protection and enforcement of their rights.

"Just Cause" Checklist

Before deciding to discipline or discharge an employee, employers should ask themselves the following seven questions.

☐ 1. *Notice:* Did the Employer put the employee on notice of the rule and possible consequences of violating the rule?

☐ 2. *Reasonableness:* Was the Employer's rule or work order reasonably related to the orderly, efficient and safe operation of the business, and the performance that the Employer might properly expect of the employee?

☐ 3. *Investigation:* Did the Employer, before imposing discipline, make an effort to discover whether the employee did in fact violate a rule or commit misconduct? Did the employer confront the employee and obtain "their story"?

☐ 4. *Fair & Objective:* Was the Employer's investigation conducted fairly and objectively?

☐ 5. *Proof:* Did the investigation produce substantial evidence that the employee was guilty of misconduct?

☐ 6. *Equal Treatment:* Has the Employer applied its rules and penalties evenhandedly, treating similarly situated employees in a similar manner?

☐ 7. *Appropriate Penaly:* Did the penalty fit the crime – was the level of discipline reasonably related to the seriousness of the offense and the employee's past record?

While these seven questions do not constitute a recognized legal standard, honest "yes" answers to all seven questions establishes a solid framework for going forward. The more "no" answers that must be given, the greater the risk of liability for imposing discipline or taking other action.

Mistake 6

If the real reason you are terminating an employee might hurt their feelings (e.g., poor and declining performance), come up with a kinder, gentler explanation, such as a decline in business.

The Truth

Do not give employees a false explanation for the reason for their discharge – even to spare their feelings. Remember, an employee can establish a claim by proving the proffered reason for their discharge is a "pretext". Pretext is a fancy word for a false reason or as my cousin Vinny would say, a reason that does not "hold water". Pretext is usually a question for the jury and can be established in many ways:

- The employee was given different reasons for discharge;

- The employee was treated differently from others;

- Handbook procedures or policies were not followed;

- The employee had performance evaluations or other documentation (e-mails, memos, letters, commendations) inconsistent with the reason given;

- Employee was not previously warned or counseled;

- The employer's reason for discharge is false;

- Statistics are inconsistent with the reason given and/or consistent with the claim being made;

- Documentation does not support the discharge;

- Timing.

It is important that in verbal and written communications concerning the reason for a discharge (termination meeting, termination letter, unemployment insurance form, internal termination documentation, etc.) the same language be used to describe the reason for the discharge.

Mistake 7

A jury will believe everything you say so do not bother documenting everything.

The Truth

When it comes to documentation, your bumper sticker should read, "If it's not in writing, it did not happen." It is not enough that you did not violate the law -- you must be able to prove it. Jurors, EEOC investigators, unemployment insurance judges and everyone in between expect employers to keep good records and produce them when there is an issue about the actions that were taken and the reasons for doing so. Remember, consistent, contemporary documentation is corroborative. On the other hand, missing documentation undermines credibility; contradictory documentation destroys credibility; and after-the-fact documentation is not nearly as helpful.

There are also a number of practical reasons to maintain proper documentation. Documents do not have bad memories – they never forget. While business organizations are dynamic, and individuals may come and go, as well as their feelings towards the employer, the documents will remain. Also, creating a written record helps to focus one's attention and thinking and leads to better decision making. Good documentation should explain three things: (i) what the employee did wrong; (ii) the reasons for the employer's decision; and (iii) the timing of the decision.

When documenting a termination decision, consider the following:

- Documentation showing when and how the employee was put on notice;

- Documentation showing each progressive disciplinary step or the seriousness of an offense requiring summary dismissal;

- Documentation showing a fair, objective and thorough investigation;

- Documentation showing substantial evidence of guilt; and

- Documentation showing that similarly situated employees have been treated in a similar manner.

Mistake 8

Be quick to terminate employees who are grappling with health problems and issues at home. Fire people right before Thanksgiving, Christmas, their birthday and make sure a guard walks them to the door in front of their coworkers.

The Truth

Remember, employment lawsuits are decided by jurors who are or were EMPLOYEES. The ultimate measuring test for jurors, and other decision makers, is whether the employee was treated fairly.

We need a proven, documented record of fairness. Performance evaluations should candidly, and in detail, describe performance problems. When appropriate, there should be progressive discipline which provides notice of the problem and the consequences of failing to correct it. As with many things in life, the timing of a termination is important. If an employee should be terminated – do it. Do not wait until the employee checks into a rehabilitation program or helps start a union campaign – stay away from a termination right before the holidays unless it would be inappropriate to wait.

Litigation breeds out of humiliation and a lack of respect and dignity, like bacteria grows out of a Petri dish. Whether a terminated employee sues their employer often depends on how they are treated during the termination process. Security guard escort from the premises is an extreme measure. There are times it is appropriate depending upon the employee, nature of the offense and nature of the business. It is not, however, a preferred method and should be used sparingly and only when necessary.

Mistake 9

We have had a very good handbook for many years and all we need to do is make sure we follow it.

The Truth

Unfortunately, while many employers adopted good handbooks twenty or more years ago, they have not reviewed and updated them in as many years. Handbooks need to be reviewed regularly to ensure:

- They are consistent with any significant changes or developments in the law; and

- The employer's current practices and policy statements are consistent with the handbook.

A provision of a handbook that is no longer followed or inconsistently followed, can be worse than having no policy at all. Jurors, and other fact finders, expect employers to follow their handbook. Therefore, it needs to be accurate.

Mistake 10

As long as the Human Resources Department is familiar with the law, the employer is protected and in compliance. There is no need to train everyone.

The Truth

Supervisors and managers are the employer's agents. Therefore, what they know is imputed to the employer and their actions are considered the actions of the employer. Supervisors need to understand that their actions have legal consequences and be trained in the law of discrimination and harassment. They need to be adequately trained in issues involving the treatment of injured and disabled employees; performance evaluations and discipline. They need to understand the employer's policies, the importance of acting upon complaints, the complaint procedure, their role in the organization, the importance of setting a good example and the importance of seeking advice and guidance from Human Resources.

What type of workplace an employer maintains is dictated more by the actions, attitude and conduct of the supervisors and managers than the charisma level of the CEO or how well the handbook reads. TRAIN YOUR SUPERVISORS.

Mistake 11

If the employer gets a threatening letter or complaint, it can wait until a Request to Produce Documents or a Subpoena is served upon it by the plaintiff before worrying about gathering documents.

The Truth

The employer needs to preserve relevant documents as soon as it has a reasonable basis to conclude a claim is or will be made. A "litigation hold" letter should be sent to each person potentially involved in the allegations of the claim or potential claim. The letter should also be sent to any record or data custodians (electronic and hard copy) to ensure all relevant records are preserved and not destroyed pursuant to any routine procedures. A failure to stop the destruction of relevant records, including email, may constitute a violation of the law, and result in sanctions, penalties and/ or an adverse jury instruction.

Appendices

263

INSTRUCTIONS
PLEASE READ ALL INSTRUCTIONS CAREFULLY BEFORE COMPLETING THIS FORM.

Anti-Discrimination Notice. It is illegal to discriminate against any individual (other than an alien not authorized to work in the U.S.) in hiring, discharging, or recruiting or referring for a fee because of that individual's national origin or citizenship status. It is illegal to discriminate against work eligible individuals. Employers **CANNOT** specify which document(s) they will accept from an employee. The refusal to hire an individual because of a future expiration date may also constitute illegal discrimination.

Section 1- Employee.
All employees, citizens and noncitizens, hired after November 6, 1986, must complete Section 1 of this form at the time of hire, which is the actual beginning of employment. **The employer is responsible for ensuring that Section 1 is timely and properly completed.**

Preparer/Translator Certification. The Preparer/Translator Certification must be completed if Section 1 is prepared by a person other than the employee. A preparer/translator may be used only when the employee is unable to complete Section 1 on his/her own. However, the employee must still sign Section 1 personally.

Section 2 - Employer.
For the purpose of completing this form, the term "employer" includes those recruiters and referrers for a fee who are agricultural associations, agricultural employers or farm labor contractors.

Employers must complete Section 2 by examining evidence of identity and employment eligibility within three (3) business days of the date employment begins. If employees are authorized to work, but are unable to present the required document(s) within three business days, they must present a receipt for the application of the document(s) within three business days and the actual document(s) within ninety (90) days. However, if employers hire individuals for a duration of less than three business days, Section 2 must be completed at the time employment begins. **Employers must record: 1)** document title; **2)** issuing authority; **3)** document number, **4)** expiration date, if any; and **5)** the date employment begins. Employers must sign and date the certification. Employees must present original documents. Employers may, but are not required to, photocopy the document(s) presented. These photocopies may only be used for the verification process and must be retained with the I-9. **However, employers are still responsible for completing the I-9.**

Section 3 - Updating and Reverification.
Employers must complete Section 3 when updating and/or reverifying the I-9. Employers must reverify employment eligibility of their employees on or before the expiration date recorded in Section 1. Employers **CANNOT** specify which document(s) they will accept from an employee.

- If an employee's name has changed at the time this form is being updated/reverified, complete Block A.

- If an employee is rehired within three (3) years of the date this form was originally completed and the employee is still eligible to be employed on the same basis as previously indicated on this form (updating), complete Block B and the signature block.

- If an employee is rehired within three (3) years of the date this form was originally completed and the employee's work authorization has expired **or** if a current employee's work authorization is about to expire (reverification), complete Block B and:

- examine any document that reflects that the employee is authorized to work in the U.S. (see List A **or** C),

- record the document title, document number and expiration date (if any) in Block C, and

- complete the signature block.

Photocopying and Retaining Form I-9. A blank I-9 may be reproduced, provided both sides are copied. The Instructions must be available to all employees completing this form. Employers must retain completed I-9s for three (3) years after the date of hire or one (1) year after the date employment ends, whichever is later.

For more detailed information, you may refer to the Department of Homeland Security (DHS) Handbook for Employers, (Form M-274). You may obtain the handbook at your local U.S. Citizenship and Immigration Services (USCIS) office.

Privacy Act Notice. The authority for collecting this information is the Immigration Reform and Control Act of 1986, Pub. L. 99-603 (8 USC 1324a).

This information is for employers to verify the eligibility of individuals for employment to preclude the unlawful hiring, or recruiting or referring for a fee, of aliens who are not authorized to work in the United States.

This information will be used by employers as a record of their basis for determining eligibility of an employee to work in the United States. The form will be kept by the employer and made available for inspection by officials of the U.S. Immigration and Customs Enforcement, Department of Labor and Office of Special Counsel for Immigration Related Unfair Employment Practices.

Submission of the information required in this form is voluntary. However, an individual may not begin employment unless this form is completed, since employers are subject to civil or criminal penalties if they do not comply with the Immigration Reform and Control Act of 1986.

Reporting Burden. We try to create forms and instructions that are accurate, can be easily understood and which impose the least possible burden on you to provide us with information. Often this is difficult because some immigration laws are very complex. Accordingly, the reporting burden for this collection of information is computed as follows: **1)** learning about this form, 5 minutes; **2)** completing the form, 5 minutes; and **3)** assembling and filing (recordkeeping) the form, 5 minutes, for an average of 15 minutes per response. If you have comments regarding the accuracy of this burden estimate, or suggestions for making this form simpler, you can write to U.S. Citizenship and Immigration Services, Regulatory Management Division, 111 Massachusetts Avenue, N.W., Washington, DC 20529. OMB No. 1615-0047.

NOTE: This is the 1991 edition of the Form I-9 that has been rebranded with a current printing date to reflect the recent transition from the INS to DHS and its components.

EMPLOYERS MUST RETAIN COMPLETED FORM I-9
PLEASE DO NOT MAIL COMPLETED FORM I-9 TO ICE OR USCIS

Form I-9 (Rev. 05/31/05)Y

Please read instructions carefully before completing this form. The instructions must be available during completion of this form. **ANTI-DISCRIMINATION NOTICE:** It is illegal to discriminate against work eligible individuals. Employers **CANNOT** specify which document(s) they will accept from an employee. The refusal to hire an individual because of a future expiration date may also constitute illegal discrimination.

Section 1. Employee Information and Verification. To be completed and signed by employee at the time employment begins.

Print Name: Last	First	Middle Initial	Maiden Name

Address (Street Name and Number)	Apt. #	Date of Birth (month/day/year)

City	State	Zip Code	Social Security #

I am aware that federal law provides for imprisonment and/or fines for false statements or use of false documents in connection with the completion of this form.

I attest, under penalty of perjury, that I am (check one of the following):

☐ A citizen or national of the United States
☐ A Lawful Permanent Resident (Alien #) A _____
☐ An alien authorized to work until _____
   (Alien # or Admission #)

Employee's Signature	Date (month/day/year)

Preparer and/or Translator Certification. *(To be completed and signed if Section 1 is prepared by a person other than the employee.) I attest, under penalty of perjury, that I have assisted in the completion of this form and that to the best of my knowledge the information is true and correct.*

Preparer's/Translator's Signature	Print Name

Address (Street Name and Number, City, State, Zip Code)	Date (month/day/year)

Section 2. Employer Review and Verification. To be completed and signed by employer. Examine one document from List A OR examine one document from List B and one from List C, as listed on the reverse of this form, and record the title, number and expiration date, if any, of the document(s).

	List A	OR	List B	AND	List C
Document title:					
Issuing authority:					
Document #:					
Expiration Date (if any):					
Document #:					
Expiration Date (if any):					

CERTIFICATION - Iattest, under penalty of perjury, that I have examined the document(s) presented by the above-named employee, that the above-listed document(s) appear to be genuine and to relate to the employee named, that the employee began employment on *(month/day/year)* _____ **and that to the best of my knowledge the employee is eligible to work in the United States. (State employment agencies may omit the date the employee began employment.)**

Signature of Employer or Authorized Representative	Print Name	Title

Business or Organization Name	Address (Street Name and Number, City, State, Zip Code)	Date (month/day/year)

Section 3. Updating and Reverification. To be completed and signed by employer.

A. New Name (if applicable)	B. Date of Rehire (month/day/year) (if applicable)

C. If employee's previous grant of work authorization has expired, provide the information below for the document that establishes current employment eligibility.

Document Title:	Document #:	Expiration Date (if any):

I attest, under penalty of perjury, that to the best of my knowledge, this employee is eligible to work in the United States, and if the employee presented document(s), the document(s) I have examined appear to be genuine and to relate to the individual.

Signature of Employer or Authorized Representative	Date (month/day/year)

NOTE: This is the 1991 edition of the Form I-9 that has been rebranded with a current printing date to reflect the recent transition from the INS to DHS and its components.

Form I-9 (Rev. 05/31/05)Y Page 2

LISTS OF ACCEPTABLE DOCUMENTS

LIST A		LIST B		LIST C
Documents that Establish Both Identity and Employment Eligibility	**OR**	**Documents that Establish Identity**	**AND**	**Documents that Establish Employment Eligibility**

LIST A
Documents that Establish Both Identity and Employment Eligibility

1. U.S. Passport (unexpired or expired)

2. Certificate of U.S. Citizenship *(Form N-560 or N-561)*

3. Certificate of Naturalization *(Form N-550 or N-570)*

4. Unexpired foreign passport, with *I-551 stamp or* attached *Form I-94* indicating unexpired employment authorization

5. Permanent Resident Card or Alien Registration Receipt Card with photograph *(Form I-151 or I-551)*

6. Unexpired Temporary Resident Card *(Form I-688)*

7. Unexpired Employment Authorization Card *(Form I-688A)*

8. Unexpired Reentry Permit *(Form I-327)*

9. Unexpired Refugee Travel Document *(Form 1-571)*

10. Unexpired Employment Authorization Document issued by DHS that contains a photograph *(Form I-688B)*

OR

LIST B
Documents that Establish Identity

1. Driver's license or ID card issued by a state or outlying possession of the United States provided it contains a photograph or information such as name, date of birth, gender, height, eye color and address

2. ID card issued by federal, state or local government agencies or entities, provided it contains a photograph or information such as name, date of birth, gender, height, eye color and address

3. School ID card with a photograph

4. Voter's registration card

5. U.S. Military card or draft record

6. Military dependent's ID card

7. U.S. Coast Guard Merchant Mariner Card

8. Native American tribal document

9. Driver's license issued by a Canadian government authority

For persons under age 18 who are unable to present a document listed above:

10. School record or report card

11. Clinic, doctor or hospital record

12. Day-care or nursery school record

AND

LIST C
Documents that Establish Employment Eligibility

1. U.S. social security card issued by the Social Security Administration *(other than a card stating it is not valid for employment)*

2. Certification of Birth Abroad issued by the Department of State *(Form FS-545 or Form DS-1350)*

3. Original or certified copy of a birth certificate issued by a state, county, municipal authority or outlying possession of the United States bearing an official seal

4. Native American tribal document

5. U.S. Citizen ID Card *(Form I-197)*

6. ID Card for use of Resident Citizen in the United States *(Form I-179)*

7. Unexpired employment authorization document issued by DHS *(other than those listed under List A)*

Illustrations of many of these documents appear in Part 8 of the Handbook for Employers (M-274)

U.S. Department of Labor
Employment Standards Administration
Wage and Hour Division

(Family and Medical Leave Act of 1993)

Date: _____

OMB No. : 1215-0181
Expires : 08-31-07

To: _____
(Employee's Name)

From: _____
(Name of Appropriate Employer Representative)

Subject: REQUEST FOR FAMILY/MEDICAL LEAVE

On _____ , you notified us of your need to take family/medical leave due to:
(Date)

☐   The birth of a child, or the placement of a child with you for adoption or foster care; or

☐   A serious health condition that makes you unable to perform the essential functions for your job: or

☐   A serious health condition affecting your ☐ spouse, ☐ child, ☐ parent, for which you are needed to provide care.

You notified us that you need this leave beginning on _____ and that you expect
(Date)
leave to continue until on or about _____ .
(Date)

Except as explained below, you have a right under the FMLA for up to 12 weeks of unpaid leave in a 12-month period for the reasons listed above. Also, your health benefits must be maintained during any period of unpaid leave under the same conditions as if you continued to work, and you must be reinstated to the same or an equivalent job with the same pay, benefits, and terms and conditions of employment on your return from leave. If you do not return to work following FMLA leave for a reason other than: (1) the continuation, recurrence, or onset of a serious health condition which would entitle you to FMLA leave; or (2) other circumstances beyond your control, you may be required to reimburse us for our share of health insurance premiums paid on your behalf during your FMLA leave.

This is to inform you that: *(check appropriate boxes; explain where indicated)*

1. You are ☐ eligible ☐ not eligible for leave under the FMLA.

2. The requested leave ☐ will ☐ will not be counted against your annual FMLA leave entitlement.

3. You ☐ will ☐ will not be required to furnish medical certification of a serious health condition. If required, you must furnish certification by _____ *(insert date)* (must be at least 15 days after you are notified of this requirement), or we may delay the commencement of your leave until the certification is submitted.

4. You may elect to substitute accrued paid leave for unpaid FMLA leave. We ☐ will ☐ will not require that you substitute accrued paid leave for unpaid FMLA leave. If paid leave will be used, the following conditions will apply: *(Explain)*

5. (a) If you normally pay a portion of the premiums for your health insurance, these payments will continue during the period of FMLA leave. Arrangements for payment have been discussed with you, and it is agreed that you will make premium payments as follows: *(Set forth dates, e.g., the 10th of each month, or pay periods, etc. that specifically cover the agreement with the employee.)*

(b) You have a minimum 30-day *(or, indicate longer period, if applicable)* grace period in which to make premium payments. If payment is not made timely, your group health insurance may be cancelled, *provided* we notify you in writing at least 15 days before the date that your health coverage will lapse, or, at our option, we may pay your share of the premiums during FMLA leave, and recover these payments from you upon your return to work. We ☐ will ☐ will not pay your share of health insurance premiums while you are on leave.

(c) We ☐ will ☐ will not do the same with other benefits (*e.g.*, life insurance, disability insurance, etc.) while you are on FMLA leave. If we do pay your premiums for other benefits, when you return from leave you ☐ will ☐ will not be expected to reimburse us for the payments made on your behalf.

6. You ☐ will ☐ will not be required to present a fitness-for-duty certificate prior to being restored to employment. If such certification is required but not received, your return to work may be delayed until certification is provided.

7. (a) You ☐ are ☐ are not a "key employee" as described in § 825.217 of the FMLA regulations. If you are a "key employee:" restoration to employment may be denied following FMLA leave on the grounds that such restoration will cause substantial and grievous economic injury to us as discussed in § 825.218.

(b) We ☐ have ☐ have not determined that restoring you to employment at the conclusion of FMLA leave will cause substantial and grievous economic harm to *us. (Explain (a) and/or (b) below. See §825.219 of the FMLA regulations.)*

8. While on leave, you ☐ will ☐ will not be required to furnish us with periodic reports every _____ _____ *(indicate interval of periodic reports, as appropriate for the particular leave situation)* of your status and intent to return to work *(see § 825.309 of the FMLA regulations).* If the circumstances of your leave change and you are able to return to work earlier than the date indicated on the reverse side of this form, you ☐ will ☐ will not be required to notify us at least two work days prior to the date you intend to report to work.

9. You ☐ will ☐ will not be required to furnish recertification relating to a serious health condition. *(Explain below. if necessary, including the interval between certifications as prescribed in §825.308 of the FMLA regulations.)*

This optional use form may be used to satisfy mandatory employer requirements to provide employees taking FMLA leave with Written notice detailing spectfic expectations and obligations of the employee and explaining any consequences of a failure to meet these obligations. (29 CFR 825.301(b).)

Note: Persons are not required to respond to this collection of information unless it displays a currently valid OMB control number.

Public Burden Statement

We estimate that it will take an average of 5 minutes to complete this collection of information, including the time for reviewing instructions. searching existing data sources, gathering and maintaining the data needed, and completing and reviewing the collection of information. If you have any comments regarding this burden estimate or any other aspect of this collection of information, including suggestions for reducing this burden. send them to the Administrator, Wage and Hour Division, Department of Labor, Room S-3502. 200 Constitution Avenue, N.W., Washington. D.C. 20210.

DO NOT SEND THE COMPLETED FORM TO THE OFFICE SHOWN ABOVE.

Certification of Health Care Provider
(Family and Medical Leave Act of 1993)

U.S. Department of Labor
Employment Standards Administration
Wage and Hour Division

---

*(When completed, this form goes to the employee, **Not to the Department of Labor**.)*

| OMB No.: 1215-0181 |
| Expires: 08-31-2007 |

| 1. Employee's Name | 2. Patient's Name *(If different from employee)* |

---

3. Page 4 describes what is meant by a **"serious health condition"** under the Family and Medical Leave Act. Does the patient's condition[1] qualify under any of the categories described? If so, please check the applicable category.

   (1) _____ (2) _____ (3) _____ (4) _____ (5) _____ (6) _____ , or None of the above _____

---

4. Describe the **medical facts** which support your certification, including a brief statement as to how the medical facts meet the criteria of one of these categories:

---

5. a. State the approximate **date** the condition commenced, and the probable duration of the condition (and also the probable duration of the patient's present **incapacity**[2] if different):

   b. Will it be necessary for the employee to take work only **intermittently or to work on a less than full schedule** as a result of the condition (including for treatment described in Item 6 below)?

   If yes, give the probable duration:

   c. If the condition is a **chronic condition** (condition #4) or **pregnancy**, state whether the patient is presently incapacitated[2] and the likely duration and frequency of **episodes of incapacity**[2]:

---

[1] Here and elsewhere on this form, the information sought relates **only** to the condition for which the employee is taking FMLA leave.

[2] "Incapacity," for purposes of FMLA, is defined to mean inability to work, attend school or perform other regular daily activities due to the serious health condition, treatment therefor, or recovery therefrom.

Form WH-380
Revised December 1999

270

6. a. If additional **treatments** will be required for the condition, provide an estimate of the probable number of such treatments.

If the patient will be absent from work or other daily activities because of **treatment** on an **intermittent** or **part-time** basis, also provide an estimate of the probable number of and interval between such treatments, actual or estimated dates of treatment if known, and period required for recovery if any:

b. If any of these treatments will be provided by **another provider of health services** (e.g., physical therapist), please state the nature of the treatments:

c. **If a regimen of continuing treatment** by the patient is required under your supervision, provide a general description of such regimen (*e.g.*, prescription drugs, physical therapy requiring special equipment):

7. a. If medical leave is required for the employee's **absence from work** because of the **employee's own condition** (including absences due to pregnancy or a chronic condition), is the employee **unable to perform** work of any kind?

b. If able to perform some work, is the employee **unable to perform any one or more of the essential functions of the employee's job** (the employee or the employer should supply you with information about the essential job functions)? If yes, please list the essential functions the employee is unable to perform:

c. If neither a. nor b. applies, is it necessary for the employee to be **absent from work for treatment**?

8. a. If leave is required to **care for a family member** of the employee with a serious health condition, **does the patient require assistance** for basic medical or personal needs or safety, or for transportation?

    b. If no, would the employee's presence to provide **psychological comfort** be beneficial to the patient or assist in the patient's recovery?

    c. If the patient will need care only **intermittently** or on a part-time basis, please indicate the probable **duration** of this need:

Signature of Health Care Provider

Type of Practice

Address

Telephone Number

Date

To be completed by the employee needing family leave to care for a family member:

State the care you will provide and an estimate of the period during which care will be provided, including a schedule if leave is to be taken intermittently or if it will be necessary for you to work less than a full schedule:

Employee Signature

Date

A **"Serious Health Condition"** means an illness, injury impairment, or physical or mental condition that involves one of the following:

1. Hospital Care

   Inpatient care (*i.e.*, an overnight stay) in a hospital, hospice, or residential medical care facility, including any period of incapacity[2] or subsequent treatment in connection with or consequent to such inpatient care.

2. Absence Plus Treatment

   (a) A period of incapacity[2] of **more than three consecutive calendar days** (including any subsequent treatment or period of incapacity[2] relating to the same condition), that also involves:

      (1) **Treatment[3] two or more times** by a health care provider, by a nurse or physician's assistant under direct supervision of a health care provider, or by a provider of health care services (*e.g.*, physical therapist) under orders of, or on referral by, a health care provider; or

      (2) **Treatment** by a health care provider on **at least one occasion** which results in a **regimen of continuing treatment[4]** under the supervision of the health care provider.

3. Pregnancy

   Any period of incapacity due to **pregnancy**, or for **prenatal care**.

4. Chronic Conditions Requiring Treatments

   A **chronic condition** which:

      (1) Requires **periodic visits** for treatment by a health care provider, or by a nurse or physician's assistant under direct supervision of a health care provider;

      (2) Continues over an **extended period of time** (including recurring episodes of a single underlying condition); and

      (3) May cause **episodic** rather than a continuing period of incapacity[2] (*e.g.*, asthma, diabetes, epilepsy, etc.).

5. Permanent/Long-term Conditions Requiring Supervision

   A period of **Incapacity[2]** which is **permanent or long-term** due to a condition for which treatment may not be effective. The employee or family member must be **under the continuing supervision of, but need not be receiving active treatment by, a health care provider**. Examples include Alzheimer's, a severe stroke, or the terminal stages of a disease.

6. Multiple Treatments (Non-Chronic Conditions)

   Any period of absence to receive **multiple treatments** (including any period of recovery therefrom) by a health care provider or by a provider of health care services under orders of, or on referral by, a health care provider, either for **restorative surgery** after an accident or other injury, **or** for a condition that **would likely result in a period of Incapacity[2] of more than three consecutive calendar days in the absence of medical intervention or treatment**, such as cancer (chemotherapy, radiation, etc.), severe arthritis (physical therapy), and kidney disease (dialysis).

This optional form may be used by employees to satisfy a mandatory requirement to furnish a medical certification (when requested) from a health care provider, including second or third opinions and recertification (29 CFR 825.306).

Note: Persons are not required to respond to this collection of information unless it displays a currently valid OMB control number.

---

[3] Treatment includes examinations to determine if a serious health condition exists and evaluations of the condition. Treatment does not include routine physical examinations, eye examinations, or dental examinations.

[4] A regimen of continuing treatment includes, for example, a course of prescription medication (*e.g.*, an antibiotic) or therapy requiring special equipment to resolve or alleviate the health condition. A regimen of treatment does not include the taking of over-the-counter medications such as aspirin, antihistamines, or salves; or bed-rest, drinking fluids, exercise, and other similar activities that can be initiated without a visit to a health care provider.

Public Burden Statement

We estimate that it will take an average of 20 minutes to complete this collection of information, including the time for reviewing instructions, searching existing data sources, gathering and maintaining the data needed, and completing and reviewing the collection of information. If you have any comments regarding this burden estimate or any other aspect of this collection of information, including suggestions for reducing this burden, send them to the Administrator, Wage and Hour Division, Department of Labor, Room S-3502, 200 Constitution Avenue, N.W., Washington, D.C. 20210.

DO NOT SEND THE COMPLETED FORM TO THIS OFFICE; IT GOES TO THE EMPLOYEE.

273

Note: These instructions and Forms 300, 300A, and 301 replace the older Forms 101 and 200 in use prior to 2002. The Forms reprinted here are for use after January 1, 2004. They are available for download in their full 8.5 x 14 inch size from the OSHA website:

http://www.osha.gov/recordkeeping/new-osha300form1-1-04.pdf

OSHA
Forms for Recording
Work-Related Injuries and Illnesses

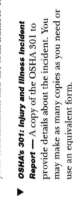

What's Inside...

In this package, you'll find everything you need to complete OSHA's *Log* and the *Summary of Work-Related Injuries and Illnesses* for the next several years. On the following pages, you'll find:

▶ *An Overview: Recording Work-Related Injuries and Illnesses* — General instructions for filling out the forms in this package and definitions of terms you should use when you classify your cases as injuries or illnesses.

▶ *How to Fill Out the Log* — An example to guide you in filling out the *Log* properly.

▶ *Log of Work-Related Injuries and Illnesses* — Several pages of the *Log* (but you may make as many copies of the *Log* as you need.) Notice that the *Log* is separate from the *Summary*.

▶ *Summary of Work-Related Injuries and Illnesses* — Removable *Summary* pages for easy posting at the end of the year. Note that you post the *Summary* only, not the *Log*.

▶ *Worksheet to Help You Fill Out the Summary* — A worksheet for figuring the average number of employees who worked for your establishment and the total number of hours worked.

▶ *OSHA's 301: Injury and Illness Incident Report* — A copy of the OSHA 301 to provide details about the incident. You may make as many copies as you need or use an equivalent form.

Take a few minutes to review this package. If you have any questions, *visit us online at www.osha. gov* **OR** *call your local OSHA office.* We'll be happy to help you.

Dear Employer:

This booklet includes the forms needed for maintaining occupational injury and illness records for 2004. These new forms have changed in several important ways from the 2003 recordkeeping forms.

In the December 17, 2002 Federal Register (67 FR 77165-77170), OSHA announced its decision to add an occupational hearing loss column to OSHA's Form 300, Log of Work-Related Injuries and Illnesses. This forms package contains modified Forms 300 and 300A which incorporate the additional column M(5) Hearing Loss. Employers required to complete the injury and illness forms must begin to use these forms on January 1, 2004.

In response to public suggestions, OSHA also has made several changes to the forms package to make the recordkeeping materials clearer and easier to use:

- On Form 300, we've switched the positions of the day count columns. The days "away from work" column now comes before the days "on job transfer or restriction."

- We've clarified the formulas for calculating incidence rates.

- We've added new recording criteria for occupational hearing loss to the "Overview" section.

- On Form 300, we've made the column heading "Classify the Case" more prominent to make it clear that employers should mark only one selection among the four columns offered.

The Occupational Safety and Health Administration shares with you the goal of preventing injuries and illnesses in our nation's workplaces. Accurate injury and illness records will help us achieve that goal.

Occupational Safety and Health Administration
U.S. Department of Labor

U.S. Department of Labor
Occupational Safety and Health Administration

274

An Overview:
Recording Work-Related Injuries and Illnesses

The Occupational Safety and Health (OSH) Act of 1970 requires certain employers to prepare and maintain records of work-related injuries and illnesses. Use these definitions when you classify cases on the Log. OSHA's recordkeeping regulation (see 29 CFR Part 1904) provides more information about the definitions below.

The *Log of Work-Related Injuries and Illnesses* (Form 300) is used to classify work-related injuries and illnesses and to note the extent and severity of each case. When an incident occurs, use the *Log* to record specific details about what happened and how it happened. The *Summary* — a separate form (Form 300A) — shows the totals for the year in each category. At the end of the year, post the *Summary* in a visible location so that your employees are aware of the injuries and illnesses occurring in their workplace.

Employers must keep a *Log* for each establishment or site. If you have more than one establishment, you must keep a separate *Log* and *Summary* for each physical location that is expected to be in operation for one year or longer.

Note that your employees have the right to review your injury and illness records. For more information, see 29 Code of Federal Regulations Part 1904.35, *Employee Involvement.*

Cases listed on the *Log of Work-Related Injuries and Illnesses* are not necessarily eligible for workers' compensation or other insurance benefits. Listing a case on the *Log* does not mean that the employer or worker was at fault or that an OSHA standard was violated.

When is an injury or illness considered work-related?

An injury or illness is considered work-related if an event or exposure in the work environment caused or contributed to the condition or significantly aggravated a preexisting condition. Work-relatedness is presumed for injuries and illnesses resulting from events or exposures occurring in the workplace, unless an exception specifically applies. See 29 CFR Part 1904.5(b)(2) for the exceptions. The work environment includes the establishment and other locations where one or more employees are working or are present as a condition of their employment. See 29 CFR Part 1904.5(b)(1).

Which work-related injuries and illnesses should you record?

Record those work-related injuries and illnesses that result in:

- death,
- loss of consciousness,
- days away from work,
- restricted work activity or job transfer, or
- medical treatment beyond first aid.

You must also record work-related injuries and illnesses that are significant (as defined below) or meet any of the additional criteria listed below.

You must record any significant work-related injury or illness that is diagnosed by a physician or other licensed health care professional. You must record any work-related case involving cancer, chronic irreversible disease, a fractured or cracked bone, or a punctured eardrum. See 29 CFR 1904.7.

What are the additional criteria?

You must record the following conditions when they are work-related:

- any needlestick injury or cut from a sharp object that is contaminated with another person's blood or other potentially infectious material;
- any case requiring an employee to be medically removed under the requirements of an OSHA health standard;
- tuberculosis infection as evidenced by a positive skin test or diagnosis by a physician or other licensed health care professional after exposure to a known case of active tuberculosis.
- an employee's hearing test (audiogram) reveals 1) that the employee has experienced a Standard Threshold Shift (STS) in hearing in one or both ears (averaged at 2000, 3000, and 4000 Hz) and 2) the employee's total hearing level is 25 decibels (dB) or more above audiometric zero (also averaged at 2000, 3000, and 4000 Hz) in the same ear(s) as the STS.

What is medical treatment?

Medical treatment includes managing and caring for a patient for the purpose of combating disease or disorder. The following are not considered medical treatments and are NOT recordable:

- visits to a doctor or health care professional solely for observation or counseling;

What do you need to do?

1. Within 7 calendar days after you receive information about a case, decide if the case is recordable under the OSHA recordkeeping requirements.

2. Determine whether the incident is a new case or a recurrence of an existing one.

3. Establish whether the case was work-related.

4. If the case is recordable, decide which form you will fill out as the injury and illness incident report.

   You may use *OSHA's 301: Injury and Illness Incident Report* or an equivalent form. Some state workers compensation, insurance, or other reports may be acceptable substitutes, as long as they provide the same information as the OSHA 301.

How to work with the Log

1. Identify the employee involved unless it is a privacy concern case as described below.

2. Identify when and where the case occurred.

3. Describe the case, as specifically as you can.

4. Classify the seriousness of the case by recording the **most serious outcome** associated with the case, with column G (Death) being the most serious and column J (Other recordable cases) being the least serious.

5. Identify whether the case is an injury or illness. If the case is an injury, check the injury category. If the case is an illness, check the appropriate illness category.

U.S. Department of Labor
Occupational Safety and Health Administration

275

▸ diagnostic procedures, including administering prescription medications that are used solely for diagnostic purposes; and

▸ any procedure that can be labeled first aid. (*See below for more information about first aid.*)

What is first aid?

If the incident required only the following types of treatment, consider it first aid. Do NOT record the case if it involves only:

▸ using non-prescription medications at non-prescription strength;

▸ administering tetanus immunizations;

▸ cleaning, flushing, or soaking wounds on the skin surface;

▸ using wound coverings, such as bandages, BandAids™, gauze pads, etc., or using SteriStrips™ or butterfly bandages.

▸ using hot or cold therapy;

▸ using any totally non-rigid means of support, such as elastic bandages, wraps, non-rigid back belts, etc.;

▸ using temporary immobilization devices while transporting an accident victim (splints, slings, neck collars, or back boards).

▸ drilling a fingernail or toenail to relieve pressure, or draining fluids from blisters;

▸ using eye patches;

▸ using simple irrigation or a cotton swab to remove foreign bodies not embedded in or adhered to the eye;

▸ using irrigation, tweezers, cotton swab or other simple means to remove splinters or foreign material from areas other than the eye;

▸ using finger guards;

▸ using massages;

▸ drinking fluids to relieve heat stress

How do you decide if the case involved restricted work?

Restricted work activity occurs when, as the result of a work-related injury or illness, an employer or health care professional keeps, or recommends keeping, an employee from doing the routine functions of his or her job or from working the full workday that the employee would have been scheduled to work before the injury or illness occurred.

How do you count the number of days of restricted work activity or the number of days away from work?

Count the number of calendar days the employee was on restricted work activity or was away from work as a result of the recordable injury or illness. Do not count the day on which the injury or illness occurred in this number. Begin counting days from the day *after* the incident occurs. If a single injury or illness involved both days away from work and days of restricted work activity, enter the total number of days for each. You may stop counting days of restricted work activity or days away from work once the total of either or the combination of both reaches 180 days.

Under what circumstances should you NOT enter the employee's name on the OSHA Form 300?

You must consider the following types of injuries or illnesses to be privacy concern cases:

▸ an injury or illness to an intimate body part or to the reproductive system,

▸ an injury or illness resulting from a sexual assault,

▸ a mental illness,

▸ a case of HIV infection, hepatitis, or tuberculosis,

▸ a needlestick injury or cut from a sharp object that is contaminated with blood or other potentially infectious material (see 29 CFR Part 1904.8 for definition), and

▸ other illnesses, if the employee independently and voluntarily requests that his or her name not be entered on the log.

You must not enter the employee's name on the OSHA 300 *Log* for these cases. Instead, enter "privacy case" in the space normally used for the employee's name. You must keep a separate, confidential list of the case numbers and employee names for the establishment's privacy concern cases so that you can update the cases and provide information to the government if asked to do so.

If you have a reasonable basis to believe that information describing the privacy concern case may be personally identifiable even though the employee's name has been omitted, you may use discretion in describing the injury or illness on both the OSHA 300 and 301 forms. You must enter enough information to identify the cause of the incident and the general severity of

the injury or illness, but you do not need to include details of an intimate or private nature.

What if the outcome changes after you record the case?

If the outcome or extent of an injury or illness changes after you have recorded the case, simply draw a line through the original entry or, if you wish, delete or white-out the original entry. Then write the new entry where it belongs. Remember, you need to record the most serious outcome for each case.

Classifying injuries

An injury is any wound or damage to the body resulting from an event in the work environment.

Examples: Cut, puncture, laceration, abrasion, fracture, bruise, contusion, chipped tooth, amputation, insect bite, electrocution, or a thermal, chemical, electrical, or radiation burn. Sprain and strain injuries to muscles, joints, and connective tissues are classified as injuries when they result from a slip, trip, fall or other similar accidents.

Classifying illnesses

Skin diseases or disorders

Skin diseases or disorders are illnesses involving the worker's skin that are caused by work exposure to chemicals, plants, or other substances.

Examples: Contact dermatitis, eczema, or rash caused by primary irritants and sensitizers or poisonous plants; oil acne; friction blisters, chrome ulcers; inflammation of the skin.

Respiratory conditions

Respiratory conditions are illnesses associated with breathing hazardous biological agents, chemicals, dust, gases, vapors, or fumes at work.

Examples: Silicosis, asbestosis, pneumonitis, pharyngitis, rhinitis or acute congestion; farmer's lung, beryllium disease, tuberculosis, occupational asthma, reactive airways dysfunction syndrome (RADS), chronic obstructive pulmonary disease (COPD), hypersensitivity pneumonitis, toxic inhalation injury, such as metal fume fever, chronic obstructive bronchitis, and other pneumoconioses.

Poisoning

Poisoning includes disorders evidenced by abnormal concentrations of toxic substances in blood, other tissues, other bodily fluids, or the breath that are caused by the ingestion or absorption of toxic substances into the body.

Examples: Poisoning by lead, mercury, cadmium, arsenic, or other metals; poisoning by carbon monoxide, hydrogen sulfide, or other gases; poisoning by benzene, benzol, carbon tetrachloride, or other organic solvents; poisoning by insecticide sprays, such as parathion or lead arsenate; poisoning by other chemicals, such as formaldehyde.

Hearing Loss

Noise-induced hearing loss is defined for recordkeeping purposes as a change in hearing threshold relative to the baseline audiogram of an average of 10 dB or more in either ear at 2000, 3000 and 4000 hertz, and the employee's total hearing level is 25 decibels (dB) or more above audiometric zero (also averaged at 2000, 3000, and 4000 hertz) in the same ear(s).

All other illnesses

All other occupational illnesses.

Examples: Heatstroke, sunstroke, heat exhaustion, heat stress and other effects of environmental heat; freezing, frostbite, and other effects of exposure to low temperatures; decompression sickness; effects of ionizing radiation (isotopes, x-rays, radium); effects of nonionizing radiation (welding flash, ultra-violet rays, lasers); anthrax; bloodborne pathogenic diseases, such as AIDS, HIV, hepatitis B or hepatitis C; brucellosis; malignant or benign tumors; histoplasmosis; coccidioidomycosis.

When must you post the Summary?

You must post the *Summary* only — not the *Log* — by February 1 of the year following the year covered by the form and keep it posted until April 30 of that year.

How long must you keep the Log and Summary on file?

You must keep the *Log* and *Summary* for 5 years following the year to which they pertain.

Do you have to send these forms to OSHA at the end of the year?

No. You do not have to send the completed forms to OSHA unless specifically asked to do so.

How can we help you?

If you have a question about how to fill out the *Log*,

☐ *visit us online at www.osha.gov* or

☐ *call your local OSHA office.*

U.S. Department of Labor
Occupational Safety and Health Administration

Calculating Injury and Illness Incidence Rates

What is an incidence rate?

An incidence rate is the number of recordable injuries and illnesses occurring among a given number of full-time workers (usually 100 full-time workers) over a given period of time (usually one year). To evaluate your firm's injury and illness experience over time or to compare your firm's experience with that of your industry as a whole, you need to compute your incidence rate. Because a specific number of workers and a specific period of time are involved, these rates can help you identify problems in your workplace and/or progress you may have made in preventing work-related injuries and illnesses.

How do you calculate an incidence rate?

You can compute an occupational injury and illness incidence rate for all recordable cases or for cases that involved days away from work for your firm quickly and easily. The formula requires that you follow instructions in paragraph (a) below for the total recordable cases or those in paragraph (b) for cases that involved days away from work, *and* for both rates the instructions in paragraph (c).

(a) *To find out the total number of recordable injuries and illnesses that occurred during the year,* count the number of line entries on your OSHA Form 300, or refer to the OSHA Form 300A and sum the entries for columns (G), (H), (I), and (J).

(b) *To find out the number of injuries and illnesses that involved days away from work,* count the number of line entries on your OSHA Form 300 that received a check mark in column (H), or refer to the entry for column

(H) on the OSHA Form 300A.

(c) *The number of hours all employees actually worked during the year.* Refer to OSHA Form 300A and optional worksheet to calculate this number.

You can compute the incidence rate for all recordable cases of injuries and illnesses using the following formula:

Total number of injuries and illnesses x 200,000 ÷ Number of hours worked by all employees = Total recordable case rate

(The 200,000 figure in the formula represents the number of hours 100 employees working 40 hours per week, 50 weeks per year would work, and provides the standard base for calculating incidence rates.)

You can compute the incidence rate for recordable cases involving days away from work, days of restricted work activity or job transfer (DART) using the following formula:

(Number of entries in column H + Number of entries in column I) x 200,000 ÷ Number of hours worked by all employees = DART incidence rate

You can use the same formula to calculate incidence rates for other variables such as cases involving restricted work activity (column (I) on Form 300A), cases involving skin disorders (column (M-2) on Form 300A), etc. Just substitute the appropriate total for these cases, from Form 300A, into the formula in place of the total number of injuries and illnesses.

What can I compare my incidence rate to?

The Bureau of Labor Statistics (BLS) conducts a survey of occupational injuries and illnesses each year and publishes incidence rate data by various classifications (e.g., by industry, by employer size, etc.). You can obtain these published data at www.bls.gov/iif or by calling a BLS Regional Office.

Worksheet

Total number of injuries and illnesses [ ] X 200,000 ÷ Number of hours worked by all employees [ ] = Total recordable case rate [ ]

Number of entries in Column H + Column I [ ] X 200,000 ÷ Number of hours worked by all employees [ ] = DART incidence rate [ ]

How to Fill Out the Log

The *Log of Work-Related Injuries and Illnesses* is used to classify work-related injuries and illnesses and to note the extent and severity of each case. When an incident occurs, use the *Log* to record specific details about what happened and how it happened.

If your company has more than one establishment or site, you must keep separate records for each physical location that is expected to remain in operation for one year or longer.

We have given you several copies of the *Log* in this package. If you need more than we provided, you may photocopy and use as many as you need.

The *Summary* — a separate form — shows the work-related injury and illness totals for the year in each category. At the end of the year, count the number of incidents in each category and transfer the totals from the *Log* to the *Summary*. Then post the *Summary* in a visible location so that your employees are aware of injuries and illnesses occurring in their workplace. **You don't post the Log. You post only the Summary at the end of the year.**

OSHA's Form 300 (Rev. 01/2004)
Log of Work-Related Injuries and Illnesses

Year 20___
U.S. Department of Labor
Occupational Safety and Health Administration
Form approved OMB no. 1218-0176

You must record information about every work-related death and about every work-related injury or illness that involves loss of consciousness, restricted work activity or job transfer, days away from work, or medical treatment beyond first aid. You must also record significant work-related injuries and illnesses that are diagnosed by a physician or licensed health care professional. You must also record work-related injuries and illnesses that meet any of the specific recording criteria listed in 29 CFR Part 1904.8 through 1904.12. Feel free to use two lines for a single case if you need to. You must complete an injury and illness incident Report (OSHA Form 301) or equivalent form for each injury or illness recorded on this form. If you're not sure whether a case is recordable, call your local OSHA office for help.

Attention: This form contains information relating to employee health and must be used in a manner that protects the confidentiality of employees to the extent possible while the information is being used for occupational safety and health purposes.

Establishment name *XYZ Company*
City *Anywhere*   State *MA*

(A) Case no.	(B) Employee's name	(C) Job title (e.g. Welder)	(D) Date of injury or onset of illness	(E) Where the event occurred (e.g. Loading dock north end)	(F) Describe injury or illness, parts of body affected, and object/substance that directly injured or made person ill (e.g. Second degree burns on right forearm from acetylene torch)
1	*Mark Bagin*	*Welder*	5/25 month/day	*basement*	*fracture, left arm and left leg, fell from ladder*
2	*Shana Alexander*	*Foundry man*	7/2 month/day	*pouring deck*	*poisoning from lead fumes*
3	*Sam Sander*	*Electrician*	8/15 month/day	*2nd floor storeroom*	*broken left foot, fell over box.*
4	*Ralph Biocelli*	*Laborer*	9/17 month/day	*packaging dept*	*Back strain lifting boxes*
5	*Jarrod Daniels*	*Machine opr.*	10/23 month/day	*production floor*	*dust in eye*

Classify the case
CHECK ONLY ONE box for each case based on the most serious outcome for that case:
(G) Death
(H) Days away from work
Remained at Work
(I) Job transfer or restriction
(J) Other recordable cases

Enter the number of days the injured or ill worker was:
(K) Away from work — 12 days, ___ days, 7 days, 3 days
(L) On job transfer or restriction — 15 days, 30 days, 30 days, ___ days

(M) Check the "Injury" column or choose one type of illness:
(1) Injury
(2) Skin disorder
(3) Respiratory condition
(4) Poisoning
(5) Hearing loss
(6) All other illnesses

Be as specific as possible. You can use two lines if you need more room.

Revise the log if the injury or illness progresses and the outcome is more serious than you originally recorded for the case. Cross out, erase, or white-out the original entry.

Choose ONLY ONE of these categories. Classify the case by recording the most serious outcome of the case, with column G (Death) being the most serious and column J (Other recordable cases) being the least serious.

Note whether the case involves an injury or an illness.

OSHA's Form 300 (Rev. 01/2004)

Log of Work-Related Injuries and Illnesses

U.S. Department of Labor
Occupational Safety and Health Administration

Year 20 ___

Form approved OMB no. 1218-0176

Attention: This form contains information relating to employee health and must be used in a manner that protects the confidentiality of employees to the extent possible while the information is being used for occupational safety and health purposes.

You must record information about every work-related death and about every work-related injury or illness that involves loss of consciousness, restricted work activity or job transfer, days away from work, or medical treatment beyond first aid. You must also record significant work-related injuries and illnesses that are diagnosed by a physician or licensed health care professional. You must also record work-related injuries and illnesses that meet any of the specific recording criteria listed in 29 CFR Part 1904.8 through 1904.12. Feel free to use two lines for a single case if you need to. You must complete an Injury and Illness Incident Report (OSHA Form 301) or equivalent form for each injury or illness recorded on this form. If you're not sure whether a case is recordable, call your local OSHA office for help.

Establishment name _____

City _____ State _____

Identify the person

(A) Case no.	(B) Employee's name	(C) Job title (e.g., Welder)

Describe the case

(D) Date of injury or onset of illness	(E) Where the event occurred (e.g., Loading dock north end)	(F) Describe injury or illness, parts of body affected, and object/substance that directly injured or made person ill (e.g., Second degree burns on right forearm from acetylene torch)
___/___ month/day		

Classify the case

CHECK ONLY ONE box for each case based on the most serious outcome for that case:

		Remained at Work	
Death (G)	Days away from work (H)	Job transfer or restriction (I)	Other recordable cases (J)

Enter the number of days the injured or ill worker was:

Away from work (K)	On job transfer or restriction (L)
___ days	___ days

Check the "Injury" column or choose one type of illness:

(M)

Injury (1)	Skin disorder (2)	Respiratory condition (3)	Poisoning (4)	Hearing loss (5)	All other illnesses (6)

Page totals ▶

Be sure to transfer these totals to the Summary page (Form 300A) before you post it.

Page ___ of ___

Public reporting burden for this collection of information is estimated to average 14 minutes per response, including time to review the instructions, search and gather the data needed, and complete and review the collection of information. Persons are not required to respond to the collection of information unless it displays a currently valid OMB control number. If you have any comments about these estimates or any other aspects of this data collection, contact: US Department of Labor, OSHA Office of Statistical Analysis, Room N-3644, 200 Constitution Avenue, NW, Washington, DC 20210. Do not send the completed forms to this office.

OSHA's Form 300A (Rev. 01/2004)

Summary of Work-Related Injuries and Illnesses

Year 20 ___ ___

U.S. Department of Labor
Occupational Safety and Health Administration

Form approved OMB no. 1218-0176

All establishments covered by Part 1904 must complete this Summary page, even if no work-related injuries or illnesses occurred during the year. Remember to review the Log to verify that the entries are complete and accurate before completing this summary.

Using the Log, count the individual entries you made for each category. Then write the totals below, making sure you've added the entries from every page of the Log. If you had no cases, write "0."

Employees, former employees, and their representatives have the right to review the OSHA Form 300 in its entirety. They also have limited access to the OSHA Form 301 or its equivalent. See 29 CFR Part 1904.35, in OSHA's recordkeeping rule, for further details on the access provisions for these forms.

Number of Cases

Total number of deaths	Total number of cases with days away from work	Total number of cases with job transfer or restriction	Total number of other recordable cases
(G)	(H)	(I)	(J)

Number of Days

Total number of days away from work	Total number of days of job transfer or restriction
(K)	(L)

Injury and Illness Types

Total number of . . .
(M)

(1) Injuries _____
(2) Skin disorders _____
(3) Respiratory conditions _____

(4) Poisonings _____
(5) Hearing loss _____
(6) All other illnesses _____

Establishment Information

Your establishment name _____

Street _____

City _____ State _____ ZIP _____

Industry description (e.g., Manufacture of motor truck trailers) _____

Standard Industrial Classification (SIC), if known (e.g., 3715) _ _ _ _

OR

North American Industrial Classification (NAICS), if known (e.g., 336212) _____

Employment Information (If you don't have these figures, see the Worksheet on the back of this page to estimate.)

Annual average number of employees _____

Total hours worked by all employees last year _____

Sign here

Knowingly falsifying this document may result in a fine.

I certify that I have examined this document and that to the best of my knowledge the entries are true, accurate, and complete.

_____
Company executive   Title _____

(___) _____   Date _ / _ / _
Phone

Post this Summary page from February 1 to April 30 of the year following the year covered by the form.

Public reporting burden for this collection of information is estimated to average 50 minutes per response, including time to review the instructions, search and gather the data needed, and complete and review the collection of information. Persons are not required to respond to the collection of information unless it displays a currently valid OMB control number. If you have any comments about these estimates or any other aspects of this data collection, contact: US Department of Labor, OSHA Office of Statistical Analysis, Room N-3644, 200 Constitution Avenue, NW, Washington, DC 20210. Do not send the completed forms to this office.

Optional

Worksheet to Help You Fill Out the Summary

At the end of the year, OSHA requires you to enter the average number of employees and the total hours worked by your employees on the summary. If you don't have these figures, you can use the information on this page to estimate the numbers you will need to enter on the Summary page at the end of the year.

How to figure the average number of employees who worked for your establishment during the year:

❶ **Add** the total number of employees your establishment paid in all pay periods during the year. Include all employees: full-time, part-time, temporary, seasonal, salaried, and hourly.

The number of employees paid in all pay periods = _____ ❶

❷ **Count** the number of pay periods your establishment had during the year. Be sure to include any pay periods when you had no employees.

The number of pay periods during the year = _____ ❷

❸ **Divide** the number of employees by the number of pay periods.

$$\frac{❶}{❷} = \text{_____} ❸$$

❹ **Round the answer** to the next highest whole number. Write the rounded number in the blank marked *Annual average number of employees.*

The number rounded = _____ ❹

For example, Acme Construction figured its average employment this way:

For pay period…	Acme paid this number of employees…	
1	10	
2	0	
3	15	
4	30	
5 ►	40	
►	20	
24	20	
25	15	
26	+10	
	830	

Number of employees paid = 830 ❶

Number of pay periods = 26 ❷

$\frac{830}{26} = 31.92$ ❸

31.92 rounds to 32 ❹

32 is the annual average number of employees

How to figure the total hours worked by all employees:

Include hours worked by salaried, hourly, part-time and seasonal workers, as well as hours worked by other workers subject to day to day supervision by your establishment (e.g., temporary help services workers).

Do not include vacation, sick leave, holidays, or any other non-work time, even if employees were paid for it. If your establishment keeps records of only the hours paid or if you have employees who are not paid by the hour, please estimate the hours that the employees actually worked.

If this number isn't available, you can use this optional worksheet to estimate it.

Optional Worksheet

Find the number of full-time employees in your establishment for the year.

_____

Multiply by the number of work hours for a full-time employee in a year.

X _____

This is the number of full-time hours worked.

_____

Add the number of any overtime hours as well as the hours worked by other employees (part-time, temporary, seasonal)

+ _____

Round the answer to the next highest whole number. Write the rounded number in the blank marked *Total hours worked by all employees last year.*

OSHA's Form 301

Injury and Illness Incident Report

Form approved OMB no. 1218-0176

U.S. Department of Labor
Occupational Safety and Health Administration

Attention: This form contains information relating to employee health and must be used in a manner that protects the confidentiality of employees to the extent possible while the information is being used for occupational safety and health purposes.

This *Injury and Illness Incident Report* is one of the first forms you must fill out when a recordable work-related injury or illness has occurred. Together with the *Log of Work-Related Injuries and Illnesses* and the accompanying *Summary*, these forms help the employer and OSHA develop a picture of the extent and severity of work-related incidents.

Within 7 calendar days after you receive information that a recordable work-related injury or illness has occurred, you must fill out this form or an equivalent form. Some state workers' compensation, insurance, or other reports may be acceptable substitutes. To be considered an equivalent form, any substitute must contain all the information asked for on this form.

According to Public Law 91-596 and 29 CFR 1904, OSHA's recordkeeping rule, you must keep this form on file for 5 years following the year to which it pertains.

If you need additional copies of this form, you may photocopy and use as many as you need.

Completed by _____

Title _____

Phone (____) ____ – ____   Date ___ / ___ / ___

Information about the employee

1) Full name _____

2) Street _____

   City _____ State _____ ZIP _____

3) Date of birth ___ / ___ / ___

4) Date hired ___ / ___ / ___

5) ☐ Male
   ☐ Female

Information about the physician or other health care professional

6) Name of physician or other health care professional _____

7) If treatment was given away from the worksite, where was it given?

   Facility _____

   Street _____

   City _____ State _____ ZIP _____

8) Was employee treated in an emergency room?
   ☐ Yes
   ☐ No

9) Was employee hospitalized overnight as an in-patient?
   ☐ Yes
   ☐ No

Information about the case

10) Case number from the Log _____ *(Transfer the case number from the Log after you record the case.)*

11) Date of injury or illness ___ / ___ / ___

12) Time employee began work _____ AM / PM

13) Time of event _____ AM / PM   ☐ Check if time cannot be determined

14) **What was the employee doing just before the incident occurred?** Describe the activity, as well as the tools, equipment, or material the employee was using. Be specific. *Examples:* "climbing a ladder while carrying roofing materials"; "spraying chlorine from hand sprayer"; "daily computer key-entry."

15) **What happened?** Tell us how the injury occurred. *Examples:* "When ladder slipped on wet floor, worker fell 20 feet"; "Worker was sprayed with chlorine when gasket broke during replacement"; "Worker developed soreness in wrist over time."

16) **What was the injury or illness?** Tell us the part of the body that was affected and how it was affected; be more specific than "hurt," "pain," or sore." *Examples:* "strained back"; "chemical burn, hand"; "carpal tunnel syndrome."

17) **What object or substance directly harmed the employee?** *Examples:* "concrete floor"; "chlorine"; "radial arm saw." *If this question does not apply to the incident, leave it blank.*

18) **If the employee died, when did death occur?** Date of death ___ / ___ / ___

Public reporting burden for this collection of information is estimated to average 22 minutes per response, including time for reviewing instructions, searching existing data sources, gathering and maintaining the data needed, and completing and reviewing the collection of information. Persons are not required to respond to the collection of information unless it displays a current valid OMB control number. If you have any comments about this estimate or any other aspects of this data collection, including suggestions for reducing this burden, contact: US Department of Labor, OSHA Office of Statistical Analysis, Room N-3644, 200 Constitution Avenue, NW, Washington, DC 20210. Do not send the completed forms to this office.

If You Need Help...

If you need help deciding whether a case is recordable, or if you have questions about the information in this package, feel free to contact us. We'll gladly answer any questions you have.

▼ **Visit us online at www.osha.gov**

▼ **Call your OSHA Regional office and ask for the recordkeeping coordinator**

or

▼ **Call your State Plan office**

Federal Jurisdiction

Region 1 - 617 / 565-9860
Connecticut; Massachusetts; Maine; New Hampshire; Rhode Island

Region 2 - 212 / 337-2378
New York; New Jersey

Region 3 - 215 / 861-4900
DC; Delaware; Pennsylvania; West Virginia

Region 4 - 404 / 562-2300
Alabama; Florida; Georgia; Mississippi

Region 5 - 312 / 353-2220
Illinois; Ohio; Wisconsin

Region 6 - 214 / 767-4731
Arkansas; Louisiana; Oklahoma; Texas

Region 7 - 816 / 426-5861
Kansas; Missouri; Nebraska

Region 8 - 303 / 844-1600
Colorado; Montana; North Dakota; South Dakota

Region 9 - 415 / 975-4310

Region 10 - 206 / 553-5930
Idaho

State Plan States

Alaska - 907 / 269-4957

Arizona - 602 / 542-5795

California - 415 / 703-5100

*Connecticut - 860 / 566-4380

Hawaii - 808 / 586-9100

Indiana - 317 / 232-2688

Iowa - 515 / 281-3661

Kentucky - 502 / 564-3070

Maryland - 410 / 767-2371

Michigan - 517 / 322-1848

Minnesota - 651 / 284-5050

Nevada - 702 / 486-9020

*New Jersey - 609 / 984-1389

New Mexico - 505 / 827-4230

*New York - 518 / 457-2574

North Carolina - 919 / 807-2875

Oregon - 503 / 378-3272

Puerto Rico - 787 / 754-2172

South Carolina - 803 / 734-9669

Tennessee - 615 / 741-2793

Utah - 801 / 530-6901

Vermont - 802 / 828-2765

Virginia - 804 / 786-6613

Virgin Islands - 340 / 772-1315

Washington - 360 / 902-5554

Wyoming - 307 / 777-7786

*Public Sector only

U.S. Department of Labor
Occupational Safety and Health Administration

Have questions?

If you need help in filling out the *Log* or *Summary*, or if you have questions about whether a case is recordable, contact us. We'll be happy to help you. You can:

▶ Visit us online at: **www.osha.gov**

▶ Call your regional or state plan office. You'll find the phone number listed inside this cover.

Model Statement - Health Insurance Continuation
Very Important Notice

Federal law [Public Law 99-272, Title X] requires that most employers sponsoring group health plans offer employees and their families the opportunity for a temporary extension of health coverage (called "continuation coverage") at group rates in certain instances where coverage under the plan would otherwise end. This notice is intended to inform you, in a summary fashion, of your rights and obligations under the continuation coverage provisions of the law. [Both you and your spouse should take the time to read this notice carefully.]

If you are an employee of [Name of Employer] covered by [Name of Group Health Plan] you have a right to choose this continuation coverage if you lose your group health coverage because of a reduction in your hours of employment or the termination of your employment (for reasons other than gross misconduct on your part). This right to choose continuation coverage also applies to any individual who is in the military reserves and is called up for active duty. (A military health plan does not cut off one's right to continuation coverage.)

If you are the spouse of an employee covered by [Name of Group Health Plan], you have the right to choose continuation coverage for yourself if you lose group health coverage under [Name of Group Health Plan] for any of the following reasons:
1. The death of your spouse;
2. A termination of your spouse's employment (for reasons other than gross misconduct) or reduction in your spouse's hours of employment;
3. Divorce or legal separation from your spouse; or
4. Your spouse becomes eligible for Medicare.

In the case of a dependent child of an employee covered by [Name of Group Health Plan], he or she has the right to continuation coverage if group health coverage under [Name of Group Health Plan] is for any of the following five reasons:
1. The death of a parent;
2. The termination of a parent's employment (for reasons other than gross misconduct) or reduction in a parent's hours of employment with [Name of Employer];
3. Parents' divorce or legal separation;
4. A parent becomes eligible for Medicare; or
5. The dependent ceases to be a "dependent child" under [Name of Group Health Plan].

Under the law, the employee or a family member has the responsibility to inform [Name of Plan Administrator] of a divorce, legal separation, or a child losing dependent status under [Name of Group Health Plan]. [Name of Employer] has the responsibility to notify [Name of Plan Administrator] of the employee's death, termination of employment, or reduction in hours, or Medicare eligibility.

When [Name of Plan Administrator] is notified that one of these events has happened, [Name of Plan Administrator] will in turn notify you that you have the right to choose continuation coverage. Under the law, you have at least 60 days from the date you would lose coverage because of one of the events described above to inform [Name of Plan Administrator] that you want continuation coverage.

If you do not choose continuation coverage, your group health insurance coverage will end. If you choose continuation coverage, [Name of Employer] is required to give you coverage which, as of the time coverage is being provided, is identical to the coverage provided under the plan to similarly situated employees or family members. The law requires that you be afforded the opportunity to maintain continuation coverage for 3 years unless you lost group health coverage because of a termination of employment or reduction in hours. In that case, the required continuation coverage period is 18 months. However, the law also provides that your continuation coverage may be cut short for any of the following five reasons:
1. [Name of Employer] no longer provides group health coverage to any of its employees;
2. The premium for your continuation coverage is not paid;
3. You become an employee covered under another group health plan (unless that plan excludes or limits coverage of a pre-existing condition the person had);
4. You become eligible for Medicare;
5. You were divorced from a covered employee and subsequently remarry and are covered under your new spouse's group health plan.

You do not have to show that you are insurable to choose continuation coverage. However, under the law, you may have to pay all or part of the premium for your continuation coverage. [The law also says that, at the end of the 18 months or 3-year continuation coverage period, you must be allowed to enroll in an individual conversion health plan provided under [Name of Group Health Plan].

The Health Insurance Portability Law (1996) provides that a person who is disabled at the time of a termination of employment or reduction in the hours of employment, together with his nondisabled family members is entitled to 29 months of COBRA continuation coverage. Beginning January 1, 1997, the disability extension will also apply if the individual becomes disabled at any time during the first 60 days of COBRA continuation coverage.

A child who is born to a covered employee, or who is placed for adoption with the covered employee, during a period of COBRA continuation coverage is also a qualified beneficiary. This law applies to [Name of Group Health Plan] beginning on [applicable date under §10002(d) of COBRA]. If you have any questions about the law, please contact [Name and Business Address of Plan Administrator]. Also, if you have changed marital status, or you or your spouse have changed addresses, please notify [Name of Plan Administrator] at the above address.

State Government Websites

The following is a list of State website addresses that provide information on state employment laws and other labor-related information.

Alabama Department of Labor	www.alalabor.state.al.us
Alaska Department of Labor	www.labor.state.ak.us
Arkansas Department of Labor	www.ark.org/labor
Arizona	www.az.gov
California Department of Industrial Relations	www.dir.ca.gov
Colorado Department of Labor	www.coworkforce.com
Connecticut Department of Labor	www.ctdol.state.ct.us
Delaware Department of Labor	www.delawareworks.com
District of Columbia Employment Services	www.does.ci.washington.dc.us
Florida Department of Labor	www.stateofflorida.com/labem
Georgia Department of Labor	www.dol.state.ga.us
Hawaii Department of Labor	www.hawaii.gov/labor
Idaho Commerce & Labor	www.cl.idaho.gov
Illinois Department of Labor	www.state.il.us
Indiana Department of Labor	www.in.gov/labor
Iowa Division of Labor	www.iowaworkforce.org/labor
Kansas Department of Labor	www.dol.ks.gov
Kentucky Department of Labor	www.labor.ky.gov
Louisiana Department of Labor	www.idol.state.la.us
Maine Department of Labor	www.state.me.us/labor
Maryland Department of Labor	www.dllr.state.md.us
Massachusetts	www.mass.gov
Michigan Department of Labor	www.michigan.gov/cis
Minnesota Department of Labor	www.doli.state.mn.us
Mississippi Department of Labor	www.dol.gov/esa/contacts/state
Missouri Department of Labor	www.dolir.mo.gov
Montana Department of Labor	www.dli.mt.gov

Nebraska Department of Labor	www.dol.state.ne.us
Nevada Office of Labor	www.laborcommissioner.com
New Hampshire Department of Labor	www.labor.state.nh.us
New Jersey Department of Labor	www.state.nj.us/labor
New Mexico Department of Labor	www.dol.state.nm.us
New York State Department of Labor	www.labor.state.ny.us
North Carolina Department of Labor	www.dol.state.nc.us
North Dakota Department of Labor	www.nd.gov/labor
Ohio Division of Labor	www.198.234.41.198/w3/websh.nsf?opendatabase
Oklahoma Department of Labor	www.state.ok.us
Oregon Bureau of Labor	www.boli.state.or.us
Pennsylvania Department of Labor	www.dli.state.pa.us
Rhode Island Department of Labor	www.dlt.state.ri.us
South Carolina Department of Labor	www.llr.state.sc.us
South Dakota Department of Labor	www.state.sd.us
Tennessee Department of labor	www.state/tm/us/labor
Texas	www.twe.state.tx.us
Utah Labor Commission	www.labor.state.ut.us
Vermont Department of Labor	www.labor.vermont.gov
Virginia Department of Labor	www.doli.state.va.us
Washington State Department of Labor	www.ini.wa.gov
West Virginia Division of Labor	www.labor.state.wv.us
Wisconsin Department of Workforce Development	www.dwd.state.wi.us
Wyoming Department of Employment	www.wydoc.state.wy.us

Index

About The Authors –

Louis P. DiLorenzo, Esq.

Mr. DiLorenzo has practiced Labor and Employment Law for 30 years and is Co-Chair of the Labor and Employment Law Department of the law firm of Bond, Schoeneck & King, PLLC. He also is Chair of the firm's Compensation Committee and Managing Partner of its New York City and Garden City Offices.

A graduate of Syracuse University and the University of Buffalo Law School, he represents employers and management in all aspects of Labor and Employment Law. His areas of expertise include collective bargaining, workplace investigations, NLRB proceedings, labor audits, supervisory training, wage and hour issues, arbitration, jury trials in both state and federal courts, wage incentive plans, OFCCP audits and proceedings, employment litigation before the EEOC and alternative dispute resolution techniques. Mr. DiLorenzo also serves several insurance companies as panel counsel with respect to employment litigation matters and served as General Counsel and Secretary to a Fortune 500 Company.

Mr. DiLorenzo is a Fellow of the College of Labor and Employment Lawyers, a New York representative of the worldwide Employment Law Alliance, listed in *Best Lawyers in America* (for over ten years), listed in *Who's Who in American Law*, *Who's Who in America* and *Chambers USA*. He has served as an adjunct professor at Syracuse University's School of Management, a member of the Editorial Board of the *New York State Bar Journal* and Chair of the New York State Bar Association's Labor and Employment Law Section. He has co-authored and contributed to a long list of treatises and has published articles on a variety of labor-related topics for a number of legal journals, educational publications, and HR-related periodicals and publications. He has been a keynote speaker at numerous seminars throughout the United States and other countries, and continues to lecture to university groups and local, state and national business associations.

Corporate Counsel Magazine named him "The Great Negotiator" and *Forbes* Magazine featured him in a cover story on Sexual Harassment.

Sheldon I. London, Esq.

Sheldon I. London in his 37 year legal career served some of the leading national trade associations as a principal in a Washington, D.C. based law firm. He carved a special niche for himself when in 1978, he wrote **How to Comply with Federal Employee Laws**. It was to become one of the important books in helping employers understand the complex area of compliance with federal employee laws.

The initial success of that publication was followed by a number of revised editions he authored over the next 25 years. As the Congress passed a dizzying array of new legislation, as the federal labor regulatory agencies issued complex new regulations, and the federal judiciary continually reviewed these new initiatives and established new judicial precedents, employers were anxiously looking for guidance. Mr. London earned the reputation of a lawyer who could write for the non-lawyer and make sense of the confusing myriad of laws, regulations and court decisions.

As he conducted seminars with employers and human resource professionals across America, he became keenly aware of their questions and needs. In his writing, he strove to keep it simple, while offering helpful suggestions to insure that his book would foster understanding and not add to confusion. His was a singular goal: provide employers with solid, accurate guidance for compliance in an understandable way.

Mr. London is a graduate of Dartmouth College. He earned an MBA from the Amos Tuck School of Business Administration, and a JD degree from the University of Connecticut School of Law.

Bond, Schoeneck & King – Firm Profile

Bond, Schoeneck & King, PLLC was founded in 1897 and developed a reputation for professional excellence, integrity, and success that lives on, more than a century later. These hallmarks of the firm have played an important role in attracting quality clients and legal work; have allowed BS&K to participate in the evolution and growth of the communities it serves; and have been the basis, not only for the noteworthy cases won, but for acknowledged leadership in the marketplace, the breadth of its practice and the talent BS&K has to offer.

From three attorneys a century ago, BS&K has grown to more than 160, making it one of the nation's largest 300 law firms. From its original Syracuse, New York location, BS&K has expanded to eight locations in New York, two in Florida, and one in Kansas. From a general law firm, BS&K has developed 27 discrete practice areas:

Administrative/Legislative/Regulatory	Estate & Financial Planning	Mergers and Acquisitions
Agribusiness	Environmental & Energy Law	Municipalities
Banking and Financial Services	Healthcare	Public Finance
Business Law	Higher Education	Real Estate
Collegiate Sports	Immigration	School Districts
Commercial Lending	Intellectual Property and Technology	Securities
Construction	**Labor & Employment Law**	Small Business
Creditors' Rights	Litigation	Tax
Employee Benefits	Media and Communications	Tax Assessment, Condemnation & Valuation

BS&K's high quality work product is also recognized as a great value, offering "big city" expertise at business-friendly rates, an attraction for a surprisingly varied clientele. BS&K represents clients from across the nation in the areas of Labor & Employment Law, Employee Benefits, and Collegiate Sports. In other areas, such as Business, Higher Education, Intellectual Property, and Litigation, BS&K's representation is more regional or statewide in scope.

BS&K's practice is a blend of the sophisticated legal work encountered by large metropolitan law firms, and the more personal legal problems associated with family and privately-owned businesses common in mid to small city environments. Clients include agribusinesses, banks, colleges and universities, construction companies and developers, energy suppliers, engineering firms, entrepreneurs and inventors, large and small family businesses, government development authorities, health care facilities, insurance companies, manufacturers, media corporations, municipalities, natural resource companies, not-for-profit organizations, physicians and physician practice groups, retailers, school districts, technology-based companies, transportation companies, and utilities, as well as individuals.

BS&K attorneys have distinguished themselves by serving as New York State Lieutenant Governor, Majority Leader and Legislator, Insurance Commissioner, and in various judicial appointments; three times as President of the New York State Bar Association (including the second woman elected to the post); twice as President of the National Association of College and University Attorneys; as Corporation Counsel for various governmental entities; as Dean of the Syracuse University College of Law and President and CEO of the Albany (New York) Medical Center; as members of the boards of directors of numerous corporations and not-for-profit organizations; and as members of a multitude of local, state, and American Bar Association sections and committees.

BS&K's **Labor & Employment Law Department** is well known, locally, state-wide, and beyond. With 60 attorneys in this department along with the Employee Benefits Practice Group, BS&K has one of the largest practices of its kind in the Northeast. In addition to sheer numbers, the attorneys in the Department have distinguished themselves by having 14 selected to The Best Lawyers of America, more than any other practice in New York State, having 3 selected to Chambers USA, one of the most prestigious listings of its kind in the world, and having 4 selected as Fellows to the American College of Labor and Employment Law Lawyers.

The firm has a long history of providing timely information to keep clients, professional associations and industry groups current with new trends and case law as well as to provide practical tools to help meet the myriad challenges they face every day. In addition to print publications like this book, the firm provides seminars ranging from short "breakfast briefings" to full-day conferences with break out sessions that cover topics across its practice areas.

How to Order:

Additional copies of
***What Every Business Manager and
HR Professional Should Know About
Federal Labor and Employment Law***
can be ordered online at:

www.WMEBooks.com

Or, by calling toll-free: 1-877-947-BOOK (2665)

Ask for it at your local bookstore by title, author name, or ISBN 0-9777297-3-7

For more information on quantity purchases, discounts, and special programs, please contact:

Special Book Orders
Windsor Media Enterprises, LLC
282 Ballad Avenue
Rochester, NY 14626

info@wmebooks.com

Additional resources online:

The authors invite your comments and questions. Really.

Visit them on the accompanying blog at:

www.LaborAndEmploymentLawBlog.com